Genealogical record of the descendants of Thomas Brownell, 1619 to 1910

George Grant Brownell

GEORGE GRANT BROWNELL

Genealogical Record of the Descendants of Thomas Brownell

1619 to 1910

George Grant Brownell

Heritage Books
2024

HERITAGE BOOKS

AN IMPRINT OF HERITAGE BOOKS, INC.

Books, CDs, and more—Worldwide

For our listing of thousands of titles see our website
at
www.HeritageBooks.com

A Facsimile Reprint
Published 2024 by
HERITAGE BOOKS, INC.
Publishing Division
5810 Ruatan Street
Berwyn Heights, MD 20740

Jamestown, New York
1910

International Standard Book Number
Paperbound: 978-0-7884-3058-9

PREFACE

~~~~~~~

Of Thomas Brownell and his wife Ann, the ancestors of our family very little is known except that they were of English descent It is claimed that he was born in Derbyshire England about 1618 Was married in 1638 to Ann, his wife whose maiden surname is unknown, and came to America in 1639 Austin in his Genealogical Dictionary of Rhode Island states that he was the son of Sir Edward or Edmund Brownell, of this we have been unable to find any proof To substantiate the fact that Thomas Brownell was a descendant of the Brownells of Derbyshire, it has been claimed by one of his descendants, that some of their ancestors who lived in Rhode Island during the seventeenth century possessed plate upon which was engraved the Coat of Arms of the Brownells of Derbyshire, England

That he came to this country about the time of his marriage seems very reasonable, as our earliest knowledge of him in this country, is that in 1647, he was living in Aquidneck, a settlement at the northern end of the island of Rhode Island, now known as Portsmouth This settlement had been made nine years before this date by a little group of men and women who had been driven out of Boston, Mass, because,

Hutchinson and Mrs. Hutchinson had seduced them into dangerous errors." There in Aquidneck they had made that famous compact of government, which is in these words: "The seventh day of the first month, 1638. We whose names are underwritten, do hereby solemnly, in the presence of Jehova, Incorporate ourselves into a bodie Politick, and, as He shall help, will submit our persons, lives and estates unto our Lord Jesus Christ, the King of Kings and Lord of Lords, and to all those perfect and most absolute laws of His, given us in His Holy Word of Truth, to be guided and judged thereby.—Exod. 24, 2-3. 2 Chron 2-3. 2 Kings 2-17."

This compact had been signed by William Coddington, John Clark and seventeen others. Twelve of the signers were members of the Boston church, and all except two were among those who had been required to give up their arms in Boston in the previous year, on account of their adherence to the doctrines of Mrs. Hutchinson.

It was among these people, who had been driven from Massachusetts colony for their religious opinions, that he cast his lot, and we may judge somewhat of him and his character, from that circumstance.

In 1895 the compiler became interested in collecting genealogical data of the descendants of Thomas and Ann Brownell. Having been very successful in accumulating a large amount of data, and as he was in receipt of many inquiries from other members of the family, he decided to publish the results of his labor in book form for the benefit of present and future generations, which he has been able to accomplish with the assistance of Mr. Simeon Brownell, Dewittville, N. Y., who so kindly backed him in this enterprise.

Great pains have been taken to avoid errors in names or dates, but as they are liable to occur in compiling a work of this kind, the compiler would be thankful if anyone finding mistakes, no matter how trivial, would inform him, giving number of page on which they occur, so that he may be able to make proper corrections in the next volume

We desire to express to those who have so kindly assisted us in our work of collecting data used in this book, our sincere appreciation of their services in our behalf, and wish that they may join us in the enjoyment of the fact of being able to hand down to posterity the genealogy of our ancestors, Thomas and Ann Brownell.

COAT OF ARMS

HISTORICAL RECORD OF THOMAS BROWNELL

THOMAS BROWNELL.

(1)

Thomas Brownell, of Derbyshire, England, born about 1619, died 1665, married about 1638, Ann, (surname unknown), and had eight children MARY, born 1639, died January 12, 1739, married Robert Hazard   SARAH, died September 6, 1676, married Gideon Freeborn.   MARTHA, born May, 1643, died February 15, 1744. married Jeremiah Wait, (2) Charles Dyer   GEORGE, born 1646 died April 20, 1718, married Susanna Pearce   WILLIAM, born 1648, died 1715, married Sarah Smiton   THOMAS born 1650, died May 18, 1732, married Mary Pearce   ROBERT, born 1652, died July 22, 1728, married Mary, (surname unknown) ANN, born 1654 died April 2, 1747, married Joseph Wilbur

March 18, 1647, he was one of the witnesses to the will of John Walker, of Portsmouth, R I   On May 20, 1647, he was appointed Water Bailey. In 1655, he became Freeman   1655-61-62-63, he was member of Court of Commissioners   April 4, 1658, he sold Thomas Lawton 35 acres of land   He was Deputy in General Assembly in 1664.

On November 6, 1665, Ann Brownell, widow and executrix of Thomas Brownell, exchanged certain lands with William Brenton, fulfilling a contract made by her husband previous to his decease

9

About the middle of the Seventeenth century there died in England, one Thomas Wilson, described in his will as "the elder sometime citizen and clothmaker of London, but now resident at Ryecroft in the Parish of Rawmarsh and County of York." This will was dated February 25, 1657, and proved on the 14th day of February, 1658. In it, he made the following bequest "I give to my cousin, George Brownell of London twenty pounds to be paid him out of the rents of Ryecroft To Mary daughter of George Brownell ten pounds at day of her marriage, it with her father's consent; it not, to her father I give to my cousin, Thomas Brownell of Portsmouth, R I, in New England, and to his children twenty pounds, to be paid either to himself if he shall come over to receive the same or else to such person or persons in his behalf as he shall lawfully assign to receive same."

Concerning this Thomas Brownell, of whom this is the only English reference which I have met with, very little is known, save that he is the ancestor of all the Brownells in the United States, except some of recent immigration He was born in 1619 He came from Derbyshire, England He married in 1638, Ann, his wife whose maiden surname is unknown It has been stated that he came to America in 1639 but I know of no authority for the statement. I have been unable to find his name in any of the lists of passengers to America in the 17th century which has been collected and printed

Our earliest knowledge of him after he immigrated is that, in 1647 he was living in Aquilneck a settlement at the northern end of the island of Rhode Island, now known as Portsmouth This settlement had been made nine years before this date by a little group of men and women who had been driven out of Boston because as was stated at the time "the opinions and revelations of Mr Hutchinson and Mrs Hutchinson had seduced them into dangerous errors"

There in Aquilneck they had made that famous compact of government, which is in these words· "The seventh day of the first month 1638 We, whose names are underwritten do hereby solemnly in the presence of Jehovah incorporate ourselves into a bodie politick and as He shall help will submit our persons, lives and estates unto our Lord Jesus Chirst, the King of Kings and Lord of Lords, and to all those perfect and most absolute laws of his, given us in His most holy word of truth to be guided and judged thereby" Exod 24 3-4 2 Corn. 2 3 2 Kings 11 17

10

This compact had been signed by William Coddington John Clarke and seventeen others. Twelve of the signers were members of the Boston church, and all except two were among those who had been required to give up their arms in Boston in the previous year, on account of their adherence to the doctrines of Mrs Hutchinson

It was among these people who had been driven from Massachusetts colony for their religious opinions, that Thomas Brownell cast his lot, and we judge somewhat of him and his character from that circumstance. The earliest mention of his name in the records of Portsmouth is under date of March 10th 1647, when he witnessed the will of John Walker of Portsmouth. He signed "with his mark" John Walker was one of the nineteen signers of the compact of March 7th, 1638 (that being "first month"). Among the old records of the Superior Court of Newport, R I for a term of court held in March 1723 about seventy-six years after the date of John Walker's will, we find the depositions taken in a controversy about this John Walker's homestead. These depositions are of interest to the descendants of Thomas Brownell. They were taken in an action of trespass brought by Mary Borden, widow, grand-daughter of John Walker of Portsmouth against Gideon Freeborn of Portsmouth

Mary Gatchell of Tiverton, widow, age seventy-seven years, testified in her deposition taken in August, 1721, that she remembered John Walker and more especially Katherine his wife who survived him, that Katherine when she went to the water mill of William Freeborn, she used to leave the house of said John Walker to go to said Freeborn's on the right hand, that said Walker's land, as was called lay to the southward of the land of Robert Hazard that said mill was southward of said Walker's land, that said Walker's land extended westward to the sea and eastward up to the common and that the White Rocks to the northward of the corner thereof and as deponent used to go by water to said mill in a canoe she hath often heard the people with her say, when they were against the lands butting upon the sea, that is Brownell's land, etc, and there is goodman Walker's land, etc. she understood the land to be John Walker's by general decree

Martha Dyer, widow, of Portsmouth, aged seventy-four years, also made a deposition. She was a daughter of Thomas Brownell, and widow of Charles Dyer of Newport, her second husband. It may be stated in passing, that her deceased husband, Charles Dyer,

11

FIRST ANNUAL REUNION OF THE BROWNELL FAMILY.

was a son of Mary Dyer, the Quakeress who returning to Boston after having been expelled, was hanged on Boston Commons June 1, 1660, in the Quaker persecution, and that all of the name of Brownell have therefore reason to feel more than a historic interest in that tragedy. Martha Dyer's deposition was taken August 28, 1721 She testified that she had some knowledge of the widow Walker, and where said Walker lived, which was in a house between the lands of the deponent's father's and after, of Robert Hazard, and lands of William Freeborn, said house stood on the right hand of an old path that led from Robert Hazard's house and land unto a grist mill of James Sands or William Freeborn

Robert Brownell of Little Compton, a son of Thomas Brownell "aged seventy years past" made his deposition in August, 1721 He deposed that he formerly lived in Portsmouth, had knowledge of land called John Walker's, that James Sands lived upon the lower part next the sea He also deposed that said land lay between land of William Freeborn and land of Thomas Brownell, the deponent's father, joining northward on said Thomas Brownell's land, which after was Robert Hazard's land, that there was a water grist mill stood on the southward side of said Walker's land or near it Soon after Phillip's War, Gideon Freeborn by two Indians erected a stone wall, etc Deponent further says that his brother-in-law, Robert Hazard and James Sands made an exchange of lands, etc

I have quoted somewhat at length from the quaintly phrased evidence in this old land case, because it shows with some exactness where Thomas Brownell's farm was, and who was his nearest neighbors It shows to one familiar with the locality or any one examining a map of Rhode Island, that his farm was on the western side of the northwestern end of Rhode Island; that it extended down to the water and looked out on Narragansett Bay, probably not far from where now is situated the Old Coal mine, that his next neighbor on the south was John Walker, whose will he witnessed; and next south of John Walker lived William Freeborn, whose son Gideon—above mentioned as building a wall "by two Indians"—married June 1st, 1658, Sarah Brownell, Thomas Brownell's second daughter The Robert Hazard who afterwards owned the Brownell land was a son of Thomas Hazard and a son-in-law of Thomas Brownell, having married Mary Brownell, who was Thomas Brownell's eldest daughter

I have no earlier reference to Thomas Brownell than the date

13

of 1647, when he acted as a witness to John Walker's will   The
next reference to him in the Rhode Island records is that, on May
20, 1647, he became "water bailey"   I have been unable to find out
the duties and functions of this office   He was six times elected Commissioner or Deputy, in May and June, 1655, May, 1661, October, 1662, May, 1663, and May, 1664

He became Freeman of Portsmouth in 1655   On April 4, 1658
he sold to one Thomas Lawton thirty-five acres of land   On April
17, 1657, Casanaquant, Chief Sachem of the Narragansett, in consideration of "gifts of value received" and one hundred pounds,
deeded the island Quononquot, opposite Newport—now known as
Conneaut—to William Coddington and Benedict Arnold, Sen.,—
both of Newport—"for themselves and such others of the free inhabitants of Rhode Island and others of their friends as are in covenant
with them," by writings bearing date March 10, 1657 or 1658.
The grantor agreed at his own charge to remove all Indians and
clear them off from the island

The agreement of March 10, 1657 or 1658, above referred to,
was signed by Governor Coddington, Robert Hazard, John Greene,
Jr., of Warwick, and sixty and more others   One of its many pro-
visions for the allotment among the purchasers of land so bought,
provided as follows: "Thomas Brownell (and many others mentioned by name) shall each of them pay one sixty-seventh part of the
whole charge, and shall receive each of them one sixty-seventh part
of the promised premises"   Among the many signatures to this
agreement is that of Thomas Brown, signed "by his mark"   As no
Thomas Brown is mentioned in the body of the instrument, I have
no doubt that this signature is that of Thomas Brownell   We do
not know the exact date of Thomas Brownell's death, or what pro-
visions he made in his will   On November 6, 1665, Ann Brownell,
his widow and executrix, exchanged certain lands with William Brenton, fulfilling a contract made by her husband previous to his death
We only know that he died between May, 1664, when he was elected
Deputy, and November 6, 1665, when this exchange was made by his
widow.   I have now given all that is known of our ancient ancestor.
The story is a very short one.   I trust further research may give us
much further information, not only of him and his life in Portsmouth,
but of his relatives and ancestry in England

14

(11)

Mary Brownell, daughter of Thomas and Ann Brownell, born 1639, died January 12, 1739, married Robert Hazard, son of Thomas and Martha Hazard, born 1635, died 1710, and had nine children. THOMAS, born 1660, died November, 1746, married Susanna (surname unknown). GEORGE, died 1743; married Penelope Wilbur. STEPHEN, died September 29, 1727, married Elizabeth Helme. MARTHA, died 1753; married Thomas Wilcox. A daughter (given name unknown), married Edward Wilcox. ROBERT, died 1718, married Amey (surname unknown). JEREMIAH, born March 25, 1675, died February 2, 1768, married Sarah Smith. MARY, born 1676, died 1722, married John Robinson. HANNAH, married Jeffery Champlin.

In 1655, Robert Hazard, husband of Mary Brownell, became a Freeman. On January 2, 1658, he sold John Roome of Portsmouth all his interest in Conanicut and Dutch Islands (1-300 part). He and his wife sold James Sands eight acres of land March 13, 1659. He was a member of Court of Commissioners in 1662-70. He bought twenty-five acres of land of Abel Potter March 1, 1663. He was a Deputy in General Assembly in 1664-65-67-70-71. On October 31, 1667, the court of Plymouth ordered, in reference to a controversy between the English and Indians about bounds in Dartmouth, that in case Robert Hazard of Rhode Island, might be procured he should run the line, etc. He was a Juryman in 1670-71. In 1671 he bought five hundred acres of land in Kings Town of the Pellaquanscott purchasers. On November 24, 1671, he sold Gideon Freeborn for eighteen pounds two-thirds of ten acres of land in Narragansett, having sold the other third to George Brownell.

On March 13, 1676, he and three others of Portsmouth were a committee who were ordered by Assembly to appoint their own men as keepers of Indians above twelve years of age (in custody of several inhabitants), that the Indians should be so secured as that they might be hindered from doing damage to the inhabitants in this juncture of time, etc. The Indians were to have sufficient keepers in company with them by day, and were to be locked up at night in a sufficient place of security. Any master offending was to pay a fine of five pounds.

On April 4, 1676, Robert Hazard was on a committee to pro-
to be four boats with five or six men in each   At same date, he and
three others were empowered to take the exact account of all inhab-
cure boats for the colony's defence "for the present," and there were
itants on the island—English, Negroes and Indians, and make a list
of the same; also to take account how all persons were provided with
corn, guns, powder, shot and lead   A barrel of powder was put in
charge of himself and three others, and two great guns in the yard
of late deceased William Brenton were to be pressed for country's
service, carried to Portsmouth, and placed one in the ferry neck and
one near the house of John Borden   They were to cause said guns
to be set on carriages and fitted for service

On April 11, 1676, he and others were appointed as commissioners to take care and order the several watches and wards on this
island, and appoint the places   In 1680, he was taxed one pound and
five shilling   On January 6 1686 he signed in full consent a deed
given by his nephew Edward Wilcox of Westerly to Isaac Lawton of
Portsmouth of sixty acres of land, buildings, etc., in Portsmouth
On September 6, 1687, he was taxed in Kings Town, eleven shillings
and seven pence

On January 14 1693, he deeded son Stephen for love etc., certain
land at Point Judith Neck   (He called himself late of Portsmouth,
now of Kings Town).   On May 2, 1698, he deeded son Jeremiah
for love, etc., right in two hundred acres of land at Tiverton   On
December 9, 1710, he deeded son Robert for three hundred pounds
land "where I now dwell," one hundred acres with housing, orchard,
etc   On January 29, 1734, Mary Brownell Hazard had a legacy
from will of her sister, Martha Dyer, of a third of her wearing
apparel

In 1739, her estate was divided by agreement of her heirs, as
appears by deposition of Stephen Hull   The deponent stated that
some time in January or February he was at the house where Robert
Hazard, son of Robert, now lives, there were several people gathered,
it being after the death of Mary Brownell Hazard widow, and they
were about dividing her estate   The persons concerned in the division
were Thomas, George and Stephen Hazard, Sarah Watson, and
Stephen Champlin all of South Kings Town; Jeremiah Hazard,
Martha Wilcox and Jeffery Hazard all of North Kings Town, and
Stephen Wilcox of Charlestown.   It was debated whether they
should divide the estate without proving the will of said Mary

16

Brownell Hazard. Thomas Hazard said he was very free to do it either way, and they all agreed the estate should be divided without proving the will. Robert Wilcox deposed that in said will, which was read, half of said Mary's estate within doors was given Martha Wilcox, and that the executor of the will was Thomas Hazard Robert Hazard deposed that he read the will to Martha Wilcox, widow, daughter of Mary Brownell Hazard. The above depositions were brought in as evidence in the suit of Martha Wilcox against Thomas Hazard for concealing the will, and the Court of Common Pleas having decided against her she appealed the case to the Supreme Court

SARAH BROWNELL FREEBORN

(12)

Sarah Brownell, daughter of Thomas and Ann Brownell, died September 6, 1676, married June 1, 1658, Gideon Freeborn, son of William and Mary Freeborn, died February 28, 1720, and had six children. MARY, born February 12, 1664, died October 25, 1676. SARAH, born January 14, 1667, died July 10, 1739, married Joseph Wanton. ANN, born March 28, 1669, died 1729; married Thomas Durfee. MARTHA, born August 8, 1671, died November 15, 1748; married Thomas Cornell. SUSANNA, born March 24, 1674, died January 21, 1723. PATIENCE, born March 4, 1676 died April 27, 1757, married William Anthony

Her husband became a deputy in 1675-90-1703-4-13, and an Overseer of the Poor in 1687. On March 5, 1690, he bought of James Sweet and Jane, his wife, of Prudence Island, for twelve pounds, a quarter of twenty acres of land in Portsmouth, given by Jane's grandfather, William Freeborn, to the mother deceased of Jane. On September 27, 1697, he deeded to his son-in-law, (ie. stepson), George Lawton of Portsmouth, a quarter share in Misquamicut, for love, etc. In May, 1708, he and his wife Mary (second wife) deeded to daughter Mercy Coggeshall, wife of Thomas of Newport, and her child or children, a half share in East Greenwich On August 1, 1709, he and his wife Mary deeded to daughter Mary Brayton, wife of Thomas of Portsmouth, a half share in East Greenwich, for love, etc., the whole of said tract being one hundred and eighty acres. On July 26, 1712, he deeded kinsman William Man-

SECOND ANNUAL REUNION OF THE BROWNELL FAMILY.

chester, son of Thomas of Portsmouth, for love, etc., ten acres of land in Potonomut

Her husband's will dated January 27, 1715, was proven March 14 1720, the executor was his son Gideon, the overseers his sons-in-law, Joseph Wanton, and Thomas Cornell He willed to son Gideon all homestead farm for life, and at death half to male heir and other half to rest of son's children, (at disposal of said son Gideon) and whoever enjoys farm at death of Gideon shall pay their mother twenty pounds a year while widow. If son Gideon die without male issue, then next male heir to have and to pay each female issue of son Gideon fifty pounds, and to grand-daughter Sarah, daughter of William deceased, fifty pounds, to wife Mary, fifteen pounds yearly while widow, use of great lower room in my new house and lodging room adjoining, firewood, fruit of orchard, use of riding horse, feather bed, etc and to her a good bed at her disposal,—if she marries only ten pounds a year, to grandson Gideon Wanton, one hundred and twenty acres of land in Tiverton, to daughters, Sarah Wanton, Ann Durfee, Martha Cornell. Susanna Freeborn and Patience Anthony, five hundred acres of land in Pennsylvania equally, to daughter Comfort Freeborn, one hundred acres of land in Freehold, East New Jersey, to grandson, John Freeborn and his children, farm in Coweset, Warwick, of two hundred acres and negro boy Samson, when grandson is of age, to grandson, Gideon Durfee, one hundred acres of land in Coweset, to daughters, Mary Broyton, Mercy Coggeshall and Comfort Freeborn, each three acres of land in Coweset, etc ; to grand-daughters, Elizabeth Borden, Sarah Wanton, Mary Wanton, Ann, Sarah, Patience, Mary, Martha, Susanna and Elizabeth Durfee, Susanna and Sarah Cornell, Abigail and Susanna Anthony, Mary and Hannah Broyton Elizabeth and Comfort Coggeshall, each forty shillings at eighteen to grand-daughter, Sarah Freeborn, one hundred acres of land in Coweset, to grandsons, William, George and Gideon Cornell, each fifty acres of land in Coweset, to grandsons Gideon and David Anthony each fifty acres of land in Tiverton, and to grandson William Anthony, forty-five acres of land in Tiverton, to grandsons Thomas and Job Durfee, each fifty acres of land in Coweset, to grandson Edward Wanton, twenty-five acres of land in Tiverton, to grandsons Gideon and Thomas Freeborn, each fifty acres of land in Tiverton, to grandson William Freeborn, land in Portsmouth at decease of said William's father.

and if he dies before his father, then to brother Thomas; to grand-daughter Susanna Freeborn, fifty acres of land in Coweset, to wife's two grand-daughters, the daughters of George Lawton, each twenty shillings at age, to wife's grandson, John Lawton, forty shillings; to my daughter Susanna Freeborn, twenty-five pounds; to daughter Ann Durfee, twenty-five pounds, son Gideon to care for negro woman Betty for life to son Gideon, negro man Eben, to grandson Thomas Freeborn, one hundred acres of land in Coweset; to daughter Susanna Freeborn, twenty shillings a year while unmarried, paid her by son Gideon, to daughter Patience Anthony, ten pounds, to daughters Sarah Wanton and Martha Cornell each ten pounds, to wife Mary, two cows and keep of same by son Gideon, who is to maintain his mother while widow; to Quakers, ten cords of wood delivered at meeting house, a cord each year for ten years; to grandson Gideon Freeborn, silver spoon and silver cup; to grandson William Freeborn, silver spoon, to son-in-law Joseph Wanton, land in Tiverton, to son Gideon, rest of real estate, two cows, a pair of oxen black mare, fifty sheep, two swine, husbandry gear, bed, silver tankard, etc., to daughters Susanna Freeborn, Comfort Freeborn and Mercy Coggeshall, each a share of personal, to son Gideon and daughters Sarah Wanton, Ann Durfee, Martha Cornell, Patience Anthony and Mary Broxton, rest of movables

The inventory amounted to six hundred and seventy-six pounds, twelve shillings and two pence, viz wearing apparel, bible, and spectacles twenty-five pounds and one shilling; gun, silver money thirty-five pounds, four shillings and four pence; plate, eleven pounds, twelve shillings and eight pence, warming pan feather bed, pewter cider, two pounds and fourteen shillings, pair of oxen, eight cows, five yearlings, a bull, four horses, sheep, lambs, seventy-eight pounds, swine, two pounds and five shillings, three negroes (man, woman and boy), one hundred and two pounds, etc.

MARTHA BROWNELL WAIT DYER.

(13)

Martha Brownell, daughter of Thomas and Ann Brownell, born May, 1643, died February 15, 1744, married Jeremiah Wait, son of Thomas Wait, died 1677. She married second Charles Dyer, son of William and Mary Dyer, born 1650 died May 15, 1709

On May 10, 1677, she bought of Daniel and Elizabeth Wilcox

of Dartmouth for sixteen pounds, an eighth of a share there. On March 8, 1690, she bought of Robert and Mary Brownell, for twenty pounds, thirty acres of land in Little Compton, they calling her sister.

Her will, dated January 29, 1734, was proven March 12, 1744. The executors were her nephews, Joseph and Stephen Brownell, the overseers, her cousins, John Reed and William Hall. She willed "to cousin George Borden, son of cousin Sarah Reed, twenty pounds; to three sisters, Mary Hazard, Ann Wilbur and Susanna Brownell all wearing apparel, to cousins John Reed of Freetown and William Hall of Portsmouth, each three pounds, to cousins Joseph and Stephen Brownell, sons of brother George Brownell, late deceased, three pounds, to all my cousins, children of my brothers and sisters balance of estate."

GEORGE BROWNELL

(14).

George Brownell, son of Thomas and Ann Brownell, born 1646 died April 20, 1718, married December 4, 1673, Susanna Pearce, daughter of Richard and Susanna Wright Pearce, born 1652, died December 24, 1743, and had eight children. SUSANNA, born January 25, 1676, died August 25, 1735, married John Reed, Jr. SARAH, born June 14, 1681, married (given name unknown) Borden MARY, born December 8, 1683; married William Hall MARTHA, born February 18, 1685; married Samuel Forman THOMAS, born June 1, 1688. JOSEPH, born December 5 1690, married Ruth Cornell WAITE, born October 3, 1693; married Joshua Sanford STEPHEN, born December 3, 1695, married Martha Earle

He was a deputy 1699-1702, and an Assistant Deputy 1706-7-8-9-10-11 In April, 1708, he was appointed on a committee in regard to vacant lands in Narragansett. His will, dated April 17, 1717 was proven May 12, 1718 His wife Susanna was named executrix He willed "to son Joseph, all housing and lands where I dwell, except lower room, and that at death of wife, to son Stephen, land in Portsmouth and all my new house building thereon, except north end of house reserved for use of my sister, Martha Dyer, and my daughters Susanna and Waite Brownell; to sons Joseph and Stephen, land in Tiverton and Little Compton, to son Joseph, a pair of oxen, to son Stephen, a pair of oxen and two cows to daughter Susanna Brownell fifty pounds; to daughter Sarah Borden thirty pounds, to daughter Mary, wife of William Hall, thirty pounds; to daughter Martha, wife of Samuel Forman, thirty pounds, to daughter Waite Brownell, fifty pounds, a good feather bed, etc , to my sister, Martha Dyer, and daughters Susanna and Waite Brownell, use of north end of new house while unmarried, to wife Susanna, the newest lower room in new dwelling for life, and the rest of movable estate to be at her disposal, she paying legacies"

The inventory amounted to nine hundred and sixty-one pounds, five shillings and ten pence, viz: wearing apparel, silver money, three hundred and forty-four pounds, sixteen shillings and four pence, plate, six pounds, tables, chairs, wheel loom, weaving gear, one pound and ten shillings, carpenter's tools, etc, seven pounds, a horse, sheep, fifty pounds, two oxen, ten cows, nine two year olds, five yearlings, swine, geese, seven beds warming pan, etc

WILLIAM BROWNELL

(15)

William Brownell, son of Thomas and Ann Brownell, died 1715, married Sarah Smiton, daughter of William and Sarah Smiton, and had eleven children THOMAS, born May 25, 1674, married Esther Taber SARAH, born November 25, 1675. MARTHA, born May 24, 1678, married Jonathan Tripp, (2) Samuel Hart ANN, born June 4, 1680 WILLIAM, born August 11, 1682 BENJAMIN, born October 20, 1684 ROBERT, born April 11, 1688 MARY, born February 13, 1691 SMITON, born February 13 1691 GEORGE, born April 13, 1693, married Elizabeth Davol ALICE, born December 3, 1695

He became a Freeman in 1677 June 9, 1683, he became Surveyor of Highway at Little Compton. In 1684, he was a constable On December 4, 1706, at Dartmouth, he took administration on his son-in-law, Jonathan Tripp's estate, the widow, Martha and her second husband Samuel Hart, refusing

November 6, 1714 he made his will which was proven August 1, 1715 The executrix was his wife Sarah, the overseers, his friend Nathaniel Soule and son Smiton Brownell, "to wife produce of all my land in Little Compton, and all movables for life, except a feather bed to daughter Alice, to son Smiton, all horsekind and cattle, left at wife's decease, and half of household stuff, to son Smiton, all land in Little Compton at wife's decease, to four sons, Thomas, William, Benjamin and Robert, twenty shillings equally, to three daughters, Martha, Ann and Mary, fifteen shillings equally."

Inventory, sixty-eight pounds and five shillings, viz ten acres of land, seven pounds; cow, five heifers, pair of steers, three yearlings two horsekind, six swine eight geese, four beds, warming pan, gun, sword loom and cheesepress.

THOMAS BROWNELL. Jr

(16)

Thomas Brownell son of Thomas and Ann Brownell, born 1650, died May 18, 1732, married 1678, to Mary Pearce, daughter of Richard and Susanna Wright Pearce, born May 6, 1654, died May 4, 1736, and had six children THOMAS, born February 16, 1679; died January, 1752, married Mary Crandall JOHN, born February 21, 1682; died March, 1759; married Mary Carr GEORGE, born January 19, 1685, died September 22, 1756 married Mary Thurston. JEREMIAH, born October 10, 1689, died June, 1756, married Deborah Burgess MARY, born March 22, 1692, died July 31 1717, married E Carr CHARLES, born December 23, 1694; died February, 1774, married Mary Wilbur

His will, dated 1730, was proven June 20, 1732 Executors were wife Mary and son Thomas He willed "to wife, half of dwelling house and half of orchard, for life, use of all bills and bonds or forty pounds a year instead, all my negroes and half of chattels, for life, and use of household goods, to son Thomas, ten pounds at decease of wife, and confirmation of deed of gift formerly made, and like legacy to sons John, George and Jeremiah, to son Charles, all farming tools, and half of outdoor stock, ten pounds and confirmation of deed, he bringing his mother firewood for life, etc.; to grand-daughter Mary Carr, one hundred pounds, two feather beds, trunk, etc, and at death of grandmother, rest of household goods, but if said grand-daughter die before eighteen, then five sons of testator to have"

Inventory, one thousand eight hundred and seven pounds, one shilling and six pence, viz. wearing apparel and sword thirty-four pounds, fourteen shillings and six pence, five beds, churn, pair of cards, loom, shoemaker's tools, silver money fourteen shillings and eight pence, English half pence eleven pounds, twelve shillings and

23

five pence, (at two pence a piece), money scales tankard, bonds one thousand and fitty-two pounds, twelve shillings and five pence mare, pair of oxen six cows, four young cattle, twenty-six sheep, twelve lambs, three calves, twenty-three geese, eleven swine, old negro man and woman ninety pounds, hives of bees, etc

His wife's will, dated June 9, 1735, proven November 19, 1736 Executor, brother George Pearce "To sons Thomas, George, Jeremiah and Charles, one shilling each to grandson Samuel, son of Charles, a feather bed, to brother George Pearce, a mare, he paying eight pounds to son John Brownell, to grand-daughter Mary Carr, money bills bonds etc

Inventory one hundred and seventy-five pounds, twelve shillings and four pence

---

ARTICLE BY MRS MARCIA BROWNELL BRADY.

In 1672, the Plymouth Colony obtained from the General Court of Plymouth a grant of that tract of land called by the Indians "Sogkonate" or the "Haunt of the Wild Goose," lying on the east side of Narragansett Bay and adjoining the ocean This land was bought of Awashonks the squaw sachem of the Sogkonate Indians, the latter remaining in the country Colonel Benjamin Church was the first Englishman to build on this peninsula in 1674. The breaking out of Phillips' war, however, interrupted the settlement and attention was given to defence until the ending of the war in 1676 Settlers then poured in, not only from Massachusetts, but from Rhode Island, which had been rapidly filling up for forty years

In 1682, Little Compton became an organized township, the records of whose meetings are still preserved The preponderance of Massachusetts settlers brought into existence a Congregational Church, and the proprietors granted one thirty-secondth of the township to the exclusive use of the ministry, but Rhode Island influence was shown by the vote that a minister be called 'provided that he be content with voluntary offerings and the product of his land, without a rate or tax upon the people,' thus comparatively separating Church from State

The soil was fertile the location beautiful, and Little Compton was known as the land of stone walls built by Indians, and with windmills on every eminence

Among those attracted to Little Compton was Thomas Brownell of Portsmouth third son of Thomas Brownell the immigrant His

24

wife, Mary Pearce, was the daughter of Richard Pearce of Portsmouth, who belonged to the twentieth generation of the Percy family of Northumberland England

Thomas Brownell held no public office, but he gathered the largest fortune, one thousand pounds in bonds, of any of the sons of Thomas Brownell the immigrant   Whether he made it by buying and selling land, or by means of his well stocked farm, is not known.   Following the English law of primogeniture, his eldest son received the chief inheritance of land   An Englishman's weapon was the sword, found among his effects, while the chest of shoemaker's tools, suggest the means of earning a livelihood, supplied him in his youth   His two negro slaves were willed to his wife, with forty pounds per year, a home, etc

———————

It is stated that the Percy family of Northumberland, England, mentioned by Mrs. Bready were originally of French stock from Percie a small place in France   Recently the statement has been made in print that "Richard Pearce was the son of Jeremiah the younger brother of Captain William Pearce or Pierce"   It seems very probable that this is true, for Mary, his daughter, gave the name to her son and it was handed down for several generations and was perpetuated even in Nova Scotia

ROBERT BROWNELL

(17).

Robert Brownell, son of Thomas and Ann Brownell, born 1652 died July 22, 1728, married Mary (surname unknown), and had six children   THOMAS, born 1687 ANNA, born January 27, 1690 BENJAMIN, born April 11, 1697,   married Hannah Manchester PATIENCE   MARGARET   MARY

He became a Freeman in 1673.   In June, 1689, he was a Selectman of Little Compton, R I   On December 25, 1689, he became Ensign   He and his wife Mary, sold his sister Martha Wait, of Portsmouth, R I, thirty acres of land in Little Compton for twenty pounds, on March 8, 1690

His will was dated January 29, 1718 and was proven August 20 1728   Executrix, wife Mary, overseers, Thomas Brownell, Jr and Joseph Wilbur, Jr   "To son Thomas, land on west side of highway where I live, and forty-two acres of other land, to son

Benjamin, all housing and land where I live, east of highway, only wife to have one room in the house and income of half the lands, with firewood provided by son Benjamin, to son Benjamin, half of all stock, he paying legacies; to daughter Mary's three children, five pounds each, to three daughters Patience, Margaret and Anna, ten pounds each to grandson Wilbur, five pounds, to wife Mary, the other half of stock, and all houshold goods for life, and at her death to be divided to daughters."

Inventory, two hundred and fifty-five pounds, eighteen shillings and six pence, viz two beds, wearing apparel, broadsword, cheese-press, eighteen sheep, eleven lambs, pair of oxen, two cows, bull, heifer two calves, colt, young horse, mare, five swine, churn, etc

ANN BROWNELL WILBUR

(18)

Ann Brownell, daughter of Thomas and Ann Brownell, born 1654, died April 2, 1747; married Joseph Wilbur, who died May 4, 1729, and had ten children   MARTHA, born August 20, 1684; married Timothy Closson   ANN, born May 8, 1686, married George Wood   WILLIAM born March 25, 1688, died, April 7 1775, married Jane Crandall.   JOSEPH, born December 30, 1689, died May 1754, married Emeline Champlain.   JOHN, born December 15, 1691   THOMAS born January 14, 1694, died September, 1783, married Susanna Irish, (2) Susanna Carr   MARY, born January 4, 1696, married William Eldridge.   BENJAMIN, born June 20, 1699, married Deborah Gifford.   STEPHEN, born March 22, 1701, married Priscilla Irish   ABIGAIL, born August 21, 1703, married Jonathan Hilliard   (2) Joseph Rathbone

Her husband Joseph Wilbur made a will dated June 11, 1728, which was pro en June 5, 1729, with his son Joseph Wilbur as executor, which read as follows: "to wife Ann, all household stuff, money, debts, etc, improvements of big room for life ten pounds per annum paid by son Thomas Wilbur, victuals and drink provided by said son and ten cords of firewood provided yearly by son Joseph, to son William, certain land and building, he paying legacies of one hundred pounds, to son Joseph, certain land and buildings, he paying legacies of eighty pounds; to son John, twenty-five acres of land, to son Thomas, land and my dwelling house, etc, benefit of certain stock of creatures while wife lives, which then go equally to children;

26

to son Benjamin, five shillings, to son Stephen, five shillings, to daughter Ann Wood, fifty pounds, to daughters Mary Eldridge and Abigail Wilbur, fifty pounds, to grandson Joseph Closson, fifteen acres of land, forty pounds and a cow, to grandson Timothy Closson, twenty acres of land, forty pounds and a cow, to son-in-law Thomas Burgess, five shillings, to nine children the rest of estate'

Inventory, six hundred and forty-three pounds, five shillings and three pence, viz wearing apparel, books, thirty shillings, beds, pewter, pair of cards, seventy sheep, twenty-four lambs, three mares, two colts, ten cows, two oxen, two heifers three two-year olds, three yearlings, five hogs, three hives of bees, cider-mill.

Her will dated December 12, 1739, was proven April 7, 1747, with her son Joseph as executor. She willed "to six sons William, Joseph, John, Thomas, Benjamin and Stephen, five shillings, each to daughter Ann, wife of George Wood fifty pounds, feather bed and pair of blankets, to daughter Mary Eldridge, widow of William, bond for fifty-one pounds; to daughter Abigail, wife of Joseph Rathbone, sixty pounds; to grandsons Joseph and Timothy Closson, ten shillings each, to five grandchildren, Joseph, John, Thomas and Jacob Burgess and Mary Wood, wife of John Wood, five shillings each; the rest of estate to go to grand-children, but none to great-grandchildren. Inventory, two hundred and seventy-one pounds, eleven shillings and eight pence."

THOMAS HAZARD

(111).

Thomas Hazard, son of Robert and Mary Brownell Hazard, born 1660, died November, 1746, married Susanna (surname unknown), died 1746, and had ten children. MARY, born October 3 1683 HANNAH, born April 14, 1685 SARAH, born July 15, 1687 ROBERT, born May 23, 1689. THOMAS, born May 11 1691 STEPHEN,, born June 13, 1693 JEREMIAH, born June 5. 1697. GEORGE, born January 18, 1699 BENJAMIN, born November 2, 1702 JONATHAN, born October 1, 1704.

On March 23, 1738, he testified calling himself aged 78 years and upwards, that his father was formerly a surveyor and was employed by the purchasers of Pallaquanscott, etc

His will, dated November 12, 1746, was proven November 27 1746, his son Robert was appointed executor. He willed "to sons

27

Jeremiah, George, Benjamin and Jonathan, five shillings each, all having had their portion, to grandson Thomas Hazard, two hundred and sixty acres and one hundred sixteen acres of land, and if he died then to my four sons, Robert, George, Benjamin and Jonathan, to daughter Hannah Easton, five shillings; to grand-daughters Mariam Hazard and Hannah Easton, children of daughter Mary Easton of Newport, deceased, one hundred pounds each, in ten years after my decease, to grand-daughter Mary Hazard, fifty pounds, in ten years, to children of my grand-daughter Ruth Underwood deceased, fifty pounds equally, to grand-daughter Susanna Gardner fifty pounds, in ten years, to my daughter Mary Easton, two hundred pounds, in ten years, if she needs it before, executor to pay her and if she die then to go to her sons James and John Easton, to the children of my grand-daughter Sarah Gardner, which she had by Ichabod Potter, deceased, fifty pounds equally, to son Robert, five shillings and all remaining part of estate of all kinds."

Inventory, three thousand seven hundred and forty-five pounds one shilling and nine pence, viz: wearing apparel, forty pounds and fifteen shillings, bed, large bible and other books, two pounds and fifteen shillings, money scales, silver buttons five shillings and one penny, silver spoon, bonds three thousand four hundred and eighty-three pounds and seventeen shillings, desk, looking glass, warming pan, two cows, etc.

GEORGE HAZARD.

(112)

George Hazard, son of Robert and Mary Brownell Hazard, died 1743, married Penelope Arnold, daughter of Caleb and Abigail Arnold, born August 3, 1669, died 1742, and had six children ABIGAIL, born March 19 1690   ROBERT, born November 3, 1694 CALEB, born November 27, 1697   GEORGE born October 9, 1700 THOMAS born March 30, 1704   OLIVER, born September 13, 1710

In 1696 he became a Freeman   He was a Deputy in 1701-2-6-7-8-9-12-13, and Assistant Deputy in 1702-3.   On May 6, 1713 he was appointed by the Assembly on a committee to make the public road leading through this colony from Pawtucket River to Pawcatuck River more straight, fair and passable.   In 1719-20, he was Lieutenant Colonel of Militia for the mainland.

His will, dated November 3, 1742, was proven November 13

28

1743, with his son Thomas as executor. He willed "to wife, Penelope, half my house for life, two negroes, Jack and Jane, three cows kept for her by son Thomas in summer and son Oliver in winter, a riding beast kept by son Thomas, and twenty pounds per year paid by said son, he also providing for her forty pounds of wool, one fat beef, two fat hogs, firewood cut for her on his land, and son Thomas further to allow her two acres of good corn, to wife also two good beds, and what household stuff necessary; to son Thomas homestead where I live, housing, etc., all goods, chattels and credits, and he to have profits till 1747 of northern part of Backside farm and profits of land given to grandsons Robert and Caleb till said Caleb is twenty-one years old to son Oliver three hundred acres of other land, negroes Caesar, Mingo and Prish, two cows and money he oweth the colony, to grandson William ten shillings, and to grandsons Robert and Caleb, certain land, their father Caleb having had before his death one hundred and seventy acres deeded to him to grandson Ebenezer Niles five shillings, he having had his portion, to grand-daughter Penelope Niles, negro girl Betty and one hundred pounds, to grand-daughter Sarah Niles, five shillings, she having had her portion, to grand-daughter Abigail negro Jeney and one hundred pounds, to grand-children Mary George, Abigail, Sarah, Penelope and Carder each ten shillings, to son Thomas, all estate, both real and personal remaining"

Inventory, three thousand three hundred and twenty-one pounds seventeen shillings and eight pence, viz wearing apparel seventy-one pounds and sixteen shillings, silver tankard, thirty-five pounds, eleven silver spoons, twenty-two pounds and ten shillings; beds, pewter, two pair stillyards, linen wheel, gin, negro Joe, one hundred and twenty pounds, Jack, one hundred and fifty pounds, Paro, one hundred and forty pounds, Harry, one hundred and twenty pounds, Will, one hundred and ten pounds, Jacob seventy pounds, John, fifty-five pounds Dirah, forty pounds, Jeney, one hundred and thirty pounds, Betty one hundred pounds, Cuff and infant, twenty pounds, Moll, one hundred and twenty pounds, thirty-one cows pair of oxen, two pair of steers, eight yearlings, one hundred and sixty-five sheep, five fat pigs, five store pigs, seven pigs, mare four colts, twenty calves, sixty loads of hay, two hundred and forty pounds, etc.

FOURTH ANNUAL REUNION OF THE BROWNELL FAMILY.

Stephen Hazard, son of Robert and Mary Brownell Hazard, died September 29, 1727, married Elizabeth Helme, daughter of Rouse and Mary Helme, died 1727, and had nine children. MARY, born July 20, 1695. HANNAH born April 20, 1697 SUSANNA, born April 23, 1699 STEPHEN, born November 29, 1700 ROBERT, born September 12, 1702. SAMUEL, born June 29, 1705. THOMAS, born July 28, 1707. ELIZABETH SARAH

He was taxed one shilling, September 6, 1687. In 1696, he became a Freeman. A Deputy in 1702-6-8-9-15, and an Assistant Deputy in 1708-18-19-20-21-22 On June 13, 1715, he was allowed eighteen shillings by the Assembly, for running a line between Eldred's purchase and Hall's purchase

His will, dated September 19, 1727, was proven October 9, 1727, with his sons Stephen and Robert as executors He willed "to son Stephen, land where I live in Point Judith Neck, one hundred and fifty acres, housing, etc, he paying to my son Samuel, fifty pounds, and to my daughter Hannah Mumford, fifty pounds, to son Stephen, also fifty acres of land in northwest corner of said homestead; to son Robert, remaining part of homestead, he paying son Samuel, one hundred and fifty pounds, to son Robert, also negro called Long Joe, to son Samuel, land in North Kings Town, two hundred acres called Middleport Neck, part of Mumford Island, etc, to son Thomas, three hundred acres of land in North Kings Town and rest of Mumford Island in Point Judith Pond, to son Samuel, negro Short Joe and negro woman Megg, to son Thomas, negro boy Jeffery: to daughter Hannah Mumford, two hundred and fifty pounds, to daughter Susanna Perry, two hundred and fifty pounds, to daughter Elizabeth Hazard, six hundred pounds, to daughter Sarah Hazard, six hundred pounds at eighteen"

Inventory, two thousand seven hundred and sixty pounds and fifteen shillings, viz: suit of wearing apparel with silver buttons and new beaver hat, nineteen pounds, fifteen shilling and six pence, rest of apparel, ten pounds, sixteen shillings and six pence; bond five hundred and twenty-two pounds, other bonds, book debts, one hundred and twenty-six pounds, nineteen shillings and one penny, silver tankard, twenty-four pounds, eighteen shillings and eight pence; four silver spoons, five pounds, eight shillings and two pence, pair of silver shoe buckles etc, case of bottles with some methegline, one pound and ten shillings, pewter, seven feather beds, stillyards, warming pan, woolen and linen wheel, canoe, four apprentices, forty pounds, negro Long Joe, one hundred pounds, Megg, eighty pounds, boy slave Jeffery, eighty-five pounds, books twenty-one pounds, seven horses, four fat oxen fat cow, thirty-six milch cows and heifers, four working oxen, twenty-two fat cattle and a fat bull, all on the Great Island, a three year old, thirty-one two year old, twenty-nine yearlings twenty-four calves, four working neat cattle cows, fifteen horsekind, twenty-one swine, five shoats, twenty-four geese, turkeys and other fowls, four hives of bees, etc

MARTHA HAZARD WILCOX

(114)

Martha Hazard, daughter of Robert and Mary Brownell Hazard died 1753, married Thomas Wilcox, died 1743, and had eight children ROBERT born 1687 married Catherine Lillibridge STEPHEN JEFFERY THOMAS, born October 24 1693 ABRAHAM GEORGE. EDWARD HANNAH

On May 17, 1710, he and seventeen others at Kings Town bought two thousand acres of land ordered sold by the Assembly

Her husband's will, dated April, 1728 appointed her as executrix, and her brother-in-law, Stephen Hazard, overseer He willed "to seven sons certain land equally, viz Eldest son Robert, Stephen, Jeffery, Thomas, Abraham, George and Edward, to sons George and Edward, the part of land where house stands, the north side being Edward's part, and neither to sell except to the other, to wife the stock and household goods and negro man, and also housing till youngest son Edward is of age, and after that she to have best room, the young children to be brought up by my wife"

On October 18, 1743, she made her will which was proven January 9, 1753, calling herself, widow, Martha of Exeter In it Thomas Sweet of North Kings Town was named as executor She willed "to her daughter Hannah Place, interest of two hundred pounds for life, and to said daughter's heirs at death, to eldest daughter of Hannah, if she happen to have any, bed, chest, etc., and to second daughter, a brass kettle to sons Robert, Stephen, Jeffery, Thomas, George, Edward and Abraham five shillings each, to

32

daughter Hannah Place, rest of estate." (Enoch Place receipted for legacy).

MARY HAZARD WILCOX.

(115)

Mary, daughter of Robert and Mary Brownell Hazard, married Edward Wilcox, born 1662, died November 5, 1715, and had four children. MARY, married Joseph Lewis HANNAH, married Ezekiel Garrett STEPHEN, married Mercie Randall EDWARD

On January 6, 1686, he of Misquanacut alias Westerly, sold Isaac Lawton sixty acres of land in Portsmouth, for one hundred and thirty-five pounds, said land being bounded partly by land of grandfather Thomas Hazard and including buildings, orchard, etc. His uncle, Robert Hazard, signed the deed in full consent. He also sold Joseph Johnson one hundred acres of land February 28, 1708. He was on the Grand Jury on December 29, 1714

On November 15, 1715, the administration of his personal estate was granted to widow, Tamsen Wilcox Said Edward Wilcox leaving ten children, four by his first wife, the daughter of Robert and Mary Brownell Hazard, and six by his second wife, Tamsen, some young and incapable of taking care of themselves The Town Council authorized the widow after paying debts to draw forth fifty pounds for the trouble to bring up children that are under age She was to have the choice of the best room in the house and a third income of real estate The eldest son Stephen, to enter forthwith into possession of the rest of the house and the orphans to have the rest of movables according to law

His widow, on December 17, 1716, asked for a division to be made of eighty-three pounds and three shillings, left of estate and it was made as follows: to widow, seven pounds and fourteen shillings, to each child, five pounds and ten shillings, viz: Mary Lewis, wife of Joseph Lewis, Hannah Garrett, wife of Ezekiel Garrett, Stephen, Edward, Sarah, Thomas, Hezekiah, Elisha, Amey and Susanna Wilcox.

Inventory, two hundred and eighty-three pounds and three shillings, viz four beds, four cots, bible and two small books given Tamsen by her father and brother, other books, pewter, gun, two oxen, two steers, twelve cows, six two year olds, eight calves, bull four mares, horse, four colts, sow, twelve shoats, nine hogs, etc.

33

Robert Hazard

(116)

Robert Hazard, son of Robert and Mary Brownell Hazard, died 1718; married Amey (surname unknown), and had seven children JEFFERY, born September 29, 1698. SUSANNA, born January 16, 1701. HANNAH, born February 26, 1703. ROBERT, born January 19, 1709. THOMAS, born June 18, 1713. AMEY, born September 20, 1715. MARY, born May 14, 1718.

He became a Freeman in 1696. His will, dated September 30, 1718, was proven November 10, 1718, executor his son Jeffery Hazard, with his brother Thomas Hazard, overseer. He willed "to wife Amy, great room of dwelling house where I live, twenty pounds a year while widow, a cow, riding beast bed, keep of cow and what household stuff is convenient; to son Jeffery, farm where I live of three hundred acres, to son Robert, land in Kings Town where my mother liveth, one hundred acres, housing, etc, after his grandmother's death, to son Thomas, two hundred acres of land in Kings Town and one hundred and sixty-five acres in Westerly at eighteen, to daughter Susanna Hazard, one hundred pounds, and a like amount each to daughters Amey and Mary at seventeen, to son Jeffery, rest of real and personal estate, he bringing up the children, etc."

Inventory, seven hundred and forty-eight pounds, nine shillings and eight pence, viz: wearing apparel, two bibles, and other books, three pounds and fifteen shillings, beds, loom, spinning wheel, churn, two guns, warming pan, three Indian children servants, twenty-three pounds, five swine, four shoats, eleven pigs, thirty geese and turkeys, two hundred and nineteen sheep and lambs, six working oxen, nine steers, twenty-six cows, eight yearlings, riding beast, bull, eight calves, horse, six mares, five colts, four yearlings, jades, etc

Jeremiah Hazard

(117).

Jeremiah Hazard, son of Robert and Mary Brownell Hazard, born 1675, died February 2, 1768, married Sarah Smith, daughter of Jeremiah and Mary Gereardy Smith, born April, 1678, died March 12, 1765, and had seven children. MARY, born March 16, 1699. ANN, born February 28, 1701. ROBERT, born April 11,

34

1703 SARAH, born January 11, 1706. MARTHA, born October 8, 1708. HANNAH, born April, 1714. SUSANNA, born May 21, 1716.

On April 18, 1707, he and his wife Sarah, of Kings Town, sold land to William Browning. May 17, 1710, he and his brother-in-law Edward Wilcox, and sixteen others bought two thousand acres of the vacant lands ordered sold by the Assembly.

MARY HAZARD ROBINSON

(118)

Mary Hazard, daughter of Robert and Mary Brownell Hazard, born 1676, died 1722, married John Robinson, born 1680; died April 6, 1712, and had four children. MARY, born September 30, 1705. SARAH, born January 22, 1707. RUTH, born March 12, 1709. SUSANNA, born February 9, 1712.

Her husband was buried in Clifton burial grounds at Newport, R. I. The inscription on tombstone calls him thirty-two years of age.

HANNAH HAZARD CHAMPLIN

(119)

Hannah Hazard, daughter of Robert and Mary Brownell Hazard, married Jeffery Champlin, and had three children. THOMAS, born September 3, 1708. STEPHEN, born February 16 1710. WILLIAM, born March 3, 1713.

SARAH FREEBORN WANTON

(122).

Sarah Freeborn, daughter of Gideon and Sarah Brownell Freeborn, born January 14, 1667, died July 10, 1739, married January 29, 1690, Joseph Wanton, son of Edward Wanton, born May 1, 1664, died March 3, 1754, and had six children. ELIZABETH, born January 5, 1691. EDWARD, born April 20, 1692. GIDEON, born October 20, 1693. SARAH, born April 27 1696. JOSEPH, born June 9, 1698. MARY, born June 10, 1700.

Both her husband and herself were public speakers of the Quaker denomination. Her husband was a shipbuilder living in Tiverton at its organization, March 2, 1692   Her son Gideon Wanton, became governor of Rhode Island

Her husband's will, dated August 14, 1749, was proven April 1, 1754, the executors were his sons Gideon and Edward   He willed "to son Gideon, land in Tiverton and a cow, to daughter Elizabeth Borden, of Newport, widow, a cow and eight hundred pounds, to daughter Mary Richardson, wife of Thomas of Newport, a feather bed, a cow and eight hundred pounds   to daughter Sarah Spencer, wife of Thomas of East Greenwich, (practioner of physics) use of house and lot at Tiverton where she formerly lived and after her death to go to my grandsons Benjamin and Wanton Howland, sons of said daughter Sarah, to daughter Sarah Spencer, also three hundred pounds, to son Edward, homestead farm where I live and buildings etc, except house and lot given above, to be for him and his heirs, if no heirs then to go to my son Gideon and daughters Elizabeth Borden, Mary Richardson and Sarah Spencer equally, to son Edward, other land and to him for life use of all my stock of cattle, horses, sheep, hogs, household goods and negroes, if he have no heirs to go to Gideon and three daughters of testator equally, except silver tankard, if son Edward dies without issue the silver tankard to go to grandson Joseph son of Gideon if grandson Joseph died before son Edward then to the wife that now is of Joseph if she should die then to grandson Joseph's daughter Sarah "

Inventory, five thousand and seventy-eight pounds, two shillings and seven pence, viz   two hundred and twenty-six sheep, ten cows, two four-year-olds, six three-year-olds, eight two-year-olds, ten yearlings nine swine, six geese, cider mill and press, cider in cellars, eighteen pounds, beds, two wheels, pewter, bonds, eight hundred and twenty-three pounds, fourteen shillings and seven pence; five hundred and twenty-three and one-fourth ounces of wrought plate one hundred and sixty-eight pounds and sixteen shillings, six negroes, Domine, Rose, Peter, Jenny, Hagar and Solomon, one thousand one hundred and sixty-five pounds, ten shillings, etc   The rooms named were east great room, west great room, bedroom store bedroom, kitchen, shop kitchen, chamber, porch chamber, east chamber, west chamber and garret

(123).

Ann Freeborn, daughter of Gideon and Sarah Brownell Freeborn, born March 28, 1669; died 1729, married Thomas Durfee, son of Thomas Durfee, died February 11, 1729, and had eleven children ANN, born August 25, 1691 SARAH, born March 1, 1693 FREEBORN born December 15, 1695 PATIENCE, born June 12, 1697 MARY, born January 22, 1701. MARTHA, born February 20, 1702 GIDEON, born January 15, 1704 THOMAS, born June 6, 1706. SUSANNA. JOB. ELIZABETH.

In 1707-9-13, her husband was a Deputy On October 13 1715, she and her husband mortgaged certain land for three hundred and fifty pounds On June 18, 1717, her husband petitioned the Assembly for a good and sufficient highway to be laid out to his farm at Common Fence Point, he having already applied to the committee of the town of Portsmouth, but did not obtain it The Assembly ordered the committee to lay out, within one month's time a good lawful and passable highway fit for horses and carts to pass and repass On October 13, 1720, he answered the suit of Stephen Broyton for impounding an ox, saying that said ox was unruly and broke into his meadow with other cattle.

May 25, 1728, her husband deeded to son Gideon for love, etc., my farm called Common Fence Point farm, being the most northeastern part of Rhode Island, of sixty acres May 29, 1728, her husband deeded to son Thomas for love, etc., fourteen acres, and two months later twenty-five acres

Her husband's will, dated February 9, 1729, was proven February 24, 1729, with his son Gideon as executor He willed "to son Gideon four parcels of land, viz the land where house standeth, called the homestead, where I now dwell, a piece called Spink's ground, a parcel called the Wind Mill Hill land and another called Jenning's land In consideration of this legacy, Gideon was to give deed to testator's son Job of the tract called Common Fence Point farm formerly deeded son Gideon by his father, and if Gideon fail to give deed within a month of testator's decease, the said four parcels were to be for son Job When Job is of age and possesses deed of farm he and son Thomas are to come to an equal division of all lands in Common Fence Point, both afore mentioned farm and that which I have given to Thomas already by two deeds of gift. The house

37

FIFTH ANNUAL REUNION OF THE BROWNELL FAMILY.

and rest of lands in Common Fence Point farm to be equally shared by sons Thomas and Job, certain land was to be sold by executor and money equally divided between seven daughters, viz: Ann Estes, Sarah Dennis, Patience, Mary, Martha, Susanna and Elizabeth Durfee; to daughters Mary, Susanna and Elizabeth, a feather bed each their sisters Patience and Martha having already received each a bed; to five unmarried daughters all pewter, brass, iron pots and rest of household goods undisposed of, and to each a good cow, and to them while unmarried the privilege of eastward chamber to live in, to sons Gideon, Thomas and Job the rest of cattle, horses, sheep and swine, husbandry gear and other movables."

Inventory, five hundred and fifty pounds and twelve shillings, viz: wearing apparel, twenty-three pounds and ten shillings, pocketbook, razor, spectacles, etc, thirteen pounds; books, one pound; money scales, his tailor shears, goose, box iron heaters, stillyards, spinning wheel, half a pair of worsted combs, negro man and bed, forty pounds; poultry, three pounds and five shillings, horsekind, fifty-three pounds, neat cattle and hay, one hundred and fifty-eight pounds and ten shillings; sheep, twenty-two pounds and ten shillings; swine, eleven pounds and ten shillings, etc   The rooms named were outward room, bedroom, kitchen, bed chamber, outward room chamber, garret an dcellar   His son Job being under age chose his Uncle Gideon Freeborn, for guardian and his daughter Elizabeth chose her uncle William Anthony.

MARTHA FREEBORN CORNELL

(124).

Martha Freeborn, daughter of Gideon and Sarah Brownell Freeborn, born August 8, 1671, died November 15, 1748, married March 26, 1696. Thomas Cornell, born November 30, 1674; died June 18, 1728, and had seven children   THOMAS, born February 3, 1698. SUSANNA, born July 22, 1702.   GIDEON, born March 12, 1704. WILLIAM, born July 26, 1705   GEORGE, born December 11, 1707. GIDEON, born July 11, 1710   SARAH, born February 20, 1713

SUSANNA FREEBORN.

(125)

Susanna Freeborn, daughter of Gideon and Sarah Brownell Freeborn, born March 24, 1674, died January 21, 1723. She was never married

Her will dated November 16, 1723, was proven February 10, 1724 In it were mentioned brother Gideon and wife, sisters Patience Anthony, Mary Brown, Mercy Coggeshall, Comfort Coggeshall, Sarah Wanton and Martha Cornell, also sister Sarah Wanton's three daughters, viz Elizabeth Borden, Sarah Wanton and Mary Wanton, sister Ann Durfee's seven daughters, viz Ann Estes, Sarah Dennis, Patience, Mary, Martha, Susanna and Elizabeth Durfee, sister Martha Cornell's daughter Susanna Bennett, sister Patience Anthony's two daughters Susanna and Abigail Anthony She further mentioned cousin (ie nephew) David Anthony and cousins (nieces) Susanna and Elizabeth Freeborn and Sarah Freeborn "To Susanna Dow, named for my sake, a silver spoon, to the woman's meeting of Friends, called Quakers, six pounds, etc"

PATIENCE FREEBORN ANTHONY

(126)

Patience Freeborn, daughter of Gideon and Sarah Brownell Freeborn, born March 4, 1676, died April 27, 1757, married September 7, 1698, William Anthony, son of John and Frances Wodell Anthony, born July 18, died November 9 1757, and had six children WILLIAM, born March 13, 1702. ABIGAIL, born June 23, 1704 GIDION, born August 14, 1706 DAVID, born September 19, 1709 SUSANNA, born September 26, 1712. JOSEPH, born September 4, 1715

SUSANNA BROWNELL READ

(141)

Susanna Brownell daughter of George and Susanna Pearce Brownell, born January 25, 1676, died August 25, 1735, married March 29, 1727, John Read, son of John Read Her husband was Town Clerk and a Freeman for thirty-five years.

SARAH BROWNELL BORDEN.

(142).

Sarah Brownell, daughter of George and Susanna Pearce Brownell, born June 14, 1681, married February 24, 1703, Joseph Borden, son of John and Mary Earle Borden, born December 3, 1680, died 1715, and had five children. STEPHEN, born August 10, 1705, married Penelope Read WILLIAM, born 1707 GEORGE, born 1709; married Priscilla Wilcox. JOSEPH, born 1712, married Susanna Read. JOB, (The blind Baptist Minister).

She married second October 31, 1719 John Read, and married third September 15, 1739, Peleg Thurston

MARY BROWNELL HALL.

(143).

Mary Brownell, daughter of George and Susanna Pearce Brownell, born December 8, 1683, married February 25, 1702, William Hall, son of Benjamin and Frances Parker Hall, and had son Benjamin, and, I think, other children

MARTHA BROWNELL FORMAN.

(144)

Martha Brownell, daughter of George and Susanna Pearce Brownell, born February 18, 1686, married November 27, 1712, Samuel Forman.

JOSEPH BROWNELL.

(146).

Joseph Brownell, son of George and Susanna Pearce Brownell, born December 5, 1690, married January 5, 1717, Ruth Cornell, daughter of George and Philadelphia Estes Cornell, and had seven children GEORGE, born June 13, 1718, died January 17, 1730 JOSEPH, born April 26, 1720, married Rebecca Tripp. THOMAS born October 23, 1722, married Abigail Slocum WAIT, born December 12, 1725. PHILADELPHIA, born December 15, 1726. MARTHA, born March 17, 1729 GEORGE, born September 27, 1736

He was a Representative to the General Court in 1720-22-24-27.

WAITE BROWNELL SANDFORD

(147).

Waite Brownell daughter of George and Susanna Pearce Brownell, born October 3, 1693, married September 27, 1717, Joshua Sandford.

STEPHEN BROWNELL.

(148)

Stephen Brownell, son of George and Susanna Pearce Brownell, born December 3, 1695, married December 12, 1726, Martha Earle, daughter of John and Mary Waite Earle, and had nine children SUSANNA born January 11, 1728, married Giles Slocum MARY, born December 5, 1729, GEORGE, born December 10, 1731, married Elizabeth Cornell. PHOEBE, born March 7, 1736, married Jonathan Cornell. SARAH, born December 2, 1739, married William Howland MARTHA, born March 24, 1742. HANNAH, born November 6, 1744 STEPHEN, born December 20, 1749, married Susanna Sherman JOHN, born January 16, 1753

THOMAS BROWNELL

(151).

Thomas Brownell son of William and Sarah Smiton Brownell, born May 25, 1674, married May 1698, Esther Taber, daughter of Philip and Mary Cook Taber, and had seven children JOSEPH, born February 13, 1699 ELIZABETH, born May 13, 1700 THOMAS, born February 15, 1702; married Hannah (surname unknown) SARAH, born February 20 1704. ESTHER, born February 10, 1706. CONTENT, born February 11, 1708. REBECCA, born February 28, 1710.

42

Martha Brownell, daughter of William and Sarah Smiton Brownell, born May 24, 1678; married August 22, 1695, Jonathan Tripp, son of Joseph and Mehitable Fish Tripp, and had four children JOSEPH, born January 7, 1696. THOMAS, born February 10, 1699. ABIGAIL, born August 8, 1701 – WILLIAM, born December 23, 1702; married Ruth Mosher.

She married second Samuel Hart, son of Richard Hart, and had three children JONATHAN, born January 6, 1706. SAMUEL, born December 10, 1708 SMITON, born January 24, 1712.

ANN BROWNELL DAVOL

(154).

Ann Brownell, daughter of William and Sarah Smiton Brownell, born June 4, 1680, married Benjamin Davol, son of Jonathan and Hannah Audley Davol, died 1735, and had eight children PETER, married Susanna Tripp. SARAH, married Mosher ELIZABETH. REBECCA, married Ichabod Brownell FREELOVE. ANN. MARY. JOHN.

Her husband's will was dated December 16, 1734, and was proven February 10, 1735. She was named as executrix. "To wife, use of all my homestead farm, etc., till son John is twenty-one, and she to bring up children To son Peter, five pounds, paid by son John when latter inherits gift To son John, at age, homestead farm, housing and orchard, and all personal and rights to undivided lands, he paying one hundred and twenty-five pounds, in legacies to brothers and sisters when he arrives at age To sons Peter and John, right in cedar swamp. To daughter Sarah Mosher, twenty pounds, and like legacies to daughters Elizabeth Davol (in two years), Rebecca Brownell (in three years), Freelove Davol (in four years), Ann Davol (in five years), and Mary Davol (in six years). If son John dies before twenty-one without issue, then Peter to have his legacy, he paying thirty pounds, to sisters, and if Peter dies, half of the property to go to Peter's children and half to mine." Inventory, one thousand three hundred and forty pounds, four shillings, viz: pewter, books, cattle hay, forty-five sheep, three horsekind, nine swine, homestead nine hundred pounds, etc   She lived at Dartmouth, Mass

WILLIAM BROWNELL

(155).

William Brownell, son of William and Sarah Smiton Brownell, born August 11, 1682, married 1704, Lydia (surname unknown), and had seven children   DEBORAH, born October 30, 1705   REJOICE, born July 29, 1707: died March 17, 1735, married Benjamin Macomber   SARAH, born June 26, 1709   MARY, born June 18, 1712; died November 17, 1732   WILLIAM, born February 2, 1715   MARTHA, born February 22, 1718   BENJAMIN, born June 24, 1720

GEORGE BROWNELL.

(159a).

George Brownell, son of William and Sarah Smiton Brownell, born April 13, 1693, married June 22, 1716, Elizabeth Davol, and had ten children   WILLIAM   JONATHAN, married Hannah Hiller   GEORGE   BENJAMIN   TIMOTHY   ELIJAH   HANNAH, SARAH   ELIZABETH.   PHOEBE

THOMAS BROWNELL.

(161)

Thomas Brownell, son of Thomas and Mary Pearce Brownell, born February 16, 1679, died January, 1752, married December 15, 1714, Mary Crandall, born 1689, and had six children   RICHARD, born December 10, 1715; married Mary Wilbur   MARY born July 15, 1717, married Peleg Simmons.   THOMAS, born February 5, 1720   SARAH, born July 31, 1722, married Thomas Brownell   GIDEON, born October 5, 1724   died October 25, 1741   Phoebe born February 16, 1726

JOHN BROWNELL

(162)

John Brownell, son of Thomas and Mary Pearce Brownell, born February 21, 1682; died March, 1759: married December 20, 1715,

44

Mary Carr, and had four children SUSANNA, born December 5, 1716. MARY, born September 11, 1719 MARTHA, born February 17, 1723. JOHN, born August 4, 1725, probably died young.

GEORGE BROWNELL.

(163).

George Brownell, son of Thomas and Mary Pearce Brownell, born January 19, 1685, died September 22, 1756, married July 6, 1706, Mary Thurston, daughter of Jonathan and Sarah Thurston, born March 20, 1685, died February 23, 1740, and had nine children GILES, born March 1, 1707, married Elizabeth Shaw PHOEBE, born June 19, 1708. MARY, born November 9, 1709; died October 6, 1791 GEORGE, born June 21, 1711, died June 30, 1800, 'married Sarah Bailey. THOMAS, born February 1, 1713. ELIZABETH, born September 15, 1717. JONATHAN, born March 19, 1719, died June 11, 1776, married Elizabeth Richmond. PAUL, born June 12, 1721, died May 20, 1760. STEPHEN, born November 29, 1726, married Edith Wilbur. (2) Mary Eldridge.

He married second April 18, 1745, Comfort Dennis Taylor, a widow, and had one child MARY, born March 3, 1747

JEREMIAH BROWNELL

(164)

Jeremiah Brownell, son of Thomas and Mary Pearce Brownell, born in Little Compton. R. I., October 10, 1689; died June, 1756, married November 6, 1712, Deborah Burgess, daughter of Thomas and Esther Richmond Burgess, born 1694; died July 1, 1779, and had twelve children. JEREMIAH, born in Little Compton, R. I, December 12, 1713, died December 17, 1738, married Ruth Irish. PEARCE, born in Little Compton, R. I., March 30, 1715, died February 7, 1740; married Ruth Thurston EDWARD, born in Little Compton, R. I. August 8, 1716. MARY, born in Little Compton, R. I, January 8, 1718, married Isaac Wilbur. GEORGE, born in Little Compton, R. I., August 2, 1719. DEBORAH, born in Little Compton, R. J, April 8, 1721 AARON, born in Little Compton, R. I., August 11, 1722, died September 17, 1754, married Alice Southworth THOMAS, born in Little Compton, R. I,

SIXTH ANNUAL REUNION OF THE BROWNELL FAMILY.

March 8, 1724. DAVID, born in Little Compton, R. I., November 29, 1725, married Grace Church JOSHUA, born in Little Compton, R. I., December 18, 1727; married Martha Peckham. JOHN, born in Little Compton, R. I., October 10, 1729, married Susannah Borden. ESTHER, born in Little Compton, R. I., August 23, 1732; married Samuel Howland.

It is stated that his wife, Deborah Burgess, was a grand-daughter of Thomas of Newport, R. I., and great-grand-daughter of Thomas, one of the founders of Sandwich, Mass., who was, according to Savage, "chief man among them." It is also stated, that her maternal grandfather was Captain Edward Richmond, son of John of Taunton, Mass

CHARLES BROWNELL.

(166).

Charles Brownell, son of Thomas and Mary Pearce Brownell, born December 23, 1694, died February, 1774; married July 6, 1717, Mary Wilbur, daughter of Joseph and Ann Brownell Wilbur, born January 4, 1696, and had five children. SAMUEL, born October 12, 1719; died December 1780. JAMES, born May 30, 1722; died December 29, 1736. MARY, born November, 1724. RUTH, born December 29, 1727 PHOEBE, born September 22, 1730.

He married second Mary Wood, and hand one child. CHARLES, born April 13, 1745, married Content Shaw.

THOMAS BROWNELL.

(171).

Thomas Brownell, son of Robert and Mary (surname unknown) Brownell, born 1687; married Grace (surname unknown), and had six children. SUSANNA, born September 5, 1708. ROBERT, born September 29, 1710; married Priscilla or Abigail Pattee BRIDGET, born December 5, 1713, married Benjamin Shrives. JOB, born July, 1717, married Ruth Manchester THANKFUL, born April 23, 1719. ELIZABETH, born July 16, 1725.

47

ANN BROWNELL BLY.

(172).

Ann Brownell, daughter of Robert and Mary (surname unknown) Brownell born January 27, 1690, had a son ICHABOD, who married Rebecca Davol. She afterwards married a Bly, and had several children.

BENJAMIN BROWNELL.

(173)

Benjamin Brownell, son of Robert and Mary (surname unknown) Brownell, born May 11, 1697, married December 27, 1721, Hannah Manchester, and had one child JOSEPH, born December 1, 1722, married (2) Elizabeth Crandall.

MARTHA WILBUR CLOSSON.

(181).

Martha Wilbur, daughter of Joseph and Ann Brownell Wilbur, born August 20, 1684, married June 16, 1702, Timothy Closson, son of Josiah Closson and had two children. JOSIAH, born October 1, 1703 TIMOTHY, born July 5, 1705, married Margaret Carr, (2) Grace Church

ANN WILBUR WOOD

(182)

Ann Wilbur, daughter of Joseph and Ann Brownell Wilbur, born May 8, 1686, married December 4, 1717, George Wood, son of William and Martha Earle Wood, and had two children. WILLIAM, born November 11, 1720; married Deborah Rogers. GEORGE, born May 4, 1723, married Sarah Davol

WILLIAM WILBUR

(183)

William Wilbur son of Joseph and Ann Brownell Wilbur, born March 25, 1688; died April 7, 1775; married Jane Crandall, born August 23, 1692, died January 20 1782, and had ten children. SARAH, born February 28, 1713 ANNA, born September 11, 1715 MARTHA, born January 8, 1719. WILLIAM, born July 2, 1721 MARY, born June 29, 1723 EDITH, born July 11, 1725, died April 28, 1726 EDITH, born April 22, 1727 PHOEBE, born February 23, 1729. ELIZABETH, born March 17, 1731 ABIGAIL, born September 7, 1734, died October 31, 1822

JOSEPH WILBUR.

(184).

Joseph Wilbur, son of Joseph and Ann Brownell Wilbur, born December 30 1689; died May, 1754, married Emeline Champlin, died 1731, and had five children. WALTER, born October 24, 1722, died January 16, 1792. SUSANNA born May 24, 1724, died March, 1773 MARTHA, born March 26, 1727; died June, 1817. EMELINE, born January 31, 1729, died January 10, 1823 HANNAH, born July 18, 1731, died January 10, 1822

THOMAS WILBUR.

(186).

Thomas Wilbur, son of Joseph and Ann Brownell Wilbur, born January 14, 1694; died September, 1783; married Susanna Irish, born 1703: died April 18, 1729 and had three children. GEORGE, born January 28, 1723 JONATHAN, born December 5, 1724. JOSEPH, born November 19, 1728.

He married second Susanna Carr, and had two children. THOMAS, born September 20, 1738, died January, 1792 JOB, born April 2, 1740

BENJAMIN WILBUR

(188).

Benjamin Wilbur, son of Joseph and Ann Brownell Wilbur, born June 20, 1699, married Deborah Gifford, and had six children. CHRISTOPHER, born December 23, 1726 LYDIA, born May 3, 1729. JUDITH, born November 23, 1730 JOHN, born January 31, 1733 JOSEPH, born September 23, 1736. DAVID, born 1738

STEPHEN WILBUR

(189).

Stephen Wilbur son of Joseph and Ann Brownell Wilbur, born March 22, 1701, married Priscilla Irish, born 1707, died 1732, and had four children ANN, born July 7, 1726 JOB, born 1728. ABNER, born 1730 JOHN, born 1731.

MARY HAZARD ROBINSON EASTON.

(1111)

Mary Hazard, daughter of Thomas and Susannah Nichols Hazard, born October 3, 1683; died 1722, married October 19, 1704 John Robinson, son of Rowland and Mary Allen Robinson, died April 6, 1712 and had four children MARY, born September 30, 1705 married Stephen Hazard SARAH, born January 22, 1707, married Ichabod Potter, (2) George Gardiner RUTH, born March 12 1709, married Joseph Underwood SUSANNAH, born February 9, 1712, married Peregrine Gardiner.

She married second Peter Easton son of James Easton, and had two children MIRIAM born December 23, 1718; married Fones Hazard HANNAH, born October 1, 1720

HANNAH HAZARD EASTON

(1112)

Hannah Hazard, daughter of Thomas and Susannah Nichols Hazard born April 14, 1685; died October 1, 1765, married Nicholas Easton, son of James Easton, born December 27, 1683, died November 10, 1743, and had two children. NICHOLAS, born January 1, 1717; died March 14, 1772. JONATHAN, born November 24, 1719, died December 9, 1795 married Ruth Coggeshall

SARAH HAZARD EASTON

(1113).

Sarah Hazard, daughter of Thomas and Susannah Nichols Hazard, born July 15, 1687, married Stephen Easton son of James Easton, born April 5 1682, died 1732, and had two children JAMES,

50

born August 8, 1710. JOHN, born 1713, married Patience Red-wood.

ROBERT HAZARD

(1114)

Robert Hazard, son of Thomas and Susanna (surname un-known) Hazard, born in South Kings Town, R. I., May 23, 1689 died 1762, married Sarah Borden, daughter of Richard and Innocent Wodell Borden, born July 31, 1694, died 1762, and had six chil-dren MARY, born February 23, 1716, died March 13, 1773; mar-ried Stephen Champlin. THOMAS, born May 9, 1718, died Decem-ber 2, 1719 THOMAS, ("College Tom") born September 15, 1720, died August 26, 1798, married Elizabeth Robinson JONATHAN, born August, 1726 married Mary Gardner RICHARD, born De-cember 3, 1730, married Susan Hazard SARAH, born June 27, 1734, married Job Watson

STEPHEN HAZARD

(1116).

Stephen Hazard, son of Thomas and Susannah Nichols Hazard, born June 13, 1693, died December 24, 1718, married Margaret Fones, daughter of John and Lydia Smith Fones, and had three chil-dren. FONES, born May 9, 1715, died in infancy SUSANNAH, born May 9, 1715, died June 8, 1717. FONES, born September 22, 1717, married Miriam Easton

His tombstone gives his age at twenty-five years He willed "all my estate both real and personal, to my beloved wife Margaret"

GEORGE HAZARD.

(1118)

George Hazard, son of Thomas and Susannah Nichols Hazard, born January 18, 1699; died 1746; married November 17, 1721, Mary Place, daughter of Enoch and Mary Sweet Place, born Octo-ber 16, 1697, and had seven children BENJAMIN, born May 2, 1723, died 1748, married Mary (surname unknown). SIMEON born August 8, 1725, married Abigail Mumford. MARY, born

November 23, 1727, died 1777   GEORGE, born April 16, 1730, married Sarah Hazard   SUSANNAH, born December 18, 1732, married Richard Hazard   ENOCH, born December 6, 1735, married Mary Potter   THOMAS, born October 11, 1738, married Mary Easton

His will was dated October 11, 1746, about a month previous to the date of his father's will.

BENJAMIN HAZARD.

(1119)

Benjamin Hazard, son of Thomas and Susannah Nichols Hazard, born November 2, 1702; died 1768, married September 13, 1739 Mehitable Redwood, daughter of Abraham and Patience (surname unknown) Redwood, born in Salem, Mass., September 16, 1722, died June 18, 1761, and had seven children   JONATHAN, born August 25, 1740   THOMAS, born December 25 1742, died in infancy   HANNAH, born July 7, 1744, married James Tanner   MEHIT-ABLE   BENJAMIN, died on board a prison ship   REDWOOD, born June 18, 1745; died June 24, 1836   THOMAS, born January 23, 1756, married Hannah Knowles

He was admitted Freeman of South Kings Town in 1722, and in 1744-45-46-47-48, he was Assistant   In 1745, he and two others were appointed a committee in regard to a controversy about the boundaries between Massachusetts and Rhode Island   In 1749 he was on a committee appointed to burn the old tenor notes as fast as received

JONATHAN HAZARD.

(1119a).

Jonathan Hazard, son of Thomas and Susannah Nichols Hazard, born October 7 1704, died 1746; married Abigail MacCoon, daughter of Daniel and Sarah Place MacCoon born December 14, 1707, and had seven children   THOMAS, born February 22, 1726, married Mary Preston Bowdoin, (2) Eunice Rhodes   SUSANNAH, born March 24 1729; died in Prince Edward Island, December 27, 1815   MARY born March 22, 1737; married Colonel Charles Dyre   GEORGE, born May 22, 1742   SARAH, ABIGAIL   JONA-THAN married Patience Hazard

52

He was admitted Freeman of South Kings Town in 1728, and was chosen a Deputy in 1742. He was one of the early shipbuilders of South Kings Town

ABIGAIL HAZARD NILES.

(1121)

Abigail Hazard, daughter of George and Penelope Arnold Hazard, born March 19, 1690, married Ebenezer Niles, son of Nathaniel and Sarah Sands Niles, born December 3, 1683, and had three children. EBENEZER, born March 4, 1710. PENELOPE SARAH

CALEB HAZARD.

(1123).

Caleb Hazard, son of George and Penelope Arnold Hazard, born November 24, 1697, died January 15, 1726, married November 19, 1719, Abigail Gardiner, daughter of William Gardiner, and had four children WILLIAM, born April 12, 1721, married Phebe Hall. ROBERT, born May 1, 1723, married Elizabeth Hazard CALEB, born January, 1724; died young. CALEB, born September 22, 1726, died March 4, 1784, married Mary (surname unknown). He was buried on the farm given him by his father.

GEORGE HAZARD.

(1124).

George Hazard, son of George and Penelope Arnold Hazard, born October 9, 1700; died 1738, married Sarah Carder, daughter of James and Mary Whipple Carder, born May 14, 1705, died 1738, and had seven children. MARY, born July 16, 1722, married Benjamin Peckham. GEORGE, born June 15, 1724; married Martha Wanton, (2) Jane Tweedy. ABIGAIL, born March 12, 1726, married Rev. Peter Bours, (2) Rev Samuel Fayerweather SARAH, born September 15, 1729, married George Wanton. PENELOPE, born May 7, 1732. CARDER, born August 11, 1734; married Alice Hull, (2) Alice Hazard ARNOLD, born May 15, 1738, married Alice Potter

He was admitted Freeman of the colony in 1721, and was chosen

Deputy of the General Assembly in 1729, and held that position six
years. In 1733, he was Speaker of the House of Representatives, and
in 1734, he was elected Deputy Governor of the colony, and was re-
elected four years in succession, and was holding the office at the time
of his death.

THOMAS HAZARD

(1125).

Thomas Hazard, son of George and Penelope Arnold Hazard,
born March 30 1704, died about 1787, married December 11,
1729, Alice Hull, daughter of Teddiman and Sarah Sands Hull,
died 1737, and had four children   PENELOPE, born February 11,
1731, married William Potter   HANNAH, born August 5, 1732;
married Colonel John Wilson   SARAH, born January 27, 1734;
married George Hazard   ALICE, born August 30, 1737; married
Carder Hazard.
    He was a Deputy in 1745-48-52-53-55-56, and in 1757 he was
Assistant   He was appointed Major in 1745, and Colonel in 1748

OLIVER HAZARD

(1126)

Oliver Hazard, son of George and Penelope Arnold Hazard,
born in South Kings Town, R I, September 13, 1710, died April
14, 1792, married December 9 1736, Elizabeth Raymond, daughter
of Joshua and Elizabeth Christopher Raymond, of North Parish,
New London, Conn, and had three children   ELIZABETH, born in
South Kings Town, R I, September 1, 1737   Oliver, born in
South Kings Town, R I, March 30 1739, married Patience
Greene, a widow   MERCY, born in South Kings Town, R I, Jan-
uary 21, 1740 died 1810, married Freeman Perry   SARAH,
LUCRETIA
    He was admitted Freeman from South Kings Town in 1734

HANNAH HAZARD MUMFORD

(1132)

Hannah Hazard, daughter of Stephen and Elizabeth Helme

54

Hazard, born April 20, 1697 married Joseph Mumford, son of Thomas and Abigail (surname unknown) Mumford, born September 17, 1691, and had one child. STEPHEN, born March 2, 1718

Her husband became a Freeman in 1722

SUSANNAH HAZARD PERRY.

(1133).

Susannah Hazard, daughter of Stephen and Elizabeth Helme Hazard, born April 23, 1699, died 1756, married Samuel Perry, son of Samuel Perry, and had twelve children ELIZABETH, born November 3, 1719; married Elisha Babcock. MARY, born June 10, 1721, married a Dodge. SAMUEL, born April 19, 1723, married Ann Clarke. SIMION, born May 31, 1726, died December 2, 1801, married Anne Browning HANNAH, born April 13, 1728, married Joseph Clarke EDWARD, born June 15, 1730, married Deliverance Moore JOHN, born May 15, 1732; married Meribah Soule. STEPHEN, born January 6, 1736, married Elizabeth Borden, (2) a Whitfield. SARAH, born March 30, 1738; married David Babcock. RUTH, born 1740, married Edward Perry. SUSANNAH, born March 30, 1742, married Jonathan Babcock. MERIBAH, born 1744; married Jeremiah Pierce

Her husband became a Freeman in 1722. In 1740-41-42-46, he was Deputy for Charleston. In 1744, "it was voted and resolved that Joseph Whipple, Deputy Governor Stephen Hopkins, Stephen Brownell, Robert Hazard, Job Randall and Samuel Perry be, and they are hereby, appointed a committee to determine what is ratable estate, and prepare a bill for the same, and present it to the next session of this Assembly "

STEPHEN HAZARD

(1134)

Stephen Hazard, son of Stephen and Elizabeth Helme Hazard, born November 29, 1700, died 1746, married January 9 1723. Mary Robinson, daughter of John and Mary Hazard Robinson born September 30, 1705, died 1780, and had four children STEPHEN, born 1723: married Sarah Nichols MARY, born September 18, 1725, married John Potter. ELIZABETH, born July 26, 1729, married John Potter JOHN, born June 26, 1731 died 1772

55

He was appointed Justice of the Interior Court of Common Pleas
in 1735. His will was proven July, 1746

ROBERT HAZARD.

(1135)

Robert Hazard son of Stephen and Elizabeth Helme Hazard,
born September 12, 1702, died 1751, married Esther Stanton,
daughter of Joseph and Esther Gallup Stanton, and had nine children JOSEPH, born May 21 1728, married Hannah Nichols
ELIZABETH, born May 31, 1730, married Robert Hazard ESTHER,
born December 7, 1732, married Jonathon Babcock. STEPHEN,
born January 13, 1736. ROBERT, born January 13, 1736
SAMUEL, born about 1739, married Hannah Perry JOSHUA
STANTON, born January 8, 1743, married Elizabeth Wickham.

In 1722 he was admitted Freeman of the colony, and in 1734
he was Deputy from South Kings Town, this position he held until
1749 In 1750 he was chosen Deputy Governor and held the office
until his death

SAMUEL HAZARD

(1136).

Samuel Hazard son of Stephen and Elizabeth Helme Hazard,
born June 29, 1705, married Abigail (surname unknown), and had
three children SAMUEL married Catherine (surname unknown)
GEORGE, married Mary Mumford. SARAH, born November 26,
1736

He became a Freeman in 1728 In 1729, he and his brother
Thomas established a fulling-mill in North Kings Town

THOMAS HAZARD

(1137)

Thomas Hazard, son of Stephen and Elizabeth Helme Hazard,
born July 28 1707 married February 22, 1727, Hannah Slocum,
daughter of Samuel Slocum, died January 24, 1737, and had one
child and probably more. STEPHEN, married Elizabeth Carpenter.

He married second May, 1738 Hannah Updike, and had two
children THOMAS, born November 30 1741 HANNAH, born

56

ELIZABETH HAZARD PERRY

(1138).

Elizabeth Hazard, daughter of Stephen and Elizabeth Helme Hazard, born 1709; married July 16, 1729, Benjamin Perry, son of Samuel Perry, and had six children   DORCAS, married Henry Potter.   SUSANNAH.   ELIZABETH   SARAH   ALICE.   BENJAMIN married Ruth Potter.

Her husband was admitted Freeman of Westerly on March 1, 1731-2.

December 22, 1745, died March 30, 1798

ROBERT WILCOX.

(1141)

Robert Wilcox, son of Thomas and Martha Hazard Wilcox, born 1687; married Catherine Lillibridge, daughter of Thomas and Mary Hobson Lillibridge, born in Newport, R I, and had six children   SUSANNA, married John Knowles   ROBERT, JR   HANNAH, married William Reynolds   MARTHA, married a Stanton.   CATHERINE, died March 30, 1773, married Barney Davis   HOBSON, married Elizabeth Holway

STEPHEN WILCOX.

(1153).

Stephen Wilcox, son of Edward and (given name unknown) Hazard Wilcox, born in Westerly; married July 12, 1716, Mercie Randall, daughter of Matthew Randall, of Stonington, and had six children   DAVID, born February 3, 1720.   MERCIE, born August 6, 1724   EUNICE, born May 22, 1726.   STEPHEN, born April 21, 1728   VALENTINE, born February 14, 1733.   ISAIAH, born about 1738.

JEFFREY HAZARD.

(1161)

Jeffrey Hazard, son of Robert and Amey (surname unknown) Hazard, born September 29, 1698, died 1767, married Mary (surname unknown), and had six children. JEREMIAH, born August 13, 1726, married Mary Hazard. SUSANNAH, died February, 1793, married Wilkinson Browning. ROBERT, married Hannah Greene. JEFFRY. HANNAH, married Thomas Champlin. PATIENCE, died March 19, 1800, married Jonathan Hazard.

He was Deputy from Kings Town, from 1735 to 1758.

ROBERT HAZARD

(1164).

Robert Hazard, son of Robert and Ann (surname unknown) Hazard, born January 19, 1709; died 1775; married March 1727 Martha (surname unknown), and had eight children. ROBERT, born September 19, 1728, married Alice Thomas. AMEY, born November, 1733, married a Wilcox. SARAH, born May 6, 1734, married John Richmond. JEREMIAH, born July 25, 1736, married Phebe Tillinghast. MARY, born December 21, 1738, married Adam Richmond. HANNAH, born March 19, 1741. JEFFRY, born October 6, 1743. THOMAS, died 1784.

AMEY HAZARD SHERMAN

(1166)

Amey Hazard, daughter of Robert and Amey (surname unknown) Hazard, born September 20, 1715, married May 30, 1734, Eber Sherman, and had one child. EBER.

ANN HAZARD BROWNING

(1172)

Ann Hazard, daughter of Jeremiah and Sarah Smith Hazard, born February 28, 1701, died 1770, married April 21, 1721 John Browning, son of William and Rebecca Wilbur Browning, and had ten children. THOMAS married Anne Hoxsie. JEREMIAH. HANNAH, married Jedediah Frink. SARAH, married a Stanton. JOHN. EPHRIAM. MARTHA, married a Powers. ANN, married John Browning. MARY, married Robert Champlin. EUNICE, married a Clarke.

58

Robert Hazard

(1173).

Robert Hazard, son of Jeremiah and Sarah Smith Hazard, born April 11, 1703, died October 8, 1789, married Patience Northup, daughter of Stephen and Mary Thomas Northup, born June 27, 1705, died June 26, 1795, and had four children. MARY, married Jeremiah Hazard. EPHRIAM, born 1729, died May 28, 1825 GIDLON, born 1734; died June 15, 1814. JEREMIAH, born 1735

Hannah Hazard Watson

(1176)

Hannah Hazard, daughter of Jeremiah and Sarah Smith Hazard, born April 17, 1714, married Samuel Watson, and had three children SAMUEL. FREEBORN HAZARD

Stephen Champlin

(1192).

Stephen Champlin, son of Jeffrey and Hannah Hazard Champlin, born February 16, 1710, died July 22, 1771, married Mary Hazard, daughter of Robert and Sarah Borden Hazard, died March 13, 1773, and had eight children. STEPHEN, born September 29, 1734, married Dinah Browning HANNAH, born 1735, married Nicholas Gardiner SARAH, born August 18, 1737, married Samuel Congdon. MARY, born 1739, married Joseph Browning. SUSANNAH, born March 26, 1742, married Arnold Wilcox JEFFREY. born March 21, 1744; married Mary (surname unknown) ROBERT born April 12, 1747. THOMAS

Elizabeth Wanton Borden.

(1221)

Elizabeth Wanton, daughter of Joseph and Sarah Freeborn Wanton, born in Tiverton, R. I., January 5, 1691, married Abraham Borden

TENTH ANNUAL REUNION OF THE BROWNELL FAMILY.

GIDEON WANTON

(1223).

Gideon Wanton, son of Joseph and Sarah Freeborn Wanton, born in Tiverton, R. I., October 20, 1693, died September 12, 1767, married February 6, 1718 Mrs Mary Cadman, widow of Christopher Cadman, died September 3, 1780, and had four children GIDEON JOHN G., born 1729, died July 2, 1799, married Mary Bull. JOSEPH, born February 8, 1730 EDWARD

He was the third of the name of Wanton to become Governor of Rhode Island He and his wife are both buried in the Friends Burial Ground at Newport, R. I.

SARAH WANTON SPENCER HOWLAND
(1224).

Sarah Wanton, daughter of Joseph and Sarah Freeborn Wanton, born in Tiverton R. I., April 27, 1696, married Thomas Spencer, (2) Benjamin Howland

MARY WANTON RICHARDSON
(1226)

Mary Wanton, daughter of Joseph and Sarah Freeborn Wanton born in Tiverton, R I., June 10, 1700, married Thomas Richardson, a wealthy and refined gentleman of Newport, R I He was General Treasurer of the colony for many years, and an influential member of the Friends Society

ANN DURFEE ESTES
(1231).

Ann Durfee, daughter of Thomas and Ann Freeborn Durfee, born in Portsmouth, R. I., August 25, 1691, died in Dartmouth, Mass, April 27, 1734, married in Portsmouth, R I, December 22, 1715, Robert Estes of Lynn, Mass, son of Richard and Elizabeth Beck Estes, born in Salem, Mass, August 27, 1694, died in Portsmouth, R. I., 1780 and hand four children RICHARD, born July 2, 1717. SARAH, born February 13, 1720. THOMAS, born April 17, 1725 ANN, born March 8, 1726.

Robert Estes grandfather, was Robert Estes of Dover, England.

SARAH DURFEE DENNIS

(1232).

Sarah Durfee, daughter of Thomas and Ann Freeborn Durfee, born in Portsmouth, R I March 1 1693, died in Portsmouth R. I April 21 1759; married April 20, 1721. Joseph Dennis, son of Robert and Sarah Howland Dennis, born in Portsmouth, R. I., May 25 1689 died in Portsmouth, R I., October 24, 1759, and had eight children SARAH, born in Portsmouth R I., July 1, 1723, died there in infancy SARAH, born in Portsmouth, R. I, April 1, 1725 ROBERT, born in Portsmouth, R I., September 12, 1727 JOSEPH born in Portsmouth, R. I., June 15, 1730 ANNA, born in Portsmouth, R I, December 19, 1731 RUTH, born in Portsmouth, R I, December 6 1733 LYDIA born in Portsmouth, R I, October 12, 1735 FREEBORN, born in Portsmouth, R. I, August 18, 1739

Her husband was admitted a Freeman in Portsmouth, R I., in 1710, and was chosen a Deputy in the General Assembly in 1720-21-31

MARTHA DURFEE READ

(1236)

Martha Durfee, daughter of Thomas and Ann Freeborn Durfee, born in Portsmouth R I, February 20, 1702, married in Portsmouth, R I, December 27, 1730, Oliver Read, son of John and Mary (surname unknown) Read, born in Freetown, Mass., October 14, 1701, and had eight children. JOSEPH born in Freetown, Mass December 11, 1732, died in Freetown, Mass 1791, married Mary Knowles OLIVER born in Freetown, Mass, August 21, 1734, married Patience Brayton MARY, born in Freetown, Mass., March 31, 1736, died in Swansea, Mass, March 12, 1806, married Philip Slade JONATHAN, born in Freetown, Mass, November 13, 1737, married Eunice Weaver. WAIT, born in Freetown, Mass December 6, 1739, married Samuel Weaver NATHAN, born in Freetown, Mass, June 16, 1742 BENJAMIN, born in Freetown, Mass, March 28, 1744 GIDEON, born in Freetown, Mass., February 5, 1746.

Her husband's will, dated June 3, 1777, mentions sons Joseph, Oliver, Jonathan, Nathan and Benjamin, daughters Wait Weaver and Mary Slade, granddaughter Elizabeth, daughter of son Gideon, deceased

GIDEON DURFEE.

(1237)

Gideon Durfee, son of Thomas and Ann Freeborn Durfee, born in Portsmouth, R I., January 15, 1705, died in Portsmouth, R I., May 5, 1766, married November 11, 1725, Waite Tripp, daughter of Abiel and Eleanor Waite Tripp, born in Portsmouth, R I, April 19, 1705, and had six children FREEBORN, born in Portsmouth, R. I, December 28, 1726 SARAH, born in Portsmouth, R. I, September 22, 1728 ELEANOR, born in Portsmouth R. I, November 22, 1730 JOB, born in Portsmouth, R I, August 19, 1735 ANN, born in Portsmouth, R I, February 23, 1736. WAITE, born in Portsmouth, R I, September 9, 1738; died young.

He married second Eleanor Tripp, daughter of Abiel and Eleanor Waite Tripp, born in Portsmouth, R I, December 26, 1715, and had six children. WAITE, born in Portsmouth, R I, April 16, 1741 ELIZABETH, born in Portsmouth, R. I, March 7, 1743 RUTH, born in Portsmouth, R I, September 20, 1744. SUSANNA, born in Portsmouth, R I, July 30, 1748 CHRISTOPHER, born in Portsmouth, R I, April 18, 1753, married October 18 1773, Mary Fisher of Portsmouth, R I ELEANOR, born in Portsmouth, R I, February 18, 1756.

An abstract of the will of Gideon Durfee, dated at Portsmouth, R I, July 9, 1754, and probated June 9, 1766 is given in the Durfee Genealogy by Winthrop C Durfee.

THOMAS DURFEE

(1238)

Thomas Durfee, son of Thomas and Ann Freeborn Durfee, born in Portsmouth, R I, June 6, 1706, died in Middletown, R I., April, 1784, married in Portsmouth, R I., June 15, 1729, Sarah Briggs, daughter of Job and Eleanor Briggs of Portsmouth, R. I, born in Little Compton, R. I., died in Portsmouth, R. I, May 2, 1737, and had three children. SARAH, born in Portsmouth, R I,

March 30 1730 ELIZABETH, born in Portsmouth, R. I., May 11, 1732 JOSEPH born in Portsmouth R I June 29, 1734.

He married second March 16 1740, Mary Tripp daughter of Abiel and Eleanor Waite Tripp, born in Portsmouth, R. I., March 9, 1711, died in Middleton, R. I., May 28, 1789, and had four children JAMES born in Bristol, R. I., January 11, 1742 BENJAMIN, born in Bristol R I, January 6, 1744, died in Portsmouth, R I, March 27 1817. OLIVER born in Bristol, R. I., March 19, 1746, died young OLIVER, born in Portsmouth, R. I., February 27, 1754

JOB DURFEE

(1230?)

Job Durfee, son of Thomas and Ann Freeborn Durfee, born in Portsmouth R I, 1710, died in Tiverton R I April 1744; married in Portsmouth, R I September 17, 1730, Elizabeth Chase, daughter of Benjamin and Amy Borden Chase of Tiverton R I born in Portsmouth, R I, June 16, 1701, died in Portsmouth, R. I., about 1734, and had one child. THOMAS, born in Portsmouth R I, March 25 1732, was "probably lost at sea when a young man"

He married second at Portsmouth, R. I., Mary Earle, daughter of John and Mary Wait Earle, born February 19, 1703, and had five children ELIZABETH, born in Tiverton, R I, July 12, 1735. JOHN, born in Tiverton, R I, August 3, 1736, died in Tiverton R I August 31, 1812, married Phebe Gray. GIDEON, born in Tiverton, R I, February 17, 1738, died in Palmyra, N Y, September 12, 1814, married Anna Bowen. EARLE, born in Tiverton, R I September 16 1740, lost at sea with his half brother Thomas Durfee JOB, born in Tiverton, R I, August 26, 1744

He married third in Freetown, Mass, April 8, 1762, Sarah Brayton of Freetown, Mass He became a Freeman of Portsmouth, R. I, in May, 1731 He was chosen a Deputy to the General Assembly of Rhode Island in 1761-62-64 His will, dated July 31, 1769 was proven May 16, 1774 In it he mentions sons John, Gideon and Job Durfee, also sons Thomas and Earle, if they ever return from sea, daughter Elizabeth Chase and wife Sarah

SUSANNAH CORNELL BENNETT.

(1242).

Susannah Cornell, daughter of Thomas and Martha Freeborn Cornell, born May 22, 1702, married February 6, 1722, John Bennett, son of Jonathan Bennett

WILLIAM CORNELL.

(1244).

William Cornell, son of Thomas and Martha Freeborn Cornell, born July 26, 1705; married in Newport, R. I., July 18, 1723, Hannah Thurston, daughter of Samuel and Abigail Clark Thurston, born December 17, 1701, died November 23, 1753, and had nine children. SARAH, born April 26, 1724, died September 10, 1730. THOMAS born January 13, 1726, married Rachel Allen. ABIGAIL, born July 11, 1728, died September 4, 1730. HANNAH, born November 22, 1730; married Thomas Coggeshall. ABIGAIL, born February 2, 1732 SARAH, born September 10, 1736 ELIZABETH, born May 17, 1740; died January 3, 1804, married Peleg Allen. SUSANNAH, born July 29 1742 WILLIAM, born October 23, 1744.

It is stated that he married second, March 27 1754, Freelove Dring of Middletown.

GEORGE CORNELL

(1245).

George Cornell, son of Thomas and Martha Freeborn Cornell, born December 11, 1707, married in Newport, R I., January 16, 1728, Elizabeth Thurston, daughter of Samuel and Abigail Clark Thurston, born December 22, 1708, and had seven children WALTER, born October 11, 1729, married Sarah Anthony THOMAS, born September 22, 1731; married Jennie Foster LATHAM, born October 22, 1733, died May 55 1734 LATHAM, born April 2, 1735, lost at sea. GIDEON, born December 6, 1737; died May 30, 1801; married Susannah Brownell EDWARD born October 7, 1740; married Elizabeth Coggeshall MATTHEW, born November 11, 1745, died March 4, 1807, married Elizabeth Shieve.

GIDION CORNELL.

(1246).

Gideon Cornell, son of Thomas and Martha Freeborn Cornell, born July 5, 1710; died 1766, married in Newport, R. I., February 22, 1732, Rebecca Vaughan, and had two children GIDION, born October 10, 1740, died at the age of nine months. REBECCA, born February 17, 1755, married Colonel Clement Biddle

He became a Freeman of Portsmouth, R. I., in 1731. He was a Deputy in 1732, and Assistant Deputy in 1740-46. In 1754, he sold land on execution in Freetown, Mass. In 1746, he was on a committee to run boundary line between Massachusetts and Rhode Island. He died in Kingston, Island of Jamaica.

JOSEPH BROWNELL

(1462)

Joseph Brownell, son of Joseph and Ruth Cornell Brownell, born in Portsmouth R. I., April 26, 1720, married December 22, 1742, Rebecca Tripp, daughter of Abial and Eleanor Wait Tripp, and had ten children. STEPHEN, born in Portsmouth, R. I. February 12, 1744, died in Providence, R. I., November 23, 1815, married Susannah Fish. CAPTAIN JONATHAN, born in Portsmouth, R. I., May 30, 1746. NATHAN, born in Portsmouth, R. I., February 7, 1747, married Elizabeth Fish. OLIVER, born in Portsmouth, R. I. February 17, 1749. PHILADELPHIA, born in Portsmouth, R. I., May 17, 1752, married Richard Sisson. SUSANNA, born in Portsmouth, R. I. March 17, 1754, married Giles Slocum. MARY, born in Portsmouth, R. I., December 6, 1757. AMEY, born in Portsmouth, R. I., September 8, 1760, married Captain Benjamin Weaver. THOMAS, born in Portsmouth, R. I., December 16, 1762, married Mercy Shaw. REBECCA, born in Portsmouth, R. I., February 19, 1765, married Major Jacob Mann

He was a Deputy in the General Assembly in 1744-45-74, and Assistant Deputy in 1755-57-58. He was Ensign in 1761.

THOMAS BROWNELL

(1463).

Thomas Brownell, son of Joseph and Ruth Cornell Brownell, born October 23, 1722, married Abigail Slocum, and had six children RUTH, born January 11, 1745 ANNA born August 3, 1747 JOSEPH, born February 21, 1754. ANN, born January 9, 1757 BENJAMIN, born April 23, 1759 GEORGE, born October 20, 1761

PHILADELPHIA BROWNELL HOWLAND.

(1465).

Philadelphia Brownell, daughter of Joseph and Ruth Cornell Brownell born December 15, 1726, married Daniel Howland, and had a daughter MERCY, born December 30, 1745, died January 26, 1824, married Gideon Greene, and I think other children

GEORGE BROWNELL

(1467)

George Brownell, son of Joseph and Ruth Cornell Brownell, born in Portsmouth, R. I., September 27, 1736, died in Portsmouth, R. I.; married March 20, 1760, Waite Durfee, daughter of Gideon and Eleanor Tripp Durfee, and had one child MARTHA, born in Portsmouth, R. I., October 5, 1761, married Doctor Elijah Cobb of Dartsmouth, Mass.

GEORGE BROWNELL.

(1483).

George Brownell, son of Stephen and Martha Earle Brownell born December 10, 1731, married December 8, 1768, Elizabeth Cornell, daughter of Clark and Priscilla Lawton Cornell.

PHOEBE BROWNELL CORNELL

(1484)

Phoebe Brownell, daughter of Stephen and Martha Earle

67

Brownell, born March 7, 1730, died May 13, 1830, married October 23, 1760, Jonathan Cornell, son of Walter and Mary Nicholls Cornell, born August 5, 1730, died 1809, and had four children MARY, born June 31, 1761, died young. WALTER, born April 7, 1764 married Ruth Earle. HANNAH BROWNELL, born March 10, 1767; married Oliver Cornell, (2) Thomas Townsend STEPHEN BROWNELL, born November 22, 1773, died January 17, 1840, married Catherine Sherman.

THOMAS BROWNELL

(1513)

Thomas Brownell, son of Thomas and Esther Taber Brownell, born February 15 1702 married Hannah (surname unknown), and had eleven children KEZIAH, born June 12 1727, married George Tibbets THANKFUL, born April 15, 1730, married Isaac Tripp. HANNAH, born July 22, 1732, married Obadiah Mosher. THOMAS, born September 27 1734 MERCY, born October 13 1736. BENJAMIN born February 7, 1739, married Martha Closson PATIENCE, born July 29, 1741, married Job Chase DOROTHY, born May 14, 1744, married John Sanford GEORGE, born December 9, 1746, married Rhoda Milks ELIZABETH born October 13, 1749 married Peleg Peckham.

His will was probated November 5, 1754

CONTENT BROWNELL CORNELL

(1516).

Content Brownell, daughter of Thomas and Esther Taber Brownell, born February 11, 1708 married May 11, 1732, Richard Cornell, son of Stephen and Hannah Mosher Cornell, born January 28, 1702, died 1761, and had five children EZEKIEL, born March 7 1733, married Rachel Wood. PHILIP, born October 5, 1735, died October 27, 1765, married Lillis Thomas PATIENCE, born January 14, 1740, married Thomas Tripp RICHARD, born March 4, 1742, married Alice Anthony GIDEON, born December 1 1745 died 1830 married Prudence Winslow, (2) widow Thornton

68

JONATHAN BROWNELL

(159a2).

Jonathan Brownell, son of George and Elizabeth Davol Brownell, married Hannah Hiller, and had six children. DAVID, married Rhoda Brownell JONATHAN, born in Cold Spring, Dutchess County, N. Y., November 2, 1768, married Desire Lake. BENJAMIN, born June 18, 1771, died May 15, 1826, married Huldah Bullock. HANNAH married Tracy Pratt MARY, married Amos Knapp ELIZABETH

It has been stated that he was married twice, and that he had three girls by his first wife and three boys by his second wife I have been unable to find such records, but am satisfied he had these six children and may have had others

BENJAMIN BROWNELL.

(159a4).

Benjamin Brownell, son of George and Elizabeth Davol Brownell, married Waite Brownell, daughter of Gideon and Eleanor Tripp Durfee and widow of George Brownell, and had three children. GEORGE, born December 30, 1765; married Sarah Burrington. GIDEON, born May 22, 1770. ELIZABETH, born September 10, 1773.

The following was taken from the diary of Elisha Fish ' "The seventh day of December, 1794, Wait, wife of Benjamin Brownell, departed this life after a long and gradual decline She was a woman remarkable for her service among her neighbors in sickness as well as in many other cases of difficulty."

RICHARD BROWNELL.

(1611).

Richard Brownell, son of Thomas and Mary Crandall Brownell, born December 10, 1715, married 1741, Mary Wilbur, born 1719, and had three children PRISCILLA, born December 20, 1741. JAMES, born July 5, 1743; died 1811 GIDEON, born December 28, 1745, died 1749.

GILES BROWNELL

(1631)

Giles Brownell, son of George and Mary Thurston Brownell, born March 1, 1707 married May 19, 1726, Elizabeth Shaw, daughter of Israel and (given name unknown) Tallman Shaw, born February 7 1706 and had ten children Isaac, born October 15, 1726 CHARLES born March 8 1728 GILES, born August 4, 1729, died October 19 WILLIAM, born February 14, 1731. ALICE, born October 28, 1733 PHOEBE, born June 10, 1735 GEORGE, born April 27, 1737 MARY, born December 1, 1741 JAMES, born March 15, 1743 JOSEPH, born July 15, 1744 died February 24, 1824 married Deborah Briggs

PHOEBE BROWNELL TABER

(1632).

Phoebe Brownell, daughter of George and Mary Thurston Brownell, born June 19 1708, married October 1, 1724, Philip Taber.

MARY BROWNELL WOOD

(1633).

Mary Brownell, daughter of George and Mary Thurston Brownell, born November 9, 1709; died October 6, 1791, married August 31, 1727, Joseph Wood

GEORGE BROWNELL

(1634)

George Brownell, son of George and Mary Thurston Brownell, born in Little Compton, R. I., June 21 1711. died June 30, 1800, married October 21, 1731, Sarah Bailey daughter of William and Dorothy Graves Bailey born June 30, 1710, died 1811, and had nine children DOROTHY, born in Little Compton, R. I., June 11, 1733 MARY, born in Little Compton, R. I., August 8, 1735 SAMUEL, born in Little Compton, R I, July 18, 1738 married Ruth Briggs ELIZABETH, born in Little Compton, R. I August

1, 1741. GEORGE, born in Little Compton, R. I., March 31, 1744, died March 27, 1810, married Lucy Richmond. EZRA, born in Little Compton, R. I., October 20, 1746, died 1818, married Hope Borden SARAH, born in Little Compton, R. I., October 1, 1748 NATHANIEL, born in Little Compton R I, December 21, 1751, died in Westport, Mass, December 30, 1825, married Sarah Tompkins PRISCILLA, born in Little Compton, R I, May 21, 1754.

He was a Sergeant in Captain Thomas Kempton's company of Colonel Timothy Danielson's regiment in the alarm of Lexington. He received order for bounty coat or its equivalent in money, dated at Roxbury, October 30, 1775 Date of company's return was October 6 1775 His three sons Samuel, George and Nathaniel served in the Revolutionary War

THOMAS BROWNELL.

(1635)

Thomas Brownell, son of George and Mary Thurston Brownell, born February 1, 1713, married Mary Blackman.

ELIZABETH BROWNELL STODDARD.

(1636)

Elizabeth Brownell, daughter of George and Mary Thurston Brownell, born September 15, 1717; married Israel Stoddard.

JONATHAN BROWNELL

(1637).

Jonathan Brownell, son of George and Mary Thurston Brownell, born March 19, 1719; died June 11. 1776, married January 14, 1742, Elizabeth Richmond, daughter of William and Ann Gray Richmond, born February 26, 1725, died June 11, 1806, and had seven children ANNA, born February 2, 1743, died January 4, 1791; married Nathaniel Richmond PARDON, born July 6, 1745 died January 24, 1799; married Prudence Shaw ELIZABTH, born June 12, 1748, married Ichabod Wood PEREZ, born October, 1750; died October, 1751. RUTH, born November 24, 1753, married Joseph Wilbur LYDIA, born November 7, 1755, died August

14, 1785, married Samuel Taylor   SYLVESTER, born November 20,
1757, died March 21, 1840, married Mercy Church

Lieutenant Jonathan Brownell was in the battle of Bunker Hill,
and received a wound from which he died.   He is buried at Westport, Mass

PAUL BROWNELL

(1638).

Paul Brownell, son of George and Mary Thurston Brownell,
born June 12, 1721, died May 20, 1760, married January 6, 1745,
Deborah Dennis daughter of Robert and Susannah Briggs Dennis,
born March 21, 1721

STEPHEN BROWNELL

(1639)

Stephen Brownell, son of George and Mary Thurston Brownell,
born November 26, 1726, married Edith Wilbur, and had eight
children   PHOEBE, born September 4, 1747   WILLIAM, born July
17 1749 died 1810 married Elizabeth Peirce, (2) Eunice Palmer,
(3) Betsey Grinnell. ABIGAIL, born March 15, 1751   EDITH,
born November 2, 1752, married William Earle.   MARY, born
July 5, 1754, married Rouse Pearce   GEORGE, born October 29,
1756, married Elizabeth Peckham.   STEPHEN, born March 18,
1762   ELIZABETH, married Israel Stoddard

He married second February 21, 1771, Mary Eldridge, daughter of William Eldridge of North Kings Town

PEARCE BROWNELL

(1642)

Pearce Brownell, son of Jeremiah and Deborah Burgess Brownell,
born at Little Compton, R. I, March 30, 1715, married February
7, 1740, Ruth Thurston, daughter of Edward and Sarah Carr Thurston, born October 3, 1722, and had eleven children   PEARCE born
1743. GIDEON, born 1746, died September 2, 1818, married Phoebe
Brown   HOPE, born 1750; married Restcome Palmer. SUSANNA,
born 1755; married Nathaniel Doring. SARAH. RUTH. GEORGE,

72

born July 5, 1763; died March, 1792 Lois, born 1765, married Seth Church ESEK. WANTON. EVA

His wife was the great-grand-daughter of Edward Thurston, and his wife, Elizabeth Mott Thurston, whose brother Jacob Mott was the great-grandfather of the noted General Nathaniel Greene of the Revolutionary Army, making Ruth Thurston Brownell the third cousin of the General The Thurstons lived at Newport, R. I., and are there buried in the Coddington Burial Grounds

AARON BROWNELL.

(1647).

Aaron Brownell, son of Jeremiah and Deborah Burgess Brownell, born in Little Compton, R I, August 11, 1722, died September 17 1754, married March, 1745, Alice Southworth, daughter of Edward and Elizabeth Palmer Southworth, born November 24, 1720, and had seven children EDWARD, born in Little Compton, R I, January 10, 1746, married Susannah Wells ELIZABETH, born in Little Compton, R I, March 26, 1747, married Benjamin Bulkeley. JEREMIAH, born in Little Compton, R. I, April 21, 1749, married a Copp ICHABOD, born in Little Compton, R I, August 30, 1750, married Elizabeth Stanley LUCY, born in Little Compton, R I March 16, 1752, married a Minor CYNTHIA, born in Little Compton, R I, September 22, 1753, married a Stevens AARON born in Little Compton, R. I, February 2, 1755.

His wife Alice Southworth was grand-daughter of William and Rebecca Paybodie Southworth, and great-grand-daughter of William and "Betty" Alden Paybodie the daughter of John and Priscilla Mullins Alden of the Mayflower Her paternal grandfather, William Southworth, was the son of Constant Southworth, whose mother, Alice Carpenter (widow of Edward Southworth) married as second wife, Governor William Bradford of the Plymouth Colony. Constant came to New England in 1628, when but fourteen years of age, and was brought up under the influence of his step-father and became a man of importance in the colony He married November 2, 1637, Elizabeth Collier, daughter of William Collier "the richest man of the colony." The Southworth family trace back to the de Southworths of Samlesbury Hall County of Lancaster, England The name was variously spelled in early English and American records, Sotherworth. Southworth. Southwood.

73

Southward and in some cases in later generations it was pronounced and spelled Southard, but the original name was Southworth as in the church yard inscriptions, County of Lancaster, where the Southworths of Samlesbury Hall (their home for more than three hundred years) are buried

JOSHUA BROWNELL

(1649a)

Joshua Brownell, son of Jeremiah and Deborah Burgess Brownell, born December 18 1727, married Martha Peckham daughter of Joseph and Elizabeth Wilbur Peckham, born May 28, 1730, and had ten children ELIZABETH, born April 2, 1751, married Edward Brownell LYDIA, born February 2, 1753, married Abraham Wing AARON born December 24, 1754, married Mary Gardner LUTHAN. JOSHUA, married Elizabeth Reasoner DANIEL SIMION, born June 4, 1759, died June 29 1832, married Sarah Hoag RHODA, married David Brownell JEREMIAH HANNAH, married a Wilcox

JOHN BROWNELL

(1649b).

John Brownell, son of Jeremiah and Deborah Burgess Brownell, born October 10, 1729 married Susanna Borden, daughter of Stephen and Penelope Borden, born May 19, 1737, and had twelve children PATIENCE, born March 25, 1755 HANNAH, born March 28 1757 ESTHER, born March 29, 1759. JEREMIAH, born March 2 1761 SUSANNA, born February 26 1763 MERIBAH born May 31 1765 ELIPHLL born June 2, 1767 ISAAC, born February 23 1769. ANNA, born February 3, 1771 JOHN born May 6, 1773 LAURA, born May 6, 1773. RICHMOND, born October 26 1775. ROBERT, born August 4 1778, married Roby Fuller

It is stated that he was born in Little Compton R I His last days were spent at Fairhaven, Mass, and he was buried in the Quaker Cemetery, at the head of the river (Acushnet) Robert Brownell, son of John, had a commission from the King of England appointing John Brownell a Major in the English Army, he gave this commission to Captain John A Hawes who before he died

74

RESIDENCE OF DAVID BROWNELL.

deposited it in some public collection His old family Bible, now in possession of Miss Helen Mar Brownell, one of his great-grand-daughters, was printed in Edenburgh by Alexander Kincaid in 1749.

CHARLES BROWNELL

(1666)

Charles Brownell, son of Charles and Mary Wood Brownell, born April 13, 1745, married February 22, 1770 Content Shaw, daughter of Israel and Sarah Wilbur Shaw, and had ten children. THOMAS, born January 2, 1771, died in Sandgate, Vt, December 8, 1838, married Milly Grey PHOLBE, born December 13, 1772; married Peter Garrett JEDADIAH, born October 11, 1774, died February 20, 1847, married Eunice Watkins ELIZABETH, born March 28, 1776 AARON, born January 27, 1778 EPHRIAM, born March 27, 1779. PRISCILLA, born June 4, 1783 BORDEN, born December 18, 1787 CHARLES, born November 18, 1789 ISABEL

It is said that either Priscilla or Isabel married John Hicks Charles Brownell moved his family from Rhode Island to Trenton, Oneida County, N Y, and died there

JOB BROWNELL

(1714).

Job Brownell, son of Thomas and Grace (surname unknown) Brownell born July 1717, married June 25, 1747, Ruth Manchester, daughter of Edward and Ann Williston Manchester, and had five children SUSANNA, born October 10, 1748. ROBERT, born April 7, 1750, married Priscilla or Abigail Pattee ELIZABETH, born April 6, 1753 GRACE, born March 26, 1757. THOMAS, born January 6, 1760.

ICHABOD BROWNELL

(1721)

Ichabod Brownell, son of Ann Brownell, married February 21, 1732, Rebecca Davol, daughter of Benjamin and Ann Davol, and had ten children WILLIAM, died young ICHABOD, married De-

76

lilah Tripp BENJAMIN, born June 13, 1734, died December 3, 1816; married Phoebe Potter GEORGE, married Mary Tripp PRINCE, married Mary Manchester, (2) Delilah Haskins. JUDITH, married Ephriam Potter. MARY, married John Davol. SARAH, married Benjamin Davol ANN, married David Cornell PRUDENCE, married Barzano Davol

JOSEPH BROWNELL.

(1731)

Joseph Brownell, son of Benjamin and Hannah Manchester Brownell, born December 1, 1722, married (intentions published August 30, 1746) Elizabeth Crandall, daughter of Eber and Content Manchester Crandall, born June 20, 1731, and had three children STEPHEN, born November 21, 1747; married Margaret Church. MARGARET, born May 7, 1749 HANNAH, born July 16, 1751

SARAH ROBINSON POTTER GARDINER.

(11112).

Sarah Robinson, daughter of John and Mary Hazard Robinson, born January 22, 1707, married January 16, 1722, Ichabod Potter, son of Ichabod Potter, and had four children JOHN born July 29, 1724. SIMEON, born September 25, 1726. RUTH, born January 19, 1728. ROUSE, born December 10, 1729.

She married second February 19, 1742, George Gardiner, and had five children. SUSANNAH born June 16, 1743 GEORGE, born March 18, 1745. RUFUS, born March 9, 1747 WILLIAM, born September 8, 1749. LEVI, born September 29, 1751

RUTH ROBINSON UNDERWOOD

(11113).

Ruth Robinson, daughter of John and Mary Hazard Robinson, born March 12, 1709, married April 27, 1731, Joseph Underwood, and had two children JOHN, born December 24, 1732 JOSEPH, born April 12, 1734

Miriam Easton Hazard

(11115)

Miriam Easton, daughter of Peter and Mary Hazard Easton, born December 23, 1718, married Fones Hazard, son of Stephen and Margaret Fones Hazard, born September 22, 1717, and had three children. STEPHEN, born May 18, 1740, died May, 1800, married Hannah Sandford. NICHOLAS born August 12 1741; married Mary Lulucina. FONES born 1744, died 1803, married Rebecca Briart

Jonathan Easton

(11122)

Jonathan Easton, son of Nicholas and Hannah Hazard Easton, born November 24, 1719, died December 9 1795, married Ruth Coggeshall, daughter of Benjamin and Sarah Easton Coggeshall, and had eleven children. MARY, born May 20, 1743; died November 20, 1794, married Thomas G Hazard. NICHOLAS, born June 29, 1744, died June 21, 1789; married Elizabeth Potter. JONATHAN, born August 6, 1747, died March 13, 1813, married Sarah Thurston. SARAH, born August 16, 1749, died November 3, 1827. HANNAH, born 1750; died October 29, 1797. BENJAMIN born August 28, 1752, died September 16, 1807. RUTH, born May 21, 1754, married Godfrey Hazard. PATIENCE, born September 24, 1756, died August 30, 1811. JOHN, born March 26, 1758, died August 21, 1823, married Ruth Taylor, (2) Hannah Taylor. STEPHEN, born October 18 1759 died October 19, 1759. REBECCA born October 18, 1759, died October 19, 1759. His wife died October 20, 1759

John Easton

(11132)

John Easton, son of Stephen and Sarah Hazard Easton, born 1713, married April 17, 1735, Patience Redwood, daughter of Abraham and Patience Howland Redwood and had seven children. NICHOLAS, born May 4, 1752, died November 28, 1825. MARY, married Joseph Thurston (And five other children names not given).

78

Thomas Hazard

(11143)

Thomas Hazard, son of Robert and Sarah Borden Hazard, born September 15, 1720, died 1798, married March 27, 1742, Elizabeth Robinson, daughter of William and Martha Potter Robinson, born June 16, 1724; died February 5, 1804 and had five children. Sarah, born January 10, 1747, died May 26, 1753 Robert, born November 17, 1753. Thomas, born January 13, 1755, died May 15, 1756. Thomas born January 15 1758. Rowland, born June 4, 1763

In 1742, he became a Freeman from South Kings Town In 1748, he was clerk of the Council. It is stated that he was one of the founders of Brown University. He was a member of the Friends Society, and a preacher of that faith for forty years before his death In 1783, it was voted by the General Assembly 'that the draft of an act authorizing the manumission of slaves, presented to this Assembly by the committee appointed to consider the petition of a committee of the people called Quakers, be referred to the third day of the next session for further consideration,'' etc. Thomas Hazard was one of the signers of this petition, which was the opening wedge to the Emancipation Act passed February, 1784 He entered Yale University, and for this reason he was called "College Tom," a name by which he was distinguished from the other Thomas Hazards of his generation.

Richard Hazard

(11145).

Richard Hazard, son of Robert and Sarah Borden Hazard, born December 31, 1730, died September 30, 1762, married Susanna Hazard, died 1767, and had six children. Hannah, born April 14, 1753, died May 22, 1784 Robert, born April 11, 1755, died 1795 married Hannah Gardiner George, born September 22, 1756, married Sarah Scott. (2) Sarah Knowles. Benjamin, born December 26, 1757, married Hannah Hazard Susannah, born April 11, 1760. Richard, born November 15, 1761, married, after the death of his brother Benjamin, his widow, Hannah Hazard.

His will dated September 18, 1762, and proven October 11, 1762 gave to his wife the use of his estate.

SARAH HAZARD WATSON

(11146).

Sarah Hazard, daughter of Robert and Sarah Borden Hazard, born June 27, 1734, died January, 1811, married February 11, 1760, Job Watson, son of John and Isabel (surname unknown) Watson, and had six children. ISABEL, born September, 1760 JOB, born October 25, 1767; married Phebe Weeden. ROBERT, born February 28, 1769, died December 30, 1790, married Catherine Weeden. WALTER, born June 10, 1770, married Mary Carr BORDEN, born February 9, 1772 married Isabella Babcock JOHN, born November 1, 1774, married Sarah Brown. (2) Isabel Watson

BENJAMIN HAZARD.

(11181).

Benjamin Hazard son of George and Mary Place Hazard, born May 2 1723· died 1748, married Mary (surname unknown), and had one child JOHN, born 1746 died June 20 1813, married Sarah Gardner, (2) Martha Clarke In 1746, his father willed him four hundred acres of land in North Kings Town

SIMEON HAZARD.

(11182)

Simeon Hazard, son of George and Mary Place Hazard, born August 8, 1725, died 1790, married February 6, 1745, Abigail Mumford, and had eight children GODFREY, married Alice Hazard (2) Ruth Easton SIMEON MUMFORD, died June 24, 1811, married Elizabeth Robinson HANNAH, married Benjamin Hazard, (2) Richard Hazard ABIGAIL, died June 17, 1839 married Robert Rodman. GEORGE, died November 29, 1836, married Content Wilbur. ELIZABETH. MARY, married Jonathan Carpenter

GEORGE PLACE HAZARD.

(11184)

George Place Hazard, son of George and Mary Place Hazard, born April 16, 1730; married November 7, 1752. Sarah Hazard, daughter of Thomas and Alice Hull Hazard, born January 23, 1734 and had four children ALICE born November 15, 1754, married Godfrey Hazard THOMAS, born October 3, 1756, died November 14, 1761. GEORGE, born April 8, 1762; died August 11, 1786 THOMAS, born March 30, 1765, married Abigail Robinson.

He owned farm of one hundred and thirty acres known as the "Little Point Judith Neck Farm"

ENOCH HAZARD

(11186)

Enoch Hazard, son of George and Mary Place Hazard, born December 6, 1735, died 1785, married Mary Potter, daughter of John and Mary Perry Potter, died January 23, 1781, and had four children MARY, born September 6, 1763, married George Corliss SARAH, born August 13, 1768, married Jeremiah Niles Potter ENOCH, born December 28, 1775, died April, 1855. ALICE, born January 1, 1778 died 1868, married Jeremiah Niles Potter

He became a Freeman of South Kings Town in 1758 In 1777-8 he was Deputy, and in 1779-80-81-82-83, he was Assistant He served on several committees and was a prominent man in the colony

THOMAS HAZARD

(11187)

Thomas Hazard, son of George and Mary Place Hazard, born October 11, 1738, died December 27 1820, married Mary Easton, daughter of Jonathan and Ruth Coggeshall Easton, born May 20 1743, died November 26, 1794, and had eight children. GEORGE PLACE, born 1763, died April 16, 1839 JONATHAN EASTON, born 1764, died January 31, 1849 THOMAS G., married Patience Borden BENJAMIN, born September 9, 1774, married Harriet Lyman MARY ENOCH, married Mary Easton JOHN ALFRED, died July 21, 1799 RUTH, died February 8, 1806

He served a short time in the General Assembly.

HANNAH HAZARD TANNER

(11193)

Hannah Hazard, daughter of Benjamin and Mehitable Redwood Hazard, born July 7, 1744; died May 8, 1801, married July 7, 1771, James Tanner, died September 6, 1778, and had one child, JAMES

THOMAS HAZARD

(11197)

Thomas Hazard, son of Benjamin and Mehitable Redwood Hazard, born January 23, 1756, died in Westerly, R. I., September 28, 1845, married October 2, 1783, Hannah Knowles, daughter of Joseph and Bathsheba Seager Knowles, and had five children. BENJAMIN born December 4, 1784, married Joanna Carr. THOMAS, born May 8, 1787, married Ruth Carpenter. HANNAH, born December 14, 1791. ISAAC SENTER, born March 27, 1795, died March 29, 1795. ISAAC SENTER, born May 10, 1796, died May 11, 1796. He was a Senator for two years and was quite a politician.

THOMAS HAZARD

(11191).

Thomas Hazard, son of Jonathan and Abigail MacCoon Hazard, born February 22, 1726, died April 27, 1804, married about 1746, Mary Preston Bowdoin, daughter of Peter Bowdoin of Virginia, died April 17 1760, and had nine children. A child, born September 27, 1747; died March 26, 1748. A child, born August, 1748, died August 10, 1749. JONATHAN, born July, 1750; married Esther Watson. ABIGAIL, born December 25, 1751; married Walter Watson. MARY, born August 14, 1753; died August 31, 1754. MARY born 1755, died November 29, 1759. A daughter, born 1757, died 1757. A son, born 1757, died 1757. SUSANNAH, born August 24, 1758, died September 18, 1841, married William Cole, (her name was changed to Mary)

He married second Eunice Rhodes, daughter of William and Mary Sheldon Rhodes, born December 12, 1741, died January 22, 1809 and had eight children. THOMAS RHODES, born March 1, 1768, died 1839, married Jane Bagnall. EUNICE, born February

82

14, 1764; died March 9, 1832, married John Gardiner. A daughter, born 1766, died 1766. WILLIAM, born May 3, 1767; died March 14, 1847, married Ann Farrant Jones SARAH, born July 18, 1769, married William Townsend. WAITSTILL C., born March 12, 1772; died May 23, 1804; married James Douglas. BOWDOIN, born 1774; died July 29, 1832. RHODES, born September 17, 1777; died 1806

He moved to Newport, R. I., and became a merchant, making a large fortune His second wife was a granddaughter of Roger Williams.

MARY HAZARD DYRE.

(1119a3).

Mary Hazard, daughter of Jonathan and Abigail MacCoon Hazard, born March 24, 1737, married 1762, Colonel Charles Dyre, and had seven children BOWDOIN, CHARLES, HAZARD, CHRISTOPHER CORNWALLIS, married a Foster ISABEL, married a Powel. MARY, married a Foster. ABIGAIL, born July 14, 1766, married Arthur Aylesworth

Her husband served in the Revolutionary Army He was appointed Major of Militia in 1775, and promoted to Colonel in 1776

JONATHAN HAZARD

(1119a7)

Jonathan Hazard, son of Jonathan and Abigail MacCoon Hazard, born about 1744; died later than 1824, for he married after he was eighty years old He married Patience Hazard, daughter of Jeffrey and Mary (surname unknown) Hazard, and had six children JONATHAN J., married Tacy Burdick. GRIFFIN BARNEY, born 1765; died 1822; married Mary Parker. JOSEPH HOXSIE, born June 16, 1777, died October 22, 1838, married Amey Williams THOMAS JEFFERSON, died aged twenty years SUSANNAH, married Rowland Champlin ABIGAIL, married Enoch Sherman.

He married second Hannah Brown, and third Marian Gage, daughter of Moses Gage He was a politician of great tact and talent, and one of the most efficient leaders of the Paper Money party in 1786. He was a member of the General Assembly for many years, and a leader in the Anti-Federal party He was a natural orator, with a ready command of language, subtle and ingenious in debate

WILLIAM HAZARD

(11231)

William Hazard, son of Caleb and Abigail Robinson Hazard, born April 12, 1721, married September 12, 1744, Phebe Hull, daughter of John and Damaris (surname unknown) Hull, and had seven children Lydia, married John Field Josiah, born December 20, 1748, married Mary Carr. Abigail, married Sylvanus Wyatt William, born March 21, 1753. John, born January 20, 1755 Benedict, born January 26 1758. Mary, born March 24, 1762

He kept a tavern in Jamestown and was a representative of his town in the General Assembly in 1756-57-60-62, and an Assistant in 1768-70 He was a Councilman of Jamestown many years He was a sea captain and was called Captain William Hazard

ROBERT HAZARD

(11232)

Robert Hazard son of Caleb and Abigail Robinson Hazard, born May 1, 1723, died February, 1771, married April 19, 1752, Elizabeth Hazard, daughter of Robert and Esther Stanton Hazard, born May 31, 1730, and had seven children Abigail, born August 29 1753, married Jared Starr. Esther born July 26, 1755, died March 25, 1831, married Silas Niles, (2) Jared Starr. Elizabeth, born November 28, 1757. Sylvester Gardiner, born July 27 1760, died February 14, 1812, married Elizabeth Greene Nancy, born April 20, 1764 Charles born July 14, 1766, married Ann Bours Francis born 1769 died 1814, married Rebecca Truman

He studied medicine with his uncle Dr. Sylvester Gardiner, and was the leading physician in his community He accumulated a large property and his will disposed of the same and was very carefully worded

MARY HAZARD PECKHAM

(11241)

Mary Hazard, daughter of George and Sarah Carder Hazard, born July 16, 1722 died April, 1805, married March 2, 1737, Benjamin Peckham, son of Benjamin and Mary Carr Peckham born

March 22, 1715, died March, 1791, and had seven children.
GEORGE HAZARD, born April 14, 1739-40, married Sarah Taylor
JOSEPHUS, born February 11, 1742, died March 27, 1814, married Mary Babcock SARAH, married John Robinson. JOHN
PAINE ; WILLIAM, born 1752, married Mercy Perry. MARY, married Joshua Perry. PELEG, born June 11, 1762, married Desire
Watson

In 1786, the town council of South Kings Town voted that "William Potter, Benjamin Peckham, Freeman Perry and Paul Mumford,
or part of them, be a committee to consider of proper measures to
recommend to the inhabitants of this town for encouraging industry,
frugality and American manufactories, and make a report" etc

GEORGE HAZARD

(11242).

George Hazard, son of George and Sarah Carder Hazard, born
June 15, 1724, died August 11, 1797, married November 24, 1745,
Martha Wanton, daughter of George and Abigail Church Wanton,
died March, 1763, and had four children EDWARD born 1746,
married Sarah Cranston ABIGAIL, born 1748, married John Channing SARAH, born 1751, married Daniel Gardiner, (2) George
Hazard GEORGE born March 30, 1758, married Martha Babcock

He married second July 28, 1769, Jane Tweedy and had five
children ELIZABETH, born 1771, died January 12, 1788 SOPHIA
FREELOVE, died 1790 CARDIR, born 1774, died March 18, 1823,
married Sarah Coggeshall NATHANIEL, born 1776, died December 17, 1820, married Sarah Fales WILLIAM TWEEDY, born 1777,
died October 26, 1794

He was admitted Freeman in 1745, and in early life settled in
Newport, R I, where he became a merchant. He was elected the
first Mayor of Newport, R I, resigning the position of Chief Justice of the Court of Common Pleas He was one of the incorporators of the Brown University and served as one of the Trustees

CARDER HAZARD.

(11246).

Carder Hazard, son of George and Sarah Carder Hazard, born

85

August 11, 1734, died November 24, 1792; married September 23, 1756, Alice Hull, daughter of Robert and Thankful Ball Hull, born September 26, 1739, died July 1, 1760 and had two children. ROBERT HULL, born April 10, 1758. PETER BOURS, born December 5 1759, died May 15, 1807

He married second March 5, 1761, Alice Hazard, daughter of Thomas and Alice Hull Hazard, born August 30, 1737, died January 13, 1793, and had nine children THOMAS, born December 5, 1761, married a Browning. (2) Eliza Arnold GEORGE, born April 13, 1763; died September 29, 1829, married Sarah Gardner, (2) Mary Hoxsie (3) Jane Hull. WILLIAM, born March 6, 1766 EDWARD. born July 7, 1768 RICHARD WARD, born November 1, 1770. CARDER, born July 21, 1773. ARNOLD, born January 9, 1776. SARAH, born May 13, 1780, married Patee Clarke. ALICE, born May 13 1780 married George Condon.

He was admitted Freeman of South Kings Town in 1757, and held the offices of Deputy, Assistant or Judge, until 1787, when he was chosen Chief Justice His death was caused by a fall from a chair, upon which he had mounted to take a book from the top of the bookcase He died at the home of his son Doctor George Hazard

ARNOLD HAZARD

(11247)

Arnold Hazard son of George and Sarah Carder Hazard, born May 15 1738, married November 30, 1777. Alice Potter, daughter of William and Penelope Hazard Potter, and had two children. MARTHA, born 1790, died March 28, 1861, married Asabel Russell. BRENTON W., born 1793, died October 4, 1864, married February 16, 1831; Harriet Brown

PENELOPE HAZARD POTTER.

(11251).

Penelope Hazard, daughter of Thomas and Alice Hull Hazard, born February 11, 1730-31, married November 18, 1750, William Potter, son of John and Mercy Robinson Potter, born January 21, 1722, and had thirteen children. MERCY, born November 26, 1751, died 1794; married Joshua Perry THOMAS HAZARD, born Decem-

ber 8, 1753, died September 11, 1807, married Patience Wilkinson
ALICE, born April 20, 1756, died 1818, married Arnold Hazard.
SUSANNAH, born April 25, 1758. WILLIAM ROBINSON, born July
13, 1760, died young BENEDICT ARNOLD, born September 12,
1761, died 1810: married Sarah Brown. PENELOPE, born March
7, 1764, died 1813, married Benjamin Brown. WILLIAM PITT,
born April 10, 1766, died November 6, 1800; married Mary Hazard EDWARD, born February 15, 1768; died August 12, 1849; married Eliza Johnson. SIMEON, born April 25, 1770; died February
1, 1817, married Catherine Klice. SARAH, born December 13, 1771,
died 1830, married George Brown JOHN, born May 24, 1774,
died 1815, married Catherine Garrison PELHAM, born December
7, 1776

HANNAH HAZARD WILSON.

(11252).

Hannah Hazard, daughter of Thomas and Alice Hull Hazard,
born August 5, 1732; married November 21, 1762, John Wilson,
son of Jeremiah and Mary (surname unknown) Wilson, born May
11, 1726, and had three children. JOHN, born July 24, 1763
THOMAS HAZARD ROBERT ARNOLD

OLIVER HAZARD

(11262)

Oliver Hazard, son of Oliver and Elizabeth Raymond Hazard,
born March 30, 1739; married Patience Cook Greene daughter of
Ebenezer and Patience Gorton Cook, died July 9, 1809, and had
three children MARY born March 15, 1762. SAMUEL GREEN,
born February 15 1764, died April 4, 1765 ELIZABETH, born
April 12, 1767.

He kept a tavern in Jamestown and was Councilman for many
years

MERCY HAZARD PERRY

(11263).

Mercy Hazard, daughter of Oliver and Elizabeth Raymond
Hazard, born in South Kings Town, R. I. January 21, 1740, died

ANDREW S. BROWNELL'S RESIDENCE.

1810, married 1755, James Freeman Perry, son of Benjamin and Susannah Barber Perry, born in South Kings Town, R. I., January 23, 1733, died October 15, 1813, and had three children   JOSHUA, born 1756; died November, 1802; married Mary Peckham   OLIVER HAZARD, lost at sea about 1783.   CHRISTOPHER RAYMOND, born in South Kings Town, R. I., December 4, 1761, married Sarah Wallace Alexander

Her husband was a physician and surgeon and held high offices in the colony

STEPHEN HAZARD

(11341)

Stephen Hazard, son of Stephen and Mary Robinson Hazard born September 12, 1723, died August 6, 1800, married April 29 1759, Sarah Nichols, daughter of Jonathan Nichols, born 1739, and had ten children   STEPHEN, born September 12, 1760, died March 17, 1788   JONATHAN NICHOLS, born October 18, 1761, married Mary Robinson. SARAH, born July 14, 1763, died June 17 1793. MARY, born September 18, 1764, died August 26, 1851, married Robert Babcock   ELIZABETH, born April 10, 1767, died 1820, married Gideon Hazard   NICHOLS, born March 20, 1770, died May 13, 1848, married Phebe Anthony   MARTHA, born March 20 1774, married Benjamin Hazard.   JOSEPH, born March 22, 1775, died April 1, 1776   APLIN, born July 20, 1777, died January 20 1778   JOHN, born December 10, 1778, died January, 1805

MARY HAZARD POTTER

(11342).

Mary Hazard, daughter of Stephen and Mary Robinson Hazard, born September 18, 1725, married August 30, 1752, John Potter, son of Ichabod and Sarah Robinson Potter, and had five children   ABIGAIL, born July 20, 1756, died March 1, 1784, married Rufus Wheeler   SARAH, born April 12, 1762, died May 9, 1787 HANNAH.   ELIZABETH   RUTH, married Benjamin Perry

ELIZABETH HAZARD POTTER.

(11343).

Elizabeth Hazard, daughter of Stephen and Mary Robinson Hazard, born July 17, 1729, married John Potter, and had seven children. SAMUEL J., married Ann Seager STEPHEN, died 1793, married Abigail Robinson GEORGE, died 1787 HENRY, married Dorcas Perry CHRISTOPHER. MARTHA, died 1819, married Hazard Browning ELIZABETH, died June 17, 1800, married Nicholas Easton

JOHN HAZARD

(11344).

John Hazard, son of Stephen and Mary Robinson Hazard, born June 26, 1731; died 1772; married Mary (surname unknown), and had one child. JOHN.

JOSEPH HAZARD

(11351).

Joseph Hazard, son of Robert and Esther Stanton Hazard, born May 21, 1728, died April 31, 1790, married September 28, 1760, Hannah Nichols, daughter of Jonathan Nichols, and had eight children. ROBERT, born January 31, 1762; died August 12, 1851; married Alice Anthony. MARY, born May 29, 1764; died April 15, 1833 LUCY, born July 6, 1766, died September 23, 1804; married Teddiman Hull RUTH, born February 4, 1769; died June 27, 1852 JOSHUA, born October 7, 1771, died November 12, 1823, married Elizabeth Niles. STANTON, born February 3, 1774, lost at sea in 1798. EVAN MALBONE, born March 6, 1776, died at sea in 1805 HANNAH born August 10, 1778, died August 26, 1827, married Stephen Griffen

He was Deputy from South Kings Town in 1756, and was appointed Lieutnant Colonel of militia the same year. He was Assistant from 1761 to 1777, with scarcely an interval. In 1786 and 1787, he was Associate Judge of the Supreme Court

ESTHER HAZARD BABCOCK

(11353).

Esther Hazard, daughter of Robert and Esther Stanton Hazard, born December 7, 1732; died March 25, 1831; married 1758, Jonathan Babcock, son of James Babcock, born October 11, 1736, and had four children. ESTHER, born June 23, 1759, married Nathan Brand. JONATHAN, born May 30, 1762; married Ruth Rodman ROBERT, born December 18, 1763; died February 11, 1848, married Mary Hazard. HANNAH, born February 11, 1768

SAMUEL HAZARD

(11356).

Samuel Hazard, son of Robert and Esther Stanton Hazard, born about 1739, married May 3, 1763, Hannah Perry, daughter of Benjamin Perry, died December 12, 1772, and had five children BENJAMIN, born March 11, 1764; died July 12, 1849; married Martha Hazard GIDEON, born November 25, 1765; died April, 1806, married Elizabeth Hazard. ESTHER, born October 5, 1767 ELIZABETH, born December 2, 1769, died July 25, 1801; married Atherton Wales. JOSEPH STANTON, born March 7, 1772, died in Havana while unloading his vessel.

He married second March 5, 1774, Susannah Perry, daughter of Benjamin Perry, and had five children. SAMUEL, born October 10, 1776, died in Middleport Center, N. Y., June 22, 1836 JAMES, born August 27, 1778. SUSANNAH, born August 21, 1780, died in South Kings Town, 1817 PATRICK, born May 10, 1782, died 1805. JOSHUA, born December 21, 1784, died in infancy

He married third December 11, 1785, Elizabeth Nichols, daughter of Jonathan Nichols, died April 4, 1815 and had two children HENRY. THOMAS. He became a Freeman from South Kings Town in 1760.

STANTON HAZARD.

(11359).

Stanton Hazard, son of Robert and Esther Stanton Hazard, born January 8, 1743, died in Honduras, 1789; married July 3, 1785,

Elizabeth Wickham, died September 22, 1801, and had one child, who died in infancy

He was Captain in the British Navy. His death was caused by a wound from a sword, given by an adversary in a duel, in which he killed his opponent

SAMUEL HAZARD

(113.1)

Samuel Hazard son of Samuel and Abigail (surname unknown) Hazard, born about 1739, died about 1787, married Catherine (surname unknown), and had nine children SAMUEL GEORGE ELIZA LODOWICK, married a daughter of William Robinson of Westerly, R I ROBERT BRISEY married a Worthington. NANCY ABBY married Ichabod Taylor HARRIET, married a Laverott

GEORGE HAZARD

(11362)

George Hazard son of Samuel and Abigail (surname unknown) Hazard born in Newport R I about 1745, died August 12, 1797 married Mary Mumford, daughter of John Mumford and had ten children JAMES, born 1770, died 1794 MARY, born 1773, died 1807, married Nathaniel Richmond ESTHER, married Benjamin Pearce CALEB born 1783 died 1804. SALLY, born 1785, died 1877 CATHERINE born 1787, died June 11 1819 JOHN, born 1790, died 1800 A daughter married a Dolbear HANNAH married John Newman, (2) Erastus P Allen JAMES AUGUSTUS born 1798, died June 11 1819.

STEPHEN HAZARD

(11371)

Stephen Hazard son of Thomas and Hannah Slocum Hazard, born about 1730, died October 24, 1804, married about 1760 Elizabeth Carpenter, daughter of Daniel and Renewed Smith Carpenter and had six children THOMAS married Silence Knowles MARY, born 1765, married Joseph Oatley MARTHA SARAH, married Asa Carpenter   ROUSL, lost at sea   ELIZABETH, born 1783, married Robert Rodman.

CATHERINE WILCOX DAVIS

(11415).

Catherine Wilcox daughter of Robert and Catherine Lillibridge Wilcox, died March 30 1773, married September 26, 1759, Barney Davis, son of John and Sarah Barney Davis, born August 18 1733, died April 3, 1822, and had two children   MARY, born April 1, 1770, married John Chase   BARNEY, born March 27, 1773, died July 9, 1774.

REV ISAIAH WILCOX

(11536)

Rev Isaiah Wilcox, son of Stephen and Mercie Randall Wilcox, born in Westerly, about 1638, (possibly earlier), died March 3, 1793 or 1795; married October 15, 1761, Sarah Lewis, daughter of John Lewis of Westerly, and had twelve children. ISAIAH, born in Westerly, January 31, 1763; died July 13, 1844, married Polly Pendleton   ASA, born in Westerly, September 1, 1764, died in Essex, Conn. NATHAN, born in Westerly, April 10, 1766 SARAH, born in Westerly, December 19, 1767, married John Barber   MERCY, born in Westerly, March 23, 1769, died September 18, 1789 STEPHEN, born in Westerly, October 10, 1770 OLIVER, born in Westerly, June 26, 1773 PRUDENCE, born in Westerly, March 10, 1775, married Joshua Vose   MARY, born in Westerly, January 8, 1777, died June 13, 1789. LEWIS, born in Westerly, November 17, 1780, died in the south. ENOCH, born in Westerly, January 4, 1785, died in Georgetown, S C, January 29, 1829 MERCY, born in Westerly, November 27 1789, died in Newville, N. Y., July 20, 1879, married Hezekiah Lewis

He was baptised February, 1766, and ordained February 14 1771, and was the first pastor of the "Wilcox Church," Baptist of Westerly In 1785, under his ministry, occurred a great revival in which more than two hundred were added to his church He was a man of much power and influence, and his death at the untimely age of fifty-five years, of small-pox, taken in ministering to one of his church, was much mourned

93

JEREMIAH HAZARD.

(11611).

Jeremiah Hazard, son of Jeffery and Mary (surname unknown) Hazard, born August 13, 1720; died June 23, 1795, married Mary Hazard, daughter of Robert and Patience Northup Hazard, born 1720, died October 22, 1816, and had one child THOMAS, born 1753, died February 15, 1815, married Lucy Congdon

SUSANNAH HAZARD BROWNING.

(11612)

Susannah Hazard daughter of Jeffery and Mary (surname unknown) Hazard, died February, 1795, married February 4 1753, Wilkinson Browning, son of William and Mary Wilkinson Browning, died October 28, 1805, and had three children HAZARD, married Martha Potter. AMEY, married Gideon Hoxsie MARY, married Thomas Hoxsie

ROBERT HAZARD

(11613).

Robert Hazard, son of Jeffrey and Mary (surname unknown Hazard married Hannah Greene, and had two children. JEFFERY, born March 24, 1771, died 1828 ROBERT, born August 29, 1785, married Abigail Seager

ROBERT HAZARD.

(11641)

Robert Hazard, son of Robert and Martha, (surname unknown) Hazard, born September 19, 1728, married December 13 1753, Alice Thomas, and had four children MARTHA, born February 27, 1755. RUTH, born February 26, 1759 ABIGAIL, born January 4, 1762, married Jared Bailey. JOHN, born 1766, died 1851

94

Jeremiah Hazard.

(11644).

Jeremiah Hazard, son of Robert and Martha (surname unknown) Hazard, born July 25, 1736, died 1773; married November 6, 1760, Phebe Tillinghast, and had two children. JEFFERY, born 1762; died June 3, 1840, married Amey Tillinghast. ABIGAIL. His will, dated June 21, 1773, was probated December 14, 1773

Jeremiah Hazard

(11732)

Jeremiah Hazard, son of Robert and Patience Northup Hazard, born 1727, married Ruth Potter, died about 1770, and had three children JOHN, born August 24, 1749, married Abby Boss ROBERT. ROWLAND, born 1762, died April 3, 1834

He married second Mary Cole, daughter of John Cole, and had one child WILBOR, born December 15, 1774, died February 14, 1827, married Mary Stanton.

Ephriam Hazard.

(11733).

Ephriam Hazard, son of Robert and Patience Northup Hazard, born 1729, died August 28, 1825, married Ann (surname unknown), and had one child. EASTON, born September 13, 1783, died September 2, 1826, married Charlotte Bissell

Gideon Hazard.

(11734).

Gideon Hazard, son of Robert and Patience Northup Hazard, married Sarah Chase Congdon, daughter of Jonathan Chase, and had four children. EPHRIAM, born September 5, 1763; died April 23, 1836; married Hannah Updike, (2) Mary Smith FREEBORN, born 1765, died August 29, 1831, married Susan Sherman. ROBERT STEPHEN.

He married second Anna (surname unknown), died November

3, 1822, and had one child   ELIZABETH, born December 7 1795;
married Joseph Hammond

STEPHEN CHAMPLIN

(11921)

Stephen Champlin, son of Stephen and Mary Hazard Champlin,
born September 29, 1734 died 1778, married Dinah Browning,
daughter of William and Mary Wilkinson Browning, and had four
children   MARY, born June 26, 1760   STEPHEN, born August 3,
1763, married Elizabeth Perry.   HANNAH, born June 5, 1765
SUSANNAH, born December 9, 1772

HANNAH CHAMPLIN GARDINER

(11922).

Hannah Champlin, daughter of Stephen and Mary Hazard
Champlin, born January 20 1735, married about 1754, Nicholas
Gardiner, and had five children   STEPHEN CHAMPLIN, born De-
cember 3, 1755   GEORGE, born June 9, 1757   ROWLAND, born
March 18, 1759   HANNAH, born October 7, 1763   JEFFREY, born
November 12, 1765

SARAH CHAMPLIN CONGDON.

(11923)

Sarah Champlin, daughter of Stephen and Mary Hazard Champlin born August 18, 1737, married Samuel Congdon, and had four
children   JOSEPH, born March 1, 1758   HANNAH, born July 18,
1759   GEORGE, born December 9, 1760   SARAH married Robert
Robinson

MARY CHAMPLIN BROWNING

(11924)

Mary Champlin daughter of Stephen and Mary Hazard Champlin, born 1739, married February 12, 1761, Joseph Browning, and
had three children   MARY, born March 14, 1762   SUSANNAH,
born August 26, 1764   WILLIAM, born September 5, 1767

96

JEFFREY CHAMPLIN

(11926).

Jeffrey Champlin, son of Stephen and Mary Hazard Champlin, born March 21, 1744; married Mary (surname unknown), and had two children. MARY, born April 7, 1769. STEPHEN GARDINER, born January 31, 1771

JOHN G. WANTON

(12232)

John G Wanton, son of Gideon and Mary Cadman Wanton, born 1729, died July 2, 1799, married 1760, Mary Bull, daughter of Henry and Phebe Coggeshall Bull, born April 18, 1728, died March 12, 1821 and had two children MARY, born August 20, 1763; died December 5, 1822, married Daniel Lyman GIDEON born July 19, 1766; died in Newport, R I, November 27, 1786.

His wife was a great-grand-daughter of Governor Henry Bull, and was nearly ninety-three years of age at the time of her death Her father was Attorney General of Rhode Island

RICHARD ESTES

(12311)

Richard Estes, son of Robert and Ann Durfee Estes, born in Portsmouth, R I., July 2, 1717, died November 13 1793, married Mary Pierce, daughter of Philip and Frances (surname unknown) Pierce, born June 8, 1724, died January 19, 1782, and had six children. RICHARD, born in East Greenwich, R. I, January 25, 1739, married Johannah Edmunds ANNA, born in East Greenwich, R I, August 25, 1741, died March 3, 1813. THOMAS, born in East Greenwich, R I, November 29, 1743, died January 25, 1744 MASEY, born in East Greenwich, R I, November 8, 1744, died April 9, 1815 MARY, born April 25, 1747. PHILIP, born in Warwick, R I, February 22, 1749, married a Gage

SARAH ESTES THOMAS.

(12312)

Sarah Estes, daughter of Robert and Ann Durfee Estes, born in Portsmouth, R. I., February 13, 1720; died in Portsmouth, R. I., married in Portsmouth, R. I., March 15, 1737. Joseph Thomas, son of Joseph and Ruth (surname unknown) Thomas, died in Portsmouth, R. I., 1780, and had thirteen children ANNE, born August 26, 1739 JOSEPH, born January 3, 1742; died in Portsmouth, R. I., June 14, 1781, married Ruth Tabor. ALEXANDER, born November 25, 1743, married Ussilla Oldridge RUTH, born August 16, 1745, married Thomas Shaw. LUCINA, born March 29, 1747; died before 1777. ELIZABETH, born November 15, 1748 DANIEL, born November 3, 1750 RICHARD, born November 28, 1752; married Ann Elizabeth Decotee Brownell JEREMIAH ROBERT, born June 29, 1757, married Abigail Thurston. SETH. DAVID. JONATHAN.

THOMAS ESTES.

(12313).

Thomas Estes, son of Robert and Ann Durfee Estes, born in Portsmouth, R. I., April 17, 1725, died in 1784; married in Portsmouth, R. I., July 24, 1747, Elizabeth Thomas, daughter of Joseph and Ruth (surname unknown) Thomas, born about 1729; died May 2, 1808, and had eight children ROBERT, born in Tiverton, R. I., June 28, 1748, died 1826, married Prudence Bennett. RUTH, born in Tiverton, R. I., January 1, 1751; married Isaac Jennings. JOSEPH, born in Tiverton, R. I., November 27, 1754; died May 26, 1844; married Edith Wood ELISHA, born in Tiverton, R. I., January 12, 1757; married Sarah Bennett DANIEL, born in Tiverton, R. I., May 21, 1759, probably died young. SARAH, born in Tiverton, R. I., March 31, 1762, died July 1, 1836; married Edmund Tripp. EDMUND, born in Tiverton, R. I., September 8, 1767, died September 14, 1863, married Elizabeth Lawton. PETER, born in Tiverton, R. I., 1773, died in Tiverton, R. I., 1847, married Mercy Durfee, (2) Anna Hicks, (3) Matilda Sherman Grinnell

ANN ESTES WILCOCKS.

(12314)

Ann Estes, daughter of Robert and Ann Durfee Estes, born in Portsmouth, R. I, March 8, 1726, married in Portsmouth, R. I., July 25, 1752, Josiah Wilcocks, son of Joseph and Sarah (surname unknown) Wilcocks, born in Portsmouth, R. I., August 31, 1727, and had five children. ROBERT, born June 15, 1752. SARAH, born April 4, 1754. HANNAH, born June 14, 1757. SUSANNAH, born December 1, 1759. MARTHA, born February 5, 1763.

SARAH DENNIS EARLE

(12322)

Sarah Dennis, daughter of Joseph and Sarah Durfee Dennis, born in Portsmouth, R I., April 1, 1725, married in Portsmouth, R. I, January 15, 1741, William Earle, son of William and Mehitable Brayton Earle, born in Portsmouth, R. I, 1719-20, and had two children. ROBERT, born February 26, 1743 WILLIAM, born August 27, 1747.

Her husband was a Justice of the Peace in Portsmouth, R. I., in 1744.

ROBERT DENNIS.

(12323).

Robert Dennis, son of Joseph and Sarah Durfee Dennis, born in Portsmouth, R. I., September 12, 1727, died in Portsmouth, R. I, April 12, 1811; married in Middletown, R. I., June 21, 1750, Hannah Coggeshall, daughter of Thomas and Mercy Freeborn Coggeshall, born in Middletown, R I., May 3, 1731, died in Newport, R. I, November 22, 1811, and had twelve children. GIDEON, born July 8, 1752; married Mary Durfee. HANNAH, born May 28, 1756, married George Hall JOSEPH, born May 31, 1759 ROBERT, born January 1, 1762; married Ruth Anthony THOMAS, born April 23, 1764, died June 1, 1813. JONATHAN, born January 15, 1767; died in Portsmouth, R I, September 17, 1850; married Hannah Sherman. GEORGE, born January 26, 1769; died in Portsmouth, R. I., March 10, 1837; married Hannah Thomas. MARY, born

February 14, 1772; died in Warwick, R. I., December 27, 1816, married Asa Sisson MOSES, born June 20, 1777, married Abigail Sherman A daughter, married Ephriam Gifford.

JOSEPH DENNIS

(12324)

Joseph Dennis, son of Joseph and Sarah Durfee Dennis, born in Portsmouth, R I, June 15, 1730, died in Portsmouth, R. I., September 28, 1758, married in Portsmouth, R I, December 14, 1752, Mercy Coggeshall, daughter of Thomas and Mary Freeborn Coggeshall, born in Middletown, R I

ANNA DENNIS COGGESHALL

(12325)

Anna Dennis, daughter of Joseph and Sarah Durfee Dennis, born in Portsmouth, R. I, December 19, 1731, married in Portsmouth, R I, June 2, 1752, Joshua Coggeshall, son of Thomas and Mary Freeborn Coggeshall, born in Middletown, R I, May 11 1722, died in Middletown, R I, September 24, 1786, and had eight children. SARAH, born September 25, 1752 JOSEPH, born August 16, 1754; died October 7, 1830, married Elizabeth Horsewell ELIZABETH, born in Middletown, R. I., October 14, 1756; died in Middletown, R. I., September 3, 1828, married Gideon Anthony GEORGE, born in Middletown, R. I., March 17, 1759, died young Mary, born in Middletown, R. I, July 14, 1761, died September 15, 1837, married Peleg Brown. MERCY, born in Middletown, R. I., September 14, 1762; died March, 1844, married Thomas Manchester. ANNA, born in Middletown, R. I., June 1, 1764, died December, 1842 GEORGE, born in Middletown. R I, June 8, 1767 died in Portsmouth, R. I, August 14, 1843, married Cynthia Sherman

RUTH DENNIS CORY

(12326)

Ruth Dennis, daughter of Joseph and Sarah Durfee Dennis, born in Portsmouth, R I, December 6, 1733, died in Portsmouth, R

I March 1, 1817, married in Portsmouth, R. I., June 22, 1748, John Cory, son of William and Deliverance Durfee Cory, born in Portsmouth, R. I., September 7, 1731, died in Portsmouth, R I., July 13, 1818, and had ten children ANN, born November 15, 1758; died November 11, 1762 DENNIS, born September 11, 1760; died February 7, 1761. SUSANNAH, born October 12, 1761, died May, 1763. ELIZABETH, born October 26, 1763; married William Borden. DENNIS, born September 11, 1765. JOSEPH, born September 11, 1765, died February 7, 1766. CYNTHIA, born October 20, 1766. JOSEPH DENNIS, born June 18, 1768 WILLIAM, born January 30, 1770. NANCY, born July 28, 1772; married Isaac Peckham.

LYDIA DENNIS FISH

(12327)

Lydia Dennis, daughter of Joseph and Sarah Durfee Dennis, born in Portsmouth, R I, October 12, 1735; died in Portsmouth, R I., December 3, 1779, married in Portsmouth, R. I, December 16, 1757, David Fish, son of David and Jemima Tallman Fish, born in Portsmouth, R. I., March 15, 1734, and had twelve children. SARAH, born in Portsmouth, R I., July 26, 1758, married Robert Hazard CHRISTOPHER, born in Portsmouth, R. I, December 25, 1759. JEMIMA, born in Portsmouth, R. I, May 6, 1761; married Thomas Richardson MARY, born in Portsmouth, R. I., January 23, 1763, married Andrew Nichols HANNAH, born in Portsmouth, R I, December 14, 1764. HANNAH, born in Portsmouth, R I., October 24, 1766 STEPHEN, born in Portsmouth, R I, October 24, 1768 JOSEPH, born in Portsmouth, R. I, April 13, 1770, married Amey Chase LYDIA, born in Portsmouth, R I, May 2, 1772 SUSANNAH, born in Portsmouth, R. I, February 20, 1773. RUTH, born in Portsmouth, R I, March 7, 1776 RACHEL, born in Portsmouth, R I, March 12, 1779

FREEBORN DENNIS CHASE

(12328)

Freeborn Dennis, daughter of Joseph and Sarah Durfee Dennis born in Portsmouth, R I, August 18, 1739; married in Portsmouth,

R. I., February 21, 1760, Holder Chase, son of Nathan and Elizabeth Shaw Chase, born in Portsmouth, R. I., August 24, 1733, died February, 1820, and had ten children. NATHAN, died in childhood. SARAH, born 1765, died January 19, 1848, married Benjamin Mott. NATHAN, born 1766, died November 12, 1827, married Anne Sherman. ANNA, born 1768, died in Smithfield, R. I., February 7, 1849, married John Weeden. ELIZA. BORDEN, married Sarah Folger, (2) Ruth Bunker. AMLY, died in childhood. ABNER, born in Portsmouth, R. I., married Deborah Chase. CLARK, born in Portsmouth, R. I., married Anna Borden. FREEBORN, died November 23, 1819.

JOSEPH READ

(12361)

Joseph Read, son of Oliver and Martha Durfee Read, born in Freetown, Mass., December 11, 1732, died in Freetown, Mass., 1791; married in Swansea, Mass., January 10, 1760 Mary Knowles, died in Freetown, Mass., 1816, and had two children. JOSEPH, born 1761; died 1791. JAMES, born 1768, died 1791.

OLIVER READ

(12362)

Oliver Read, son of Oliver and Martha Durfee Read, born in Freetown, Mass., August 21, 1734, died in Freetown, Mass., married in Swansea, Mass., February 14, 1754, Patience Brayton, and had eight children NANCY, married Thomas Freelove RUTH STEPHEN OLIVER THOMAS DEBORAH, married William Gifford PHEBE ANNE, married George Read, (2) Perley Willson. He was a Captain in the Revolutionary Army

MARY READ SLADE.

(12363)

Mary Read, daughter of Oliver and Martha Durfee Read, born in Freetown, Mass., March 31 1736, died in Swansea Mass., March 12, 1806, married in Swansea, Mass., October 9, 1755, Philip Slade, son of Edward and Phebe Chase Slade, born in Swansea,

Mass., April 19, 1732, died in Pittstown, N Y, July 31, 1803, and had twelve children. MARTHA, born September 11, 1756, died November 18, 1822. EDWARD, born April 9, 1758; died June 22, 1805 OLIVER, born January 8, 1760. PHILIP, born August 11, 1761. JOSEPH, born March 31 1763 SIBEL, born August 19, 1765, died August 24, 1805. SARAH, born August 17, 1767 PHEBE, born January 18, 1773 DEBORAH, born January 22, 1775 GIDEON, born June 11, 1777. WAIT, born February 16, 1781.

JONATHAN READ

(12364).

Jonathan Read, son of Oliver and Martha Durfee Read, born in Freetown, Mass., November 13, 1737, married Eunice Weaver, and had nine children. FREEMAN, born September 27, 1757 ICHABOD, born April 26, 1760 died December 5, 1796; married Elizabeth Law. JAMES, born June 7, 1762 LYDIA, born September 7, 1764; married Sheffield Weaver ELIZABETH, married Robert Gibbs SUSANNA, born July 3, 1767, married Luther Wilson EUNICE HANNAH, born August 1, 1769, married James Whitewell JONATHAN, born September 7, 1771, married Eleanor Law.

WAIT READ WEAVER.

(12365).

Wait Read, daughter of Oliver and Martha Durfee Read, born in Freetown, Mass., December 6, 1739, married in Freetown, Mass., January 9, 1761, Samuel Weaver, and had son SHEFFEL, born in Somerset, Mass, 1764; died in Fall River, Mass., July 26, 1839, married Hannah Durfee

SARAH DURFEE ALLEN.

(12372).

Sarah Durfee, daughter of Gideon and Wait Tripp Durfee, born in Portsmouth, R I, September 22, 1728; married in Portsmouth, R I, April 9, 1747, John Allen, son of John and Rebecca (surname unknown) Allen, born in Prudence Island, R. I, October 26, 1725, and had ten children. WAIT, born June 17, 1748; married Ebenezer

Matteson. REBECCA, born August 14, 1750 GIDEON, born November 21, 1752. died June 12, 1754 DURFEE. born May 31,
1755 SARAH, born April 7, 1758. SUSANNAH, born June 21,
1760 JOHN, born October 14, 1762 JOB, born July 20, 1765
SILVIA, born June 12, 1768 PATIENCE, born April 9, 1770

JOB DURFEE.

(12374)

Job Durfee, son of Gideon and Wait Tripp Durfee, born in
Portsmouth, R I, August 19, 1733, died in Portsmouth, R I, September 10, 1810, married October 25, 1753 Sarah Easton of South
Kings Town, R I., and had ten children. GIDEON, born in Portsmouth, R I., March 27, 1755, died in Brimfield, Mass, October
21, 1828, married Susanna Freeborn. WAIT, born March 3, 1757
STEPHEN, born May 12, 1759 MARY, born in Portsmouth, R I.,
September 30, 1761, married Samuel Dyre. JAMES, born in Portsmouth, R I, January 29, 1764, died in Cannonsville, N Y., October 5, 1837, married Maribah (surname unknown). SARAH, born
in Portsmouth, R I., April 26, 1766 THOMAS, born in Portsmouth, R I., March 16, 1768, died in Portsmouth, R I, November
5, 1845 MERCY, born in Portsmouth, R I., May 2, 1770, died in
Fall River, Mass, April 13, 1835, married Aaron Borden ELIZ-
ABETH, born in Portsmouth, R I., September 18, 1772, married
David Earle SUSANNAH, born in Portsmouth, R I, 1775

He passed his life in Portsmouth, R I, and was a farmer He
was admitted Freeman from Portsmouth, R I, in May, 1757 He
represented the town in the General Assembly as a Deputy in 1775
and 1778. His will dated April 11, 1803, proven October 8, 1810,
mentions son Thomas as executor. He willed "to son Gideon, land
specified, to son Thomas, and to his mother Sarah, house and land
except that given to Gideon to son James, lower lot in Spinks so
called adjoining the land of George Brownell on the west, the same
being in the town of Portsmouth, R I.; daughter Sarah to live with
her brother Thomas, and mother Sarah, to daughters Sarah Durfee, Mercy Borden, Elizabeth Earle, and Hannah Goble, twenty
dollars each, to granddaughter Sarah Borden, wife of Joseph Borden, twenty dollars, and to grand-children John, Mercy and Stephen
Dyre, twenty dollars equally, and grandchildren Sarah, Elizabeth

and Mary Munroe, twenty dollars equally, to be paid by son Gideon;
to wife, indoor movables and horse and carriage."

ELIZABETH DURFEE ALBRO

(12378)

Elizabeth Durfee, daughter of Gideon and Eleanor Tripp
Durfee, born in Portsmouth, R. I., March 7, 1743; married in Portsmouth, R I, April 19, 1764, James Albro,
son of Samuel and Ruth Lawton Albro, born in Portsmouth, R. I., and had seven children RUTH, born February 28, 1765 SAMUEL, born January 4, 1767. GIDEON, born January 20, 1769, married Sarah Dickson JAMES, born December 30,
1771; married Rebecca Tabor CHRISTOPHER DURFEE, born May
20, 1775. ELIZABETH, born July 17, 1780. ELEANOR DURFEE,
born October 18, 1783.

RUTH DURFEE PEARSE

(12379).

Ruth Durfee, daughter of Gideon and Eleanor Tripp Durfee,
born in Portsmouth, R. I., September 20, 1744; married in Portsmouth, R. I., December 29, 1765, Jeremiah Pearse, son of Jeremiah and Submit Carpenter Pearse, born in Bristol, R. I., June 2,
1738, and had four children. ELIZABETH, born in Portsmouth, R.
I, June 13, 1766, married Henry Lawton. ELEANOR, born in Barrington, R. I, June 5, 1767; married William Pearse. SUSANNAH,
born in Rehoboth, Mass., February 8, 1771; married Samuel Shearman. BENJAMIN, born in Portsmouth, R. I, February 26, 1775;
died in Portsmouth, R. I., November 22, 1841. married Primacy
Payne

ELEANOR DURFEE BORDEN

(12379c)

Eleanor Durfee, daughter of Gideon and Eleanor Tripp Durfee,
born in Portsmouth, R I, February 18, 1756; died in Portsmouth,
R I, March 4, 1783. married John Borden, son of Joseph and
Catherine Turner Borden, born in Portsmouth R I February 16,

1752; died in Portsmouth, R. I, April 30, 1828, and had three children. WAITE, born in Portsmouth, R. I., June 8, 1776; married
Peter Lawton. ELIZABETH, born in Portsmouth, R. I, November
21, 1778 RUTH, born in Portsmouth, R. I., September 27, 1780

JOSEPH DURFEE

(12383)

Joseph Durfee, son of Thomas and Sarah Briggs Durfee, born
in Portsmouth, R. I, January 29, 1734; died in Shelburne, New
Brunswick, 1801, married in Portsmouth, R. I, December 29, 1757.
Ann Lawton, daughter of Jeremiah Lawton, and had six children
ROBERT, born September 2, 1758. HANNAH, born July 13, 1760
MARY, born July 15, 1762. ANN, born 1764 ANN, born April
9, 1766 ELIZABETH, born March 15, 1768.

He was admitted a Freeman of Middletown, R I, May, 1758
He was a prosperous merchant in Newport, R I, before the Revolutionary War He became a Captain of a company of Loyalists at
Newport, known as the "Loyal Newport Associators," he received
his commission as Captain from the British General, Pigot, January
1, 1778 At the close of the War for Independence he settled on
some lots in Shelburn, New Brunswick, which were given him by
the English government

JAMES DURFEE.

(12384)

James Durfee, son of Thomas and Mary Tripp Durfee, born
in Bristol, R I, January 4, 1742, died in Portsmouth, R I, March
27, 1817; married in Middletown, R. I., Ruth Slocum, and had five
children. MARY, born September 21, 1763; died September 18,
1827 REBECCA, born February 16, 1765, died February 5, 1834.
BENJAMIN, born September 20, 1766 ELIZABETH, born April 21,
1769. JAMES, born August 11, 1777

OLIVER DURFEE

(12387).

Oliver Durfee, son of Thomas and Mary Tripp Durfee, born

106

in Portsmouth, R. I., February 27, 1754, died in Middletown, R. I., September 11, 1798, married in Newport, R. I., October 13, 1782, Elizabeth Lowden Langley, widow of Peter Langley, and daughter of Richard and Priscilla Stafford Lowden, born November 5, 1755, died in Newport, R I, October 6, 1835, and had six children. OLIVER, born August 7, 1783. MARY, died March 20, 1809. JAMES LOWDEN, born April 11, 1788; died in Berkley, Mass, May 24, 1859. PRISCILLA, born August 1, 1790; died in Newport, R. I., April 22, 1866. THOMAS, born June 20, 1793 LUCINA, born February 17, 1796.

He was a Captain in the Revolutionary Army, and at the close of the war, May 18, 1782, he was appointed collector of rates in Middletown, R I He was chosen assistant to the Governor in 1786 and 1788; was commissioned as justice of inferior court May 12, 1788, by Governor John Collins; also by Governor Arthur Fenner, September 13, 1790 He was Deputy in 1781-2; also town clerk from 1780 to 1783.

ELIZABETH DURFEE CHASE

(1239a2)

Elizabeth Durfee, daughter of Job and Mary Earle Durfee born in Portsmouth, R. I, July 12, 1735, married in Tiverton, R I, 1757, Benjamin Chase, son of Stephen and Esther Buffington Chase, born in Swansea, Mass, January 29, 1737, and had seven children MARY, born January 20, 1758, married David Potter JOSEPH, born November 10, 1759, married Sylvia Sowle. SARAH, born May 13, 1762, married James Butts. HANNAH, born May 14, 1764, died March 24, 1768 GIDEON, born March 13, 1767, married Mrs. Sarah Purrington Briggs, (2) Louisa Slade CLARK, born August 22, 1770, died in Ontario County, N. Y., 1821, married Phebe Mason STEPHEN, born January 15, 1774; married Bethia Matteson

JOHN DURFEE

(1239a3).

John Durfee, son of Job and Mary Earle Durfee, born in Tiverton, R. I, August 31, 1736, died in Tiverton, R. I, August 31

1812, married in Tiverton, R. I., December 15, 1757, Phebe Gray, daughter of Thomas and Sarah Bennett Gray, born in Tiverton, R. I., November 14, 1740, died in Tiverton, R. I., February 12, 1819, and had nine children THOMAS, born in Tiverton, R. I., November 4, 1759; died in Tiverton, R. I., January 17, 1829, married Mary Lowden. ABNER, born in Tiverton, R. I. September 18, 1761, married Nancy Cory WILLIAM, born in Tiverton, R. I. 1763; died in Tiverton, R. I., 1845; married Alice Stafford MARY, born in Tiverton, R. I., died in Portsmouth, R. I., married Gideon Dennis. PRISCILLA, born in Tiverton, R. I., 1780; died in Portsmouth, R. I., May 14, 1860, married Ralph Earl. SILVIA, born in Tiverton, R. I., married George Tripp. JOHN, born in Tiverton, R. I., 1771; died in Tiverton, R. I., September 19, 1805, married Abigail Westgate. PHEBE, born in Tiverton, R. I., 1779, died in Tiverton, R. I., 1851; married Daniel Coggeshall SARAH.

GIDEON DURFEE

(1239a4).

Gideon Durfee, son of Job and Mary Earle Durfee, born in Tiverton, R. I., February 17, 1738 died in Palmyra, N. Y., September 12, 1814, married in Tiverton, R. I., March 10, 1757, Anna Bowen, born August 21, 1738, died in Palmyra, N. Y., October 20, 1821, and had twelve children EARLE, born in Tiverton, R. I., October 27, 1757, died in South Cambridge, N. Y., May 24, 1839, married Patience Lake, (2) Phebe Hunt LEMUAL, born in Tiverton, R. I., April 18, 1759, died in Palmyra, N. Y., August 9, 1829, married Prudence Hathaway MARY, born in Tiverton, R. I., December 2, 1761, died in Palmyra, N. Y., 1794, married Humphrey Sherman. JOB, born in Tiverton, R. I., September 19, 1763, died in Palmyra, N. Y., 1831; married Susannah Borden GIDEON, born in Tiverton, R. I., February 21, 1765; died in Palmyra, N. Y., 1809; married Hannah Wood HANNAH, born in Tiverton, R. I., July 27, 1766, died in Palmyra, N. Y., September 1, 1820; married Weaver Osband ELIZABETH, born in Tiverton, R. I., March 29, 1768, married Welcome Herendeen PARDON, born in Tiverton, R. I., January 24, 1770, died in Palmyra N. Y., April 25, 1828, married Ruth Reeves EDWARD, born in Tiverton, R. I., December 10, 1771, died in Palmyra, N. Y., September 20, 1823, mar-

108

ried Hannah Howell, (2) Susannah Brown. RUTH, born in Tiverton, R. I., March 13, 1774; died in Palmyra, N. Y., November 13, 1857, married William Wilcox STEPHEN, born in Tiverton, R. I., April 4, 1776, died in Palmyra, N. Y., April 14, 1854, married Mary Allen. ANNA, born in Tiverton, R. I., March 18, 1780, died before 1791.

On May 19, 1791, he bought the first tract of land sold in East Palmyra, Wayne County, N. Y., six hundred acres. He was a private in Captain Peleg Simmons' company of Colonel Christopher Olney's regiment, muster roll dated at Newport, R. I., October 23, 1781.

JOB DURFEE.

(1239a6)

Job Durfee, son of Job and Mary Earle Durfee, born in Tiverton, R. I., August 26, 1742; died in Tiverton, R. I., 1789, married in Portsmouth, R. I., March 10, 1765, Mary Slocum, daughter of Thomas Slocum, born in Portsmouth, R. I., 1745, died in Tiverton, R. I., June 28, 1823, and had six children THOMAS, born in Tiverton, R. I., August 2, 1766; died in Tiverton, R. I., February 26, 1790. DANIEL, born in Tiverton, R. I., November 21, 1767, married Barsheba Hart DAVID, born in Tiverton, R. I., September 5, 1770 GEORGE, born in Tiverton, R. I., September 11, 1772; died in Tiverton, R. I., November 12, 1854; married Sarah Coggeshall. JOSEPH, born in Tiverton, R. I. May 8, 1780, died in Fall River, Mass., December 16, 1865, married Elizabeth Borden WILLIAM, born in Tiverton, R. I., August 5, 1784; died in Tiverton, R. I.: married Hannah Clark.

THOMAS CORNELL.

(12442)

Thomas Cornell, son of William and Hannah Thurston Cornell, born January 13, 1726, married in Middleton, October 16, 1746, Rachel Allen, and had two children. SARAH, born July 10, 1747 ELIZABETH, born November 21, 1749, married Alex Briggs or James Anthony.

WILLIS LORD BROWNELL'S RESIDENCE.

Hannah Cornell Coggeshall.

(12444).

Hannah Cornell, daughter of William and Hannah Thurston Cornell, born November 22, 1730; married July 4, 1750, Thomas Coggeshall, son of Thomas and Mary Freeborn Coggeshall, born August 26, 1728, died January 17, 1803, and had three children. John, born May 7, 1751; died 1799. Josiah, born August 13, 1752. William, born January 7, 1757; died January, 1829, married Deborah Horswell.

Walter Cornell.

(12451).

Walter Cornell, son of George and Elizabeth Thurston Cornell, born October 11, 1729, died in Portsmouth, R. I., May 21, 1813, married April 4, 1753, Sarah Anthony, daughter of Abraham Anthony, and had two children. Thurston, married Ann Anthony, (2) Mary Perry. Elizabeth, married Robert N. Hix.

Gideon Cornell.

(12455).

Gideon Cornell, son of George and Elizabeth Thurston Cornell, born December 6, 1737, died May 30, 1801; married Susannah Brownell, died April 4, 1825, age eighty-two years, and had ten children. Edward, born 1765, died in Butternuts, Otsego County, N. Y., 1857, married Elizabeth Hoxie. William, born October 29, 1766, died 1864-5; married Content Davis, (2) Rhoda Tenny. Millicent, born October 19, 1768; died April 19, 1791, married Philip Allen. Susannah, born December, 1770; died in Union Village, Washington County, N Y, September 4 1824, married Jonathan Mooney. Sarah, born September 23, 1774, died May 28, 1802, married Abraham Briggs. Gideon, born October 17, 1776; died August 13, 1834, married Hannah Russell, (2) Harriet Sarchet. Wanton, born September 23, 1778; died in Milton, Saratoga County, N Y., March 26, 1871. Latham, born 1781; died April 17, 1876. Mary, born March 2, 1783, died March 12, 1861; married Gideon Gifford, (2) Erastus Bigelow, D. D. Walter, born

111

May 17, 1785, died in Troy, N. Y., April 14, 1877

He and his brother Matthew moved to Easton, Washington County, N. Y., in 1783.

MATTHEW CORNELL.

(12457)

Matthew Cornell, son of George and Elizabeth Thurston Cornell, born November 11, 1745, died March 4, 1807; married in Newport, R. I., about 1774. Elizabeth Shrieve, daughter of Daniel and Abigail Shrieve, born in Little Compton, R. I., November 23, 1750; died April 29 1829, and had eight children. JOHN, born June 24, 1780, died May 5, 1839, married Eunice Cheesboro. WALTER, born August 24, 1782, died March 4, 1833, married Eunice Hart. Matthew, born March 27, 1787, died January 29, 1851 AMY, born December 11, 1774, died September 14, 1814, married Anthony Lee. HANNAH, born September 10, 1784, died August 15, 1821; married Gideon Durfee. ELIZABETH, born February 19, 1788; married Wilbur Dennis MILLICENT, born June 18, 1792, died July 20, 1866; married Gideon Gifford GEORGE, born September 3, 1790; died young

He engaged in whale fishery previous to the Revolution, and in July, 1776, he sold his ship and cargo in the Dutch West Indies to avoid capture by the British ship-of-war Pomona He was subsequently captaured by the British and was a prisoner on a British ship in New York harbor, for more than two years After his release, he moved with his family to Easton, Washington County, N. Y., remaining there nine years, then moved upon a farm near Buskirk's Bridge, where he lived at the time of his death. He and his wife are buried in the Quaker burial ground at Easton, N. Y.

REBECCA CORNELL BIDDLE

(12462).

Rebecca Cornell, daughter of Gideon and Rebecca Vaughan Cornell, born February 17, 1755, married Col Clement Biddle, son of John Biddle of Philadelphia. Pa., and had nine children THOMAS, married Christiana Williams JAMES, married Elizabeth Kepling JOHN, married Mary Widdle JACOB died unmarried CLEMENT,

married Mary Barkley. MARY, married George Cadwallader RE-
BECCA, married Mathew Chapon NANCY, married Thomas Dunlop. SALLY, died unmarried.

STEPHEN BROWNELL

(14621).

Stephen Brownell, son of Joseph and Rebecca Tripp Brownell,
born in Portsmouth, R. I, February 12, 1744; died in Providence,
R I., November 23, 1815, married December 7, 1768, Susannah
Fish, daughter of David and Jemima Tallman Fish, born Novem-
ber 29, 1749, died October 20, 1820, and had ten children RE-
BECCA, born February 16, 1770 DAVID, born February 26, 1772
NANCY, born September 23, 1773. DAVID, born December 30, 1775
STEPHEN, born May 10, 1778, died August 13, 1778. ISAAC, born
July 1, 1780 MOSES, born May 10, 1782. SUSANNA, born April
10, 1784. STEPHEN FISH, born in Portsmouth, R. I, December 1,
1785, died in Smithfield, R I, April 28, 1865, married Susanna
White, (2) Mary White PETER, born July 8, 1788
He was a farmer and suffered from depredations of British in the
Revolutionary war.

NATHAN BROWNELL.

(14623)

Nathan Brownell, son of Joseph and Rebecca Tripp Brownell,
born February 7, 1747, married 1769, Elizabeth Fish.

PHILADELPHIA BROWNELL SISSON.

(14625)

Philadelphia Brownell, daughter of Joseph and Rebecca Tripp
Brownell, born in Portsmouth, R. I., May 17, 1752; married De-
cember 10, 1772, Richard Sisson, and had six children. RUTH
GRIZZEL NATHAN. REBECCA. PELEG. JAMES

SUSANNA BROWNELL SLOCUM

(14626)

Susanna Brownell, daughter of Joseph and Rebecca Tripp Brownell, born March 17 1754, married December, 1772, Giles Slocum.

AMY BROWNELL WEAVER.

(14628).

Amy Brownell, daughter of Joseph and Rebecca Tripp Brownell, born September 8, 1760, married 1784, Captain Benjamin Weaver, son of Captain Benjamin and Joanna Barnaby Weaver, and had four children GARDNER, born October 24, 1784, died January 14, 1810, married Betsey Douglass JOANNA, born May 8, 1786, died January 6, 1859, married Ebenezer Peirce. MAJOR JOSEPH, born September 17, 1787, died December 26, 1814. AMY, born October 7, 1793, died October 30, 1808

THOMAS BROWNELL

(14629).

Thomas Brownell, son of Joseph and Rebecca Tripp Brownell, born December 16, 1762, died August 21, 1811, married May 6, 1790, Mercy Shaw, born March 22, 1762, died January 15, 1829, and had six children AMY, born January 31, 1791, died May 1, 1826, married Philip Almy OLIVER, born April 15, 1793; died January 29, 1875, married Sally Green JOSEPH, born January 19, 1795, died August 19, 1879; married Lydia Almy. ANTHONY, born September 27, 1797; died February 12, 1824 REBECCA, born January 14, 1800, died June 21, 1879, married Rev. Lawton Cady WILLIAM, born June 17, 1804, died June 5, 1887, married Rebecca Child

JOSEPH BROWNELL

(14633)

Joseph Brownell, son of Thomas and Abigail Slocum Brownell, born February 21, 1754, married Elizabeth (surname unknown), and had eleven children. BORDEN, born in Portsmouth, R. I., August 5, 1776. GEORGE, born in Portsmouth, R I., October 12, 1778 HANNAH, born in Portsmouth, R I., June 24, 1780 DAVID, born in Portsmouth, R I., October 1, 1784 RUTH, born in Portsmouth, R. I., October 16, 1785 ABNER, born in Portsmouth, R. I., January 30, 1787; died in Sauquoit, N. Y., December, 1874, married Susan Macomber MERCY, born in Portsmouth, R. I., April 3, 1788 HOLDER, born in Portsmouth, R. I., May 1, 1789 ANNA, born in Portsmouth, R. I., October 31, 1792 JOSEPH, born in Portsmouth, R. I., November 25, 1796 ELIZA, born in Portsmouth, R. I., July 19, 1806.

GEORGE BROWNELL

(14636)

George Brownell, son of Thomas and Abigail Slocum Brownell, born in Rhode Island, October 20, 1761; died in Lonsdale, Susquehanna County, Pa., 1845, married a Hopkins, and had eight children. BENJAMIN, married Margaret Coil RHODA, married George Coil. PATIENCE, married George Waterman. GEORGE, born in Rhode Island, 1801, died in Clifford, Susquehanna County, Pa., about 1869, married Sarah Kelsey, (2) Amy Arnold CLARISSA, married John Coil JAMES, married Ellen Arnold. BETSEY, married a Champlin. MARY ANN, married John Stephens

It is stated that he was a butcher and meat dealer in Rhode Island and that he drove an ox team from Rhode Island to Susquehanna County, Pa., bringing his family with him The first record of him in Pennsylvania is in 1818, where he and his son Benjamin are on the tax list of Clifford, Pa

MERCY HOWLAND GREENE

(14651).

Mercy Howland, daughter of Daniel and Philadelphia Brownell Howland, born December 30, 1745, died January 26, 1824, married February 23, 1769, Gideon Greene, born about 1745, died March 10, 1832

Gideon Greene was a cousin of General Nathaniel Greene of the Revolutionary Army and a lineal descendant of John Greene, Surgeon of Warwick, R. I., who came to the Colonies in 1635, from Salisbury, England.

MARTHA BROWNELL COBB

(14671)

Martha Brownell, daughter of George and Wait Durfee Brownell, born October 5, 1761, married in Tiverton, R. I., June 6, 1781 Dr. Elijah Cobb, son of Elijah Cobb, and had five children. WAIT DURFEE, born in Portsmouth, R. I., April 24, 1782 KATHERINE DANFORTH, born in Portsmouth, R. I., August 9, 1783 MARTHA BROWNELL born in Portsmouth, R. I., August 6, 1785 RACHEL, born in Portsmouth, R. I., August 13, 1794 ELIJAH, born in Portsmouth, R. I., May 3, 1796

WALTER CORNELL.

(14842)

Walter Cornell, son of Jonathan and Phoebe Brownell Cornell, born April 7 1764, died September 1, 1819, married December 8, 1791, Ruth Earle, daughter of John and Deborah Anthony Earle, died May 23, 1812, and had seven children JOB, born November 2, 1792. DAVID EARLE, born August 23, 1794. EDWARD, born March 19 1797 MARY, born 1799, married Joshua Blanchet WALTER, born March 1, 1801. ALBERT, born October 1, 1804; died March 15, 1881 JOHN, born 1806, died in California.

KEZIAH BROWNELL TIBBETTS

(15131)

Keziah Brownell, daughter of Thomas and Hannah (surname unknown) Brownell, born June 12, 1727, married 1748, George Tibbetts

THANKFUL BROWNELL TRIPP.

(15132)

Thankful Brownell, daughter of Thomas and Hannah (surname

116

unknown) Brownell, born April 15, 1730, married January 4, 1749 or 1750, Isaac Tripp, son of James and Mary Tripp

HANNAH BROWNELL MOSHER.

(15133).

Hannah Brownell, daughter of Thomas and Hannah (surname unknown) Brownell, born July 22, 1732; married September, 1759, Obadiah Mosher, son of John and Hannah Davol Mosher

BENJAMIN BROWNELL

(15136)

Benjamin Brownell, son of Thomas and Hannah (surname unknown) Brownell, born February 7, 1739, died November 21, 1815, married 1758, Martha Closson, daughter of Josiah Closson, and had six children DEBORAH, born April 3, 1761. JOSIAH, born June 5, 1765; married Deborah Howland. EZEKIEL, born August 5, 1770, married Penelope Borden, (2) Sarah Negus, (3) Hannah Sisson MARTHA, born July 28, 1772, died 1840. HANNAH, born May 15, 1775, married Warren Dwelley

PATIENCE BROWNELL CHASE

(15137).

Patience Brownell, daughter of Thomas and Hannah (surname unknown) Brownell, born July 29, 1741; married Job Chase.

DOROTHY BROWNELL SANFORD

(15138)

Dorothy Brownell, daughter of Thomas and Hannah (surname unknown) Brownell, born May 14, 1744, married 1768, John Sanford.

George Brownell

(15139)

George Brownell, son of Thomas and Hannah (surname unknown) Brownell, born December 9, 1746, married July 12, 1770, Rhoda Milk, daughter of Lemuel and Mary Milk, and had eleven children. HANNAH, born 1771, married Peleg Sisson REBECCA, born 1772, married George Chase DOROTHY, born 1774. AMY, born 1777 ELIZABETH, born 1779; married Jeremiah Raynolds POLLY, born 1781, married Richard Lawton SALLY, born 1783; married Joseph Boomer PATIENCE, born 1786, married Thaddeus Raynolds GEORGE MILK, born November 15, 1787, died September 20, 1830, married Mary Davis. DAVID, born October 8, 1789, died December 30, 1864. DANIEL, born and died in infancy.

Elizabeth Brownell Peckham

(15139a)

Elizabeth Brownell, daughter of Thomas and Hannah (surname unknown) Brownell, born October 13, 1749, married August 20, 1767, Peleg Peckham.

Ezekiel Cornell

(15161).

Ezekiel Cornell, son of Richard and Content Brownell Cornell, born March 27, 1733, married March 25, 1760, Rachel Wood of Little Compton R I, and had two children. EZRA, born in Dartmouth, Mass, May 22, 1762 RHODA, born in Scituate, Mass, May 13, 1782, married Caleb Aldrich.

In 1775 he was appointed lieutenant-colonel of Colonel Hitchcock's regiment, and was present at the siege of Boston. He was made deputy-adjutant-general, October 1, 1776, and subsequently brigadier-general and commander of the brigade of state troops which were in service three years and three months, and were disbanded March 16, 1780 He was in the battles of Bunker Hill, Long Island and Rhode Island He was a delegate from Rhode Island to the Continental Congress in 1770-3, and chairman of the military committee

PHILIP CORNELL.

(15162).

Philip Cornell, son of Richard and Content Brownell Cornell, born October 5, 1735, died October 27, 1765, married Lillis Thomas, daughter of Simeon and Hannah (surname unknown) Thomas, and had five children. NATHANIEL, born January 1, 1759. OLIVER, born April 16, 1760. PATIENCE, born November 18, 1761. PHILIP, born October 1, 1764. SEABURY, born March 31, 1770, married Abigail Mason

RICHARD CORNELL

(15164)

Richard Cornell, son of Richard and Content Brownell Cornell born March 4, 1742, married September 15, 1763, Alice Anthony, and had four children. CONTENT, born September 23, 1764. RICHARD, born October 10, 1766. MARY, born March 20, 1769. JAMES, born June 4, 1770.

GIDION CORNELL

(15165)

Gideon Cornell, son of Richard and Content Brownell Cornell, born December 1, 1745, died November, 1830, married Prudence Winslow, and had six children. ESTHER, born August 17, 1770. GIDEON, born September 27, 1771, died September 16, 1845. THOMAS, born May 13, 1773; died in the West Indies. JOHN, born September 5, 1774. ALFRED, born July 28, 1776, died September 3, 1860, married Nancy Cadwell. WINDSOR, born May 2, 1778

He married second widow Thornton, and had four children. DANIEL A, married Mary Cauldwell. STEPHEN, married Mary Hopkins GEORGE DANIEL NILES, married Maria Cornell.

On October 1, 1776, he was First Lieutenant of Scituate Hunters, and in 1777, he became captain of the same company

DAVID BROWNELL

(159a21)

David Brownell, son of Jonathan and Hannah Hiller Brownell, married Rhoda Brownell, daughter of Joshua and Martha Peckham Brownell, and had eight children REUBEN, married Alice Sherman PICKHAM, married a Rowland DAVID, married a Tatt MARTHA, married Joel Davis LYDIA, born January 28, 1796, died February 10, 1861, married Wilson Brownell BETSEY, married Jesse Brundige ELIJAH, married a Hoag RHODA, married a Wallace.

JONATHAN BROWNELL.

(159a22)

Jonathan Brownell, son of Jonathan and Hannah Hiller Brownell, born in Cold Spring, Dutchess County, N. Y., November 2, 1768; died in Solon, Cortland County, N. Y., March 6, 1859, married in Cold Spring, N. Y., August 28 1788, Desire Lake, born July 19, 1772, died in Solon, N. Y., March 23, 1856, and had fourteen children MARY, born in Duanesburg Schenectady County, N. Y., August 12, 1790 ISRAEL, born in Duanesburg N. Y., September 7, 1792 RACHEL, born in Duanesburg, N. Y., October 6, 1794 REBECCA, born in Duanesburg, N. Y., April 15, 1796; died September 1829 ARIADNE, born in Columbus, Chenango County, N. Y., June 12, 1799 Twins, born in Columbus, N. Y., October 12, 1801, died October 12, 1801 DAVID I, born in Columbus, N. Y., December 15, 1802 AMOS KNAPP, born in Columbus, N. Y., July 23, 1805, BENJAMIN JONATHAN, born in Columbus, N. Y., September 1, 1807 DORMAN SMITH, born in Columbus, N. Y., January 10, 1810, died May 27, 1814 STEPHEN FOSTER, born in Columbus, N. Y., June 17, 1812 DORMAN LAKE, born in Columbus, N. Y., August 16, 1814 TRACY PLATT, born in Columbus, N. Y., April 26, 1817

He lived with his parents until his marriage. He then went to Duanesburg, N. Y., where he remained until about 1800, he then moved to Columbus, N. Y., and built a log house, in which he kept tavern. Later he replaced this with a large frame house which is still used as a hotel. He continued to conduct the hotel in Columbus, N. Y., until his health failed, he then went to reside with his son, David I., in Solon, N. Y., where he died. In politics he was a Democrat.

BENJAMIN BROWNELL

(159a23)

Benjamin Brownell, son of Jonathan and Hannah Hiller Brownell, born June 18, 1771, died May 15, 1826, married February 26, 1792, Huldah Bullock, daughter of Nathan and Huldah Whiton Bullock, born August 10, 1767, died August 6, 1814, and had nine children HANNAH, born August 20, 1793, died at Troy, N Y., May 29, 1865, married Russell Pack. WILSON, born July 14, 1795, died August 8, 1872; married Lydia Brownell. DAVID, born in Sand Lake, Rensselaer County, N Y, July 2, 1798, died in Ellery, Chautauqua County, N Y, December 1, 1877, married Thankful Brownell, (2) Jane Jemima Brownell Burch, (a widow). HULDAH, born February 28, 1800, married Stephen Van Rensselaer Bullock REBECCA, born August 8, 1802, died August 28, 1874, married Charles Goodrich AMOS, born July 23, 1804; died January 29, 1884, married a Smith LEAH, born March 27, 1806, died April 29, 1875: married Benjamin Gardner. ANNA, born September 23, 1808, died March 27 1810 RHODA, born August 3, 1813; died January, 1814

He married second Clarissa Riche, and had two children Charles, born October 6, 1816, died March 9, 1874 EDWIN, born June 12, 1821, died March 12, 1874.

GEORGE BROWNELL.

(159a41)

George Brownell, son of Benjamin and Waite Durfee Brownell, born December 30, 1765, married at Portsmouth, R I, March 6, 1783, Sarah Burrington, daughter of Robert and Sarah Brown Burrington, born in Portsmouth, R. I., March 26, 1759, and had three children. ANNE, born November 2, 1783, married John Lawton. RUTH, born October 14, 1785. GEORGE WASHINGTON, born December 6, 1790.

121

CHARLES BROWNELL.

(16312).

Charles Brownell, son of Giles and Elizabeth Shaw Brownell, born March 8, 1728, he married and had three children COMFORT, married Abner Wilcox RHODA JOSEPH

JOSEPH BROWNELL

(16319a).

Joseph Brownell, son of Giles and Elizabeth Shaw Brownell, born July 15, 1744, died February 24, 1824, married February 11, 1766, Deborah Briggs, daughter of Joseph and Ruth Briggs, born September 23, 1748, died September 23, 1840, and had eleven children CYNTHIA, born December 14, 1769, died November 1, 1828 ISAAC, born April 17, 1772 ROBY, born April 1, 1774, died February 22, 1824. ELIZABETH, born December 7, 1776. ELIZABETH, born February 25, 1779 JOSEPH born March 6, 1781 DEBORAH, born June 19, 1783, died June 23 1848 PARDON, born April 3, 1785, died May 1, 1836 LYDIA, born March 15, 1787 JAMES, born March 5, 1789 MARY, born January 10, 1792; died September 19, 1826

DOROTHY BROWNELL BURGESS

(16341)

Dorothy Brownell, daughter of George and Sarah Bailey Brownell, born January 11, 1733, married August 25, 1757, James Burgess, son of Joseph and Ann Tew Burgess, born January 1, 1731, died March 15, 1787, and had eight children JOSEPH, born May 15, 1758, died April, 1826; married Sarah Peckham, (2) Freelove Randall GEORGE, born October 5, 1759, died May 14, 1843. ANNA, born January 1, 1762, died February 27, 1847, married Caleb Corp JAMES, born August 14, 1763 SARAH died April 13, 1851, married Nathaniel Williams. NATHANIEL, died March, 1855, married Mary Alverson, (2) Sarah Spencer. BENJAMIN, died October 8, 1822, married Abigail Mason, (2) Eunice Dunlap. BETSEY, married Parker Brownell

Her husband's paternal grandfather Thomas Burgess, married

122

Martha Wilbur Closson, widow of Timothy Closson, and daughter of Joseph and Ann Brownell Wilbur, granddaughter of Thomas and Ann Brownell

SAMUEL BROWNELL.

(16343).

Samuel Brownell, son of George and Sarah Bailey Brownell, born in Little Compton, R. I., July 18, 1738, died 1817, married October 23, 1763, Ruth Briggs, daughter of William and Abisha Records Briggs of Little Compton, R I, and had ten children. LUCY, born February 6, 1766, married Gilbert Tompkins. WILLIAM, born April 12, 1768; drowned while at college. MARY, born July 8. 1770; died May 10, 1844, married Gilbert Tompkins. SARAH, born October 2. 1772; died July 28, 1860, married Calvin Whitcomb SUSANNA, born March 16, 1775, married Adam Simmons. FALLY, born April 2, 1777; married Philip Taylor. EUNICE, born January 25, 1780; died August 6, 1849; married Joseph Hitchcock ABISHA, born December 21, 1782, died 1813; married William Simmons. SAMUEL. born September 2, 1785; died March 6, 1865, married Abigail Barker, (2) Frances Gurnsey. LUCY, born June 16, 1788, married Ann Pease

He married second Phoebe Thompkins He came from Westport, Mass, in 1794, and settled in Madison County, N Y. He enlisted from Dartmouth, Mass., as a private in Captain William Hick's company of Colonel Pope's regiment, which marched December 7. 1777, and returned December 21, 1777, service, fifteen days, also in Captain William Hick's company of Colonel John Hathaway's regiment, enlisting August 1, 1780 and being discharged August 9. 1780, service nine days on the alarm in Rhode Island.

His wife was a sister to Captain Cornelius Briggs, who married Fallee Brownell, daughter of Paul and Deborah Dennis Brownell of Westport, Mass.

GEORGE BROWNELL

(16345)

George Brownell, son of George and Sarah Bailey Brownell, born in Little Compton, R. I., March 31, 1744; died March 27,

1816, married June 17, 1770, Lucy Richmond, daughter of Perez and Deborah Loring Richmond, born July 3, 1751, and had eleven children LORING RICHMOND, born August 28, 1771, married Betsey Burgess and was lost at sea MARY, born February 26, 1773, died February 23, 1846 CHARLOTTE, born November 15, 1774; died 1776 ISRALL PUTNAM, born May 1, 1776, lost at sea PARKER, born August 9, 1777, died July 8, 1779 CHARLOTTE, born October 11, 1779; died December 23, 1852 PERIS RICHMOND, born April 7, 1783, lost at sea PARKER, born April 29, 1785, died 1842 CUSHING, born March 25, 1787 NATHAN, born March 13, 1789, died May 22 1866, married Polly Brown. GILBERT, born April 23, 1792, died 1794

He enlisted as a private in Captain William Hick's company of Colonel Pope's regiment and marched December 7, 1777, returning December 27, 1777, service twenty-one days. About 1793, he moved with his family from Little Compton, R. I., to Oneida County, N. Y., upon his arrival he purchased a farm near Parish Hill, Oneida County, N. Y., upon which farm he lived and labored, loved and died and there the husband and father lies buried

His wife was a grand-daughter of Colonel Sylvester Richmond, who received the French flag at the capture of Louisburg, in 1744, and his wife, Elizabeth Rogers daughter of John and Elizabeth Paybodie Rogers She was great-grand-daughter of Edward Richmond, one of the incorporators of Little Compton, R. I., and afterwards Attorney General of Rhode Island and great-great-grand-daughter of John Richmond of Ashton Keynes, Wiltshire, England, who settled first at "Richmond's Island," Me, came to Taunton in 1637, and was one of the "incorporators"

EZRA BROWNELL

(16346)

Ezra Brownell, son of George and Sarah Bailey Brownell, born in Dartmouth, Mass, October 20, 1746, died 1818, married October 20 1768, Hope Borden, daughter of John and Susanna Borden, born October 28, 1747, and had fourteen children. EZRA, born January 19, 1769, died 1813, married Miss Davidson, (2) Nancy Dorn. RICHARD, WILLIAM, GEORGE, GAMER, PERCY, JOHN, CHARLOTTE, born December 25, 1776; married Nathaniel Mudge. SUSAN, married Mr. Hoyt. MARY, married Mr Hunt LUCY, mar-

ried Mr Simpson, (2) Mr. Palmer. SALLY, married Mr Shaver
PHOEBE, born November 19, 1788, died December 3, 1808, married Abner Lawton. MARTHA, married Mr Palmer

NATHANIEL BROWNELL

(16348).

Nathaniel Brownell, son of George and Sarah Bailey Brownell,
born in Westport, Mass, December 21, 1751, died December 30,
1825; married March 25, 1790, Sarah Tompkins, died in Westport,
Mass, 1855, and had seven children OSMIN B, born in Westport, Mass., September 27, 1790, died 1852; married Mary Brownell Simmons ALFRED, born in Westport, Mass, September 21,
1792; died in Westport, Mass., September 16, 1867, married Chris-
tine Stoddard CLARINDA, born in Westport, Mass, May 11, 1794
SAMUEL, born in Westport, Mass., May 25, 1798, lost at sea.
CLARK, born in Westport, Mass, June 2, 1800, lost at sea. LUCY,
born in Westport, Mass, March 31, 1802 DAVID, born in Westport, Mass., December 28, 1803

He received his education at the public schools in Westport,
Mass. He was a farmer and always resided at Westport, Mass.
In politics, he was a Whig. He was a member of the Congregational Church. He enlisted as a private in Captain William Hick's
company of Colonel Pope's regiment, and marched December 7,
1777, returning with company December 21, 1777,, service fifteen
days His two brothers, Samuel and George Brownell, served in
the same company

ANN BROWNELL RICHMOND

(16371)

Ann Brownell, daughter of Jonathan and Elizabeth Richmond
Brownell, born February 2, 1743, died January 4, 1791; married
Nathaniel Richmond, and had nine children SAMUEL BUCKMAN,
born April 4, 1767, married Eunice Mack. ELIZABETH, born
February 5, married a Jones. JONATHAN, born July 31, 1774;
married Rebecca Almy MARY, born March 19, 1776, married
John Tuttle RUTH, born April 16, 1780. JOHN, born April 16.
1780. NANCY, born February 11, 1783, married Isaac Hathway.
FALLIE, born May, 1785, married a Gifford.

PARDON BROWNELL

(16372).

Pardon Brownell, son of Jonathan and Elizabeth Richmond Brownell, born July 6, 1745, died July 24, 1799; married Prudence Shaw, born 1744; died January 9, 1823, and had eight children. PEREZ, married May Grinnell THURSTON JONATHAN, born April 24, 1768, married Mary Briggs (2) Sarah Kingsley GILBERT, born May 7, 1770, married Amy Tillinghast Grinnell ELIZABETH, married Daniel Brightman. ANNA born November 26, 1772, married Henry Chase EDMUND, born November 7, 1775, died February 1, 1840, married Mary Bailey, (2) Priscilla Briggs. LYDIA, born November 6, 1783, died July 6, 1832

SYLVESTER BROWNELL

(16377)

Sylvester Brownell, son of Jonathan and Elizabeth Richmond Brownell, born November 20, 1757, died March 21, 1840, married Mercy Church, daughter of Thomas and Ruth Bailey Church, born March 3, 1756, died March 31, 1837, and had eleven children THOMAS CHURCH, born October 19, 1776; died January 13, 1865, married Charlotte Dickenson RUTH, born August 3, 1781; died January 29, 1861; married Joseph Church MERCY born July 28, 1783, died June 22, 1860, married Samuel Almy, (2) Isaac Corey SYLVISTER, born August 12, 1785, died June 12, 1863; married Abbey Taylor PARDON, born January 13, 1788, died March 10, 1846, married Lucia Emilia De Wolf RICHMOND, born March 4, 1790, died October 29, 1866, married Harriet B Church JONATHAN, born March 31, 1792, died August 29, 1877, married Eliza Simmons LYDIA, born April, 1794, married William Richmond, (2) John L. Wendall PRUDENCE, born March 31, 1796, married William A Brown. ELIZABETH, born April 12, 1798, died May, 1892; married Nathan C. Brownell MARY, born August 3, 1800, died 1852.

Sylvester Brownell was in the battle of Bunker Hill with his father, Lieutenant Jonathan Brownell He was an officer in the Revolutionary War, and served under General Washington His "Queen Ann" was hung under the rafters, his grandchildren "adventuring" with it—it exploded with an awful bang.

WILLIAM BROWNELL.

(16392)

William Brownell, son of Stephen and Edith Wilbur Brownell, born in Little Compton, R I , July 17, 1749; died in Little Compton, R. I., 1810, married Elizabeth Pierce, daughter of Giles and Mercy Rouse Pierce, born 1751, and had two children EDITH, born in Little Compton, R I., March 1, 1772 ISAAC, born in Little Compton, R. I., July 1, 1774.

He married second Eunice Palmer, and had three children. ELIZABETH, born in Little Compton, R. I., February 13, 1779 SYLVESTER, born in Little Compton, R I , July 31, 1782 HUMPHREY, born in Little Compton, R I , July 19, 1785

He married third Betsey Grinnell, daughter of Daniel and Grace (surname unknown) Grinnell, and had six children EUNICE, born in Little Compton, R. I , September 1, 1787. WILLIAM, born in Little Compton, R. I , March 23, 1789. WALTER, born in Little Compton, R. I , September 3 1790. CLARKE, born in Little Compton, R. I , October 16, 1793 BETSEY, born in Little Compton, R. I., December 16. 1795. STEPHEN, born in Little Compton, R. I., January 2, 1798.

He was among the Rhode Island recruits of 1782, and was a drummer in Colonel Archibald Deury's regiment of the Revolutionary Army

EDITH BROWNELL EARLE

(16394).

Edith Brownell, daughter of Stephen and Edith Wilbur Brownell, born November 2, 1752, married 1776, William Earle

MARY BROWNELL PEARCE.

(16395).

Mary Brownell, daughter of Stephen and Edith Wilbur Brownell, born July 5, 1754, married December, 1776, Rouse Pearce, son of Giles and Mercy Rouse Pearce

George Brownell

(16396).

George Brownell, son of Stephen and Edith Wilbur Brownell, born October 29, 1756, married March 26, 1780, Elizabeth Peckham, daughter of John Peckham, born January 9, 1761, and had ten children RHODA, born August 6, 1781, married Christopher Taber DANIEL, born March 14, 1782, married Hannah Allen, MARY, born July 24, 1786 married Jonathan Records PRISCILLA, born October 22, 1788 married a Pierce EZRA, born December 24, 1791, married Lucy Wilbur NANCY, born August 31, 1793, married Benjamin Wilbur SALLY, born June 22, 1795, married a Sawyer, PELEG, born March 13, 1798, married Lydia Randall Church GEORGE COOK, born October 4, 1800, married Deborah Pence Hillard ELIZABETH, born July 19, 1803

Stephen Brownell

(16397)

Stephen Brownell, son of Stephen and Mary Eldridge Brownell, born March 18, 1762, died March 12, 1855; married Cynthia Wilbur. He married second December 11, 1803, Mary Coggeshall, died January 3, 1863, and had five children DWELLEY, born September 28 1804 WRIGHT, born December 17, 1806; died March 1, 1880 PERRY, born November 9, 1808, died July 20, 1885 EDITH W, born July 24, 1811, died November, 1895 ABIGAIL, born April 20, 1813

Gideon Brownell

(16422)

Gideon Brownell, son of Pearce and Ruth Thurston Brownell, born in Little Compton, R I, 1746, died September 27, 1818, married March 24, 1776, Phebe Brown, daughter of Robert and Elizabeth Palmer Brown of Tiverton, R I., born January 2, 1754, died May 22, 1844, and had three children HENRY, born 1777; died November 8, 1857, married Ruth Shaw. EDWARD, died 1855; married Rebecca Macomber ARTEMAS born about 1780, died at sea, married Sarah Grinnell.

He served in the Revolutionary Army, enlisting from Little Compton, R. I., December, 1776, under Captain George Simmons, of Colonel Cooke's Regiment According to official records, he served on alternate months from December, 1776, to December, 1779 His widow, Phebe Brownell, drew a pension for seven years until her death in 1844, in her ninetieth year. She was buried beside her husband on the farm of their son, Edward Brownell, in Little Compton, R I, where they had always resided.

Edward Brownell.

(16471).

Edward Brownell, son of Aaron and Alice Southworth Brownell, born in Little Compton, R I, January 10, 1746, died in Willistown, Vt, 1824, married in North Canaan, Conn., January 26, 1774, Susannah Wells, and had nine children Samuel, born in Canaan, Conn died in infancy Beriah Southard, born in Canaan, Conn, 1776; died in Williston, Vt, 1869, married Lucinda Sanford. Samuel Aaron, born in Canaan, Conn, 1778, died in Williston, Vt, 1869, married Zeruah Forbes Hannah, born in Canaan, Conn, 1780, married Joseph Sanford. Chauncey Wells, born in Canaan, Conn, 1782, died in Williston, Vt., 1850; married Belinda Beech. Ira, born in Sharon, Conn, 1784, died in Winterset, Iowa, 1867, married Betsey Clark. Harvey, born in Sharon, Conn, 1787, died in Essex, Vt, 1862, married Alma Rogers, (2) Maria Delano Grove Lawrence, born in Canaan, Conn, March 1, 1790, died in Sharon, Conn., April 10, 1855, married Harriet Burnham, (2) Mary Whittlesey. Edward, born in Canaan, Conn., 1792, died in Williston, Vt, July 25, 1808

The parentage of his wife, Susannah Wells, is not given, but she was probably a lineal descendant of Thomas Wells the immigrant, who came to America in 1635, it is said from the Essex branch of the de Welles family of Lincolnshire, England, who were barons of the realm. His will was dated July 3, 1666 and it is known that at the time of his death he had relatives in Colchester, County of Essex, England In the parish register there is the following entry: Thomas Wells, son of Thomas Wells, the 11th of December, 1605, which is probably the baptismal record of the above Thomas Edward Brownell was called "Captain," no doubt of the militia, but very little has been learned of him during his residence in Connecticut. He removed to Williston, Vt., as early as the winter of 1800, as the following from the town clerk's records shows. "February 26, 1800, Jonathan Crosby deeded to Edward Brownell of Canaan, Litchfield County, Conn., one hundred and three acres of land in Williston, for the sum of two hundred and fifty dollars," and on May 16, 1801, "Edward Brownell, deeded to his son Samuel Aaron Brownell one-half of the same one hundred and three acres of land. The consideration in this deed being one hundred and nine dollars and fifty-three cents," and the residence of both given as Canaan, Conn.

JEREMIAH BROWNELL

(16473).

Jeremiah Brownell, son of Aaron and Alice Southworth Brownell born in Little Compton, R. I., April 21, 1749, died in Jolicure, Province of New Brunswick, about 1835, married a Copp, and had nine children AARON JOHN JEREMIAH THOMAS WILLIAM EDWARD SARAH ANNA LAVINIA "All of whom married and had large families."

He removed as did his brothers Edward, Ichabod and Aaron, to Vermont (perhaps previously to Connecticut) and remained there for a while—was probably where his brothers first located before going to Colchester, Vt. At the time of the Revolution or about 1783, Jeremiah Brownell went to Nova Scotia and settled in Jolicure, Province of New Brunswick, where he died at the age of eighty-six years, according to the testimony of his grandson Jeremiah Brownell, now living. (Sabine in his history of the Loyalists gives the record, "Went to West Moreland, N. S., and died there in 1835 aged thirty-eight." This was undoubtedly an error, possibly eighty-eight was intended, and was the approximate age given to the historian). There is a tradition in the family that ' his brother Joshua went to Nova Scotia with him and settled at St. John, N. B., but the birth of all the children of Aaron and Alice are clearly stated in the vital records of Little Compton, R. I., and there is no Joshua among them. He may have been a cousin or nephew. It is certain that a Joshua Brownell did go to Nova Scotia about 1783, as Sabine gives the record with Jeremiah's. He was one of the grantees of Parrtown, a portion of St. John, New Brunswick, so called in honor of John Parr, then Governor of Nova Scotia, who was appointed July, 1783, "Agent for the Loyalist of New York," at the time when more than seven thousand refuges arrived there. They petitioned the Governor to grant them lands for settlement, which at a later date was arranged for. Joshua probably died at St John and the relatives "never heard of any descendants living there"

ICHABOD BROWNELL.

(16474).

Ichabod Brownell, son of Aaron and Alice Southworth Brownell, born in Little Compton, R I., August 30, 1750, married Elizabeth Stanley, daughter of Nathaniel and Sarah Baldwin Stanley, born about 1755, and had daughter Amy, and probably other children.

He moved with his brothers from Little Compton, R. I, to Connecticut, and thence to Vermont, arriving there about 1792-3 He settled at the falls between Colchester and Burlington and built a stone house in which he kept tavern—called the "Stone Tavern"—until 1811 It was said to have been "better built than any building set up at that period" He also worked at blacksmithing

His wife's maternal grandparents were Deacon Nathaniel and Elizabeth Parmelee Baldwin, and her paternal grandfather, Nathaniel Stanley, moved in 1742 from Farmington to Goshen, Conn, where he followed the business of a tanner, and became a large landholder, at one time owning seven hundred and twenty-eight and one-half acres He is described as "a prosperous and useful inhabitant until old age, and was above mediocrity in intellectual ability and wrote much more than most men of his time." His father, John Stanley, was an early settler of Waterbury, Conn, and "was the first Recorder of the town and wrote a very legible and business-like hand" He was Lieutenant of the militia and a Representative to the General Court

His wife, Elizabeth Stanley Brownell, according to her descendants was "a woman of fine character who lived to the age of eighty-five years, although she became blind." The date of his death is not given and owing to his removals from state to state a full record of children could not be obtained.

131

AARON BROWNELL.

(16477).

Aaron Brownell, son of Aaron and Alice Southworth Brownell, born nearly five months after his father's death, in Little Compton, R. I., February 2, 1755 He probably went with his older brothers in his childhood or early manhood to Connecticut—probably to Canaan—and removed thence to Colchester, Vt, in 1792, where he held the office of Town Clerk from 1797 to 1800 "He lived west of the brook and south of Center street, and worked at the forge." The name of his wife is not learned and history mentions but one child Thomas, born probably in Colchester and is referred to in local history as "our respected citizen"

AARON BROWNELL

(16493a3)

Aaron Brownell, son of Joshua and Martha Peckham Brownell, born December 24, 1754; married Mary Gardner, and had six children HANNAH, born October 18, 1786, married a Marshall EUNICE, born September 25, 1788, died 1857, married Adam Crouse, (2) Henry Ricketson. MARTHA, born May 30, 1791, married Curtis Bennett. JOSHUA, born June 9, 1793, died May 25, 1865; married Esther Denton NATHANIEL, born December 7, 1795, married Eunice Emigh. MARY, born September 25, 1798, died 1800, never married

JOSHUA BROWNELL

(16493a5)

Joshua Brownell, son of Joshua and Martha Peckham Brownell, born on Long Island near New York, N Y ; died in Chemung County, N Y 1822, married Elizabeth Reasoner, and had nine children DEBORAH, born in Dutchess County, N. Y., 1788 WILLIAM, born in Dutchess County, N. Y., 1790, died in Poughkeepsie, N. Y., 1857, married Ann Wing MORDECAI, born in Dutchess County, N Y, 1792; died in Wyoming County, N Y, married Betsey Esmond. ELIZABETH, born in Dutchess County, N Y, 1794, died December 1861 MARIA, born in Dutchess County, N.

Y, 1796; died in Dutchess County, N. Y.; married Nicholas Emigh ANN, born in Dutchess County, N. Y., 1798, died in Webster Station, Madison County, N. Y., April 2, 1881, married Henry Thompson. JOSHUA, born in Dutchess County, N. Y., 1800, died in Columbia County, N. Y., married Susan Moon JACOB REASONER, born in Beekman, Dutchess County, N. Y., January 10, 1802; died in Ellery, Chautauqua County, N. Y., April 20, 1871, married Mary M. Brownell, (2) Hannah Harrington, (3) Eliza Bemus Barney (a widow) PETER REASONER, born in Beekman, N. Y., April 20, 1806, died in Ellery, N. Y., March 31, 1895; married Rhoda Putnam, (2) Mary Van Dusen (a widow)

He attained a position of prominence and about 1812 moved to and settled near Elmira, N. Y., where he was a cattle buyer, purchasing and shipping large numbers to the New York and Philadelphia markets. Politically he was a Whig and a devoted admirer of DeWitt Clinton whom he ardently supported when he was a candidate for Governor.

SIMEON BROWNELL.

(1649a7)

Simeon Brownell, son of Joshua and Martha Peckham Brownell, born June 4, 1759, died June 29, 1832, married May 21, 1780, to Sarah Hoag, born June 3, 1764, died March 18, 1849, and had fifteen children ALICE, born April 4, 1781; died October 16, 1859, married Moses Van Namee JOSEPH, born January 14, 1783 died June 10, 1849, married Prudence Sherman, (2) Elizabeth Van Wert, (3) Mrs Phoebe Smith STEPHEN, born September 4, 1784; died October 18, 1840; married Esther Norton DANIEL, born July 3, 1786, died April 5, 1857, married Esther Miller SIMEON, born April 14, 1788, died October 6, 1862, married Elizabeth Ann Churchill. MOSES, born January 1 1790, died March 12, 1879, married Mary Brown. SARAH, born January 15 1792, died April 5, 1837, married Thomas Wing. BENJAMIN born September 16, 1793, died December 12, 1847; married Marcia S Allen MARY, born November 23, 1795, died February 15, 1877, married David Brown. NATHAN, born May 7, 1797 died December 4, 1859, married Alcha Case, (2) Orpha Case. ISAAC, born January 29, 1799, died June 26, 1886, married Anna E. Barker JOHN, born April 29, 1801; died October 12, 1803. LUTHAN, born

March 2, 1803; died August 26, 1866; married Mary A. Hustus. PHOEBE, born July 9, 1805; died July 24, 1883; married Morrison Weaver. HENRY, born October 14, 1806; died April 13, 1877; married Mary Faulkner.

SARAH HOAG BROWNELL.

He and his wife were prominent members of the Society of Friends and were both public speakers in that faith. His wife learned to read and write after she was fifty years of age. A letter to one of her daughters, dated December 30, 1844, is in possession of one of her great-granddaughters and says: "I am now at Nathan's, and have been here a week, and they have a young daughter about eight weeks old, which makes a hundred and one grandchildren. They call it Aleha Annette."

She wrote the following verses after she was seventy-five years of age.

By these lines, you may see,
What has happened unto me
When I was in my fourteenth year
Then I lost my mother dear.

It was a hard thing, to be sure:
I thought too hard for me to endure.
But hard things will be made light
If we only take them right.

I being young, and that is true,
The business came to me to do.
It was not long before I did find
A friend, according to my mind.

134

And with him, I did agree,
And bound myself before I was free.
When we are bound we must obey
And go where'ere our husband say.

If it is in some distant land,
We must go at their command
By the men it has been said
Of the wife they would be head.

Where there is a head it wants a neck no doubt,
For to turn the head about
When it is turned about to take a view
It begins to see what to do.

Then we came in this country
Some land for to see.
We had a horse worth twenty pounds,
And for some land we paid it down

When we moved and got up here,
I was in my twenty-first year
Two children we had before we come
And here it made us a little home.

The worst of all when we got here
Grain was scarce and very dear.
We had money enough to buy one bushel of corn;
We had no more when that was gone.

Then he went out to work by the day.
When he got money, he went away,
He went away for to buy
Some corn or some rye

When he came home to me did say,
I have found no grain for bread today
But tomorrow I will try once more,
I have heard of some corn in Rennsellear's store.

135

This is the way that we begun
Next fall we had another son
After that first year was gone
We was blest with enough all along.

Enough, I say, with prudent care,
To bring up our children, and something to spare.
We had to work very hard.
But that we did not regard

We have brought you up and you may see
That you have got to wait on me.
To wait on me, and your father too,
For that is your duty so to do

Fourteen children I hope we have
And one we have buried in the grave.
If they all prove good and very kind
That will satisfy my mind.

Now, dear children, if you take the care
You will have all we have to spare.
Now I write as I do feel
Unto the Good Master we must yield

If we are obedient unto Him
He will pardon us from our sins,
I think we read in that good book,
It tells us where we must look

You must seek the kingdom that is true—
He will provide all things for you.
All things necessary He will provide
If you will all come and forsake your pride

If you come humble to beg and pray
He will give you food every day
Food fit for your taste,
And so He would the human race

Remember how the multitude was fed
With a few small fishes and five loaves of bread
Five thousand men as I have read
The Good Master ordered to be fed

He commanded them to sit down,
He blest the bread and sent it round.
They all did eat and was satisfied,
And took up twelve baskets full beside.

I have another subject in my view,
I will relate it unto you
I was reading the other day
Where Jesus was taken and led away.

He was led away to be crucified
He suffered it all for the sake of mankind.
Many hard things He suffered beside
He healed the sick and cured the blind.

How hard it was to prsecute Him
That was so clear of all manner of sin.
All that do not His law obey
Persecute Him every day

Read in your book—see what was done,
How Judas betrayed the beloved Son.
He went and agreed with the high Priest
To betray his Master with a kiss

Thirty pieces of silver he would pay
If his Master he would betray.
Then Judas who had betrayed Him
When he saw that he was condemned,

Repented himself and brought again
The thirty pieces of silver that remain
To the chief priests and elders, too.
All these things we ought to view

This money never did him any good
Because he betrayed the innocent blood.
When he saw what he had done
He went out and himself he hung.

ANNA BROWNELL DURFEE

(1649b9)

Anna Brownell, daughter of John and Susannah Borden Brownell, born in Little Compton, R I, February 3, 1771; died January 28, 1843, married in Little Compton, R I, June 6, 1793, Samuel Durfee, son of Wing and Hannah (surname unknown) Durfee, born in Little Compton, R I., April 20, 1771; died August 22, 1850, and had eight children   SALLY, born August 14, 1794   CHRISTINA, born May 17, 1796   BARTON BROWNELL, born October 17, 1799   LUCY B, born October 22, 1801.   RODNEY, born April 27, 1804   ALLEN, born July 26, 1807.   HANNAH C., born August 6, 1809   SAMUEL B, born January 30, 1813; died October 16, 1838

ROBERT BROWNELL

(1649b9d.)

Robert Brownell, son of John and Penelope Borden Brownell born August 4, 1778; married Roby Fuller, daughter of Peter and Audria Fuller, born June 28, 1778, and had seven children   ALLEN, born February 16, 1801   EMILY W., born September 10, 1802. SILAS, born July 7, 1804.   ADOLPHUS, born July 19, 1806   HENRY H, born February 22, 1808   JEREMIAH, born October 27, 1809 CAROLINE G., born February 28, 1814

THOMAS BROWNELL.

(16661)

Thomas Brownell, son of Charles and Content Shaw Brownell, born in Little Compton, R. I, January 2, 1771, died in Sandgate, Vt., December 8, 1838; married Milly Grey, daughter of James and Mabel Hall Grey, born in Redding, Conn., 1775, died in Sandgate, Vt, May, 1838, and had seven children   JAMES GREY   DANIEL

LYON.   ABRAM.   MILLY   MABEL.   ELIZABETH.   MARIA
EVELINE.

He spent his youth in Little Compton, R. I , and was very fond
of hunting.   Later he moved to Hoosick, N. Y , and conducted a
tavern.   This tavern was located opposite the Old Dutch Church
and burying ground, the accredited spooks of the latter being ob-
jects of wonder and terror to the children of the family.   It is stated
that there was a swinging partition in this tavern, which opened
upward and fastened to the ceiling, thus enlarging the rooms for
public gatherings.   He was a Mason and their meeting was held in
his tavern   After conducting this tavern for many years, he sold
out and moved upon a farm at Sandgate, Vt , where lived the balance of his life.   In early life, he dressed in the fashion of the times,
with silk stockings and knee buckles and wore a long black que which
was kept in his desk for many years after the fashion had passed away.
In later life, he became a strong and ardent Methodist, and the min-
isters of that denomination always found with him a hearty welcome,
and often held meeting in his house   His two oldest grandsons were
names "John Fletcher" and "John Wesley," and in his will he made
provision that each of his seven children should be provided with a
set of Dr. Adam Clark's Commentaries, which was carried out.   One
set is now in the library of his granddaughter, Mrs Frances A
Parish, of Avon, N. Y.

Of his wife's family it is stated that her father and two brothers
were taken prisoners by the British and confined in prison, while
her mother was left to take care of other children   One of the boys
escaped but was captured and later died of privation. One of the boys
mother had her horse saddled before the door, when some British
officers came along and spying the horse, said with an oath   "That
is a good horse.   We will leave one of our old ones and take it
along"   Hearing their remarks she came out of the house, seized
the bridle, let down the bars, led the horse through, then, taking a
pitchfork, she faced the officers, declared she would run the first one
through that attempted to take the beast   "You have taken my husband and my sons, and this is all that is left to assist me in the support of my family, and I may as well die by the sword as by famine"
At this brave speech the officer replied, "She has pretty good pluck,
let her have her old horse"

JEDEDIAH BROWNELL

(16663).

Jedediah Brownell, son of Charlese and Content Shaw Brownell, born in Little Compton, R. I., October 11, 1774; died in Trenton, Oneida County, N. Y., February 20, 1847, married, August 5, 1803 Eunice Watkins, born February 6, 1782, died September 6, 1872, and had four children   JEDEDIAH, born August 25, 1811, died November 9, 1834   EUNICE, born October 19, 1813, died October 1815   MARY POTTER born September 23, 1815, died April, 1898, married Rasseles Wilcox Brown.   WILLIAM SHAW, born in Trenton. N. Y., October 27, 1818, died in Smethport, Pa., July 21, 1900, married Octavia C Howard

AARON BROWNELL

(16665)

Aaron Brownell son of Charles and Content Shaw Brownell, born in Little Compton R. I., January 27, 1778 died in Rochester, N Y., married and had seven children   GARRETT   JOHN EPHRIAM.   ADAM   CONTENT   ELIZABETH.   NANCY

BURDEN BROWNELL

(16668)

Burden Brownell, son of Charles and Content Shaw Brownell, born in Little Compton, R. I., December 18, 1787, died in Trenton, Oneida County, N. Y., married and had son HORACE and other children

ROBERT BROWNELL

(17142)

Robert Brownell, son of Job and Ruth Manchester Brownell born April 7, 1750, married Priscilla or Abigail Pattee daughter of Robert and Priscilla (surname unknown) Pattee, and had three children, and possibly more.   ROBERT PATTEE, born February 14, 1784, married Hannah Colby, (2) Catherine Webb   ABNER EPHRIAM

140

BENJAMIN BROWNELL.

(17213).

Benjamin Brownell, son of Ichabod and Rebecca Davol Brownell, born June 13, 1734, died December 3, 1816, married August 18, 1753 to Phoebe Potter, born August 29, 1733, died November 29, 1811, and had seven children. MARTHA, born December 1, 1754; died in infancy. ABNER, born June 21, 1756, died January 13, 1851, married Hannah Crary. PHOEBE, born November 6, 1758, died November 29, 1811, married Job Milk. BENJAMIN, born February 2, 1760, died April 14, 1830, married Abigail Milk. SARAH, born August 29, 1766, died April 29, 1816. MARY, born July 18, 1772, died February 20, 1867; married Dr. Eli Handy. ESTHER, born August 30, 1775; died September 3, 1835.

GEORGE BROWNELL.

(17214).

George Brownell, son of Ichabod and Rebecca Davol Brownell, married Mary Tripp, daughter of John Tripp, and had six children. RUBY JUDITH, born May 1, 1777, died February 17, 1869, married Jonathan Mayhew. POLLY. PEACE. PARDON PRISCILLA, married Pardon Manchester or Macomber.

PRINCE BROWNELL

(17215)

Prince Brownell, son of Ichabod and Rebecca Davol Brownell, married Mary Manchester, and had five children. WILLIAM, married Patience Earle. EPHRIAM ESTHER PARDON JOHN

He married second Delilah Haskins, and had four children. JOAN MARY DELILAH. JOHN

He was one of the early settlers of Dartmouth, Mass., and was a minute man in 1775. He enlisted May 6, 1775, as a private in Captain Thomas Kempton's company of Colonel Timothy Danielson's regiment, and was mustered in August 1, 1775; company's return dated October 6, 1775; service three months and two days, also order for bounty coat or its equivalent in money, dated at Roxbury, October 30, 1775 He also enlisted August 3, 1780, in Captain Jonathan Taber's company of Colonel John Hathaway's regiment, and was discharged August 7, 1780, having served five days on alarm at Rhode Island

JUDITH BROWNELL POTTER

(17216)

Judith Brownell, daughter of Ichabod and Rebecca Davol Brownell, married Ephraim Potter, son of Nathaniel and Phoebe Potter, and had seven children EDMOND DAVID WILLIAM. NATHANIEL MARTHA REBECCA SARAH

MARY BROWNELL DAVOL

(17217).

Mary Brownell, daughter of Ichabod and Rebecca Davol Brownell, married John Davol, and had one child JOB

SARAH BROWNELL DAVOL

(17218)

Sarah Brownell, daughter of Ichabod and Rebecca Davol Brownell, married Benjamin Davol, son of Reuben and Mary Ricketson Davol, and had nine children JUDITH married Prince Howland ABNER, married Lydia Milk JEREMIAH, married Maria Tripp. LYDIA, married Edward Potter. REUBEN, married Elizabeth Tripp RUTH. GEORGE, married Abigail Tripp BENJAMIN, married Elizabeth Rounds FREELOVE.

ANN BROWNELL CORNELL

(17219)

Ann Brownell, daughter of Ichabod and Rebecca Davol Brownell, married David Cornell, and had two children WILLIAM JETHRO

PRUDENCE BROWNELL DAVOL.

(17219a).

Prudence Brownell, daughter of Ichabod and Rebecca Davol Brownell, married Barzano Davol, and had three children. PATIENCE. MERIBAH. MARY.

STEPHEN BROWNELL

(17311)

Stephen Brownell, son of Joseph and Elizabeth Crandall Brownell, born November, 1747, died September 27, 1824, married January 31, 1771, by Aaron Wilbur, J P, to Margaret Church, daughter of Joseph and Lydia Randall Church, born January 1, 1750, died September 27, 1824, and had six children JOSEPH, born May 14, 1773, died April 29, 1844; married Rachel Putney ESTHER ALBRO, born September 2, 1775, died October 29, 1820 STEPHEN, born August 19, 1778, married Abby Brown. BENJAMIN, born August 19, 1778; married Mary Record. PELEG, born March 14, 1783 LYDIA SANFORD, born December 25, 1785

ROBERT HAZARD

(111432)

Robert Hazard, son of Thomas and Elizabeth Robinson Hazard, born November 17, 1753, died May 3 1833 married 1781, Sarah Fish, daughter of David and Lydia (surname unknown) Fish, died 1847, and had eleven children THOMAS, born January 14, 1782, married Lydia Rogers. ELIZABETH, died young ROWLAND, married Fanny Carpenter DAVID, married Sarah Rogers. ROBERT SARAH, married Nicholas Holmes LYDIA A, married Schuyler Lewis MARY.. WILLIAM, married Hannah Rogers, (2) Lucy Burroughs ROBINSON. STEPHEN, married Sarah Odell

He moved February 26, 1794, to Ferrisburg, Vermont.

Thomas Hazard

(111434)

Thomas Hazard, son of Thomas and Elizabeth Robinson Hazard born November 15, 1758, died in New York city, July 24, 1828, married September 6, 1780, Anna Rodman, daughter of Thomas and Mary Borden Rodman, born June 24, 1762, died June 14, 1845, and had eight children THOMAS R., died near Cincinnati, O., October 18, 1822, married Margaret Avery SAMUEL, married Rebecca Peace SARAH, born September 19, 1781, married John H Howland ELIZABETH, born December 2, 1783, died December 29, 1866, married Jacob Barker ANNA, born in Cranston, R. I., June 24, 1786, died on Skidway Island, Georgia, October 7, 1823, married Philip T Hone, (2) Charles Stephens EDWARD, died young WILLIAM, died young. MARTHA, died young

He moved to New Bedford, Mass, and made a large fortune in the whaling business He was active in politics, and was appointed postmaster of New Bedford, Mass, later he was elected State Senator He was the first president of the Bedford Bank, which commenced business in 1803.

Rowland Hazard

(111435)

Rowland Hazard son of Thomas and Elizabeth Robinson Hazard, born June 4, 1763, died July 1, 1835, married 1793, Mary Peace, daughter of Isaac Peace, died June 28, 1852, and had nine children ISAAC PEACE, born October 3, 1794, died March 2, 1879 THOMAS ROBINSON born January, 1797, married Frances Minturn ELIZA GIBSON, born March 17, 1799 ROWLAND GIBSON, born October 9, 1801, died June 24, 1888, married Caroline Newbold WILLIAM ROBINSON born December 15, 1803, married Mary Wilbur JOSEPH PEACE, born February 17, 1807, ISABELL WAKEFIELD, born August 3, 1809, died 1838 MARY PLACE, born August 15, 1814, died 1874 ANNA, born October 27, 1820

ROBERT HAZARD.

(111452).

Robert Hazard, son of Richard and Susannah Hazard Hazard, born April 14, 1753, died 1795; married December 29, 1782, Hannah Gardiner, daughter of Nicholas and Hannah (surname unknown) Gardiner born October 7, 1763, and had three children. SARAH, born January 11, 1784, married Thomas A. Hazard. A daughter, born January 11, 1784, and also a son, CHRISTOPHER

GEORGE HAZARD

(111453)

George Hazard, son of Richard and Susannah Hazard Hazard, born September 22, 1756, died August 1, 1825, married March 7, 1782, Sarah Scott, died April 12, 1783, and had one child. SARAH, born March 28, 1783, died June 17, 1818.

He married second December 8, 1786, Sarah Knowles, daughter of John and Susannah (surname unknown) Knowles, of Hopkinton, R. I. He lived and died on his farm near Worden's Pond, given him by his father.

BENJAMIN HAZARD.

(111454).

Benjamin Hazard, son of Richard and Susannah Hazard Hazard, born December 26, 1757, died in Boston Neck, October 15, 1784, married April 11, 1779, Hannah Hazard, daughter of Simeon and Abigail Mumford Hazard, and had two children. ABIGAIL born December 7, 1781, married a Snow ALICE, born 1782 died May 30, 1818, married John Allen

RICHARD HAZARD

(111456)

Richard Hazard, son of Richard and Susannah Hazard Hazard, born November 15, 1761, married 1787, Hannah Hazard, and had six children JOSEPH WANTON, married Mary Potter JOHN

MARY, died young. RICHARD, born 1802, died July 18, 1823.
ROWLAND. MARY ANN.

It is claimed that he moved to Newport, and died there at the age of one hundred and two years

JOB WATSON.

(111462).

Job Watson, son of Job and Sarah Hazard Watson, born October 25, 1767, died July 25, 1832, married June 18, 1787, Phebe Weeden, and had six children DANIEL WEEDEN, born 1790, died March 5, 1873, married Mary Condon. SALLY, married George Hall PHEBE, married Freeman Watson. HANNAH, married Arnold Hazard ARNOLD HAZARD

ROBERT H. WATSON.

(111463)

Robert H. Watson, son of Job and Sarah Hazard Watson, born February 29, 1769, married December 30, 1790, Catherine Weeden, and had eight children. ISABELLA, born July 31, 1791 JOSEPH W, born August 25, 1793. MERIBAH, born November 20, 1795 JOHN JAY, born August 13, 1797 SARAH, born September 8, 1799 DANIEL, born April 13, 1801 HANNAH, born June 19, 1803. ROBERT H, born March 4, 1806

WALTER WATSON.

(111464).

Walter Watson, son of Job and Sarah Hazard Watson born June 10, 1770; married Mary Carr, and had eight children. NICHOLAS CARR, born October 10 1794. JOB, born October 23, 1796 ISABELLA, born April 17, 1798. THOMAS HAZARD, born January 22 1800 WILLIAM, born September 15, 1803 ELISHA WALTER JOHN

BORDEN WATSON.

(111465).

Borden Watson, son of Job and Sarah Hazard Watson, born February 9, 1772, married Isabella Babcock, and had six children. JOHN BORDEN. SARAH MARY. ABIJAH ALBERT

JOHN WATSON

(111466).

John Watson, son of Job and Sarah Hazard Watson, born November 1, 1774; died September 7, 1852; married January 24, 1799, Sarah Brown, daughter of Deputy-Governor George Brown, died February 19, 1804, and had four children WILLIAM B. HENRY. GEORGE A daughter

He married second August 4, 1805, Isabella Watson, daughter of Walter and Mary Carr Watson, died January 9, 1858, and had six children. WALTER JOB. ISABELLA, born 1814, died April 6, 1856 EMILY, born July 29, 1816; died July 19, 1856 HARRIET, born January 19, 1818, died May 22, 1858. THOMAS, born July 23, 1822, died November 30, 1862

JOHN HAZARD

(111811).

John Hazard, son of Benjamin and Mary (surname unknown) Hazard, born 1746; died June 26 1813, married Sarah Gardiner, daughter of Nathan Gardiner He married second, Martha Clark, daughter of Latham and Martha Robinson Clark, and had two children. JOHN, born 1775, died 1806, married Frances Gardiner NATHAN GARDINER, married Frances Gardiner Hazard.

GODFREY HAZARD

(111821)

Godfrey Hazard, son of Simeon and Abigail Mumford Hazard, married February 22, 1778, Alice Hazard, daughter of George and Sarah Hazard Hazard, died October 29, 1778. He married second November 22, 1787, Ruth Easton, daughter of Jonathan and Ruth

147

RESIDENCE OF WILLIAM O. BROWNELL.

Coggeshall Easton, and had one child. JONATHAN EASTON, married Sarah Lawton

SIMEON HAZARD

(111822).

Simeon Hazard, son of Simeon and Abigail Mumford Hazard, married and had four children GODFREY, died November 29, 1810, aged about seven years MUMFORD, married a Jermain. ABBY, died November 9, 1819. MARY.

He lived at the upper Narrow River Bridge, and for many years kept a tavern there

GEORGE HAZARD.

(111826)

George Hazard, son of Simeon and Abigail Mumford Hazard, born May 15, 1773, died November 29, 1836, married September, 1800, Content Wilbur, died January 16, 1833, and had eleven children MUMFORD, born February, 1802, married Sarah Tilley ELIZABETH born January 19, 1804, married William Wilbur CHARLES, born July 31, 1806; married Sarah Cook ARNOLD, born October 8, 1807, married Sarah Ann Stedman ANN MATILDA, born September 30, 1808, married Stephen M Stedman WILLIAM WILBUR, born July 4, 1810, married Sarah M. Armstrong. HARRIET, born January 23, 1813, married Albert Armstrong. HENRY B., born December 23, 1815, married Eunice G Wilbur SIMEON, born January 7, 1817 married Mary Ann Stedman. JAMES LAWRENCE, born February 21, 1818, married Frances B Irish. GEORGE AUGHSTUS, born March 26, 1819; married Abby Card

THOMAS HAZARD.

(111842)

Thomas Hazard, son of George Place and Sarah Hazard, Hazard, born March 30, 1765, married February 3, 1790, Abigail Robinson, daughter of Sylvester and Alice Perry Robinson, died March, 1818, and had five children SYLVESTER, born March 3, 1791, married Hannah Congdon (2) Guhelma M Babcock, (3) Abby C Clarke ROWLAND ROBINSON, born February 20, 1792; died August 21, 1874, married Anna Collins SARAH ROBINSON, married George Congdon GEORGE, married Ann Barnet ALICE ROBINSON, married Joseph Babcock

SARAH HAZARD POTTER

(111862)

Sarah Hazard, daughter of Enoch and Mary Potter Hazard, born August 13, 1768, died September 11, 1817; married December 25, 1793, Jeremiah Niles Potter, born January 23, 1769, died February 27, 1849 and had six children MARY NILES, born October 9, 1794, died August 27, 1870, married George Champlin Robinson. JEREMIAH NILES, born October 10, 1796, died June 15, 1798 ELIZABETH S, born May 15, 1798; died May 14, 1799 NILES, born August 31, 1800, died January, 1864, married Almira Fales SARAH, born August 19, 1802 married Stephen Ayrault Robinson. ASA N, born April 27, 1806.

ALICE HAZARD POTTER

(111864)

Alice Hazard, daughter of Enoch and Mary Potter Hazard, born January 1, 1778, died 1868, married March 15, 1821, Jeremiah Niles Potter, born January 23, 1769, died February 27, 1849, and had one child. ALICE, born January 16, 1822 died May 12, 1847, married Benjamin Balch.

THOMAS G HAZARD

(111873)

Thomas G Hazard, son of Thomas and Mary Easton Hazard, died October 27, 1833; married Patience Borden, and had nine children. JOHN A, born April 11, 1804, died March 28, 1877; married Phebe Sheffield WILLIAM born October 30, 1805, married Harriet Brenton THOMAS G, born November 6, 1807, died December 20, 1866, married Mary Hazard, (2) Sarah Hazard Congdon MARY E, born April 28, 1810, died February 4 1893

GEORGE BORDEN, born December 25, 1813, married Martha Clarke, (2) Phebe Read ENOCH, born June 22, 1815, died March 3, 1854. RUTH, born June 30, 1817, died February 13, 1888; married Luther Bateman BENJAMIN, born November 15, 1819, married Hannah Davenport ISAAC, born January 31, 1823

BENJAMIN HAZARD.

(111874).

Benjamin Hazard, son of Thomas and Mary Easton Hazard, born September 9, 1774; died March 10, 1841; married October 28, 1807, Harriet Lyman, daughter of Major Daniel and Mary Wanton Lyman, and had nine children EMILY LYMAN, born October 16, 1808 PAYTON RANDOLPH, born April 9, 1810, died in St Louis, Mo, July 2, 1849 HARRIET, born March 26, 1812, married Rev. Charles T. Brooks MARY, born December 14, 1813, died April 2, 1814. MARY, born March 5, 1815 MARGARET LYMAN, born April 8, 1817, married General Isaac Ingalls Stevens. NANCY, born June 4, 1819, married John Alfred Hazard DANIEL LYMAN, born July 19, 1821; married Delia Colton. THOMAS GEORGE, born March 13, 1824, married Mary King Brooks

He graduated from Brown University in 1792, and was admitted to the bar in 1796. He began the practice of law in Newport, R. I., and followed his profession there with honor for the balance of his life In 1809, he was elected a Representative to the General Assembly, and was re-elected for sixty-five consecutive terms A contemporary says "His ability was marked, and his integrity never questioned "

ENOCH HAZARD.

(111876)

Enoch Hazard, son of Thomas and Mary Easton Hazard, married September, 1804, Mary Easton, daughter of Nicholas Easton, and had one child. JOHN ALFRED, married Nancy Hazard

Benjamin Hazard.

(111921).

Benjamin Hazard, son of Thomas and Hannah Knowles Hazard, born December 11, 1784, died June 4, 1845, married May 12, 1814, Joanna Carr, died June 3, 1820, and had two children. SARAH, born September 11, 1815, died March 29, 1838, married Dr. Amos Wilbur   Hannah, born June 9, 1817, died July 8, 1838.

He married second June 3, 1823, Eliza Earle

Thomas Hazard

(111922)

Thomas Hazard, son of Thomas and Hannah Knowles Hazard, born May 8, 1787; died April 16, 1846, married March 13, 1814, Ruth Carpenter, daughter of James and Ann Rodman Carpenter, born 1789; died August 7, 1860, and had seven children PETER BOURS, born September 2, 1815, died June 22, 1871. ABRAHAM, born December 9, 1817. BENJAMIN, died 1881. THOMAS EDWARD born August 19, 1823 JONATHAN.. RUTH. MARY ANN, born February 17, 1838, married an Adams

Jonathan Hazard.

(1119a13).

Jonathan Hazard, son of Thomas and Mary Preston Hazard, born July, 1750, married Esther Watson, daughter of Stephen and Abigail (surname unknown) Watson, and had eight children GEORGE WATSON, born August 5, 1779, died January 31, 1822, married Mary Lillibridge PATIENCE, married Elam Holloway THOMAS ARNOLD, born 1784, married Sarah Hazard. BOWDOIN, born August, 1785, married Theresa Clarke ABBY, married William H. Nye ESTHER, married Robert Champlin SAMUEL, born 1794; died January 14, 1866; married Lydia Eldred. NANCY, born March 30, 1798, died May 20, 1850; married William T. Gardiner.

ABIGAIL HAZARD WATSON.

(1119a14).

Abigail Hazard, daughter of Thomas and Mary Preston Hazard, born December 25, 1751, died February 2, 1837, married Walter Watson, born May 7, 1752, died May 1, 1808, and had three children. WALTER, died young. ISABELLA, born 1785, died January 9, 1858, married John J Watson. ABBY, born June 22, 1792, died March 31, 1843, married Wilkins Updike

SUSANNAH HAZARD COLE

(1119a19).

Susannah Hazard, daughter of Thomas and Mary Preston Hazard, born August 24, 1758 or 1759, died September 18, 1841, married William Cole, son of John Cole, died August 7, 1823, and had six children JOHN. ANN, born 1785, died August 27, 1874, married Elisha Watson ABBY, married Warren Gardiner SARAH WILLIAM, married Lydia Gerry. MARY, married William Watson

It is stated that her name was changed to Mary after the death of her sister Mary

THOMAS RHODES HAZARD

(1119a19a).

Thomas Rhodes Hazard, son of Thomas and Eunice Rhodes Hazard, born March 1, 1762; died November 30, 1839, married May 8, 1796, Jane Bagnall, died December 27, 1840, and had five children. JAMES DOUGLAS, born June 27, 1797, died August 17, 1875; married Sarah Sophia Gardiner, (2) Susanna Jane Nelmes ELIZABETH, born March 29, 1799 THOMAS RHODES, born April 17, 1801. GEORGE, born April 23, 1803, died June 17, 1824 CHARLOTTE JOANNA, born July 20, 1807, died July 1, 1890

EUNICE HAZARD GARDINER

(1119a19b).

Eunice Hazard, daughter of Thomas and Eunice Rhodes Haz-

153

ard, born February 14, 1764, died March 9, 1832, married John Gardiner, died in Prince Edward Island, January 5, 1842, and had ten children WILLIAM HAZARD, born April 25, 1786, married Ann Clark SARAH, born December 4, 1789 ANNA MATILDA, born May 29, 1791, married James Bagnall THOMAS, born May 8, 1796 BOWDOIN, born May 8, 1796. JOHN RHODES, born April 24, 1798, married Mary Gardiner, (2) Mary Hooper. GEORGE SCOTT, born September 9, 1800, died young SARAH SOPHIA, born March 17, 1804, died September 27, 1827 MARIA WAITSTILL, born April 7, 1806, married Thomas Hooper. EUNICE SUSANNAH, born May 13, 1809, married Joseph Pippy

WILLIAM HAZARD

(1119a19d)

William Hazard, son of Thomas and Eunice Rhodes Hazard, born May 3, 1767, died March 14, 1847, married Ann Farrant Jones, born February 14 1780, died January 18, 1858, and had ten children HARRIET CLARISSA, born September 28, 1798, died February 4, 1841 married William Compton. SARAH LOUISA, born May 20, 1800, died January 18, 1871, married William Cundall MILLICENT CASTLE, born April 19, 1802 died October, 1802. MILLICENT CASTLE born August 10, 1803, died May 8, 1855, married William Hodges WAITSTILL DOUGLASS born November 5, 1805, died April 23, 1844. WILLIAM JONES, born July 12, 1808, died April 18, 1879 CHARLES, born February 29, 1812, died June 4, 1862, married Margaret Longworth. HENRY BOWDOIN, born December 8, 1813, died November 24, 1872, married Hannah Catherine Cameron JOHN, born March 4, 1816, died May 8, 1878, married Amelia McNutt, (2) Jane Davenport Davis ANN FARRANT, born January 29, 1823, married Rev Andrew Lockhead, (2) Rev William Ross Frame.

WAITSTILL CURTIS HAZARD DOUGLAS

(1119a19f)

Waitstill Curtis Hazard, daughter of Thomas and Eunice Rhodes Hazard, born March 12, 1772, died May 22, 1804, married January 31, 1789, James Douglas, died September 26 1803, and

154

had eight children   SARAH, born March 27, 1790, married Major Edward Michael Dewend.   MARY, born June 4, 1791, married Robert Brown   MARGARET, born May 18, 1793.   SAMUEL JAMES, born November 7, 1794.   MARGARET, born October 20, 1796.   JOHN, born December 31, 1797, married a Gordon.   SUSANNA WILSON, born June 29, 1801.   WAITSTILL EUNICE, born June 15, 1803.

JONATHAN J. HAZARD.

(1119a71).

Jonathan J. Hazard, son of Jonathan and Patience Hazard Hazard, born 1759; died 1807, married December 29, 1781, Tacy Burdick, daughter of Edward and Thankful (surname unknown) Burdick, born 1755, and had three children   JONATHAN, born about 1782, died at sea.   GEORGE V, married Miriam Potter   DANIEL SHERMAN, married Susan Meek

He, like his father, was an active man in the affairs of the town and colony.   He was often chosen representative of the town of Charlestown, and intrusted with commissions by the colony

GRIFFIN BARNEY HAZARD

(1119a72)

Griffen Barney Hazard, son of Jonathan and Patience Hazard Hazard, born 1765, died 1822, married about 1792, Mary Parker, daughter of James Parker, died 1845, and had nine children.   JAMES PARKER, born 1794; died 1866; married Pamela Little.   PATIENCE, born 1795 married John Walton, (2) Nicholas Yost   PENELOPE, died young   JONATHAN J, born 1799, married Elizabeth Lake   GEORGE W, born 1801, died 1844 married Sarah Card.   ELIZABETH, married George J Wheeler   JOSEPH H.   THOMAS JEFFERSON, born 1807; married Susannah Champlin.   CATHERINE

He was the driver of an army wagon in the Revolutionary War, though then but a mere lad   He was a man of energy and enterprise, and was much employed in public offices.

Joseph Hoxsie Hazard.

(1119a73)

Joseph Hoxsie Hazard, son of Jonathan and Patience Hazard Hazard, born June 16, 1777, died October 12, 1838, married January 21, 1808, Amey Williams, died September 25, 1871, and had nine children Jonathan Amy Susan, born November 14, 1808, died March 6, 1838 Daniel Williams, born in Rome, N. Y., February 29, 1812, died June 27, 1888; married Ann E. Dyre. Patience Ann, born January 29, 1814, died March 4, 1819. Abby M, born May 8, 1816, died December 25, 1881, married a Williams Sarah M, born March 3, 1818, died September 16, 1887, married a Woodworth. Joseph W., born July 5, 1820, died November 8, 1860 Caroline A, born October 25, 1822, married a Lee Eliza E, born April 6, 1825, died August 6, 1825.

Abigail Hazard Sherman

(1119a76)

Abigail Hazard, daughter of Jonathan and Patience Hazard Hazard, married Enoch Sherman, and had two children. Patience, died young, married George Vosbinder Elisha W, married Pamela Sutherland.

Josiah Hazard.

(112312)

Josiah Hazard, son of William and Phebe Hull Hazard, born December 20 1748 married Mary (surname unknown), and had one child Damarias born January 6, 1782.

William Hazard.

(112314).

William Hazard, son of William and Phebe Hull Hazard, born March 21, 1753; married a Perry, and had one child Edward, married Susannah Havens.

Abigail Hazard Starr

(112321).

Abigail Hazard, daughter of Robert and Elizabeth Hazard Hazard, born August 29, 1753, married September 11 1780, Jared Starr, born 1745, died in Groton, Conn., 1839, and had nine children MARY, born July 1, 1781, died September 16, 1869, married Samuel Greene. ROBERT, born August 11, 1783, died January 20, 1808 CHARLES, born October 28, 1785; died July 17, 1817 GEORGE born June 14, 1787, died August 4, 1869. HENRY, born December 22, 1788, died September, 1789. NANCY, born July 5, 1790, died young ELIZABETH, born June 23, 1791; died October 20, 1801, married Gilbert Saltonstall. FRANCIS HENRY, born August, 1793, died April 3, 1836 NANCY, born January 11, 1796, died December 19, 1869, married Hon. Hume R Field.

Esther Hazard Niles

(112322).

Esther Hazard, daughter of Robert and Elizabeth Hazard, Hazard, born July 26, 1755, died March 25, 1831, married December 25, 1775, Silas Niles, and had five children ROBERT HAZARD, born September 30, 1776; died in infancy MARY, born January 13, 1779; died 1868; married Ezekiel Watson Gardiner. WILLIAM, born August 3, 1780; lost at sea. ELIZABETH, born December 7, 1784, died June 30, 1833. CHARLES, born June 30, 1786, died July 31, 1855

She married second March 5, 1805, Captain Jared Starr.

Sylvester Gardiner Hazard

(112324).

Sylvester Gardiner Hazard, son of Robert and Elizabeth Hazard Hazard, born July 27, 1760; died February 14, 1812 married March 5, 1786, Elizabeth Greene, daughter of Richard and Sarah (surname unknown) Greene, and had twelve children RICHARD, born March 7, 1787, died at sea, March 7, 1811 HARRIET, born 1788, died May 15, 1856 ELIZA, born May 5, 1790, died

May 5, 1874. HENRY, born April, 1792; died, 1871; married Eliza Essex ESTHER, born October 1, 1793, died April 26, 1874; married Edmund Bailey HANNAH, born May 26 1796; died February 9, 1878. LUKE, born October 20, 1797; died June 9, 1878; married Julia Miller. JOB ABBY, married Jonathan Remington. LYDIA, born February, 1802, died July 1, 1802 MARY ANN, born February, 1802 ROBERT, born 1807; died September 11, 1811

CHARLES HAZARD

(112326).

Charles Hazard, son of Robert and Elizabeth Hazard Hazard, born July 24, 1766; married February, 1795, Ann Bours, died in New London, Conn., October 17, 1810, and had six children. JARED, born 1798, died 1833 Charles Courtland, born 1800, died in Mobile, Ala, November, 1857, married Cornelia Livingston. JOHN BOURS, born 1802, died in St. Stephen, Ala, September, 1833, married Mary F Avott ABBY, born November 3, 1804, married Henry Snow CAROLINE, born November 3, 1906, died in Syracuse, N Y, January 20 1866 ANN BOURS, born 1809, married William Hampton

FRANCIS HAZARD

(112327)

Francis Hazard, son of Robert and Elizabeth Hazard Hazard, born 1769; died 1814, married Rebecca Truman, and had seven children MARIA, born in New London, Conn, 1799, died 1864 HENRY TRUMAN, born 1801; died on the Ohio River, 1827 ELIZABETH, born 1803, died 1880; married Dr George Kiefer. ROBERT, born 1805; died 1865, married Sarah M Greene CHARLOTTE, born 1807, died 1880 GEORGE STARR, born December 5, 1809; married Sarah Mercer WILLIAM SYLVESTER, born 1812, died 1890, married Marion Snelling

158

George Hazard Peckham

(112411).

George Hazard Peckham, son of Benjamin and Mary Hazard Peckham, born April 14, 1739, died November 26, 1799, married January 7, 1763, Sarah Taylor, daughter of Robert and Rebecca Coggeshall Taylor, died June 13, 1795, and had seven children. SARAH, married Wheeler Watson. ABIGAIL, REBECCA, married Robert Potter. BENJAMIN, born October 22, 1773, married Abigail Oatley. GEORGE, married a Lawton CARDER, married Achsa Brown WILLIAM

Josephus Peckham

(112412)

Josephus Peckham, son of Benjamin and Mary Hazard Peckham, born February 11, 1742, died March 27, 1814, married May 25, 1774, Mary Babcock, daughter of Hezekiah Babcock, died March, 1807, and had seven children. MARY, born May 27, 1793, married Richard Ward Hazard. BENJAMIN. HEZEKIAH JOSEHUS, married Mary Champlin. GEORGE, married Betsey Cornell. WILLIAM HANNAH, born May 17, 1795; married Freeman Perry.

Sarah Peckham Robinson.

(112413).

Sarah Peckham, daughter of Benjamin and Mary Hazard Peckham, born 1744, died 1775, married January 13, 1761, John Robinson, son of William Robinson, born January 13, 1742-43; died June 23, 1805, and had six children BENJAMIN, born August 5, 1763, married Elizabeth Brown SARAH, born December 10, 1764; married Samuel Tabor WILLIAM, born April 25, 1766, married Phebe Dennison. JOHN, born December 16, 1767, married Abigail Robinson. SYLVESTER, born July 12, 1769; died 1807, married Eliza Rodman. THOMAS, born May 5, 1771; died 1786

WILLIAM PECKHAM.

(112415)

William Peckham, son of Benjamin and Mary Hazard Peckham, born 1752; died May 19 1820, married Mercy Perry, daughter of James and Mercy Potter Perry, died July 24, 1810, and had eight children SARAH born November 28, 1777, married Acors Rathbun ALICE, born January 19, 1780, married Rowland Rathbun WILLIAM, born November 11, 1781, married Susannah Stanton. MERCY, born July 11, 1783 married John Bigland Dockray DORCAS, born February 7, 1787, married Hezekiah Babcock PERRY, born June 30, 1789 ELIZABETH, born December 9 1792, died March 1, 1878 MARY, born March 27, 1795, died January 27, 1827

MARY PECKHAM PERRY

(112416).

Mary Peckham, daughter of Benjamin and Mary Hazard Peckham, married October 17, 1780 Doctor Joshua Perry, son of Judge Freeman and Mercy Hazard Perry, born 1756, died November, 1801 and had four children SARAH, married Doctor Joseph Comstock ABBY, married Thomas Rose ELIZABETH, married John Boss MARTHA, married James or Joshua Barker

PELEG PECKHAM

(112417).

Peleg Peckham, son of Benjamin and Mary Hazard Peckham, born June 11, 1762, married August 25 1785, Desire Watson, daughter of John Watson and had nine children. ELIZABETH, born in South Kings Town, R I., July 25, 1786, married Elijah Griggs RUFUS WHEELER, born September 27, 1789, died young. PELEG BENJAMIN born July 17, 1792, married Laura Griggs GEORGE WILLIAMS, born February 24 1796, married Mary Watson. MIRANDA, married Brockholst Livingston. WALTON HAZARD, married Margaret A Milderburger RUFUS WHEELER, born December 20, 1809, married Isabella Lacy, (2) Mary Foote HENRIETTA, married Joseph S. Colt ORRIN, married a Thompson

Edward Hazard.

(112421).

Edward Hazard, son of George and Martha Wanton Hazard, born about 1746; died March 22, 1830, married May, 1770, Sarah Cranston, daughter of Thomas Cranston, and had one child THOMAS CRANSTON

Sarah Hazard Gardiner

(112423)

Sarah Hazard, daughter of George and Martha Wanton Hazard, born 1750, married April 18, 1775, Daniel Gardiner, son of Nathan Gardiner, and had three children FRANCES, married John Hazard, (2) Nathan G Hazard MALBONE. NILES.
She married second October, 1790, George Hazard

George W. Hazard.

(112424)

George W Hazard, son of George and Martha Wanton Hazard, born March 30, 1758, died November 6, 1834, married Martha Babcock, daughter of Christopher and Martha Perry Babcock, and had four children SALLY born June 14, 1780, married David Larkin MARTHA, born January 25, 1782; married Marlbury Stanton BRENTON, born January 15, 1784; married Ann G Childs GEORGE CHAMPLIN, born July 4 1787, married Eliza Butter

Carder Hazard

(112427).

Carder Hazard, son of George and Jane Tweedy Hazard, born 1774; died March 18, 1823; married April 4, 1804, Sarah Coggeshall, and had seven children JULIA SOPHIA, born in Middletown, R. I, February 6, 1806, married Abiel Sherman. WILLIAM COGGESHALL, born in Middletown, R. I., August 15, 1807, died November 6, 1807 ANGELINE MARGARET, born in Norwich, Conn, January 3, 1810. ALMIRA JANE born in Norwich,

Conn., August 11, 1811, died in Norwich, Conn., February 16, 1884. SARAH ELIZA, born in Norwich, Conn., March 5, 1813, died in New York, N. Y., July 3, 1858. CARDER, born in Norwich, Conn., September 3, 1815. GEORGE CARDER, born in Norwich, Conn., October 18, 1817, died March 5, 1840.

NATHANIEL HAZARD

(112428)

Nathaniel Hazard, son of George and Jane Tweedy Hazard, born 1776, died December 17, 1820, married November 2, 1801, Sarah Fales, daughter of Judge Fales, and had five children. SAMUEL, died 1865, married Martha DeWolfe. GEORGE, died young. WILLIAM, died about 1879, married a Nailor. SARAH, married Charlese DeWolfe. JANE, married David Bugbee.

He graduated from Brown University about 1792. In 1818, he was a member of the General Assembly and Speaker of the House. In 1820, he was a Rpresentative in Congress. He died in office, and was buried in the Congressional burying ground.

THOMAS HAZARD

(112463)

Thomas Hazard, son of Carder and Alice Hazard Hazard, born December 5, 1761, died November 1, 1834, married January 3, 1790, a Browning, and had two children. JOSEPH, married Ruhama Champlin. SUSAN, married Judge Nathan Kenyon.

He married second January 8, 1812, Eliza Arnold, daughter of Thomas Arnold of Newport, R. I.

GEORGE HAZARD

(112464)

George Hazard, son of Carder and Alice Hazard Hazard, born April 13, 1763; died September 29, 1829; married Sarah Hazard Gardiner, daughter of George and Martha Wanton Hazard, and widow of Captain Daniel Gardiner. He married second December 25, 1804, Mary Hoxsie, died March 30, 1806, and had one child.

Mary Hoxie, born March 20, 1806; died March 6, 1808.

He married third May 16, 1807, Jane Hull, daughter of Robert Hull, and had eight children. William Henry, born February 12, 1808, married Louisa Arnold. Carder, born August 20, 1809; married Eliza Watson. Jane, born December 5, 1810; married Dr. Daniel Howland Greene Edward Hull, born September 29, 1812 George, born August 25, 1813; died February 12, 1864 Mary Hoxie, born March 10, 1815, married Rev James Carpenter. Laura, born November 4, 1819, married Attmore Robinson. Alice Joanna Fitzgerald, born September 7, 1821 died April 11, 1881

Richard Ward Hazard

(112467)

Richard Ward Hazard, son of Carder and Alice Hazard Hazard, born November 1, 1770, died December 2, 1844, married Mary Peckham, daughter of Josephus and Mary Babcock Peckham, died September 27, 1869, and had ten children Benjamin, died in infancy Elizabeth, died in infancy Mary, married John Nichols. Joseph, born September 14, 1814; married Susan Congdon. Daniel. Joshua, born November, 1820, died January 19, 1877. Alice, married Jonathan Allen. Hannah, born October, 1827; married Hezekiah Babcock, (2) Jonathan Allen Charlotte, died young. Jane Maria, died young

He was a farmer and always lived on his farm in Matunuck He was for years an honored member of the Baptist communion, and was always in his seat on Sunday morning, with a pew full of children He was respected by his townspeople, and was a good type of the honest, upright country gentleman.

Sarah Hazard Clarke

(112469)

Sarah Hazard daughter of Carder and Alice Hazard Hazard, born May 13, 1780, died January 10, 1852; married January 2, 1807, Peter Clarke, born 1788, and had four children James E, born March 3, 1809 Carder Hazard, born July 21, 1811, married Hannah Allen. Peter, born March 12, 1815 Nicholas, born 1818 died September 2, 1844

163

ALICE HAZARD CONGDON

(112469a)

Alice Hazard, daughter of Carder and Alice Hazard Hazard, born May 13, 1780, died December 25, 1831, married September 18, 1800, George Congdon, and had two children. CARDER HAZARD MARY, married Lee Perkins

CHRISTOPHER RAYMOND PERRY

(112633)

Christopher Raymond Perry, son of Freeman and Mercy Hazard Perry, born in South Kings Town, R I., December 4, 1761, died June 4, 1818, married August, 1784, Sarah Wallace Alexander, who came from Scotland in the vessel commanded by Captain Perry and there formed the acquaintance which led to their marriage They had eight children. OLIVER HAZARD, born in South Kings Town. R I, August 20, 1785: died in Port Spain, Isle of Trinidad, August 23, 1819, married Elizabeth Champlin Mason RAYMOND, born in South Kings Town, R I, February 11, 1789, died March 2, 1826, married Mary Ann DeWolf. SARAH WALLACE, born in South Kings Town, R. I., April 28, 1791, died January, 1851. Matthew Calbraith, born in Newport, R I., April 10, 1794, died March 4, 1858, married Jane Slidell ANN MARIA, born November 10, 1797, died December 7, 1856, married Commodore George W Rogers, U. S. N. JANE TWEEDY, born December 15, 1799, died July, 1875, married Doctor William Butler, U S N JAMES ALEXANDER, born June 26, 1801, drowned in harbor of Valparaiso, March 9, 1822 in the attempt to save the life of a friend NATHANIEL HAZARD, born November 27, 1802, married Lucretia Mumford Thatcher of New London, Conn

He served with distinction in the Revolutionary War upon armed vessels fitted out in the colony He was commissioned captain in the United States navy in 1799 and discharged under the Peace Establishment Act, April 3, 1801 Subsequently he was Collector of Internal Revenue at Newport and Bristol, R. I, and in 1812, was appointed Commander of the United States navy yard at Charlestown, Mass

Elizabeth Perry Champlin.

(112634)

Elizabeth Perry, daughter of Freeman and Mercy Hazard Perry born August 20, 1762, died March 12, 1811; married December 20, 1782, Stephen Champlin, and had seven children MERCY, born September 19, 1783, died August 14, 1857; married Rev. James Rogers WILLIAM B., born February 13, 1785, married Olive Manning ELIZABETH, born December 2, 1786, married Sherman Loomis HANNAH, born June 19, 1788, died 1878 STEPHEN, born November 17 1789 married Minerva Pomeroy MARY PERRY, born April 17, 1791, died in infancy MAY PERRY, born February 7, 1793, married Gordon Bailey.

Susan Perry Watson.

(112636)

Susan Perry, daughter of Freeman and Mercy Hazard Perry, married 1784, Elisha Watson, and had four children. FREEMAN PERRY, born May 16, 1787, married Phebe Watson SUSANNA, born March 13, 1789, married George Watson. ELIZABETH, born June 24 1790; married Benjamin Brown MIRIAM, born October 30 1793, married Stephen Browning

George Hazard Perry.

(112637)

George Hazard Perry, son of Freeman and Mercy Hazard Perry, married Abigail Cheesborough, and had three children. GEORGE HAZARD FREEMAN, married Hannah Peckham GIDEON, born in South Kings Town, R. I., October 11, 1800, died in Hopkinsville, Ky., September 30, 1879, married Abby Stewart.

Jonathan Nichols Hazard.

(113412)

Jonathan Nichols Hazard, son of Stephen and Sarah Nichols Hazard, born October 18, 1761; died 1802; married Mary Robinson, daughter of Sylvester and Alice Perry Robinson, born 1763, died 1837, and had six children JAMES ROBINSON, born February 10, 1789, married Sarah Barney ALICE ROBINSON, born December 12, 1790, died January 1, 1837 STEPHEN, born September 10, 1792 JONATHAN NICHOLS, born January 16, 1795, married Mary Congdon SYLVISTER ROBINSON, married Alice Hull. MARY A., born July 3, 1799, died April 6, 1855

NICHOLS HAZARD

(113416)

Nichols Hazard, son of Stephen and Sarah Nichols Hazard, born March 11, 1770, died May 13, 1848, married Phebe Anthony, and had eight children. ALICE, born 1801, died March 11, 1868 MARY, born July 16, 1805: died November 5, 1883 PHEBE, born July 12, 1807. RUTH, born February 11, 1809: died September 9, 1882. SARAH born March 4, 1811, died February 21, 1843. HANNAH, born April, 1813. NICHOLAS, born November 21, 1815, died November 21, 1836 EDWARD, born February 9 1820, died April 10, 1878

SAMUEL J POTTER.

(113431)

Samuel J Potter, son of John and Elizabeth Hazard Potter, born about 1752, died September 26, 1804; married Ann Seager, and had seven children SAMUEL J. ANN FENNER. MARY JOSEPH SARAH. ELIZABETH.

He was Deputy-Governor of the state from 1790 to 1799, and was chosen again in 1800 and served until 1803

STEPHEN POTTER

(113432)

Stephen Potter, son of John and Elizabeth Hazard Potter, born about 1754, died 1793, married about 1772, Abigail Robinson, daughter of Christopher and Ruhamah (surname unknown) Robinson, born 1754, died 1803, and had four children ROBINSON

ABIGAIL A daughter, married Captain Gardiner A daughter, married a Chadwick.

LUCY HAZARD HULL

(113513).

Lucy Hazard, daughter of Joseph and Hannah Nichols Hazard, born July 6, 1766, died September 23, 1804, married December 25, 1801, Teddiman Hull, and had one child LUCY, born September 7, 1804, married Harry Clarke.

JOSHUA HAZARD

(113515)

Joshua Hazard, son of Joseph and Hannah Nichols Hazard, born October 7, 1771; died November 12, 1823, married October 7, 1807 Elizabeth Niles, daughter of Silas and Esther Hazard Niles, and had six children STANTON, born April 21, 1809; died August 16, 1892, married Bethany Brattle Aborn EVAN MALBONE, born October 1, 1811, married Jane Hume MARY NILES, born October 13, 1813, married Ebenezer Dennison. ROBERT, born March 11, 1815; died June 8, 1815 ESTHER, born May 30, 1817; died August 31, 1851, married Captain Waterman Cliff CHARLES PHILIPS, born November 25, 1820, died in Memphis, Tenn, October 17, 1847

HANNAH HAZARD GRIFFEN

(113518).

Hannah Hazard, daughter of Joseph and Hannah Nichols Hazard, born August 10, 1778; died August 26, 1827, married November 16, 1807, Doctor Stephen Griffen, and had six children EVAN MALBONE, born January 4, 1809; died in infancy. JOSEPH HAZARD, born July 25, 1810 died June 27, 1879. CHARLOTTE R., born October 23, 1812; died September 16, 1884, married Captain William Montgomery HANNAH HAZARD, born July 14, 1814. MARY C., born May 14, 1816; died April 5, 1886 STEPHEN AUGUSTUS, born August 21, 1818, married Eliza Card.

167

JONATHAN BABCOCK

(113532)

Jonathan Babcock, son of James and Esther Hazard Babcock, born May 30, 1762, married January 29, 1795, Ruth Rodman, daughter of Benjamin and Hannah Niles Rodman, died December 16, 1795, and had one child RUTH HANNAH born November 26, 1795, married Solomon Harley.

ROBERT BABCOCK

(113533)

Robert Babcock, son of James and Esther Hazard Babcock, born December 18, 1763; died February 11, 1848, married May 11, 1793, Mary Hazard, daughter of Stephen Hazard, and had four children JARED, died October 16, 1838, married Diadema Douglass SARAH, died May 21, 1870, married John Wiltrey. ESTHER, married Robert Tripp NICHOLAS, married Maria Hamblin

BENJAMIN HAZARD

(113561).

Benjamin Hazard, son of Samuel and Hannah Perry Hazard, born March 11, 1764, died July 12, 1849, married April 4, 1804, Martha Hazard, daughter of Stephen Hazard, and had two children MARTHA, born May 31, 1805; died July 15, 1889 BENJAMIN, born July 3, 1808, died May 10, 1876

GIDEON HAZARD

(113562).

Gideon Hazard, son of Samuel and Hannah Perry Hazard, born November 25, 1765, died April 18, 1806, married Elizabeth Hazard, daughter of Stephen Hazard, died November 21, 1818, and had two children. JOHN G. JOSEPH STANTON.

ELIZABETH HAZARD WALES

(113564).

Elizabeth Hazard, daughter of Samuel and Hannah Perry Hazard, born December 2, 1769; married July 25, 1798, Atherton Wales, son of Peter F. and Lydia Potter Wales, born May 26, 1773, and had two children ROUSE POTTER, born July 21, 1802 LYDIA POTTER, born May 17, 1804.

LODOWICK HAZARD

(113614)

Lodowick Hazard, son of Samuel and Catherine (surname unknown) Hazard, married Susan Robinson, daughter of Doctor William Robinson, and had six children LODOWICK JAMES WILLIAM ABBY. GEORGE NANCY

ROBERT HAZARD.

(113615).

Robert Hazard, son of Samuel and Catherine (surname unknown) Hazard, married and had one child SAMUEL

ABBY HAZARD TAYLOR

(113617)

Abby Hazard, daughter of Samuel and Catherine (surname unknown) Hazard, married Ichabod Taylor, and had two children ROBERT. DUDLEY.

ESTHER HAZARD PEARCE.

(113623).

Esther Hazard, daughter of George and Mary Mumford Hazard, born in Newport, R I., about 1775; married October 22, 1803, Benjamin Pearce, and had five children GEORGE WALTER. JOHN. JAMES CATHERINE, married a Liscomb

Hannah Hazard Allen.

(113629)

Hannah Hazard, daughter of George and Mary Mumford Hazard, married May 12, 1822, John Newman She married second Erastus P Allen, son of William S. N Allen, and had three children ABBY WILLIAM S N, married a Lyon. ERASTUS P., married Sarah Barker

Thomas Hazard

(113711)

Thomas Hazard, son of Stephen and Elizabeth Carpenter Hazard, born about 1760, married about 1782, Silence Knowles, daughter of Hazard and Margaret Congdon Knowles, died November 25, 1827, and had eight children. WILLIAM, born 1785, died in Columbia, Conn, July 28, 1849 MARGARET, died October 20, 1812 MARY, married John Knowles STEPHEN, married Abby Knowles. ROUSE. ELIZA STANTON, married a Gridley AUGUSTUS GEORGE, born April 28, 1802, died May 7, 1868; married Salome Goodwin Merrill

Mary Hazard Oatley

(113712)

Mary Hazard daughter of Stephen and Elizabeth Carpenter Hazard, born 1765, died May 20, 1857, married January, 1781, Joseph Oatley, son of Benedict and Betsey Ladd Oatley, died November 29, 1815, and had ten children MARY, died young. HANNAH, born November 6, 1783, married Rodman Carpenter BETSLY, born February 16, 1786, married Jonathan Carpenter. NANCY, born March 28, 1788, married Jonathan Carpenter JONATHAN, born July 7, 1790, married Mary Champlin JOSEPH, born September 13, 1793, married Eliza Wells STEPHEN, born June 10, 1796; married Mary Carpenter MARY, born August 28 1798, married Stephen Congdon SUSAN, born May 2, 1803, married David Mumford, (2) Isaac Hopkins ROUSE, born July 30, 1806, died February 8, 1812

170

ELIZABETH HAZARD RODMAN

(113716)

Elizabeth Hazard, daughter of Stephen and Elizabeth Carpenter Hazard, born about 1783; died May 6, 1870, married July, 1799, Robert Rodman, son of Robert and Margaret Carpenter Rodman, born May 18, 1774, died April 1, 1838, and had ten children. Samuel, born May 3, 1800, died May 9, 1882, married Mary Peckham, (2) Mary Anstis Updike ELIZABETH, born July, 1801; married Henry Money ABBY, born May 21, 1804, died May 31, 1829, married Thomas Hiscox SARAH, born September 19, 1805; died August 10, 1845; married William Knowles. AMOS PEASLEY, born 1806, married Clarissa Allen. PENELOPE, born March 24, 1807, died May 1, 1856, married Daniel Gould BENJAMIN, born September 13, 1808, died April 15, 1860; married Hannah Brown. HANNAH, born 1815; married Erasmus D. Campbell. ANN, married Lorenzo Hall. ROBERT, born 1820, married Mary Gardiner

MARY DAVIS CHASE.

(114151)

Mary Davis, daughter of Barney and Catherine Wilcox Davis, born April 1, 1770, died December 4, 1858 married November 29, 1787, John Chase, son of Caleb and Mary Manchester Chase, born February 5, 1766; died December 25, 1827, and had eleven children ANNA, born December 27, 1788; married James Bosworth. COMFORT, born February 13, 1791, married Clothier Peirce. JOHN, born September 3, 1796; married William Manchester NATHAN, born March 30, 1799; married Lovisa Pitts MARY DAVIS, born November 30, 1801, married Alanson Post. BARNEY DAVIS, born February 17, 1804; married Lydia G Peirce. WESLEY, born May 7, 1806; married Lydia B Pitts SARAH BARNEY, born June 25, 1808, married Henry Pitts CLARISSA GREENE, born December 31, 1811 married Samuel Barry, (2) Alonzo L Cory AMANDA MASON, born January 5 1816, died April 3, 1893; married James Luther Peirce.

ISAIAH WILCOX

(115361).

Isaiah Wilcox, son of Isaiah and Sarah Lewis Wilcox, born January 31, 1763; died July 13, 1844, married January 22, 1788, Mary (Polly) Pendleton, daughter of William and Judith Carr Pendleton, born November 14, 1766, died November 18, 1847, and had seven children MARY, (Polly) born in Preston Conn., January 4, 1789. ISAIAH, born in Preston, Conn., November 31, 1790 WILLIAM PENDELTON, born in Danube, N Y., May 30, 1794, died in Port Allegany, April 13, 1868; married Betsey Payne ASA, born in Danube, N Y., March 9, 1797 LYDIA, born in Danube, N Y., October 10, 1799 NANCY, born in Danube N Y., January 31, 1802 NATHAN PENDLETON, born in Danube, N. Y., May 3, 1804, died April 24, 1833, married Lurancie Richardson.

Though less than fourteen years of age at the breaking out of the Revolutionary War, he nevertheless served for short periods in that contest He enlisted as a minute man about February 10, 1778, in Captain Walter White's company of Colonel Joseph Noye's regiment, at Westerly, and was under arms a number of times between that date and the close of the war. After his marriage, he removed to New London, Norwich and Preston, Conn., and later to Danube township, Herkimer County, N. Y. A specially trying experience of his here was the destruction of his house and contents by fire soon after his settlement He lived to the ripe age of eighty-two years He was a deacon in the Baptist church and a man highly esteemed in the community

ASA WILCOX

(115362).

Asa Wilcox, son of Isaiah and Sarah Lewis Wilcox, born September 1 1764, died in Essex, Conn. He was a Baptist clergyman.

NATHAN WILCOX

(115363)

Nathan Wilcox, son of Isaiah and Sarah Lewis Wilcox, born

April 10, 1766. He moved with his brother Isaiah Wilcox, to Danube, N Y

Stephen Wilcox

(115366)

Stephen Wilcox, son of Isaiah and Sarah Lewis Wilcox, born October 10, 1770 His sons Stephen, born May 7, 1796 and Thomas Jefferson, born August 15, 1800, were merchants and directors in the Phenix Bank His son Stephen was a representative, senator and was nominated for governor. His grandson Stephen, son of Stephen, was a manufacturer and inventor of note. He founded and endowed the Westerly public library.

Oliver Wilcox.

(115367).

Oliver Wilcox, son of Isaiah and Sarah Lewis Wilcox, born June 26, 1773. He bought from the other heirs the old homestead at Watch Hill. From him it descended through his daughter Hannah, to her son Enoch Wilcox Vars, of Niantic, who recently sold it.

Thomas Hazard.

(116111).

Thomas Hazard, son of Jeremiah and Mary Hazard Hazard, born 1753, died February 15, 1815; married Lucy Congdon, born 1763; died December 30, 1807, and had four children Abby, born 1789; died June 8, 1865, married Hazard Knowles, (2) Elder Chapin. Arnold, born 1792, died March 19, 1856, married Hannah Watson Lucy. Jeremiah.

Mary Browning Hoxie

(116123).

Mary Browning, daughter of Wilkinson and Susannah Hazard Browning, married October 20, 1777, Thomas Hoxsie, and had two children Hazard, born June 17, 1782: married Chloe Bailey. Mary, born April 28, 1786.

JEFFREY HAZARD

(116131)

Jeffrey Hazard, son of Robert and Hannah Greene Hazard, born March 24, 1771, died 1828, married and had one child JOHN P, born 1804

ROBERT HAZARD

(116132).

Robert Hazard, son of Robert and Hannah Greene Hazard, born August 29, 1785, married Abigail Seager, daughter of John Seager, and had four children JEREMIAH B, died July 23, 1883. JOHN S born February 14, 1810. JOSEPH P HANNAH, born 1820; married Jesse Reynolds

JOHN HAZARD

(116414).

John Hazard, son of Robert and Alice Thomas Hazard, born 1766, died 1851, married and had five children ALICE, born August 2, 1788, died March 19, 1879, married J P Stone ROBERT, born June 26, 1790 died March 21, 1871, married Amey Hazard THOMAS T, born March 2, 1792, died August 2, 1874 MARY, born May 11, 1794, died May 3, 1815. PHEBE THEODOSIA, born November 21, 1796 married Easton Lewis

JEFFREY HAZARD

(116441)

Jeffrey Hazard, son of Jeremiah and Phebe Tillinghast Hazard born 1762 died 1840, married Amey Tillinghast, daughter of Thomas Tillinghast, born 1773; died June 3, 1870, and had five children AMLY, born 1791; died 1864, married Robert Hazard THOMAS JEFFERSON, born June 17, 1795, died August 2, 1874 WILLARD married Mary Ann Hazard JOHN, married Margaret Crandall. PHEBE, married Reuben Brown

He was Lieutenant-Governor of the state from 1833 to 1835.

and again from 1836 to 1837 He was Representative in the General Assembly many years, and was Chief Justice of the Court of Common Pleas, and a Judge of the Supreme Court from 1810 to 1818

JOHN HAZARD

(117321)

John Hazard, son of Jeremiah and Ruth Potter Hazard, born August 24 1749: died November 26, 1832, married Abby Boss, died about 1800 and had ten children GEORGE, married Henrietta Freeborn. JOHN BOSS, born February 17, 1778, died May 28, 1848, married Mary Potter RUTH, married Daniel Bates, (2) John Buckover, (3) a Mitchell. SARAH, married Elisha Gardiner PATIENCE, born January 30, 1784, died March 3, 1869, married William Battey. MARY, married Henry Chapell, (2) Edward Alb, (3) Shadrach Card ABBY, born June 24 1789, died February 21, 1864; married Elisha B. Johnson HANNAH, born 1790, died November, 1840, married Benjamin Hammond. JEREMIAH, born October 10, 1792, died October 19, 1878, married Harriet Moore CATHERINE, born 1796, died October 16, 1876, married Edward Carr

He married second Sarah Cranston, and had two children CALEB, born June 24, 1804, married Susan Hazard. BETSEY, born May 24, 1809, married James Hight

ROWLAND HAZARD

(117322).

Rowland Hazard, son of Jeremiah and Ruth Potter Hazard, married Elizabeth Hammond, daughter of William and Chloe Hammond, and had five children. MARY ELIZABETH, married Nicholas Gardiner RUTH, married Elisha Potter ESTHER RODMAN, born 1797; died August 10, 1842, married Deborah Congdon, (2) Martha Congdon

175

RESIDENCES OF HENRY B. AND CHARLES H. BROWNELL.

WILBOUR HAZARD.

(117323)

Wilbour Hazard, son of Jeremiah and Mary Cole Hazard, born December 15, 1774, died February 14, 1827, married 1804, Mary Stanton, daughter of Benjamin Stanton, born December 14, 1786, died October 15, 1876, and had eleven children. ANN, born February 12, 1805, married Samuel C Cottrell. JEREMIAH, born October 12, 1807, married a Zubero RENEWED, born February 22 1808, died May 10, 1857, married Edward Slocum MARY, born September 25, 1810; married Benjamin Cottrell BENJAMIN, born August 25, 1812, married Charlotte Cole Atwood WILBUR, born February 27, 1814, married Lydia Pierce. RUTH, born April 29, 1817, married John C Gardiner SUSAN, born June 10, 1819, died April 28, 1883 SAMUEL, born October 22, 1821, died April 29, 1878, married Sarah Cole DANIEL S, born January 26, 1824, married Hannah S Congdon WILLIAM, born January 22, 1827

EASTON HAZARD

(117331)

Easton Hazard, son of Ephriam and Ann (surname unknown) Hazard, born September 13, 1783, died September 2, 1826, married Charlotte Bissell, and had two children CHARLOTTE, born November 23, 1803 VARNUM, born October 5, 1805, died 1836

EPHRIAM HAZARD.

(117341).

Ephriam Hazard, son of Gideon and Sarah Chase Congdon Hazard, born September 5, 1763; died April 23, 1836, married Hannah Updike, daughter of Richard Updike, died June 22, 1808, and had three children. NANCY UPDIKE, born November 19, 1787, married Henry Burlingame JAMES, born May 15, 1794; died at the age of nineteen years HANNAH born April 20, 1801, married Ezekiel Reynolds.

He married second Mary Smith, died 1835, and had two children MARY, born August 21, 1810, married Samuel Pierce.

LOUISA, born November 24, 1814; died June 22, 1868, married Ezekiel Pierce

FREEBORN HAZARD.

(117342).

Freeborn Hazard, son of Gideon and Sarah Chase Congdon Hazard, born 1765, died August 29, 1831, married Susan Sherman, died March 11, 1829, and had three children ROBERTSON, born August 27, 1785, married Elizabeth Marshall. STANTON, born August, 1786, married Phebe Bush SUSAN, born November 11, 1788, married Stephen Hazard.

ROBERT HAZARD

(117343)

Robert Hazard, son of Gideon and Sarah Chase Congdon Hazard, married and had three children PELEG, married Mary Northrup STEPHEN, married Sarah Hazard EDWARD, married Hannah Smith

ELIZABETH HAZARD HAMMOND

(117345)

Elizabeth Hazard, daughter of Gideon and Anna (surname unknown) Hazard, born December 7, 1795, died October 20, 1868, married Joseph Hammond, son of Benjamin Hammond, and had six children. ELIZA ANN, born 1816, married Stephen G. Slocum JOSEPH WILLETT born 1817 WAITY FRANCES, born 1820 RUTH, born 1824 BENJAMIN FRANKLIN, born 1826. GEORGE NEWTON, born 1828

MARY WANTON LYMAN.

(122521)

Mary Wanton, daughter of John G. and Mary Bull Wanton, born August 20, 1763, died December 5, 1822, married January 10, 1782, Daniel Lyman, born in Durham, Conn., January 27, 1756,

178

died in North Providence, R. I., October 16, 1830, and had thirteen children. ANNIE MARIA, born November 13, 1782; married R. K. Randolph of Virginia. HARRIET, born March 16, 1784, married Benjamin Hazard. MARGARET, born November 24, 1786, married Samuel Arnold. MARY, born 1788, married Jacob Dunwell. ELIZA, born May 30, 1790. THOMAS, born December 20, 1791, died November 4, 1832. JOHN WANTON, born May 10, 1793, married Eliza Wheaton of Providence, R. I. DANIEL, born September 28, 1794, died 1828. HENRY BULL, born November 13, 1795, married Caroline Dyer of Providence, R. I. LOUISA, born April 16, 1797, married Doctor George H. Tillinghast of Providence, R. I. SALLY, born February 14, 1799, died February 19, 1837, married Governor L. H. Arnold. JULIA MARIA, born August 30, 1801, married John H. Easton of Newport, R. I. EMILY, born December 23, 1804, died August 29, 1805.

Her husband served in the Revolutionary Army, and was a Chief Justice of the Supreme Court of Rhode Island. In the history of Durham, he is mentioned as "an able advocate, a firm, intelligent, high-minded man." His first meeting with his wife was at her father's house in Newport, R. I., in 1780, on the arrival of the French fleet, when he entertained the officers with great hospitality.

PHILIP ESTES.

(123116)

Philip Estes, son of Richard and Mary Pierce Estes, born in Warwick, R. I., February 22, 1749, married a Gage, and had nine children. ROBERT URIAH. THOMAS P., born February 28, 1778, died September 17, 1845, married Mary Burlingham. BENJAMIN RICHARD, married Rebecca Abrams. PHILIP. MARY, married a Loomis, (2) Gideon Tabor. ELEANOR, married Nathaniel Southwick. BENJAMIN, born August 17, 1791. STEPHEN, born September 22, 1793.

THOMAS ESTES.

(123117)

Thomas Estes, son of Richard and Mary Pierce Estes, born in Warwick, R. I., September 28, 1752, died 1825; married in Duchess

County, N. Y., Sarah Tripp, born in Rhode Island, April 22, 1752, died in Scipio, N. Y., and had seven children. JOSEPH, born January 10, 1775; died 1854, married Lois Sowle. REBECCA, born July 5, 1776, married Daniel Gage. ANNE, born December 30, 1779, married Henry Olin. MARY, born November 24, 1782, died May 8, 1823. THOMAS, born January 7, 1784, died September 9, 1812. JERUSHA, born March 20, 1786, married James McDonald. NATHANIEL, born May 31, 1788, died September 3, 1819; married Ruth Gage.

BENJAMIN ESTIS

(123119a).

Benjamin Estes, son of Richard and Mary Pierce Estes, born October 3, 1761, married in the state of New York, Phebe Borland, and had eleven children. MARY, born May 20, 1782; died in Canada, 1860, married Joel Thompson. REBECCA, born March 24, 1784, married Nicholas Rector. ANN, born April 28, 1786; married Alexander Gage. ANDREW, born September 5, 1788; died October 27, 1832. JAMES B., born July 14, 1791. DEZIAH, born January 20, 1794, married Solomon Dimmock. JOHN, born May 2, 1796, drowned in the St. Lawrence river. HORATIO N., born December 29, 1798, married Sarah Cummings. BETSEY, born April 6, 1801, married Alsbro Barber. WILLIAM, born September 1, 1803. LUCINDA, born October 27, 1805, married Calvin Wright.

He was a farmer and one of the early settlers of Cape Vincent, N. Y., and in 1815, moved to Johnston, N. Y.

JAMES ESTES.

(123119c)

James Estes, son of Richard and Mary Pierce Estes, born October 16, 1766, died October 11, 1828, married Catherine Pearce, born February 21, 1767, died February 25, 1807, and had eleven children. MARY, born March 4, 1788, married Roswell Herrick. JOHN, born October 18, 1789. Hannah, born August 17, 1791, married Jacob Empey. BENJAMIN, born February 15, 1793, married Sally Barber. PETER born November 14, 1794. RICHARD P., born November 14, 1794. CHARLOTTE, born April 6, 1798, married William Rowe   BETSLY, born May 14, 1800, married Epenetus Cline   SARAH, born September 14, 1801; married Leonard Herrick.   CATHLRINE, born March 1, 1803, married David Lathrop   ROSINA, born September 20, 1805, died January 6, 1844; married Charles Leonard

He married second Rachel Odell, and had three children   JANE, born July 3, married Jeremy W Rogers   EMILY, married John C Clock   JAMES, married Laura Scribner.

He moved to Lyme, N Y., in 1816, and was a farmer and hotel keeper.   He built one of the first frame houses in Three Mile Bay, N. Y., and from his farm was divided the lots on which the village of Three Mile Bay now stands.

ALEXANDER THOMAS.

(123123).

Alexander Thomas, son of Joseph and Sarah Estes Thomas, born November 25, 1743, married Ussilla Oldbridge of Bristol, R I, and had seven children.   SUSANNA, born in Portsmouth, R. I., June 25, 1767 married Joseph Anthony   SUSANNA, born in Portsmouth, R I., April 14, 1769, married John Cook.   ANNE, born in Portsmouth, R I, January 22, 1771   RHODA, born in Portsmouth, R I, July 13, 1774.   MARY, born in Portsmouth, R. I, May 18, 1777, married William Hall   ARNOLD born in Portsmouth, R. I., June 22, 1781.   PHEBE, born July 24, 1784

RICHARD THOMAS

(123128)

Richard Thomas, son of Joseph and Sarah Estes Thomas, born November 28, 1752; married in Portsmouth, R I., July 18, 1774, Ann Elizabeth Decotee Brownell, and had nine children   PHILADELPHIA, born in Portsmouth, R I., November 21, 1775, married Josiah Wood   DAVID, born in Portsmouth, R I, July 18, 1777   RUTH, born in Portsmouth, R I, February 7, 1780   STEPHEN, born in Portsmouth, R. I, January 17, 1784, married Henrietta Shearman.   HANNAH, born in Portsmouth, R. I., October 6, 1787, married Parker Hall   GARDINER, born in Portsmouth, R I, October 21, 1790, died in Portsmouth, R I., married Eleanor Borden,

(2) Amy C Monroe   SARAH, born in Portsmouth, R I, July 4, 1792   ANNE, born in Portsmouth, R. I., June 5, 1796.   JOSEPH, born in Portsmouth, R I., December 15, 1797, married Hannah Anthony

ROBERT THOMAS

(123129a).

Robert Thomas, son of Joseph and Sarah Estes Thomas, born June 29, 1757, married in Newport, R I, February 7, 1781, Abigail Thurston, daughter of Benjamin and Amy (surname unknown) Thurston, died in Portsmouth, R I, August 28, 1786, and had two children   AMY, born in Portsmouth, R I, November 28, 1781   ELIZABETH, born in Portsmouth, R. I., December 5, 1783

He married second in Portsmouth, R I, February 8, 1786, Mary Shearman daughter of Job and Martha (surname unknown) Shearman, and had one child   THURSTON, born in Portsmouth, R I, December 30, 1786

ROBERT ESTES

(123131)

Robert Estes son of Thomas and Elizabeth Thomas Estes, born in Tiverton, R. I., June 28, 1748, died in 1826, married in Tiverton, R I, 1770, Prudence Bennett, daughter of Robert Bennett of Tiverton, R I, and had five children   MARY, born in Tiverton, R.I, March 29, 1771, died young   HANNAH, born in Tiverton, R. I, December 26, 1772, died young   ZILPHA, born in Tiverton, R I, October 17, 1776, married Abel Carpenter   THOMAS, born in Tiverton R I August 2, 1780, married Catherine Brown   DAVID, born in Tiverton, R I, June 3, 1783; died in Savoy, Mass, April 19, 1842, married Eliphal Durfee

RUTH ESTES JENNINGS

(123132).

Ruth Estes, daughter of Thomas and Elizabeth Thomas Estes, born in Tiverton, R I, Jan 1, 1751, married in Tiverton, R. I. December 30, 1767, Isaac Jennings, son of John and Annie (surname

unknown) Jennings, born in Tiverton, R. I., March 9, 1742, and
had seven children DANIEL, married Elizabeth Chase. GIDEON.
ELIZABETH, married a Brownell ELISHA, married Lydia Borden
ISAAC, born in Tiverton, R. I., May 11, 1782; married Susan D
Cole PERRY, born in Tiverton, R. I., May, 1785, married Florana
Perry. ANNIE.

JOSEPH ESTES
(123133).

Joseph Estes, son of Thomas anr Elizabeth Thomas Estes, born
in Tiverton, R. I., November 27, 1754, died May 26, 1844 married in Dartmouth, Mass., April 2, 1788, Edith Wood, daughter of
Josiah and Hannah Tucker Wood, born in Dartmouth, Mass., January 13, 1769 died September 13, 1826, and had five children
ELIZABETH, born in Dartmouth, Mass., March 12, 1789, died June
19, 1872, married Allen Sisson SARAH, born in Dartmouth, Mass.,
April 22, 1791; died July 5, 1867, married George Smith HAN-
NAH, born in Dartmouth, Mass., May 10, 1794, died April 21,
1869, married Captain John Hull. EDITH, born December 25,
1796, died November 7, 1799 JOSEPH, born October 26, 1801,
died March 26, 1889, married Eunice Chase

ELISHA ESTES.
(123134)

Joseph Estes, son of Thomas and Elizabeth Thomas Estes, born
in Tiverton, R. I., January 12, 1757, married Sarah Bennett, daugh-
ter of Daniel Bennett of Tiverton, R. I., and had five children
PHEBE, born in Tiverton, R. I., April 19, 1781, died September 1,
1850; married Abner Macomber. JOSEPH, born in Tiverton, R. I.
April 3, 1783, died August 19, 1858 DANIEL, born in Tiverton,
R. I., June 1, 1785, died April 9, 1873 RUTH, born in Tiverton,
R. I., January 26, 1789, died February 6, 1881. SARAH, born in
Tiverton, R. I., October 27, 1791, died August 28, 1878, married
Christopher Lake
He married second Thankful Bennett, daughter of Daniel Ben-
nett He married third Nancy Wilcox daughter of William and
Betsey (surname unknown) Wilcox, born January 6, 1767, and
had one child CLARK, born May 2, 1808; died January 6, 1883

He married fourth Sarah Butterfield Baker, a widow

SARAH ESTES TRIPP

(123130).

Sarah Estes, daughter of Thomas and Elizabeth Thomas Estes, born in Tiverton, R. I. March 31, 1762, died July 1, 1836, married in Tiverton, R. I. December 7, 1780, Edmund Tripp, son of Tripp and Sarah Wood Tripp, born in Westport, Mass. June 1, 1755, and had ten children. ABRAHAM born in Westport, Mass. August 9, 1782, married Mary (surname unknown). PETER, born in Westport, Mass. May 17, 1784, married Margaret Kirby (2) Priscilla Snow. 3) Johannah Baker. JOSEPH, born in Westport, Mass. November 23, 1785, married Elizabeth Davis. BENJAMIN born in Westport, Mass. November 24, 1787, married Nancy Case. ELIZABETH born in Westport, Mass. November 21, 1789, married William Davis. RICHMOND, born in Westport, Mass. August 12, 1791, married Silvia Tripp. 2) Mary Potter (3) Mary Baker. HANNAH married Patrick Potter. EDMUND, born in Westport, Mass. September 16, 1797, married Cynthia Case (2) Esther Barker. DANIEL born in Westport, Mass. July 19, 1802, married Ruth Tripp. THOMAS ESTES, born in Westport, Mass. May 11, 1808, married Edith Tripp.

EDMUND ESTES

(123137)

Edmund Estes, son of Thomas and Elizabeth Thomas Estes, born in Tiverton, R. I. September 8, 1767, died September 14, 1803, married October 17, 1790, Elizabeth Lawton, daughter of William and Sarah (surname unknown) Lawton, died September 14, 1803, and had two children. EDMUND born in Tiverton, R. I. October 25, 1794, died 1823. JOB, born in Tiverton, R. I. March 24, 1797, died December 23, 1872, married Beulah Oswell.

PETER ESTES

(123138)

Peter Estes, son of Thomas and Elizabeth Thomas Estes, born

184

in Tiverton, R. I., 1773; died in Tiverton, R. I., 1847 married in Tiverton, R I, March 31, 1799, Mercy Durfee, daughter of Joseph and Abigail Borden Durfee, born in Tiverton, R. I., October 11, 1773 died in Tiverton, R I, January 4, 1811, and had seven children FLIZABETH, born in Tiverton, R I, September 16, 1799, married Holder Chase THOMAS, born in Tiverton, R. I, November 20, 1800, married Mary Snell GODFREY born in Tiverton, R I., July 15, 1802 died in Tiverton, R I, March 1, 1871, married Polly Durfee, (2) Johannah Lake, (3) Laura Carpenter Earle, a widow ABIGAIL, born in Tiverton, R. I, January 3, 1804, married Benjamin Fish MARY, born in Tiverton, R I, September 29 1805, died October 8, 1883, married Captain Samuel T Cook HOPE, born in Tiverton, R I, March 31 1807 married Ephriam Pettey MERCY, born in Tiverton, R. I., May 15, 1810, died January 4, 1866.

He married second about 1811, Anna Hicks, daughter of Stephen and Catherine Coggeshall Hicks, born in Tiverton, R I, July 14, 1780, died in Tiverton, R I, January, 1835, and had nine children CATHERINE C born in Tiverton, R I, February 21, 1812, died in Toledo, O, August 26, 1861; married Albert Swift LYDIA born in Tiverton, R I, November 7 1813, married Thomas R Sisson AMANDA M, born in Tiverton, R I, January 8, 1816 married Henry B Chase HANNAH H, born in Tiverton, R I March 21, 1818; died April 27, 1888, married Joseph T Church (2) Ephriam Willey. HARRIET, born in Tiverton, R I, March 21 1818, died young ANNA died young. PETER died young ANNA B, born in Tiverton, R I., April 28, 1822, died August 21 1877 married Thomas R. Swift HIRAM M, born in Tiverton R I, February 9, 1826, died July 10, 1854, married Mary A Jones

He married third Matilda Sherman Grinnell, widow of Stephen Grinnell, and daughter of Daniel and Hannah Pierce Sherman He was treasurer of Tiverton R I, several years, and was highly esteemed and respected by his fellow-townsmen

GIDEON DENNIS

(123231)

Gideon Dennis, son of Robert and Hannah Coggeshall Dennis born July 8, 1752, married September 29 1786, Mary Durfee daughter of John and Phebe Grey Durfee, born in Tiverton, R I and had twelve children. JOHN, born in Portsmouth, R. I., March 31 1787. ROBERT, born in Portsmouth, R I, February 25, 1789. PHEBE, born in Portsmouth, R I, November, 1790; married a Cornell. GIDEON, born in Portsmouth, R. I., February 27, 1793, married Meribah Manchester. JOB DURFEE born in Portsmouth, R. I., April 3, 1795, died in Tiverton, R. I, December 13, 1875, married Mary Borden Mosher WILLIAM, born in Portsmouth, R. I., January 20, 1797; drowned when twenty-one years of age MARY, born in Portsmouth, R .I, November 18, 1798, married Lawton Taylor EDWARD, born in Portsmouth, R. I., February 18, 1801. RICHMOND, born in Portsmouth, R. I., February 27, 1803. CHARLES, born in Portsmouth, R I, July 5, 1805; lost at sea JOSEPH CORNELL, born in Portsmouth, R. I, November 8, 1807 SARAH ANN, born in Portsmouth, R I, October 1, 1814

He was a Justice of the Peace in Portsmouth, R I

HANNAH DENNIS HALL

(123232)

Hannah Dennis, daughter of Robert and Hannah Coggeshall Dennis, born May 28, 1756, died in Portsmouth, R. I., married in Portsmouth, R I, October 22, 1773, George Hall, son of Benjamin and Deliverance Cornell Hall, born in Portsmouth, R I, November 24, 1749, and had twelve children. WILLIAM, born in Portsmouth, R I, February 2, 1774, married Mary Thomas. HANNAH, born in Portsmouth, R I, August 29, 1775, married Jeremiah Gifford BENJAMIN DENNIS, born in Portsmouth, R I, February 27, 1777, married Ruth M. Rogers. RUTH, born in Portsmouth, R I, July 24, 1778 SUSANNAH, born in Portsmouth, R. I, June 24, 1780 JOSEPH, born in Portsmouth, R. I., May 16, 1782 PARKER, born in Portsmouth, R I, July 29, 1784, died in Portsmouth, R. I., August 17, 1809, married Hannah Thomas FRELLBORN, born in Portsmouth, R I, September 11, 1786 GEORGE, born in Portsmouth, R I, January 2, 1789. ANNE born in Portsmouth, R. I, March 19, 1791 ROBERT DENNIS, born in Portsmouth, R. I, February 4, 1793 BENJAMIN born in Portsmouth, R I, November 20, 1795

ROBERT DENNIS.

(123234)

Robert Dennis, son of Robert and Hannah Coggeshall Dennis born January 1, 1762, married in Portsmouth, R. I., October 8, 1783, Ruth Anthony, daughter of Isaac Anthony, and had fourteen children. HANNAH, born July 13, 1784, married David Hall SARAH, born March 28, 1786. ISAAC A., born April 30, 1788, married Sarah Coggeshall. ROBERT born April 30, 1788. REBECCA, born November 12, 1789. RUTH born October 10, 1791, married Isaac Chase. DAVID born August 4, 1793, married Eliza Gifford. ABEL, born April 30, 1795. ANTHONY, born June 13, 1799. WALTER, born July 18, 1801. DARIUS, born June 1, 1803, died May 12, 1809. ELIZA born August 22, 1805, died May 4, 1809. ABRAHAM, born June 19, 1807. ELIZA born January 28, 1810.

JONATHAN DENNIS

(123230)

Jonathan Dennis son of Robert and Hannah Coggeshall Dennis, born January 15, 1767, died in Portsmouth, R. I. September 17, 1850 married in Portsmouth, R. I. July 12, 1791 Hannah Sherman daughter of Sampson and Ruth Fish Sherman born in Portsmouth, R. I., January 27, 1769, died in Portsmouth R. I., July 21, 1852, and had ten children. ANNA, born September 22 1792 married Paul Wing. ABIGAIL, born May 18, 1794, married Asa Arnold. SAMUEL, born February 19, 1796, married Diana Gifford. RUTH, born September 16 1797, died February 10, 1860, married Joshua Shove. MARY born April 27 1799 died in Providence, R. I., September 29, 1871, married Welcome Congdon. JAMES, born February 1, 1801, died in East Providence, R. I April 9, 1889, married Hannah Jackson. RICHARD, born September 5 1802 died in Lowell, Mass February 19, 1860, married Lucy Ann Hooper. JONATHAN, born August 21, 1805 died in Newport R. I., March 15, 1806. JONATHAN, born May 24 1809. WILLIAM, born October 10, 1811.

He was a farmer and lived near Newport, R. I. until 1828 when he moved eight miles eastward. 'All but one of his children married and lived to be aged." He and his sons were all tall, and none used tobacco or spirituous drinks

GEORGE DENNIS.

(123237).

George Dennis, son of Robert and Hannah Coggeshall Dennis, born January 26, 1769, died in Portsmouth, R I, March 10, 1837, married in Portsmouth, R I, November 6, 1793, Hannah Thomas, daughter of Joseph and Ruth Tabor Thomas, born in Portsmouth, R I March 20, 1770, died in Portsmouth, R I, March 5, 1849, and had six children JOSEPH, born September 29, 1794. AMEY, born October 29, 1795, died July 21, 1840 NATHAN, born March 26, 1798, died in Portsmouth R I, December 7, 1869, married Patience Seabrook Cook JOHN DORCAS, born July 23, 1802 JONATHAN, born October 10, 1808

He was a farmer and a member of the Society of Friends

MARY DENNIS SISSON.

(123238)

Mary Dennis, daughter of Robert and Hannah Coggeshall Dennis, born February 14, 1772 died in Warwick, R. I., December 27, 1816, married in Portsmouth, R I, August 15, 1798, Asa Sisson, son of Joseph and Ruth (surname unknown) Sisson, and had six children MARY, born in Newport, R. I., December 20, 1800. ISAAC, born in Newport, R. I., November 14, 1802, died April 22, 1803 JOSEPH, born in Newport, R. I., December 30, 1803 ROBERT, born in Newport, R I, November 16, 1805 ISAAC, born in Newport, R I, May 31, 1807, died January 17, 1808 RUTH, born in Newport R I, November 20, 1808

MOSES DENNIS

(123239)

Moses Dennis, son of Robert and Hannah Coggeshall Dennis born June 20, 1777, married in Portsmouth, R. I., September 5 1798, Abigail Sherman, and had three children JOB SHERMAN, born in Portsmouth, R I, August 30, 1800 HANNAH COGGE-

SHALL, born in Portsmouth, R. I., August 30 1800   ROWLAND HAZARD, born in Portsmouth, R. I., May 15, 1804

JOSEPH COGGESHALL

(123252).

Joseph Coggeshall, son of Joshua and Anna Dennis Coggeshall, born in Middletown, R. I., August 16, 1754; died October 7, 1830; married Elizabeth Hoisewell, and had eight children. NOEL, born March 31, 1777; died in Middletown, R. I., August 4, 1853 RUTH born August 27, 1780   JOSEPH, born June 5, 1783, died April 30, 1871, married Lydia Cornell   ANNE, born January 28, 1786; died November 4, 1856.   JOSHUA, born December 25, 1788, died in Middletown R. I., April 7, 1879, married Deborah Allen SARAH, born September 18 1791, died 1860, married Isaac A Dennis.   JOHN P, born April 13, 1794, died in Middletown, R. I., April 30, 1830, married Sarah Anthony.   ABRAHAM C, born March 15, 1797; married Annie Sisson.

ELIZABETH COGGESHALL ANTHONY.

(123253).

Elizabeth Coggeshall, daughter of Joshua and Anna Dennis Coggeshall, born in Middletown, R. I., October 14, 1756, died in Middletown, R. I., September 3, 1828, married in Middletown, R. I., November 19, 1786, Gideon Anthony, son of Philip and Mary (surname unknown) Anthony, born June 20, 1766, and had two children.   PHILIP, born 1789, died 1873, married Mary Manchester   JOSHUA, born 1798; died 1877

MARY COGGESHALL BROWN.

(123255)

Mary Coggeshall, daughter of Joshua and Anna Dennis Coggeshall, born in Middletown, R. I., July 14, 1761; died September 15, 1837; married Peleg Brown, and had thirteen children. THOMAS, born in Middletown, R. I., January 8, 1779. MERCY, born in Middletown, R. I., November 5, 1780. JOSEPH born in Middletown, R. I., September 7, 1782   JUDITH, born in Middletown, R

I, May 21, 1784. PELEG, born in Middletown, R. I, March 3, 1786. PATIENCE, born in Middletown, R I, December 8, 1787 ANNE, born in Middletown, R. I, May 3, 1790 WILLIAM COGGES-HALL, born in Middletown, R. I., April 11, 1792 JAMES HALL, born in Middletown, R. I., May 31, 1794 GEORGE COGGESHALL, born in Middletown, R. I, December 2, 1798. PARDON, born in Middletown, R. I., December 24, 1801, married Lucy Armstrong JOSHUA COGGESHALL, born in Middletown, R. I., December 24, 1801 ROBERT DENNIS, born in Middletown, R I, March 22, 1805

MERCY COGGESHALL MANCHESTER.

(123250).

Mercy Coggeshall, daughter of Joshua and Anna Dennis Coggeshall, born in Middletown, R I, September 14, 1762 died March, 1844, married April 2, 1786, Thomas Manchester, and had eight children. LYDIA, born March 31, 1787. SARAH, born May 12, 1789 ISAAC born February 9 1792 married Sally Fish FREEBORN, born November 14, 1793, married Ann Slocum ANNE, born December 12, 1795. HANNAH, born November 8, 1797 MERCY, born March 19, 1800 GEORGE, born April 22 1804

GEORGE COGGESHALL.

(123258).

George Coggeshall, son of Joshua and Anna Dennis Coggeshall, born in Middletown, R. I, June 8, 1767, died in Portsmouth R I., August 14, 1843, married in Portsmouth, R I, Cynthia Sherman, daughter of Peleg and Elizabeth (surname unknown) Sherman, born in Portsmouth, R I, September 17, 1773, and had one child PELEG married Bridget Almy

ELIZABETH CORY BORDEN.

(123264).

Elizabeth Cory, daughter of John and Ruth Dennis Cory, born October 26, 1763, married in Portsmouth, R. I, February 15, 1787, William Borden, son of Joseph and Catherine Turner Borden, born

190

in Portsmouth. R I, April 14, 1760; died in Portsmouth, R I, September 22, 1798, and had five children. JOSEPH, born February 11, 1788, died in Havana, August 19, 1809 SUSANNA, born August 8, 1790 JOHN, born March 24, 1793 THOMAS born August 11, 1795. CYNTHIA, born December 9, 1797.

JOSEPH FISH.

(123278).

Joseph Fish, son of David and Lydia Dennis Fish, born April 13, 1770; married in Portsmouth, R I., July 9, 1798, Amey Chase, and had three children. ELIZABETH, born in Portsmouth, R. I, October 12, 1799 BENJAMIN, born in Portsmouth, R. I, September 5, 1801, married Abbie Estes RACHEL, born in Portsmouth, R. I, September 11, 1803

SARAH CHASE MOTT.

(123282).

Sarah Chase, daughter of Holder and Freeborn Dennis Chase, born 1765, died January 19, 1848, married in Portsmouth, R. I., May 14, 1794, Benjamin Mott, son of Jacob and Hannah Weaver Mott, born in Portsmouth, R I, January 1, 1758; died in Portsmouth, R. I, August 29, 1838, and had four children HANNAH, born in Portsmouth, R. I., February 24, 1795, died August 29, 1839. ANNA, born in Portsmouth, R I., June 29, 1797 ELIZABETH, born in Portsmouth, R I, November 3, 1799, married John A Wadsworth, M D. JACOB, born in Portsmouth, R. I, January 21, 1804; married Eliza Anthony.

NATHAN CHASE

(123283).

Nathan Chase, son of Holder and Freeborn Dennis Chase born 1766, died November 12, 1827; married in Portsmouth, R. I, November 14, 1792, Anna Sherman, daughter of Sampson and Ruth Fish Sherman, born in Portsmouth, R. I November 19, 1770, died in Newport, R I, October 22, 1852, and had nine children HANNAH, born in Tiverton, R. I, November 22, 1793, married Daniel

Chase. AMY, born in Tiverton, R. I., July 20, 1795, married Job Weeden HOLDER, born in Tiverton, R. I., March 17, 1797; died September, 1832; married Elizabeth Estes ELIZA, born in Tiverton, R. I., February 25, 1799 MARY, born in Tiverton, R. I. September 5, 1800 ABBY, born in Tiverton, R. I., July 25, 1802, died February 3, 1803 ROWLAND, born in Tiverton, R. I., January 23, 1804 OBADIAH, born in Tiverton, R. I., March 2, 1806 RUTH ANN, born in Tiverton, R. I., September 21, 1810, died in Tiverton, R. I., December 15, 1811

ANNA CHASE WEEDEN

(123284)

Anna Chase, daughter of Holder and Freeborn Dennis Chase, born 1768 died in Smithfield, R. I., "at the residence of her son, H. C. Weeden," February 7, 1849, married in Portsmouth, R. I., John Weeden, son of Daniel and Hannah (surname unknown) Weeden, born in Jamestown, R. I., died in Jamestown, R. I., October 2, 1839, and had three children HOLDER CHASE, born in Jamestown, R. I., October 12, 1799, married Abigail Anthony. JOHN HULL, born in Jamestown, R. I., February 10, 1801 ANN ELIZA, born in Jamestown, R. I.

Her husband was known as "Farmer John," to distinguish him from his cousin of the same name He was a man of more than ordinary intelligence and great probity of character.

ABNER CHASE

(123288)

Abner Chase, son of Holder and Freeborn Dennis Chase, born in Portsmouth, R. I., married in Portsmouth, R. I., October 5, 1803, Deborah Chase daughter of Benjamin and Mary Almy Chase, and had twelve children WILLIAM ALMY, born in Portsmouth, R. I., September 15, 1804, died June, 1857 GEORGE WASHINGTON, born in Portsmouth, R. I., October 9, 1805 MARY ANN, born in Portsmouth, R. I., June 7, 1807, married Peleg Sherman ALEXANDER HAMILTON, born in Portsmouth, R. I., September 8, 1808 JANE ELIZA, born in Portsmouth, R. I. March 4, 1810 BENJAMIN FRANKLIN, born in Portsmouth, R. I., November 30, 1811; married Priscilla Anthony GILES MARTINBOROUGH, born in

Portsmouth, R I., August 24, 1813, married Elizabeth Hambly. MASON CHAMPLIN, born in Portsmouth, R I., November 7, 1814, died January 24, 1837. JAMES SCOTT, born in Portsmouth, R. I, May 10, 1816, married Mary Fish. SARAH ANN, born in Portsmouth, R I, October 15, 1818, died September 9, 1819. FANNIE SMITH, born in Portsmouth, R. I., October 25, 1822, died March 14, 1853 SAMUEL WEST, born in Portsmouth, R I, October 12, 1824, died January 18 1857, married Abbie A Thomas.

CLARK CHASE.

(123289).

Clark Chase, son of Holder and Freeborn Dennis Chase, born in Portsmouth, R. I, married in Tiverton, R I, December 26, 1811, Anna Borden, daughter of Simeon and Amey Briggs Borden, born in Fall River, Mass, September 14, 1790, and had nine children. SIMEON B, born October 5, 1812, died November 8, 1832 AMEY A, born July 9, 1814, married Humphrey Almy. BORDEN, born April 5 1816, died in Fall River, Mass, 1897; married Elizabeth A Thomas PHILIP BORDEN, born February 3, 1818, married Sarah Cook. SARAH FREEBORN, born February 17, 1820; married Stephen Davol. ELIZA, born May 3, 1822, married Charles Fowler CHARLES, born February 2, 1824, married Frances C Pearce NATHANIEL BORDEN, born November 1, 1825, married Louisa M Pierson ALFRED CLARK, born March 21, 1833; married Ruth Anthony

JONATHAN READ.

(123649).

Jonathan Read, son of Jonathan and Eunice Weaver Read, born September 7, 1771, married in Freetown, Mass., March 31, 1792, Eleanor Law, and had one child. BETSEY, married Ebenezer Spooner Winslow, (2) William Baker.

GIDEON DURFEE.

(123741)

Gideon Durfee, son of Job and Sarah Easton Durfee, born in

Portsmouth, R I, March 27, 1755, died in Brimfield, Mass, October 21, 1828; married in Portsmouth, R I, January 1, 1778, Susanna Freeborn, daughter of Jonathan and Mary Mott Freeborn, born in Portsmouth, R. I, April 7, 1755, died in Brimfield, Mass, April 9, 1829, and had seven children. THOMAS, born June 6, 1782. STEPHEN born Septemeber 24, 1789 JAMES JOSEPH, born September 16, 1892 JONATHAN, drowned at sea. MARY ANN when young, fell in spring and was drowned. WAITY.

MARY DURFEE DYRE

(123744).

Mary Durfee, daughter of Job and Sarah Easton Durfee, born in Portsmouth, R I, September 30, 1761; married in Portsmouth, R. I, April 27, 1780, Samuel Dyre of Portsmouth, R I, and had three children JOHN. MERCY STEPHEN

JAMES DURFEE

(123745)

James Durfee, son of Job and Sarah Easton Durfee, born in Portsmouth R. I, January 29, 1764, died in Cannonsville, N Y, October 5, 1837, married Meribah (surname unknown), born in Rhode Island, October, 1757, died in New York, May 23, 1805, and had six children. SALLY, born March 12, 1792 HANNAH PHEBE, POLLY STEPHEN THOMAS

He married second in Cannonsville, N. Y., Mrs Elizabeth Cannon born 1761, died in Cannonsville, N Y, July 26, 1840.

From the history of Delaware County, N Y, it says: "James Durfee came from Rhode Island in 1788 to Kortright, and stayed three years and then removed to Tompkins, first to the 'Slow and Easy' Mill, two miles below the 'city,' and afterwards to Cannonsville He had one son, THOMAS DURFEE, who became a Baptist preacher and whose long life closed in 1879 "

Mercy Durfle Borden

(123748)

Mercy Durfee, daughter of Job and Sarah Easton Durfee, born in Portsmouth, R. I., May 2, 1770; died in Fall River, Mass., April 13, 1835; married in Portsmouth, R. I., November 19, 1792, Aaron Borden, son of Joseph and Peace Borden Borden, born in Tiverton, R. I., October 5, 1758, and had three children DAVID, born in Fall River, Mass., June 1, 1796. PHILADELPHIA, born in Fall River, Mass., October 16, 1799; died in Fall River, Mass., February 20, 1887, married John Church SUSAN M., born in Fall River, Mass., January 31, 1803, married Isaac Brightman

Elizabeth Durfee Earle.

(123749).

Elizabeth Durfee, daughter of Job and Sarah Easton Durfee, born in Portsmouth, R. I., September 18, 1772; married in Portsmouth, R. I., November 18, 1792, Captain David Earle, son of John and Deborah Anthony Earle, born November 2, 1763, died 1796, and had one child RUTH HALL, born June 23, 1795

Susannah Durfee Munro

(123749a)

Susannah Durfee, daughter of Job and Sarah Easton Durfee, born in Portsmouth, R. I., 1775; died in Bristol, R. I., November 29, 1802, married in Bristol, R. I., September 24, 1795, Bateman Munro, son of Thomas and Sarah (surname unknown) Munro, born in Bristol, R. I., 1767, died in Portsmouth, R. I., February, 1840, and had three children SARAH EASTON, born in Bristol, R. I., July 22, 1798; died in Portsmouth, R. I.; married Robert Fish ELIZA PEARSE, born in Bristol, R. I., July 19, 1800, married John Burrington MARY

GIDEON ALBRO

(123783).

Gideon Albro, son of James and Elizabeth Durfee Albro, born January 20, 1769, married in Portsmouth, R. I., August 3, 1800, Sarah Dickson, daughter of Robert Dickson of North Kings Town R. I., and had nine children. RHODA, born December 24, 1800 HANNAH, born May 6, 1802 GIDEON, born September 23, 1803 ELIZABETH, born September 11, 1805 EDWARD, born October 27, 1808 GARDINER DURFEE, born October 6, 1810 CHARLES, born October 21, 1812 SARAH ANN, born February 25 1816 JAMES DURFEE, born April 9, 1818.

JAMES ALBRO

(123784)

James Albro, son of James and Elizabeth Durfee Albro, born December 30, 1771, married in Little Compton, R. I., December 8, 1793, Rebecca Tabor daughter of David Tabor of Little Compton, R. I., and had four children SARAH, born May 22, 1797 CHRISTOPHER, born January 21, 1800 ALMIRA, born July 16, 1802 OLIVER, born April 18, 1805

ELIZABETH PEARSE LAWTON

(123791)

Elizabeth Pearse, daughter of Jeremiah and Ruth Durfee Pearse, born in Portsmouth, R. I., June 13, 1766, married in Portsmouth, R. I., September 10, 1786, Henry Lawton, son of Job Lawton of Portsmouth, R. I., and had ten children HENRY, born in Portsmouth, R. I., January 13, 1787 SARAH, born in Portsmouth, R. I., October 9, 1788 JOB H, born in Portsmouth, R. I., May 27, 1790. RUTH, born in Portsmouth, R. I., March 3, 1792. ELIZABETH, born in Portsmouth R. I., March 13, 1794 MARY ANN, born in Portsmouth R. I., February 15, 1796 ALICE, born in Portsmouth, R. I., March 27, 1798 GEORGE P., born in Portsmouth, R. I., April 28, 1800. LUCY P., born in Portsmouth, R. I., March 5, 1802. GEORGE, born in Portsmouth, R. I., March 4, 1804

196

ELEANOR PEARSE PEARSE

(123792).

Eleanor Pearse, daughter of Jeremiah and Ruth Durfee Pearse, born in Barrington, R. I., June 5, 1767, married in Portsmouth, R I, August 8, 1790, William Pearse, son of James and Deborah Hunt Pearse, born in Little Compton, R I, June 7, 1766, and had five children. JONATHAN, born May 23, 1791 HENRY, born April 30, 1793 BATHSHEBA, born February 11, 1795. HARRIET, born January 14, 1799. BENJAMIN FRANKLIN, born July 2, 1801

SUSANNAH PEARSE SHEARMAN

(123793)

Susannah Pearse, daughter of Jeremiah and Ruth Durfee Pearse, born in Rehoboth, Mass., February 8, 1771; married in Portsmouth, R I, November 7, 1790, Samuel Shearman, son of John Shearman, and had thirteen children JOHN, born in Portsmouth, R I, September 14, 1791, died in Portsmouth, R I, June 9, 1864, married Mary Albro. ELEANOR DURFEE, born January 11, 1793 WAITE DURFEE born April 4, 1794, married David Shearman. GIDEON, born October 1, 1795, married Betsey Brownell BENJAMIN CLARK, born January 2, 1797. PEACE, born May 27, 1798 GEORGE SCOTT, born August 14, 1800 JEFFERSON born April 23, 1802 ABIGAIL, born August 26, 1803. CHARLES, born October 5, 1806 LYDIA MARIA, born February 12, 1808. DAVID EARLE, born September 22, 1809 IRA, born July 6, 1811, married Maria Mason Pearse.

BENJAMIN PEARSE

(123794).

Benjamin Pearse, son of Jeremiah and Ruth Durfee Pearse, born in Portsmouth, R I., February 26, 1775; died in Portsmouth, R. I., November 22, 1841; married in Freetown, Mass., Primacy Payne, daughter of Ebenezer and Waite (surname unknown) Payne, born in Freetown, Mass., February 8, 1778, died in Portsmouth, R I, December 28, 1842, and had two children. BENJAMIN, born February 11, 1812 OLIVER, born August 19, 1814.

WAITE BORDEN LAWTON.

(12379c1).

Waite Borden, daughter of John and Eleanor Durfee Borden, born in Portsmouth, R. I., June 8, 1776; married in Portsmouth, R. I., November 5, 1794, Peter Lawton, and had nine children. SUSANNAH, born October 5, 1795; married Darius Perry Lawton. ELEANOR, born June 12, 1797 RUTH, born June 25, 1800; married Stephen Chase OBIDIAH, born July 3, 1802. HANNAH, born June 17, 1804 ANNA, born August 16, 1806 ISAAC, born October 22, 1808 OBEDIAH, born January 24, 1811. CATHERINE, born October 15, 1813

BENJAMIN DURFEE

(123843).

Benjamin Durfee, son of James and Ruth Slocum Durfee, born in Middletown, R. I., September 20, 1766, died October 16, 1826; married in Middletown, R. I., August 15, 1790, Elizabeth Beebe, daughter of Daniel Beebe, born in Middletown, R. I., March 1, 1773, died in New Bedford, Mass., May 22, 1849, and had fourteen children RUTH, born December 3, 1791 REBECCA, born September 19 1793 LYDIA STANTON, born September 19, 1795 MARY, born September 21, 1797. HANNAH BEEBE, born September 3, 1799 RAYMOND P., born December 3, 1801. CATHERINE STANTON, born September 30, 1804 BETSEY, born May 1, 1806, died young ALBERT G., born March 13, 1808. WILLIAM H., born May 4, 1810. ROBERT A., born July 1, 1812 BETSEY, born December 7, 1813 BENJAMIN, born December 5, 1815 SARAH, born October 21, 1818

ELIZABETH DURFEE SEABURY

(123844)

Elizabeth Durfee, daughter of James and Ruth Slocum Durfee, born in Middletown, R. I., April 21, 1769, died in Newport, R. I., October 15, 1847, married in Middletown, R. I., Thomas Seabury, died in the West Indies June 19, 1795, and had one child. THOMAS MUMFORD, born in Newport, R. I., April 12, 1793, died in Newport, R. I. October 6, 1843, married Elizabeth Webster

James Durfel

(123845).

James Durfee, son of James and Ruth Slocum Durfee, born in Middletown, R. I., August 11, 1777, died in Portsmouth, R. I., March 22, 1830; married in South Kings Town, R I, October 21, 1799, Mary Pearse, daughter of Timothy and Nancy (surname unknown) Pearse, born in South Kings Town, R. I., 1780, died in Portsmouth, R I, February 15, 1856, and had nine children. JESSE TRIPP, born in North Kings Town, R. I, August 18, 1800 ELIZA SEABURY, born May 11, 1802 TIMOTHY PEARSE, born June 5, 1804; died in New York City, 1836 ISAAC PEARSE, born December 9, 1805. MARY ANN, born October 4, 1807, died February 12, 1810. RUTH S, born May 28, 1809, died January, 1892. MARY T., born December 23, 1811 JOSEPHINE L, born March 13, 1819. JAMES LAWRENCE, born November 21, 1821

Lucina Durfee Carr

(123876)

Lucina Durfee, daughter of Oliver and Elizabeth Lowden Langley Durfee, born in Middletown, R I., February 17, 1796, died in Newport, R. I, November 29, 1878, married in Bristol, R I, March 1, 1823, Francis Carr, son of Samuel and Damaris Underwood Carr, born in Newport, R. I, 1796; died in Tiverton, R I, November 14, 1848, and had five children. FRANCIS F., died young ELIZABETH D, born 1826; died 1833 MARY H., born 1829; died 1833 BENJAMIN MORRIS, born July 12, 1834, died in Newport, R I, April 21, 1897; married Harriet E. Underwood FRANCIS MEADER, born August, 1836; died October 8, 1840

She and her husband were members of the Society of Friends in Newport, R I. The following was said of her by the Friend who spoke at her funeral· "This dear Friend was much attached to the early testimonies of our Society, although from bodily infirmities she was for many years deprived of the enjoyment of attending meetings, she was always ready to encourage others to work in the vineyard of the Lord, her end was peace " Her husband was a lineal descendant of Governor Caleb Carr, who died in office in 1695.

199

CLARK CHASE

(1239a26)

Clark Chase, son of Benjamin and Elizabeth Durfee Chase, born August 22, 1770, died in Ontario County, N. Y., 1821, married June 21, 1792, Phebe Mason, and had ten children DURFEE, born January 24, 1793, died January 10 1872, married Almira Holmes, (2) Lucinda C. Gregg. MASON, born November 19, 1795 WILLARD, born February 1, 1798 SARAH, born October 20, 1800 EDMUND, born March 26, 1803 PURLEY, born January 3, 1806 LUCINDA, born October 18, 1808 HENRY, born April 9, 1811 ABEL D., born January 19, 1814. ASA S., born June 29 1818

THOMAS DURFEE

(1239a31)

Thomas Durfee, son of John and Phebe Gray Durfee, born in Tiverton, R. I., November 4, 1759, died in Tiverton, R. I., January 17, 1829, married in Newport, R. I., September 13, 1779, Mary Lowden, daughter of Richard and Priscilla Stafford Lowden, born August 13, 1753, died in Tiverton, R. I., November 29, 1842, and had five children GOODWIN HALVERSON, born July 19, died July 30, 1796 ELIZABETH, born October 28, 1781 LUCINDA, born May 18, 1784, drowned September 29 1809 JOB, born September 20, 1790 CHARLES, born February 26, 1793

He began his public life in the military camp of the Colonist, in 1776, as a patriot He enlisted as a private in the Revolutionary Army, and was promoted to Ensign after the battle of Rhode Island He was chosen by his fellow-townsmen to fill various town offices, and was a member of the General Assembly of Rhode Island from 1787 to 1797. He was one of the committee that canvassed the vote of the state on the adoption of the Constitution of the United States He was appointed Notary Public for Tiverton, R. I., June 23, 1801, and was elected Town Clerk in 1814, retaining the office the remainder of his life He became Chief Justice of the Court of Common Pleas of Newport County, R. I., in 1820, and continued for nine years He was Surveyor of Customs at Tiverton, R. I., from 1822 until 1829, when death closed his earthly duties

ABNER DURFEE

(1239a32)

Abner Durfee, son of John and Phebe Gray Durfee, born in Tiverton R I, September 18, 1761, married Nancy Cory, daughter of Thomas Cory, born in Tiverton, R I., 1762, died in Tiverton, R. I, July 30, 1847, and had five children CATHERINE. born October 3, 1787. ABIGAIL, born September 6, 1789 BRIDGET ANN, born September 6, 1793 HARRIET, born September 16, 1796, died June 16, 1822 BETSEY, born August 3, 1798.

WILLIAM DURFEE

(1239a33)

William Durfee, son of John and Phebe Gray Durfee, born in Tiverton, R I, 1763, died in Tiverton, R I., 1845, married in Tiverton, R I, February 16, 1800, Alice Stafford, daughter of John and Judith (surname unknown) Stafford, and had five children. ELIZABETH, born November 5, 1800. JOB, born February 22, 1802 JUDITH, born August 20, 1804. ISAAC T., born December 5, 1806, died June 5, 1830 JOHN, born June 11, 1812

PRISCILLA DURFEE EARL WATTS.

(1239a35)

Priscilla Durfee, daughter of John and Phebe Gray Durfee, born in Tiverton, R I, 1780, died in Portsmouth, R. I, May 14, 1860, married in Tiverton, R I, December 24, 1797, Ralph Earl, son of William and Edith Brownell Earl, born in Westport, Mass, August 28, 1776, and had one child. THOMAS

She married second in Tiverton. R. I., John Watts, and had five children JOHN. JEFFERSON PELEG, born July 25, 1811. ELMINA, born June 8, 1813 LORENZO, born December 8, 1820

SILVIA DURFEE TRIPP

(1239a36).

Silvia Durfee, daughter of John and Phebe Gray Durfee, born in Tiverton, R. I. married George Tripp, and had ten children

Job. Stephen. William. John Abbie, married Gardner Potter Nancy. Mary Priscilla Phebe Emma

John Durfee.

(1239a37)

John Durfee, son of John and Phebe Gray Durfee, born in Tiverton, R I, 1771; died in Tiverton, R I, September 19, 1805, married in Tiverton, R I, December 26, 1792, Abigail Westgate, daughter of George and Elizabeth Durfee Westgate, born in Tiverton, R I., June 13, 1763, died in Tiverton, R I, 1846, and had four children Elizabeth, born October 1, 1793 Richard Bordin, born February 20, 1796. Rebecca, born September 9, 1798, died January 9 1859. Elianor, born December 9, 1801, died November 20, 1875

Phebe Durfee Coggeshall.

(1239a38)

Phebe Durfee daughter of John and Phebe Gray Durfee, born in Tiverton, R. I., 1779, died in Tiverton, R. I, 1851, married Daniel Coggeshall, son of John and Elizabeth Stafford Coggeshall, born November 11, 1776, died 1849, and had fourteen children Rose, born in Tiverton, R. I, May 29, 1800, died in infancy Lizzie, born in Tiverton, R. I, May 29, 1800; died in infancy. Bethany, born in Tiverton, R I, December, 1802; died 1836, married Elias Tripp. Mary, born in Tiverton, R. I, December, 1802, married Moses Hunt Ruth, born in Tiverton R I, August 8, 1804, married Caleb Sabin, (2) Job Durfee Joshua, born in Tiverton, R. I, October 30 1805, died insane; married Mary B. Manchester Arnold, born in Tiverton, R I, June 29, 1807, married a Tripp Admiral, born in Tiverton, R. I, May, 1810 Nelson, born in Tiverton, R I., May, 1810, died December 5, 1893; married Alice Bessy Lizzie, born in Tiverton R I, March 29, 1813, married Alden Woodle Harriet, born in Tiverton, R. I., January, 1815, married Isaac Grinnell Durfel W., born in Tiverton, R I, 1817. Sally, born in Tiverton, R. I., November 5, 1819, married Jeremiah Borden Amy Ann, born in Tiverton, R I, 1820, married Welcome Clark

EARLE DURFEE.

(1239a41).

Earle Durfee, son of Gideon and Anne Bowen Durfee, born in Tiverton, R. I., October 27, 1757, died in South Cambridge, N. Y., May 24, 1839; married in Tiverton, R I., November 17, 1776, Patience Lake, daughter of Joseph Lake, died in South Cambridge, N Y, March 27, 1813, and had six children. ABRAHAM, born June 10, 1777. MARY, born July 2, 1780 GIDEON, born March 30, 1782. TABITHA, born February 14, 1784, died January 10, 1819 JOSEPH, born February 7, 1787, died September 24, 1790. BENJAMIN, born February 7, 1787, died September 24, 1790

He married second October 16, 1814, Phebe Hunt, born March 9, 1784; died in South Cambridge, N. Y, September 28, 1839, and had one child ANNE, born September 13 1819

It has been stated that he and his younger brother were soldiers in the Revolutionary Army, and were under General Sullivan at the time of the battle of Rhode Island, and that shortly after the close of the war they moved from Tiverton, R. I, to Cambridge, Washington County, N Y.

LEMUEL DURFEE

(1239a42).

Lemuel Durfee, son of Gideon and Anne Bowen Durfee, born in Tiverton, R. I, April 18, 1759 died in Palmyra, N. Y, August 9, 1829; married in Tiverton. R. I, August 29, 1784, Prudence Hathaway, died in Palmyra, N. Y, April 13, 1849, and had eleven children. ISAAC, born November 21, 1785 PHEBE, born June 9, 1788. PARDON, born July 30, 1790, died August 10, 1814 OLIVER, born August 5 1792 STEPHEN, born June 15, 1794 PRUDENCE, born March 29, 1796. MARY, born February 10, 1799. LEMUEL, born March 1, 1801 IRENE, born September 30, 1803 LUCENA, born November 29, 1805. BAILEY, born June 8, 1809

He was a private in Captain Christopher Manchester's company of Colonel Archibald Crary's regiment of Rhode Island, on duty at Bristol. R I, from November 15, 1777 to February 20, 1778. He also appears on the roll of Captain Richard Durfee's company of Colonel John Cook's regiment of Rhode Island militia in August. 1778 Soon after the war he moved with his brother,

Earle Durfee, to Cambridge, Washington County, N. Y., and in 1794, he settled on a farm about two miles north of Palmyra, where he died. He was buried in the family graveyard upon the farm

MARY DURFEE SHERMAN

(1239a43)

Mary Durfee, daughter of Gideon and Anne Bowen Durfee born in Tiverton, R. I., December 2, 1761, died in Palmyra, N. Y., 1794, married in Tiverton R. I. Humphrey Sherman, son of David Sherman born in Tiverton, R. I., 1760, died in East Palmyra, N. Y., 1812, and had eight children LEMUEL ANN. JOB. BETSEY. GIDION. STEPHEN, born 1789. ALEXANDER, born in Cambridge, Washington County, N. Y., 1790. DURFEL
She was the first person buried in East Palmyra, N. Y.

JOB DURFEE

(1239a44)

Job Durfee, son of Gideon and Anne Bowen Durfee, born in Tiverton, R. I., September 19, 1763, died in Palmyra, N. Y., 1813, married in Tiverton, R. I. July, 1782, Susannah Borden, and had eleven children. AARON, born November 18, 1784 ANNA, born August 9, 1786 PATIENCE born September 3 1788 EDWARD, born August 1 1790 SALLY, born February 15, 1794 HANNAH, born March 6, 1796 BETSEY, born May 13, 1799 BENJAMIN B., born April 19, 1801. SUSAN, born March 7, 1803 SAMANTHA, born May 13, 1805 JOB W., born December 5, 1807.
He came from Tiverton, R. I., to Palmyra, N. Y., in 1791, and purchased, March 7, 1792, three hundred acres of land, at seventy-five cents per acre

GIDEON DURFEE

(1239a45).

Gideon Durfee, son of Gideon and Anne Bowen Durfee, born in Tiverton, R. I., February 21, 1765 died in Palmyra, N. Y., 1809. married in Tiverton, R. I., February 6, 1791, Hannah Wood, daughter of George and Desire Gray Wood, born in Little Compton, R.

I , November 21, 1766, died in Nankin, Wayne County, Mich., November 25, 1859, and had eight children. GEORGE, born September 24, 1792 POLLY, born June 23, 1794 NATHAN, born August 21, 1796. BARZILLA, born November 20, 1798 HARVEY, born February 1, 1801 AUSTIN, born February 12, 1803 ELIZABETH, born February 10, 1805. MATILDA, born February 11, 1807

He and his brother Edward came from Tiverton, R I., to Farmington, N Y, in the summer of 1790. He returned with a favorable report of the country, and came back the following winter with Isaac Springer He purchased two hundred acres of land of his brother-in-law, Humphrey Sherman, in 1792 He was appointed, in 1804, an Ensign in Lieutenant-Colonel Swift's regiment of New York militia

HANNAH DURFEE OSBAND

(1239a46)

Hannah Durfee, daughter of Gideon and Anne Bowen Durfee, born in Tiverton, R I, July 27, 1766, died in Palmyra, N Y, September 1, 1820, married in Tiverton, R I, October 16, 1788, Weaver Osband, son of William and Elizabeth Shrieve Osband, born in Tiverton R I, April 17, 1756, died in Palmyra, N Y, May 21, 1805, and had nine children PHEBE, born April 12, 1789 WILSON born January 11, 1791. ANNA born August 7, 1793 WILLIAM, born June 1, 1796 ELIZABETH, born February 26, 1798. GIDEON, born January 5, 1801 DURFLE, born January 5, 1801. HANNAH, born February 9, 1803, died July 29, 1813 PATIENCE, born March 20, 1805, died July 8, 1805

ELIZABETH DURFEE HERENDEEN

(1239a47).

Elizabeth Durfee, daughter of Gideon and Anne Bowen Durfee, born in Tiverton, R I, March 29, 1768, married May, 1794, Welcome Herendeen, son of Nathan and Huldah Dillingham Herendeen born in Smithfield, R I., April 18, 1768 and had seven children. EDWARD. GIDEON, married Bersheba Willets ANNE, married Asa Smith HULDAH, born in Farmington, N Y, April 28, 1802, married William Gatchall DURFEE, born in Farmington, N. Y, July

5, 1804; married Mary Smith NATHAN. WILKINSON, married Caroline C Arnold

PARDON DURFEE

(1239a48)

Pardon Durfee, son of Gideon and Anne Bowen Durfee, born in Tiverton. R I, January 24 1770, died in Palmyra, N. Y., April 25, 1828, married in Palmyra, N Y, May, 1794, Ruth Reeves, died in Palymra, N Y., April 29, 1858, and had eight children. ELIAS. born March 9, 1796 HARRIET, born November 30, 1797 CYNTHIA, born November 6, 1799 MARIA, born December 14, 1801 SYDNEY SMITH, born January 1, 1804. NELLSON, born March 17, 1806, died July 15, 1823 CHARLES, born March 22, 1808. PHILO, born March 27, 1810

He established a rope factory in Palmyra, N Y., and carried on the business of making rope until his death

EDWARD DURFEE.

(1239a49)

Edward Durfee, son of Gideon and Anne Bowen Durfee, born in Tiverton, R I, December 10, 1771 died in Palmyra, N. Y., September 20, 1823, married in Palmyra, N Y, March 9, 1795, Hannah Howell, born September 15, 1775, died August 18, 1808, and had three children ABEL, born November 11, 1795 SETH. born May 16, 1797, died July 27, 1801 LUCENA, born January 31, 1802, died February 20, 1806

He married second October 24, 1809, Susannah Brown, daughter of Elijah and Bashua Kuffield Brown, born in New London, Conn., 1776, died in Lyons, N Y, January 11, 1854, and had five children AMANDA, born May 27, 1810 ANNA B, born May 19, 1812 MARY E, born January 14, 1814. SUSAN, born December 11, 1815 PHILENA, born July 12, 1819

He came with his brother, Gideon Durfee, on his journey from Rhode Island in 1790, as far as Farmington, N Y, and in 1791 he came to Palmyra N Y, with the Durfee family He was selected as one of the Commissioners of Highways of Palmyra, N Y., in 1796 He was First Major in Lieutenant-Colonel Gilbert

Howell's regiment of Light Infantry, New York State militia during the war of 1812.

RUTH DURFEE WILCOX.

(1239a49a).

Ruth Durfee, daughter of Gideon and Anne Bowen Durfee, born in Tiverton, R I., March 13, 1774, died in Palmyra, N. Y, November 13, 1857, married in Palmyra, N. Y, March 7, 1793, William Wilcox, died in Palmyra, N Y, November 17, 1857, and had twelve children EARL, born March 30, 1794; married Jane Stewart. GIDEON, born January 26, 1796, married Mercy Herendeen. GEORGE, born July 14, 1798, married JULIA STODDARD MARY, born June 23, 1800, died September 24, 1843 MEREBIAH, born August 22, 1802 HIRAM, born October 27, 1804 ANN, born December 17, 1806, married John Gregg WILLIAM, born June 27, 1808, died July 7, 1808 DURFEE, born October 29, 1809, died in Sodus, N. Y., April 15, 1893, married Samantha Wells. RUTH, born November 20, 1811, died September 6, 1825 ELIZA, born March 7, 1814 Infant, born July 12, 1815 died July 12, 1815

STEPHEN DURFEE

(1239a49b)

Stephen Durfee, son of Gideon and Anne Bowen Durfee, born in Tiverton, R I., April 4, 1776, died in Palmyra, N Y, April 14, 1854, married in Palmyra, N Y., January 4, 1798, Mary Allen, born in Dove Dutchess County, N Y.. June 1, 1778, and had twelve children ELIZABETH, born August 23, 1798. WILLIAM, born May 3, 1800. ALLEN, born March 4, 1802. BARTON, born March 12, 1804. ELIHU, born March 27, 1806 CHLOE, born October 15, 1808. NATHANIEL, born January 19, 1811 EMILY, born March 7, 1813: died February 9, 1815 ANNE, born July 8, 1815. MARY, born October 29, 1817. EMILY, born March 27, 1820 EMORY, born March 27, 1820

He married second January 25, 1822, Sarah Fuller, and married third December 30, 1830, Mary Bristol He was a farmer and resided near Palmyra, N Y, until his death He was a man of sound thought and exemplary in his character.

207

DANIEL DURFEE

(1239a62)

Daniel Durfee, son of Job and Mary Slocum Durfee, born in Tiverton, R. I., November 21, 1767; married in Tiverton, R. I., October 28, 1798, Barsheba Hart, daughter of Joseph and Mary Dwelly Hart, born in Tiverton, R. I., February 20, 1778; died in Michigan, March 21, 1848 and had six children BENJAMIN, born January 10, 1799 MARY, born 1804, BETSEY, born 1807 SETH, born March 20, 1810 ELEANOR, born 1812, ADDISON, born April 15, 1815.

DAVID DURFEE

(1239a63)

David Durfee, son of Job and Mary Slocum Durfee, born in Tiverton, R. I., September 5, 1770, died in Tiverton, R. I., about 1815, married in Tiverton, R. I., Elizabeth Tabor, daughter of George Tabor, born 1769, died in Tiverton, R. I., July 16, 1857, and had one child Thomas born March 18, 1802

GEORGE DURFEE

(1239a64).

George Durfee, son of Job and Mary Slocum Durfee, born in Tiverton R. I. September 11, 1772, died in Tiverton, R. I., November 12, 1854, married in Tiverton, R. I., 1793, Sarah Coggeshall, daughter of John and Elizabeth Stafford Coggeshall, born in Tiverton, R. I., August 18, 1774; died in Tiverton, R. I., August 31, 1859, and had ten children DWELLY, born September 6, 1795 JOB, born January 25, 1798 GIDEON C born December 28, 1800 ELIZABETH C, born January 1 1803 MARY, born February 19, 1805 JOSHUA C, born October 11, 1807. SUSANNAH born December 25, 1809 PETER, born October 16, 1812 DAVID, born May 3, 1815 DELANA born August 3 1818.

He was a farmer, and large owner in the Eagle Mills, located near Fall River He began life with very little that he could call his own having had very limited advantages in education He, however, came to be very apt in figures, accumulated large tracts of land in the vicinity of Fall River, New Bedford, and Tiverton. It is said that he owned more than a thousand acres at one time.

JOSEPH DURFEE

(1239a65).

Joseph Durfee, son of Job and Mary Slocum Durfee, born in Tiverton, R. I., May 8, 1780; died in Fall River, Mass., December 16, 1865, married in Fall River, Mass., January 29, 1804, Elizabeth Borden, daughter of Daniel and Anna Brightman Borden, born in Freetown, Mass., 1786, died in Tiverton, R I, June 27, 1874

WILLIAM DURFIE.

(1239a66).

William Durfee, son of Job and Mary Slocum Durfee, born in Tiverton, R I, August 5, 1784; died in Tiverton, R. I, married in Taunton, Mass, about 1807, Hannah Clark, daughter of Theophilus Clark, born in Taunton, Mass., 1774, died in Fall River, Mass, 1860, and had one child AMEY, born October 8, 1808

THURSTON CORNELL

(124511)

Thurston Cornell, son of Walter and Sarah Anthony Cornell, married Ann Anthony and had one child ANTHONY

He married second 1782, Mary Perry, daughter of Phineas and Elizabeth (surname unknown) Perry, and had eight children ANN, born March 8, 1783 WALTER, born February 10 1784, married Theresa Manchester ELIZABETH SARAH WILLIAM, married Betsey Jennings MARY. ANTHONY, married Sarah Grinnell. CLARA

EDWARD CORNELL

(124551)

Edward Cornell, son of Gideon and Susannah Brownell Cornell, born May 6, 1765, died 1857, married Elizabeth Hoxie, and had ten children. ANNA, born March 10, 1794 ISAAC, born February 29, 1796 ALICE, born April 28, 1798 SUSANNAH, born November 15, 1800 GIDEON, born November 1, 1802 GERVIS, born January 1, 1803 MARY, born June 9, 1807 DANIEL, born February 12, 1810 DOLLWYN, born April 22, 1812. WALKER, born August 11, 1814.

He was a member of Assembly in 1843 His son Gervis moved to Canada and settled in Pickering, Ontario, and was an active member of the Society of Friends and was a director of the college of that sect in Pickering.

WILLIAM CORNELL.

(124552)

William Cornell, son of Gideon and Susannah Brownell Cornell, born October 29, 1766, died 1864-5, married Content Davis, and had eleven children ISAAC, born August 18, 1789 GEORGE, born June 5, 1791 WILLIAM, born July 3 1792, died April 24, 1819 ANNA born January 29, 1794 SILVEY, born May 15, 1795 HANNAH, born May 18, 1797 ELIZABETH, born February 14, 1799 MARY, born April 24, 1801. GIDEON, born April 18, 1803 MILLICENT, born February 8, 1805. JOHN, born March 9, 1807

He married second 1839, Rhoda Tenny, and had six children EDWARD, born June, 1810 died 1850, married Dinah George SUSANNAH, born March 1, 1812. HARRIET, born June 8, 1814 CHARLES, born November 10, 1816. CHARLOTTE, born July 14, 1819 FRANCES, born February 8, 1821.

He was the second settler in Scarboro, Canada, and remarkable for his energy and upright character He was a member of the Society of Friends and a staunch supporter of the government His sons fought in the Canada Militia in 1812 He built the first sawmill in the township

GIDEON CORNELL.

(124556).

Gideon Cornell, son of Gideon and Susannah Brownell Cornell born October 17, 1776, died before 1853, married Hannah Russell of Easton, Washington County, N. Y., and had one child CHARLES

RUSSELL, born January 20, 1806, died September 12, 1866, married Maria Cornell, (2) Hannah Avery.

He married second August 13, 1834, Harriet Sarchet of Philadelphia, Pa   He was administrator to Charles Russell Cornell

WANTON CORNELL.

(124557)

Wanton Cornell, son of Gideon and Susannah Brownell Cornell, born September 23, 1778, died in Milton, Saratoga County, N Y., March 26, 1871, married September 27, 1808, Sybil Gifford, and had five children   ELIJAH, born August 6, 1809, married Fannie King of Troy, N Y   MILLICENT, born September 22, 1810. SUSANNAH, born June 27, 1815; married Rev J G Warren. DORR, born November 27, 1821, died February 23, 1825.   EMMA, born May 20, 1826.

He married second 1856 Maria Taylor

LATHAM CORNELL

(124558).

Latham Cornell, son of Gideon and Susannah Brownell Cornell, born January 18, 1781, died April 17, 1876; married October 4, 1808, Louisa Bailey White, died October 24, 1853, and had three children.   MARIA, born November 20, 1809, married Charles Russell Cornell.   WILLIAM W, born May 10, 1812, died May 26, 1894, married Margaret P Edgar.   SARAH ELIZABETH, born April 22, 1823, married Henry Wright Strong, (2) Horace Harrington

He married second 1856, Louisa Evarts, a widow   and had one child.   Louisa, born January 1, 1858, died July 3 1859.   He founded the business of stove manufacturing in Troy, N Y., 1816, and retired in 1836.

WALTER CORNELL.

(124559a)

Walter Cornell, son of Gideon and Susannah Brownell Cornell, born May 17, 1785, died April 14, 1877 married April, 1811, Mary Batty, born February, 1793, died August 4, 1853, and had five children EMMA, born December 28, 1812 EMELINE died March 11, 1853 married a Hollingsworth MARY JANE, died December 11, 1856 married a Kennedy SUSAN ALMY, married a Hutchinson, (2) a Williams ADELAIDE, died March 5, 1850.

(124572).

Walter Cornell, son of Matthew and Elizabeth Shrieves Cornell, born August 24, 1782, died in Albany, N. Y., March 4, 1833, married Eunice Hunt, daughter of William Hunt and had two children JOHN W, born in Easton, Washington County, N. Y., November 16 1816 died in Chautauqua, Chautauqua County, N. Y., January 6, 1896, married Anne Durfee MARIA JANETTE, born in Easton, N. Y., March, 1824, died in Chautauqua, N. Y., February 15, 1903, married William P. Whiteside

He became a member of the Assembly from Washington County and died while attending a term of the legislature at Albany.

MATTHEW CORNELL.

(124573)

Matthew Cornell, son of Matthew and Elizabeth Shrieve Cornell, born March 27, 1787, died January 29, 1854, married Lydia Ford, and had twelve children MERRITT I, born in Cambridge, N. Y., March 5, 1809, died August 1883, married Mercy Witman Howard ZINA born January 3, 1811 died February 3, 1893 married Mary Hunt CHARLOTTE M., born April 13, 1813, died January 8, 1851; married Isaac G Parker. CYRUS, born November 11, 1815, died August 1, 1818. THOMAS F, born June 26, 1818; married Patience Burdick, (2) Sarah Byers WALTER, born December 18 1820, died December 8, 1845 MEHITABLE F, born April 19, 1823, died April 29 1848 married Humphrey K Brownell. ELIZABETH, born January 17, 1825, died June 13, 1854 MARY D, born September 15, 1827, died July 20, 1847 AMY, born January 6, 1830, died August 6, 1849. EMMA born January 6 1830, died January 6, 1830 THOMAS J born May 11, 1832, married Mary Devel

212

born in Portsmouth, R I , July 1, 1780, married in Privodence, R I., May 5, 1803, Susan Anthony, daughter of John and Rachel Bullock Anthony, and had four children. ANN ELIZA, born January 22, 1804, died January 3, 1815 WILLIAM, born October 1, 1805; died November 25, 1892 HARRIET, born September 13, 1807, died July 13, 1902, married Malachi Rodes Gardiner SUSAN FISH, born May 30, 1810, died March 29, 1835, married Abel Lincoln.

ISAAC BROWNELL.

(146216).

Isaac Brownell, son of Stephen and Susannah Fish Brownell,
He married second January 1, 1815, Mary Anthony, daughter of John and Rachel Bullock Anthony, and had one child. ISAAC, born December 13, 1815; died December 13, 1815

MOSES BROWNELL

(146217).

Moses Brownell, son of Stephen and Susannah Fish Brownell, born in Portsmouth, R I, May 10, 1782, married and had two children Stephen Elton and ~~another son~~ *Josiah Ormsbee*   *Cel*   *Orr*

(CEB

STEPHEN FISH BROWNEII

(146219).

Stephen Fish Brownell, son of Stephen and Susannah Fish Brownell, born in Portsmouth, R I, December 1, 1785; died in Smithfield, R. I., April 28, 1865; married May 14, 1809, Susanna White, daughter of Samuel and Hannah Aldrich White of Mendon, Mass.

He married second November 24, 1811, Mary White, daughter of Samuel and Hannah Aldrich White of Mendon, Mass, and had six children ISAAC. SUSAN, married Horace Darling. HANNAH. STEPHEN, born March 14, 1822, married Henrietta Hunt. MARY DEXTER

He moved from Portsmouth, R. I, to Smithfield, R. I, when fourteen years of age He was a farmer and carpenter.

213

Peter Brownell.

(146219a).

Peter Brownell, son of Stephen and Susannah Fish Brownell, born in Portsmouth, R I, July 8, 1788; married and had two children. ROXYLANIA. THEODORE.

Joseph Brownell

(146293).

Joseph Brownell, son of Thomas and Mercy Shaw Brownell, born January 19, 1795, died in New Bedford, Mass, August 19, 1879, married Lydia Almy of Little Compton, R I., and had four children J. AUGUSTUS, married Emeline Gray REBECCA, married Dr Ira Chase ALMINA EMMA, born in New Bedford, Mass, August 22, 1834, married Charles S Cummings THOMAS FRANK, born in New Bedford, Mass, died in New York, N Y, January, 1901, married Eva Palmer.

He was a successful business man and was a member of the firm of Brownell & Ashley He and his wife were members of the Fourth Street Methodist Episcopal Church for many years, and he was a member of the Official Board. He was highly respected and a valuable member of the community.

William Brownell.

(146296).

William Brownell, son of Thomas and Mercy Shaw Brownell, born June 17, 1804, died June 5, 1887, married Rebecca Childs, and had three children WILLIAM FREDERICK, born in New Bedford, Mass, January 24, 1847, married Evelyn H Keith JOSEPH, born in Acushnet, Mass, April 15, 1853. EMILY A

Burden Brownell.

(146331).

Burden Brownell, son of Joseph and Elizabeth (surname unknown) Brownell, born in Portsmouth, R I, August 5, 1776; married and had three children. JOSEPH OLIVER. BURDEN

GEORGE BROWNELL.

(146332).

George Brownell, son of Joseph and Elizabeth (surname un-known) Brownell, born in Portsmouth, R. I., October 12, 1778, married and had two children WILLIAM. REBECCA. He lived in Pomfret, Conn.

ABNER BROWNELL

(146336)

Abner Brownell, son of Joseph and Elizabeth (surname un-known) Brownell, born in Portsmouth, R. I., January 30, 1787; died in Sauquoit, N. Y., December 27, 1874; married June 5, 1807, Susan Macomber, and had seven children. SUSAN E, born July 11, 1810, died December 17, 1816 GEORGE MACOMBER, born September 15, 1812; died July 30, 1859, married Louise Sweeting. JULIETTE V, born July 26, 1814; died August 22, 1872, married Morris Savage. EBENEZER DEAN, born November 13, 1816, died June 2, 1889, married Hannah West HENRY DWIGHT, born August 4, 1820: died March 21, 1892, married Katherine R. Fox. SUSAN EMELINE, born April 10, 1824; died October 7, 1888; married Jonah J Willard. FANNY MARIA, born March 6, 1828, died March 30, 1844

The following was taken from the Utica Morning Herald of December 28, 1874: "News was received Sunday evening of the death of Abner Brownell of Sauquoit, one of the oldest residents of the village and a pioneer in the manufacturing business of Oneida County He died of old age at the residence of his son-in-law, M S Savage, Sunday afternoon. His age was 88 years, and for more than a year his strength had been so low that when he quietly passed away his death was no sudden bereavement. For twenty years he had lived in retirement from active business, and he was known in all the vicinity for his charities and exemplary life

Abner Brownell was born January 30, 1787, at Portsmouth, Rhode Island About the year 1812 he removed to where is now Chadwick's Mills, and began the manufacture of cotton goods in company with John Chadwick, father of Hon G W Chadwick of that place. After several years had elapsed he removed two miles farther up the stream (Sauquoit Creek) and founded the cotton mill long known as the Franklin factory, and which has since developed into the present large establishment. From that time he has resided at Sauquoit, and has seen the village grow up about him, lending efficient aid in the building up of its local institutions and its general progress. He never sought nor filled public office, ever preferring to do unostentatious work in private walks. He was loved by the operatives whom he employed. He was methodic and orderly in the performance of his own work, and though he required those who worked for him to do so with order and method he was a kind master. He was a charter member of the Sauquoit Masonic Lodge. He was in old times a Whig in politics, and in later days he was a staunch though quiet Republican. He was charitable and honest, diligent in business, a loved and revered citizen, and he died full of years and honors— honors than which none are prouder those of a well spent life and the respect of one's fellow-men. He leaves two sons, who, since his retirement from business twenty years ago, have conducted the affairs of the mills, and a married daughter residing in Connecticut."

HOLDER BROWNELL

(146338)

Holder Brownell, son of Joseph and Elizabeth (surname unknown) Brownell, born in Portsmouth, R I, May 9, 1789, married and had a daughter Louise and probably other children. He lived in Utica, N Y

BENJAMIN BROWNELL.

(146361)

Benjamin Brownell, son of George and (given name unknown) Hopkins Brownell, born in Rhode Island, died in Royal, Pa , married Margaret Coil, and had eleven children HENRY, DANIEL
EBENEZER   GEORGE   JAMES   BENJAMIN   SARAH   NANCY
MARIA MARGARET MARTHA

He kept a hotel at Royal, Pa , a number of years

RHODA BROWNELL COIL

(146362)

Rhoda Brownell, daughter of George and (given name unknown) Hopkins Brownell, born in Rhode Island, died in Dundaff, Pa, married George Coil, and had nine children GEORGE. MARIA PATIENCE. JAMES JOHN MARY ANN. CHARLES HENRY. BENJAMIN.

She came with her parents from Rhode Island and settled in Dundaff Pa, where she resided until her death.

PATIENCE BROWNELL WATERMAN

(146363)

Patience Brownell, daughter of George and (given name unknown) Hopkins Brownell, born in Rhode Island, died in Rhode Island, married George Waterman and had one child A daughter

GEORGE BROWNELL

(146364).

George Brownell, son of George and (given name unknown) Hopkins Brownell, born in Rhode Island, 1801, died in Clifford, Susquehanna County, Pa, 1869, married Sarah Kelsey, and had one child. DANIEL KELSEY.

He married second Amy Arnold, and had seven children JOSEPH ARNOLD, born in Lonsdale, Pa, August 30, 1834; married Henrietta Barnum SARAH ANN. GEORGE WASHINGTON, married Maria Bennett ANN JANE, married Nelson Colman EMILINE AIWORTH, married Dr J. C. Olmstead, (2) Byron S Clark AGNES, married Sylvester Wells MARQUIS LAFAYETTE, born in Lonsdale, Susquehanna County, Pa., July 16, 1851, married Annjennette Cobb.

He was a drummer boy and at the age of twelve years was in a "tea fight" skirmish of some kind He played the drum at general training for a number of years At the age of sixteen he moved with his parents from Rhode Island to Clifford Township, Pa having covered the whole distance with an ox team He is buried in Clifford, Pa.

CLARISSA BROWNELL COIL.

(146365).

Clarissa Brownell, daughter of George and (given name unknown) Hopkins Brownell, born in Rhode Island, died in Dundaff Pa., married John Coil, died in Dundaff, Pa., and had seven children JAMES HENRY. LOCKIL MARY CLARISSA BENJAMIN. ERASTUS.

JAMES BROWNELL.

(146366)

James Brownell, son of George and (given name unknown) Hopkins Brownell, born in Rhode Island, died in Royal Pa ; married Ellen Aronld, died in Royal, Pa., and had four children. CHARLOTTE ANNA JASON. JAMES

It is stated that he would not ride on the cars and walked from Royal, Pa., to Rhode Island twice, a distance of over two hundred and fifty miles

BETSEY BROWNELL CHAMPLIN.

(146367)

Betsey Brownell, daughter of George and (given name unknown) Hopkins Brownell, born in Rhode Island; died in Rhode Island, married a Champlin, and had three children ARABELLA, and two others

MARY ANN BROWNELL STEPHENS.

(146368)

Mary Ann Brownell, daughter of George and (given name unknown) Hopkins Brownell, born in Rhode Island, died in Royal, Pa ; married John Stephens, died in Royal, Pa., and had six children JACOB, married Soluna Johnson GEORGE, married Emeline Bennett. MARTHA, married Andrew Simpson MARY, married James C Decker LOUISE, married Charles Hunter. JOHN

DEBORAH BROWNELL HOWLAND

(151361).

Deborah Brownell, daughter of Benjamin and Martha Closson Brownell, born April 10, 1759; married Henry Howland, son of Henry and Abigail Goddard Howland, and had son WILLIAM P., who married Deborah Howard, and probably other children

JOSIAH BROWNELL.

(151363).

Josiah Brownell, son of Benjamin and Martha Closson Brownell, born June 5, 1765, married Deborah Howland, daughter of Henry and Abigail Goddard Howland, and had five children DIADAMA, married a Wood. ABIGAIL, married Lawton Corey MARTHA, married Benjamin Wilcox. CHRISTOPHER, married a Crandall MAJOR, married Alice Brownell

EZEKIEL BROWNELL.

(151364).

Ezekiel Brownell, son of Benjamin and Martha Closson Brownell, born August 5, 1770, died March 4, 1855, married 1797, Penelope Borden, daughter of George and Rebecca Church Borden, born February 15, 1775, died December 29, 1812, and had six children. THOMAS, born June 30, 1798, married Nancy Case, (2) Abby Petty. ABRAHAM, born March 27, 1800; married Esther Tripp, (2) Catherine Pierce. ISAAC, born December 19, 1802; married Abbie Carpenter MARY ANN, born September 1, 1806, married Sylvester Himes. JABEZ BARKER, born May 3, 1808; married Nancy Butts Negus. JOHN AVOY, born September 10, 1810; married Lucy Ryder

He married second Sarah Negus, who died in 1818, aged thirty years. He married third January 20, 1820, Hannah Sission, born October 6, 1786, died April 14, 1870, and had five children. CHARLES F, born November 16, 1820, married Nancy Sission, (2) Almira White. ELIZABETH H'ARRIET, born November 15, 1823, died January 17, 1837. RHODA M, born April 29, 1824, married Richard Borden, (2) Rev. Gould Anthony. GEORGE HARVEY

BRADFORD, born April 12, 1826, married Nancy Bliss, (2) Louisa
Davol   JAMES A, born April 11, 1830, married Hannah N White

RLBECCA BROWNELL CHASE.

(151392)

Rebecca Brownell, daughter of George and Rhoda Milk Brown-
ell, born 1772; married George Chase, and had three children.
GEORGE B., born July 14, 1801, died October 24, 1853, married
Lorette Noyce   AMY WILLIAM.

POLLY BROWNELL LAWTON

(151396)

Polly Brownell, daughter of George and Rhoda Milk Brownell,
born 1781, married Richard Lawton, and had three children.
ISAAC   PATIENCE K, born August 24, 1817, died February 26,
1894, married Samuel G Allen   ADAM.

SARAH BROWNELL BOOMER

(151397)

Sarah Brownell, daughter of George and Rhoda Milk Brownell,
born 1783 married Joseph Boomer, and had one child. DAVID, married Hannah Wing

GEORGE MILK BROWNELL.

(151399).

George Milk Brownell son of George and Rhoda Milk Brownell born November 15, 1787, died September 20, 1830: married July
10, 1809 Mary Davis daughter of William and Elizabeth (surname
unknown) Davis of Maine, and had four children   PHILIP, born
in Westport Mass, 1810 died in infancy JOHN DAVIS born in
Westport, Mass, June 5 1812, died April 21, 1894, married Elizabeth W Little. (2) Mrs Rhoda Allen Howland (3) Almira Rathbone AMY S, born in Westport, Mass October 30, 1814: died
September 25, 1865: married Holder White. Infant.

220

He married second Mrs. Fallie Duvol Tripp of Tiverton, R. I., born October 10, 1797, died February 8, 1879, and had four children. MARY DAVIS, born May 25, 1824, died January 16, 1860, married Francis W. Tilton. GEORGE A., born September 15, 1826; died at sea. PHILIP H., born June 4, 1828, died December 29, 1891, married Emily Sowle. ANN ELIZA, born August 4, 1830; married Luther M. Dayton.

DAVID M. BROWNELL.

(151399a).

David M. Brownell, son of George and Rhoda Milk Brownell, born October 8, 1789, died December 30, 1864; married Zilpha Davol, born October 21, 1797; died May 30, 1864, and had ten children. HARRIET, married Frederick Wheeler Brownell. RHODA M., born August 26, 1825, died October 22, 1852, married Nathaniel W. Winchester. ADALAIDE, married James Harvey Sherman. GEORGE FRANK, married Nancy Jane Macomber. RUTH LOUISE, died 1858 married William Henry Gifford. EDMOND. JULIA, born October 7, 1833, married John Wady. AMELIA S., born October 7 1833, died May 27. 1869 EMILY S., born November 5. 1836, died July 12, 1868, married Charles H. Freelove MARIA, born August 9, 1842, died September 18, 1875, married George Handy

REUBEN BROWNELL.

(159a211).

Reuben Brownell, son of David and Rhoda Brownell Brownell, married Alice Sherman, and had eight children LEVI, married Esther McDonald MARY, born in Pittstown, Rensselaer County, N. Y., January 5, 1807, died in Pittstown, N. Y., June 13, 1830, married Jacob Reasoner Brownell CLINTON DAVID, married Paulina MacNames. NANCY, born in Pittstown, N. Y., April 11, 1811, died in Ellery, Chautauqua County, N Y September 29, 1855, married Ezra Haner REUBEN. PRUDENCE, born in Pittstown, N. Y.; died in Ellery, N Y; married Stephen Carpenter. SHERMAN. JOHN

ELIJAH BROWNELL.

(159a217)

Elijah Brownell, son of David and Rhoda Brownell Brownell, born March 14, 1783, married January 6, 1805, Philenor Hoag, born July 27, 1789, and had thirteen children. DEBORAH, born November 25, 1805, died October 4, 1817. RHODA JANE, born February 14, 1809, married John Lytle. PHEBE, born October 22, 1811, died September 30, 1813. ELISHA H., born June 7, 1812. DAVID E., born May 12, 1815. ELIJAH, born March 6, 1817, died September 30, 1817. LYDIA, born January 3, 1819, died January 4, 1819. CAROLINE, born February 29, 1822, died November 29, 1822. JOHN B., born October 1, 1823; died October 13, 1825. CHARLES H., born January 7, 1825, died January 7, 1825. WARREN P., born June 4, 1827. JOHN L., born April 7, 1830. LOUISA W., born May 20, 1832.

MARY BROWNELL WILLIAMS

(159a221)

Mary Brownell, daughter of Jonathan and Desire Lake Brownell, born in Duanesburg, Schenectady County, N. Y., August 12, 1790, died in Brooklyn, N. Y., August 17, 1849, married Foster Williams and had four children. FOSTER BROWNELL. WASHINGTON WARREN. JUDITH. SARAH.

She is buried beside her husband in Cypress Hill Cemetery, Brooklyn, N. Y.

ISRAEL BROWNELL

(159a222)

Israel Brownell, son of Jonathan and Desire Lake Brownell, born in Duanesburg, Schenectady County, N. Y., September 7, 1792; died in Georgetown, Madison County, N. Y., June 1, 1869, married February, 1811, Ruth Barber, born January 9, 1790, died in Georgetown, N. Y., July 5, 1874, and had nine children. ELIZA ANN, born in Solon, N. Y., July 26, 1812. J. S. BRADLEY, born in Solon, N. Y., June 28, 1815; died in Solon, N. Y., September 23, 1838. DAVID M., born in Solon, N. Y., September 11, 1817, died in Solon, N. Y, July 23, 1839 ELECTA, born in Solon, N. Y., May 11, 1820, died in Solon N. Y, August 1, 1825 JULIA, born in Solon, N. Y., March 16, 1823. RALPH PLATT, born in Solon, N Y., June 12, 1826. MARTIN VANBUREN, born in Solon, N Y., November 16, 1828, died in Solon, N Y, September 10, 1831. RUTH JANE, born in Solon, N Y, May 11, 1831 HENRY MARTIN, born in Solon, N Y, April 13, 1834.

He was a farmer and lived in Solon, N Y, until 1854, when he moved to Georgetown, N. Y, and resided there the balance of his life In politics he was a Democrat

RACHEL BROWNELL CARPENTER.

(159a223)

Rachel Brownell, daughter of Jonathan and Desire Lake Brownell, born in Duanesburg, Schenectady County, N. Y, October 6, 1794, died in Meredith, Delaware County, N Y, June 14, 1854; married about 1810, David Carpenter, born July 21, 1787; died in Meredith, N. Y., December 11, 1851, and had thirteen children. WILLIAM NELSON, born in Milan, Dutchess County, N Y, February 16, 1812, married Catherine Frances Rehner JUDITH, died in Castle Creek, Broome County, N Y, June 3, 1869, married Richard Gray. SARAH ANN, born January 3, 1818, died in Meredith, N. Y, October 11, 1842 JONATHAN BROWNELL, born in Meredith, N. Y., February 7, 1819, married Phebe Ann Hart DAVID PIERCE, born in Delhi, Delaware County, N. Y, May 8, 1820 CALEB JOSHUA, born in Meredith, N. Y., March 28, 1822, died in Cortland, Cortland County, N Y, June 5, 1898; married Paulina Caroline Reynold MARY ELIZABETH, born about 1824 married Samuel A Garrett RACHEL MATILDA, born in Meredith, N Y., June 3, 1826, died in Meredith, N Y, January 23, 1843 WASHINGTON BENJAMIN, born in Meredith, N. Y., October 27, 1829, married Frances Alice Mason. MINER M, born in Meredith, N. Y., June 1, 1831, died in Meredith, N. Y, May 28, 1849 FOSTER W., born in Meredith, N. Y, January 11, 1833 died in Meredith, N Y, November 23, 1838. JOSEPHINE, born in Meredith, N Y., March 15, 1836, died in Meredith, N. Y., March 25, 1836 MELISSA, born in Meredith, N. Y., August 27, 1839, died in Meredith, N. Y., August 27, 1839

ARIADNE BROWNELL PERKINS

(159a225).

Ariadne Brownell, daughter of Jonathan and Desire Lake Brownell, born in Columbus, Chenango County, N. Y., June 12, 1799, died in South Otselic, Chenango County, N. Y., May 4, 1876, married in Columbus, N. Y., March 2, 1818, by Stephen Howard, to Thomas Perkins, son of Daniel and Susan Phillips Perkins, born in Scituate, R. I., August 28, 1796, died in South Otselic, N. Y., April 14 1876, and had six children. MARIA LORETTE, born in Columbus, N. Y., May 6, 1819. MILES THOMAS, born in Columbus, N. Y., March 17, 1821, died in Genoa, Carson Valley, September 30, 1854. MARY JULIA, born in Columbus, N. Y., August 12, 1822, died in Taylor, Cortland County, N. Y. January 29, 1899 TRACY KNAPP, born in Columbus, N. Y., May 15, 1824, died in South Otselic, N. Y., April 28, 1881. ELSIE ARIADNE, born in Cortlandville, Cortland County, N. Y., December 28, 1834 CHARLES GRANT, born in Otselic, N. Y., July 29 1839

She lived for several years in Columbus, N. Y., after which she moved to Cortland, N. Y., and later to Otselic, N. Y. She resided in the village of South Otselic, N. Y., at the time of her death. Although not a member of any church, she was a Universalist.

DAVID I BROWNELL.

(159a228)

David I Brownell, son of Jonathan and Desire Lake Brownell, born in Columbus, Chenango County N. Y., December 15 1802, died in McGrawville, Cortland County N. Y., February 16, 1887, married in Columbus, N. Y., October 1, 1828, Harriet Leonard, daughter of Heman and Rebecca Frary Leonard born in Blandford, Hampden County, Mass., May 15, 1810, died in McGrawville, N. Y., December 29 1893 and had eleven children. ALVA HEMAN, born in Columbus, N. Y., June 27, 1829, died in Solon, Cortland County, N. Y., September 14, 1830. JOHN LEONARD, born in Solon N. Y., March 17, 1831. JONATHAN, born in Solon, N. Y., November 24, 1832. MARY, born in Solon, N. Y. March 20, 1835. CHARLES ARANZO born in Solon N. Y., July 6, 1836 DAVID I, born in Solon, N. Y., June 20 1838 CATHERINE, born in Solon,

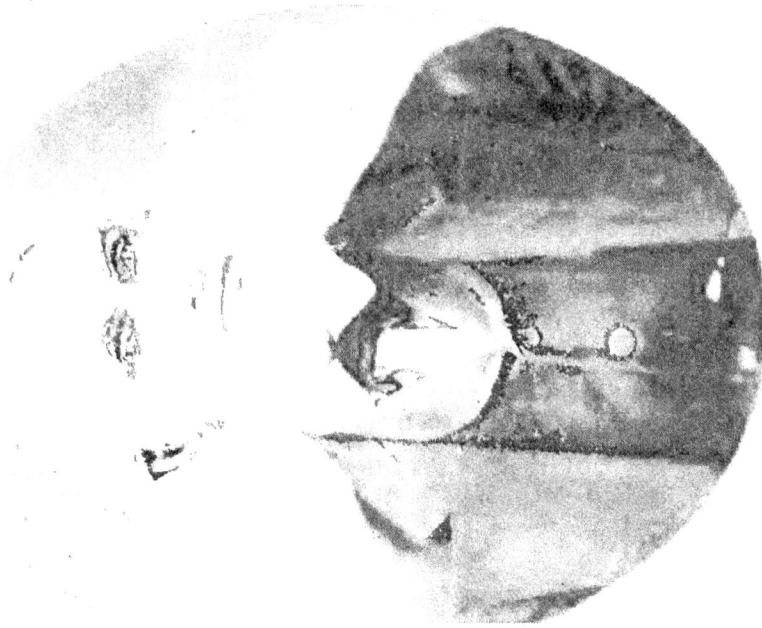

DAVID I. AND HARRIET LEONARD BROWNELL.

N Y, January 16, 1840 MARCUS, born in Solon, N Y, December 27, 1841. BENJAMIN FRANKLIN, born in Solon, N Y, February 4, 1844 HEMAN LANDAIS, born Solon, N Y, May 28, 1846 LYDIA ANN, born in Solon, N Y., July 15, 1848

He was a farmer and lived in Columbus N Y, until 1830, when he moved to Solon, N Y, where he resided for forty years. About 1870, he went to McGrawville, N Y, where he remained the balance of his life In politics he was a lifelong Democrat, having cast his first presidential vote for Andrew Jackson in 1824 He was elected to several town offices and was Supervisor a number of terms He was a man of strong character and his advice was much sought after in the community He is buried beside his wife in McGrawville, N Y

AMOS KNAPP BROWNELL

(159a229).

Amos Knapp Brownell, son of Jonathan and Desire Lake Brownell, born in Columbus, Chenango County, N Y, July 23, 1805, died in New Jersey, August 16, 1877 married Jane (surname unknown)

He lived with his aunt Mary Brownell Knapp, in Dutchess County, N. Y, for a number of year, and later moved to New York City He was janitor of Rutgers' Female Institute in New York, N Y, for many years.

BENJAMIN JONATHAN BROWNELL

(159a229a).

Benjamin Jonathan Brownell, son of Jonathan and Desire Lake Brownell, born in Columbus Chenango County, N Y, September 1 1807, died October, 1895, married Marilla Greenman, daughter of Lester and Hannah (surname unknown) Greenman, died November 22, 1885, and had two children OSCAR LAVALDIN, born in Solon N Y., June 9, 1841 WILLIAM NELSON ALONZO, born in Syracuse, N Y, August 10, 1849

226

STEPHEN FOSTER BROWNELL.

(159a229c).

Stephen Foster Brownell, son of Jonathan and Desire Lake Brownell, born in Columbus, Chenango County, N. Y., June 17, 1812; died in Hosensack, Pa, May 31, 1897, married probably in Edmeston. N.Y, about 1840, Jane Willis Schermerhorn, daughter of Peter and Rachel Edmonds Schermerhorn, born August 14, 1821, died in Otselic, N. Y., November 29, 1852, and had three children HELEN AMELIA, born in Solon, N Y., January 22, 1842. STEPHEN DUANE, born in Otselic, N Y., April 17, 1850; died in Columbus, N Y., March 12, 1858. CHARLES HOMER, born in Otselic, N. Y., November 24, 1852.

He married second probably in Georgetown, N Y, October, 1860, Irene Nichols Partridge, died in McGrawville, N Y., January 13, 1895. In politics he was a Democrat.

DORMAN LAKE BROWNELL.

(159a229d).

Dorman Lake Brownell, son of Jonathan and Desire Lake Brownell, born in Columbus, Chenango County, N Y., August 16, 1814, died in McGraw, N. Y., January 15, 1877; married Emma Hudson Fish, daughter of Eldridge Fish, born 1824, died in McGraw, N Y., October 17, 1861, and had three children HUDSON LORENDYNE, died in youth EMMA GENEVIEVE born in Solon, N Y, August 28, 1856. ADELBERT, born 1858; died in youth

He married second in Ludlowville, Cayuga County, N. Y, May, 1864, Lovinia Cornelia Owen, daughter of Harry and Permelia Matteson Owen, born March 13, 1840; died in McGraw, N. Y, January 28, 1877, and had two children. EVA GARDNER, born in Ludlowville, N Y, August 4, 1865. EDGAR DORMAN, born in Hedgesville, Berkley County, W Va, January 8, 1867.

He was a farmer and in politics a Democrat. He was a member of the Presbyterian Church.

TRACY PLATT BROWNELL

(159a229e).

Tracy Platt Brownell, son of Jonathan and Desire Lake Brownell born in Columbus, Chenango County, N Y, April 26, 1817, died in Columbus, N Y, April 9 1861, married in Edmeston, Otsego County, N Y, December 29, 1840, by the Rev. J. Tray, to Calista Stephens daughter of Elisha and Sarah Kennedy Stephens born in Edmeston N Y, June 10, 1820, and had four children J AMES AL VARO, born in Edmeston, N Y, December 21, 1842 AD LBLRT L IONARD, born in Edmeston, N Y, June 17, 1844 T R ACY KN APP, born in Edmeston, N Y, July 19, 1847. H ERMON ARCHLUS born in Columbus N Y November 28 1853

H ANN AH PROW NELL PECK

(159a231)

Hanrah Brownell, daughter of Benjamin and Huldah Bullock Brownell born in Sand Lake Rensselaer County, N Y, August 20, 1793, died in Troy, N Y May 29, 1865, married November 24, 1811 Russell Peck, son of Benjamin and Sarah (surname unknown) Peck, born in Canterbury, R. I., August 20, 1784, died in Brunswick, Rensselaer County, N Y August 23, 1862, and had four children EMILY born in Sand Lake, N Y, September 17, 1812, died in Evansville, Ind, August 7, 1842, married George W Sharpe JOHN born in Sand Lake, N Y, August 21, 1814, died in Poestenkill, N Y, July 8, 1817 CYNTHIA born in Sand Lake, N Y, November 11, 1816, died in Poestenkill N. Y. May 24, 1898 married George Wetherwax SARAH JANE, born in Sand Lake, N Y, February 7, 1819, married Caleb B. Crumb

She is buried beside her husband in New Mount Ida Cemetery at Troy, N Y

WILSON BROWNELL

(159a232)

Wilson Brownell son of Benjamin and Huldah Bullock Brownell, born in Sand Lake Rensselaer County, N Y., July 14, 1795, died August 8, 1872, married August 15, 1819 Lydia Brownell, daughter of David and Rhoda Brownell Brownell, born January 28, 1796 died February 10, 1861, and had three children A son HULDAH married John Smith ROSILLA

DAVID BROWNELL.

(150a233).

DAVID BROWNELL.

David Brownell, son of Benjamin and Huldah Bullock Brownell, born in Sand Lake, Rensselaer County, N. Y., July 2, 1798; died in Ellery, Chautauqua County, N. Y., December 1, 1877; married in Pittstown, Rensselaer County, N. Y., May 11, 1826, Thankful Brownell, daughter of Joseph and Prudence Sherman Brownell, born in Pittstown, N. Y., October 18, 1805; died in Ellery, N. Y., April 9, 1846; and had nine children. PRUDENCE JANE, born in Sand Lake, N. Y., April 16, 1827; died in Ellery, N. Y., November 3, 1847. LUCINDA, born in Sand Lake, N. Y., August 6, 1829; died in Ellery, N. Y., November 15, 1847. BENJAMIN, born in Sand Lake, N. Y., April 25, 1831; married Salina Strunk, (2) Emily Vendervort, (3) Cynthia Gardner. SIMEON, born in Ellery, N. Y., February 10, 1833; married Julia Mason. CHARLES HENRY, born in Ellery, N. Y., November 23, 1835; died in Washington C. H., Ohio, July 9, 1902; married Ruth Barnett. ESTIE MARIA, born in Ellery, N. Y., November 10, 1837; died in Dewittville, Chautauqua County, N. Y., December 12, 1882; married Perry Dexter Wood. DAVID SHERMAN, born in Ellery, N. Y., August 26, 1840; died in Washington C. H., Ohio, May 28, 1892; married Mary Ann Klever. HARRIET MINERVA, born in Ellery, N. Y., August 9, 1842; married George Mason. HULDAH EUNICE, born in Ellery, N. Y., November 28, 1844; married Amisa Ives Starr.

He married second, in Chautauqua, Chautauqua County, N. Y., March 15, 1849, Jane Jemima Brownell Burch, (a widow), daughter of Joseph and Elizabeth Van Wert Brownell, born in Ellery, N. Y., January 19, 1820; died in Panama, Chautauqua County, N. Y., December 16, 1891, and had one child. SARA ELIZABETH, born in Ellery, N. Y., May 17, 1850, died in Chautauqua, N. Y., September 16, 1905, married John C. Lewis.

He received his education at the district school in Sand Lake, N. Y., and while a young man he used to build flaxmills in the summer and would work in them winters. In the summer of 1831, he with one of his wife's uncles, came from Pittstown, N. Y., to Ellery, N. Y., with a horse and wagon, returning the same way, looking for a farm to locate upon. James McCoul had offered his farm previously, for eighteen dollars an acre but would not say what he would take now. He found one he could buy, located between Bemus Point, N. Y. and Ellery Center, N. Y., for nine dollars an acre. Before leaving Pittstown, N. Y., he had made up his mind not to buy a farm until he had returned home.

After returning to Pittstown, N. Y., he made up his mind to buy the farm for nine dollars an acre, and wrote his father-in-law, Joseph Brownell, to buy it for him. Before sealing the letter, he again thought he would like the McCoul farm, and instructed his father-in-law to buy it if he could get it for eighteen dollars an acre. Joseph Brownell saw McCoul, making a contract for his farm at eighteen dollars an acre, paying one hundred dollars to bind the bargain, McCoul saying, "that was the easiest hundred dollars he ever received as David Brownell would never come after the farm." He was to be disappointed, for David Brownell with his family started again that fall for Ellery, N. Y., going as far as Buffalo, N. Y., on the Erie canal. McCoul was digging potatoes when Brownell came in sight. Throwing down his hoe, he said "The farm's gone."

In 1851 he moved on the farm joining him on the south, and while living there he built a new house on the farm he had vacated, moving into it in 1857, living there until his death. Although of a strong Christian character, he never identified himself with any church. He never sought political preferment. He was once nominated for a town office and lost the election by one vote. Jedediah Vorce, an Ellery pioneer and intimate friend, rode with him to election, and wanting to vote for a man on the opposition ticket, voted it straight, thus causing his defeat. He was a man of very strong mind. He accumlated quite a property, owning at one time three hundred and twenty-five acres of land on the east shore of Lake Chautauqua, opposite the now famous Chautauqua Assembly. He is buried beside his wife in the Lewis Cemetery in Ellery, N. Y.

Huldah Brownell Bullock

(159a234)

Huldah Brownell, daughter of Benjamin and Huldah Bullock Brownell, born in Sand Lake, Rensselaer County, N. Y., February 28, 1800, married Stephen Van Rensselaer Bullock, and had eight children MINERVA, died September 24, 1869, married John Holcome Underwood REBECCA, married John Gilbert. NELSON CYRUS, married Ann Freeman. LEWIS, died December 18, 1864. JAMES. CHARLES, born in Hartfield, Chautauqua County, N Y, October 4, 1839, married Miriam D Sweet. LAURA, married Seeley Wilmarth.

Rebecca Brownell Goodrich.

(159a235)

Rebecca Brownell, daughter of Benjamin and Huldah Bullock Brownell, born in Sand Lake, Rensselaer County, N Y, August 8, 1802, died August 28, 1872, married Charles Goodrich, and had five children DARWIN ARMITTA, married Charles S Ogden. CAROLINE, married Harlow M. Ogden. HENRIETTA, born in Brocton, Chautauqua County, N. Y., April 13, 1836, married Charles S Ogden. FRANCES

Amos Brownell

(159a236)

Amos Brownell, son of Benjamin and Huldah Bullock Brownell, born July 23, 1804, died in Schaghticoke, N. Y., January 29, 1884; married in Johnsonville, N Y., to Susan Smith, daughter of Rensselaer and Mary Jane Burdick Smith, and had seven children. BENJAMIN, born August 27, 1830, died July 3, 1872, married Anna Stocom ANN ELIZA, born April 27, 1833, died September 30, 1876, married Christopher Andrews. MARY JANE, born in Pittstown, N. Y, November 20, 1836; died in Pittstown, N Y, August 10, 1889, married Wilson Brundige. SARAH MARIA, born in Johnsonville, N Y, March 4, 1839, married Hezekiah C Parkis EDWIN, born May 6, 1840; died July 13, 1868, married Emma Conklin. JULIA, born June 11, 1843, married Harmon (surname unknown) GEORGE R., born June 7, 1846; died February 7, 1903, married Isabelle McClellan

He attended the public schools in Rensselaer County, N. Y., and always lived near Pittstown N. Y. In politics, he was a Republican. He is buried in the Millertown Cemetery at Millertown, Rensselaer County, N. Y.

LEAH BROWNELL GARDNER.

(159a237)

Leah Brownell, daughter of Benjamin and Huldah Bullock Brownell, born in Sand Lake Rensselaer County, N. Y., March 27, 1808, died April 29 1875, married March 2 1833, Benjamin Gardner, son of Eleazer and Thankful Chamberlain Gardner, born February 9, 1810, died August 12, 1873, and had six children. HULDAH THANKFUL, born August 28, 1835, died September 28, 1872; married Alonzo Evans. JULIA LOVINA born August 11, 1837, died October 14, 1899 married Ashbel E Watrous. EMMA JANE, born May 27, 1839, married James H Funk CYNTHIA MARIA, born March 18, 1841, married Benjamin Brownell WILSON BENJAMIN born in Hanover Chautauqua County, N. Y., August 14, 1844, married Helen Moore, (2) Mrs Josephine Southerland Van Wert. GEORGE NELSON, born August 22, 1846, married Lucy A Thatcher

CHARLES BROWNELL

(159a239a)

Charles Brownell, son of Benjamin and Clarissa Baldwin Brownell, born in Sand Lake, Rensselaer County, N. Y., October 16, 1816, died in Springfield, Mo., March 9, 1874, married in Troy, N. Y., September 25, 1839 Lucy Adams, daughter of Harmon and Grace Millard Adams, born in Troy, N. Y., January 9, 1819, died in St Louis Mo, May 15 1884, and had twelve children FRANCIS EDWIN, born in Troy, N. Y., July 18, 1840, died in Washington, D C, March 15, 1894, married Cornelia Harrington BENJAMIN HARMON, born in Troy N. Y., March 16, 1842, died in St Louis, Mo, January 28, 1895, married Laura Martindale, (2) Mary F Fashender WILLIAM ADAMS born in Troy, N Y, December 17,

232

1843, died in Chattanooga, Tenn., March 24, 1875. HARRIET E., born in Troy, N. Y., March 4, 1846, died in Troy, N. Y., June 1, 1846 JANE ANN, born in Troy, N. Y., July 28, 1847; married W. J. Teed. CHARLES CARROL, born in Troy, N. Y., March 8, 1849, died in Troy, N. Y., August, 1850 FREDERIC BETTS, born in Troy, N. Y., December 20, 1851, died in Battle Creek, Mich., January 7, 1902, married Anna Jones. JAMES AMATUS, born in Troy, N. Y., December 13, 1853. JESSIE MATILDA, born in Troy, N. Y., February 20, 1856 GEORGE HENRY born in Troy, N. Y., July 7, 1859, died in St. Louis, Mo., October, 1884, married Clara Sebastian. EUGENE ELLSWORTH, born in Troy, N. Y., August 14, 1861. CHARLES, born in Troy, N. Y., June 19, 1864, died in St. Louis, Mo., December 17, 1886.

He resided in Troy, N. Y., until 1865, when he moved to St. Louis, Mo., residing there three years, then removing to Springfield, Mo., where he lived until his death. He was an architect and builder, continuing in active business until his death. He was a member of the Presbyterian Church and took an active interest in church work. In politics he was a Republican, and was Superintendent of the County House in Troy, N. Y., for a number of years

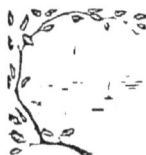

EDWIN BROWNELL.

(159a230b).

Edwin Brownell, son of Benjamin and Clarissa Baldwin Brownell, born in Sand Lake, Rensselaer County, N. Y., June 12, 1821; died in Troy, N. Y., March 14, 1874; married Catherine Witbeck, and had five children. MARY FRANCES, born in Troy, N. Y., July 2, 1846; died May 23, 1901; married James Spencer Gurnsey. ALICE C., born in Troy, N. Y., December 21, 1847; married Rynin Van Alstyne. MARGARET, born in Troy, N. Y., April 5, 1850; died in Troy, N. Y., November 18, 1893. CLARA, born in Troy, N. Y., September 28, 1852; married Rev. Edward Payson Johnson. KATHERINE, born in Lansingburgh, N. Y., October 14, 1864; married Henry Lenard Wilcox.

EDWIN BROWNELL.

COMFORT BROWNELL WILCOX.

(163121).

Comfort Brownell, daughter of Charles Brownell, married November 17, 1779, Abner Wilcox, son of William and Elizabeth Wilcox, and had one child. GEORGE, born January 26, 1781.

JOSEPH BROWNELL.

(163123).

Joseph Brownell, son of Charles Brownell, married Almy Freeborn, and had six children. SILAS, married a Simpson. MARY FREEBORN, born 1799; died March 12, 1869; married William Smith. JOSEPH, married Elizabeth Wilcox. HENRY FREEBORN. ENOS.

CHARLES, born 1807; died September 14, 1887; married Elizabeth Frances Stevens, (2) Sarah Jane Furness

SARAH BURGESS WILLIAMS.

(163415)

Sarah Burgess, daughter of James and Dorothy Brownell Burgess, died April 13, 1851, married 1787, Nathaniel Williams, and had two children CINDARILLA, born July 10, 1789, died December 17, 1863. SARAH, born November 25, 1795, died October 13, 1871, married Christopher Tanner.

LUCY BROWNELL TOMPKINS

(163431).

Lucy Brownell, daughter of Samuel and Ruth Briggs Brownell, born February 6, 1766, married July 4, 1784, Gilbert Tompkins, son of Joseph and Martha Pierce Tompkins, born October 26, and had one child BROWNELL, born November 17 1785; died October 4, 1864; married Polly Blair, (2) Matilda Tompkins.

MARY BROWNELL TOMPKINS.

(163433).

Mary Brownell, daughter of Samuel and Ruth Briggs Brownell, born July 8, 1770; died May 10, 1844; married February 5, 1788, Gilbert Tompkins, son of Joseph and Martha Pierce Tompkins, and had nine children. WILLIAM B, born November 4, 1789; died March 15, 1862, married Margaret Briggs, (2) Annis Gilbert SAMUEL, born 1793, died 1871, married Lucy Whitcomb JAMES B, married Mary White. MARIAH, born February 23, 1795, died February 8, 1881, married Gideon Manchester. PHOEBE, born 1802, died July 8, 1837, married Nathan Peck RUTH, died 1865, married William Smith PHILIP, born March 29, 1804; died March 28, 1894; married Mary A. Simmons. LUCY, born 1806; died 1864, married Chester Holcomb MARY, born 1809; died December 20, 1877, married Nathan Peck

CALVIN AND SARAH BROWNELL WHITCOMB.

SARAH BROWNELL WHITCOMB.

(163424).

Sarah Brownell, daughter of Samuel and Ruth Briggs Brownell, born October 2, 1772; died July 28, 1860; married January 4, 1798, Calvin Whitcomb, and had seven children. LUCY, born October 4, 1798; died June 8, 1836; married Samuel Tompkins. SARAH, born September 28, 1800; died March 2, 1878, married Dennis Morse. MARY, born July 5, 1803; died June 20, 1806; married Adolphus Blair. A son, who died young. RUTH, born October 29, 1810; died June 8, 1869; married Nelson D. Emmons. JUDITH, born January 23, 1814; died November 22, 1902; married Arunah Gil-

SUSANNAH BROWNELL SIMMONS

(163435).

Susannah Brownell, daughter of Samuel and Ruth Briggs Brownell, born in Westport, Mass., March 16, 1775, died in Paris Hill, N. Y., married in Westport, Mass, 1795, to Adam Simmons, born in Little Compton, R I; died in Paris Hill, N. Y., and had ten children. ALANSON, born March 25, 1796; married Mary Bartlett. PHILIP, born December 10, 1799; died May 22, 1879, married Mirinda Head. CARLOS, born January 29, 1802, married Lydia Bailey, (2) Louisa Meggs. CLARISSA born March 7, 1804, married Nathaniel Pierce. CALISTA, born March 22, 1806, died November 15, 1886, married Harvey Head. RUTH, born April 29, 1808, died November 15, 1886, married Seth Hitchcock. MEHITABLE, born February 24, 1811; died 1898, married Lysander Head. SUSANNAH, born August 8, 1813, died at the age of seven years. SAMUEL, born February 28, 1817, married Mariah (surname unknown). GAMALIEL born May 2, 1819, married Alice Prentice.

She received her education in the public schools. She was an active member of the Congregational Church and was a devoted wife and mother. She is buried beside her husband at Paris Hill, N Y

EUNICE BROWNELL HITCHCOCK

(163437).

Eunice Brownell daughter of Samuel and Ruth Briggs Brownell, born in Westport, Mass., January 25, 1780 died in Hamilton N. Y., August 6, 1850, married November 19, 1798 Capt Joseph Hitchcock, son of Deacon Joseph and Hannah Livermore Hitchcock, born in Brimfield, Mass., March 2, 1775, died in Madison, N Y, April 15, 1861, and had eleven children. RUTH, born in Hamilton, N. Y, October 23, 1799; died July 7, 1858, married Otis Simmons. HANNAH, born in Hamilton, N Y, September 4, 1801; died December 3, 1873, married Thurston Wood. SAMUEL, born in Hamilton, N Y, August 7, 1803, died April 22, 1872, married Prudence Groves. MERON, born in Lebanon, N. Y June 19, 1805, died January 29, 1862, married Ezia Campbell. FALLY, born in Lebanon, N Y, October 14, 1807, died December 2 1884, married Benjamin Simmons. JOSEPH, born in Lebanon, N. Y, April

30, 1810; died August 23, 1892; married C Maria Campbell. ISAAC, born in Lebanon, N. Y., July 18, 1812, died March 10, 1877, married Antrice Pierce. SETH, born in Lebanon, N. Y., July 17, 1814; died in Madison, N Y, November 6 1900; married Ruth Simmons, (2) Eliza Chilson. EUNICE, born in Lebanon, N Y., October 16, 1816, died October 9, 1890; married Frederick Sawdey. MARY, born in Lebanon, N. Y, January 17, 1819, died March 31, 1869, married Heman Hotchkin. WILLIAM, born in Lebanon, N Y, August 18, 1823, married Cornelia Waters (2) Mary Pierce Kron

She was a member of the Congregational Church for many years A devoted wife and mother, and is buried beside her husband at Lebanon, N Y.

ABISHA BROWNELL SIMMONS.

(163438).

Abisha Brownell, daughter of Samuel and Ruth Briggs Brownell, born 1782, died 1813, married William Simmons, and had four children FALLY, born April, 1803; died 1873, married George Pierce MELISSA, born September 9, 1805, died October 20, 1885; married John Tompkins PHOEBE, born July 4, 1807; died December 21, 1884, married Ezekiel Pierce. MARY, born September 9, 1809, married John B. Tompkins

SAMUEL BROWNELL

(163439)

Samuel Brownell, son of Samuel and Ruth Briggs Brownell, born in Westport, Mass, September 2, 1785, died in Madison, N Y., March 6, 1865, married 1812, Abigail Barker, born 1792, died in Madison, N. Y., 1850, and had eight children. RUTH, born in Madison, N Y, 1813; died in Madison, N Y, 1888; married Sidney Putnam RUSSELL, born in Madison, N Y., 1815, died in Madison, N Y., 1868, married Electa Coe SAMUEL, born in Madison, N Y., 1816 died in Clinton, N Y, 1887; married Susan Bronson WILLIAM, born in Madison, N Y, 1816, died in Waterloo, N Y., 1885; married Elvira Baldwin ELIZABETH, born in Madison N. Y, 1817, died in Hamilton, N Y, September 6, 1896, married Sanford Gardner. HAMILTON, born in Madison, N. Y., November 18, 1821, died in Oneonta, N. Y., July 31, 1900; married Lucy L. Simmons. PHILIP, died in early youth. LEVERETT, died in youth.

He married second Frances Gurnsey. He was a farmer and always resided in Madison, N. Y. He was a member of the Congregational Church

LUCY BROWNELL PEASE

(163439a)

Lucy Brownell, daughter of Samuel and Ruth Briggs Brownell, born June 16, 1788, died 1828, married 1812, Ami Pease, born 1791, died 1869, and had four children   HANNAH, born 1814; died 1831. SAMUEL B., born 1817, died 1881, married Emeline Childs ABISHA, born 1821, married Samuel Cleveland. WILLIAM.

LORING R BROWNELL.

(163451)

Loring R. Brownell, son of George and Lucy Richmond Brownell, born in Little Compton, R I, August 28, 1771, died at sea, married January 17, 1795, Betsey Burgess, daughter of James and Dorothy Brownell Burgess, and had one child. LORING

He was a seafaring man, owning the schooner of which he was captain. He came to Madison County, N. Y, with his parents and bought the farm upon which they afterward lived He then returned to his vessel to make one more voyage to the West Indies, taking with him his two brothers Peris Richmond Brownell and Israel Putnam Brownell. None of them ever returned nor were any tidings from them received. This was about 1795 He left a widow and one son, Loring Brownell, who, having been born after his father left on this last fatal voyage, was never seen by him   His son became a prominent man and died in Piqua, O, leaving five children four sons and one daughter

NATHAN BROWNELL

(163459a)

Nathan Brownell, son of George and Lucy Richmond Brownell, born in Little Compton, R. I., March 13, 1789, died in Madison County, N. Y., May 22, 1866, married December 30, 1817, Polly Brown, born January 25, 1800, died April 1, 1837, and had ten children. LUCY R. born August 28, 1819, died August 29, 1819. LUCY R., born August 17, 1820, died December 5, 1866, married Jerome Terry. (2) Alfred Babcock. NICANOR, born February 14, 1823, died October 11, 1887, married Caroline E. Hunt. GEORGE, born March 29, 1825, died April 14, 1825. GEORGE, born May 8, 1826, married Celestia Fuller. NATHAN, born June 6, 1828, married Rozella Hart. PARIS R., born April 3, 1831, died March 23, 1833. PARIS R., born August 31, 1833, married Anna C. Burdick. PUTNAM CUSHING, born June 8, 1835, married Cornelia E. Morgan. HARVEY B., born April 1, 1837, died July 9, 1839.

He followed farming for some time after his marriage, and later engaged in the mercantile business in Madison Center, N. Y., Hubbardsville, N. Y., and Brookfield, N. Y., where he resided at the time of his death. He was a man of broad ideas and a leading member of society in the community.

EZRA BROWNELL

(163461)

Ezra Brownell, son of Ezra and Hope Borden Brownell, born January 19, 1769, died 1813, married Miss Davidson, and had two children. AMANDA, born December 5, 1796, married a Bliss or a Blinn. CYNTHIA born March 3, 1799, married an Abrams.

He married second Nancy Dorn, daughter of Alexander and Rachel Egmont Dorn, born November 4, 1783, died October 12, 1865, and had six children. RACHEL, born in Florida, N. Y., July 25, 1802, married Thomas Wiltsie. MARY, born in Florida, N. Y., June 23, 1804, died July, 1881, married Joseph Earl. ALVAH, born in Florida, N. Y., March 24, 1806, died May, 1871, married Margaret Steinberg. HOPEFUL, born in Florida, N. Y., January 14, 1808, married a Segur. GEORGE born in Florida, N. Y., November 6, 1809, died June 15, 1867, married Joanna Gough.

EZRA, born in Florida, N. Y., December 6, 1811; died May 13, 1878; married Maria Sternberg.

PHOEBE MACOMBER BROWNELL LAWTON.

(163460d).

PHOEBE M. BROWNELL LAWTON.

Phoebe Macomber Brownell, daughter of Ezra and Hope Borden Brownell, born in Rhode Island, November 19, 1788; died in Skaneateles, Onondaga County, N. Y., December 30, 1868; married November 15, 1806, Abner Lawton, born in Rhode Island, April 23, 1784; died in Skaneateles, N. Y., February 20, 1855, and had thirteen children. JOHN, born in Cairo, Green County, N. Y., October 3, 1807; died December 21, 1869; married Elizabeth Giles, (2) Sarah Hoxie. ABRAM A., born in Cario, N. Y., September 8, 1809; died May 21, 1896; married Phebe Giles. MARIA, born in Cario, N. Y., September 13, 1811; died November 27, 1826. DAVID, born in Cairo, N. Y., August 7, 1813; died 1846; married Eliza E. Drake. WILLIAM B., born in Cairo, N. Y., June 23, 1815; married Hannah Macomber. HANNAH, born in Cairo, N. Y., January 7, 1818; died 1872; married Jerome B. Stillson. ELIZABETH, born in Cairo, N. Y., October 22, 1819; married Dr. George Campbell. JULIA, born in Cairo, N. Y., October 22, 1822; died 1847. ANGELICA, born in Cairo, N. Y., May 17, 1824; married Dr. William Abell. HENRY M., born in Cairo, N. Y., March 27, 1826; died in Rome, N. Y., November 9, 1901; married Adelia Ann Parker. SARAH M., born in Cairo, N. Y., February 9, 1828; died August 4, 1857; married Albert Rogers. HARRIET, born in Skaneateles, N. Y., February 1, 1830; married Henry D. McCulloch. EDWIN F., born in Skaneateles, N. Y., April 19, 1832; married Mariam Austin.

She was a member of the Society of Friends, and a woman beloved by all who knew her.

OSMIN BROWNELL.

(163481)

Osmin Brownell, son of Nathaniel and Sarah Tompkins Brownell, born in Westport, Mass, September 27, 1790, married about 1833, by the Rev Mace Shepard, to Mary Brownell Simmons, daughter of Isaac and Abisha Briggs Simmons, born in Little Compton R I, May 3, 1800, died in Fall River, Mass., December 24, 1870, and had two children ALEXANDER C, born in Westport, Mass, January 17, 1836, married Emily M. Irish WILLIAM, HENRY, born in Little Compton, R. I, November 30, 1838

He obtained his education in the public schools at Westport, Mass He was a farmer and always lived in Westport, Mass., and Little Compton, R I He was a member of the Home Guards in 1812, and was a lifelong Whig. He was much interested in the public school system and served for many years upon the school board He was a member of the Congregational Church for many years, and a man of strong character

ALFRED BROWNELL

(163482)

Alfred Brownell, son of Nathaniel and Sarah Tompkins Brownell, born September 21, 1792, died September 16, 1867, married November 22, 1818, Christina Stoddard, born September 28, 1798, and had five children. NATHANIEL, born October 1, 1821; died November 11, 1901; married Abby L Barker SUSAN, born February 29, 1824, died September, 1888, married Stephen Losey SAMUEL CLARKE, born in Madison, Madison County, N Y, April 2, 1829, married Catherine Fox. (2) Abbie Maus SARAH, born November 3, 1830, married Theo. L. Spencer. PHILIP, born March 23, 1836

SAMUEL BUCKMAN RICHMOND

(163711).

Samuel Buckman Richmond, son of Nathaniel and Anna Brownell Richmond, born April 4, 1767; married November 8, 1796, Eunice Mack, and had nine children NATHANIEL, born September

9, 1797, married Lavenia Avery. BROWNELL, born February 6, 1799, died December 25, 1803, married Jane Elliot. SAMUEL, born July 15, 1801, died March 16, 1866, married Cynthia Wood. CLARA, born October 27, 1803, married Abel Wilcox. SYLVESTER, born August 15, 1805; died February 9, 1890; married Lucy Avery. FRANKLIN, born March 2, 1808, died May 2, 1876. ALFRED, born October 23, 1811, died April, 1880, married Amanda Knapp. ANNA, born September 24, 1813 married Archimades Gray NANCY, born May 8 1816, died June 6, 1885; married John Nelson

ELIZABETH RICHMOND JONES.

(163712)

Elizabeth Richmond, daughter of Nathaniel and Anna Brownell Richmond, born about February 15, 1770, married December 25, 1794, Isaac Jones, and had eight children RICHMOND, born 1796. ELIZABETH, born 1797, died 1824 SYLVESTER, born 1800 CLARISSA, born 1802, married Alvah Chase RUTH, born 1805. MARY born 1807 NANCY, born 1812 married Isaiah Barney SARAH, born 1814, married Davis A Blake

JONATHAN RICHMOND

(163713).

Jonathan Richmond son of Nathaniel and Anna Brownell Richmond, born July 1, 1774, married February 11, 1807, Rebecca Almy daughter of William and Mary (surname unknown) Almy, and had twelve children. WILLIAM A, born January 28, 1807, married Loraine Page. SARAH ALMY, born September 30, 1809, married Jonathan Lund MARIA C, born June 7, 1811 MARY CHURCH, born May 21, 1813, married Hamilton Brownell JONATHAN, born August 23, 1815. REBECCA, born March 22, 1817, married John Marsh ELIZA JANE, born May 30 1819, married Charles Jones CHARLES H, born March 6, 1821, married Amy W Howland FREDERIC D, born September 5, 1822; married Abbey E. Swift FALIFE, born July 14, 1824 CORNELIA R., born September 21, 1825 NANCY, born August 11, 1827, married William D Eagles

PEREZ BROWNELL.

(163721).

Perez Brownell, son of Pardon and Prudence Shaw Brownell, married Mary Grinnell, and had three children Amy, married a Smith Mary Elizabeth.

The following taken from Eliott G. Storke's History of Cayuga County, N. Y., gives the early movements of Pardon Brownell and his sons Perez, Thurston, Jonathan and Gilbert "In 1790, Gilbert, Jonathan Thurston and Perez Brownell came from Little Compton, R. I., and commenced work, on the Indian Reservation, north of Aurora They were disposed by the sheriff and built a cabin near R. M. Atwater's residence in Ledyard, one and one-half miles north of the south line In the spring of 1791, Perez brought his family, Jonathan brought his in 1792. Their father, Pardon Brownell bought lot 23 in Genoa and gave Gilbert two hundred acres on the east side, Thurston two hundred acres on the west side, and Perez two hundred acres in the middle. Perez moved on his in the spring of 1793 His home was west of J. G. Burgess' stone quarry. Gilbert came and boarded with him Mrs. Brownell's sister was a member of the family November 4, 1793, Gilbert and Amy were married The marriage certificate is in the possession of their daughter, Mrs. Clarissa Chadwick and reads: This certifies that Gilbert Brownell and Amy Grinnell were joined in marriage November 4, 1793 by Aaron Kinne, minister of the gospel and missionary in the western settlement.

The incidents connected with this event are somewhat romantic. It seems a contract was made between them, but unfortunately there was neither civil officer or settled minister who could make them one. It was agreed that when the missionary came they would be married After weeks and months of delay Kinne called at Perez Brownell's Gilbert was engaged at some distance from the house, logging Amy blew a conch shell, now in possession of Mrs. Chadwick and called her soon to be husband soiled and besmeared. Gilbert came in and without change of raiment stood up before the man of God and they were married Immediately after the ceremony he went back to toil This was probably the first marriage in the town. Gilbert built his house and lived a little southeast of J. G. Burgess' residence A fine old apple tree marks the locality. Perez subsequently sold to Joseph Goodyear and then Gilbert changed

21.

farms with Goodyear Gilbert bought Thurston's lands and eventually owned a large portion of lot 23 He lived and died where H. S King now lives Of a family of nine children there only remains Edmund, Mrs. Clarissa Chadwick and Mrs John H. Carter Perez subsequently moved to Ohio and died there Thurston went to Philadelphia, Pa Jonathan remained in Ledyard He built the house where Charles E Slocum lives and died there His daughters were reigning belles in their day and much admired

THURSTON BROWNELL.

(163722)

Thurston Brownell, son of Pardon and Prudence Shaw Brownell, married and had four children and possibly more PARDON ROBERT SMITH, married Caroline Irons LAWRENCE SUSAN, married an Anthony

He was Justice of the Peace in Onondaga County, N. Y

JONATHAN BROWNELL.

(163723)

Jonathan Brownell, son of Pardon and Prudence Shaw Brownell, born in Little Compton, R. I., April 24, 1767; died in Ledyard, N. Y., October 26, 1835, married Mary Briggs, daughter of Cornelius and Mary Brownell Briggs, born April 9, 1770, died November 15, 1809, and had nine children LYDIA, born in Ledyard, N. Y., September 8, 1792, died January 16, 1836, married Charles Hubbard CLARA, born in Ledyard, N. Y., May 8, 1794, died in Ledyard, N. Y, May 11, 1796. CALISTA, born in Ledyard, N. Y., May 1, 1796; married Lancing Budlong. HARRIET, born in Ledyard, N Y, August 15, 1798, married Lewis Himrod LUCY, born in Ledyard, N Y, September 20 1800 died September 11, 1835, married William Todd. JONATHAN, born in Ledyard, N Y, August 23, 1802 HAMILTON, born in Ledyard, N Y., February 22, 1805 married Mary Richmond WILLIAM, born in Ledyard, N Y, May 12, 1805, married Clarissa Brooks, (2) Lucy Franklin CORNELIUS B., born in Ledyard, N Y, November 15, 1809, died in Ledyard, N. Y., June 14, 1810

He married second Mrs Sarah Kingsley Curtis, (a widow) born September 6, 1786, died October 7, 1864, and had four children

Mary B, born in Ledyard, N Y, April 8, 1813, married John Morgan, (2) Charles C Young Elizabeth, born in Ledyard, N. Y, July 28, 1815 died January 13 1836 married George M Richmond (2) George Marsh Richmond born in Ledyard, N Y., April 29 1820; died 1863 Cornelia Budlong, born in Ledyard, N. Y, September 12, 1823, married James Avery.

Gilbert Brownell

(163724)

Gilbert Brownell, son of Pardon and Prudence Shaw Brownell, born in Little Compton, R. I, May 7, 1770, died January 31, 1852, married November 4, 1793. Amy Tillinghast Grinnell, and had nine children Sylvester, born in Cayuga County N Y, March 24. 1795, died September 12, 1828 Phoebe Shaw, born in Cayuga County N Y, November 10, 1796, died August 28, 1865. Clarissa born in Cayuga County, N Y, November 10, 1798; died March 7, 1889, married a Chadwick. Richard Grinnell, born in Cayuga County, N Y, August 9 1801; died July 30 1867, married Mary Dunning, (2) Mrs Adaline Seymour Ann, married William Wood. Mercy Church born in Cayuga County, N Y, February 8, 1804, died August 20, 1881 married John H Carter Gilbert, born in Cayuga County, N Y, March 22, 1806; died July 7, 1850, married a Ballard Edmund, born in Cayuga County, N Y, May 5 1808, died in Cayuga County, N Y, January 26, 1880, married Ann Niblo Horatio Nilson, born in Cayuga County, N Y, October 3, 1812, died April 8, 1863; married Jane Tratalgar

Elizabeth Brownell Brightman

(163725).

Elizabeth Brownell, daughter of Pardon and Prudence Shaw Brownell, married Daniel Brightman, and had daughter Betsey and probably others

ANNA BROWNELL CHASE.

(163726)

Anna Brownell daughter of Pardon and Prudence Shaw Brownell, born in Little Compton, R I, November 26, 1772, married Henry Chase, and had five children. ANNA. ALICE. SARAH. ELIZABETH. HENRY.

EDMUND BROWNELL.

(163727)

Edmund Brownell, son of Pardon and Prudence Shaw Brownell, born in Little Compton, R I, November 7, 1775, died February 1, 1840, married Mary Bailey, and had one child. MARY.

He married second Priscilla Briggs, daughter of Job and Sarah Church Briggs, born January 10, 1785, died December 1, 1868, and had eleven children. GILBIRT, married Eliza Emmerson. HARRIET, married Dr James Peckham PARDON, married Abby White. AMEY ANN, born April 25, 1811, died March 21, 1883, married William Richmond Atwood SOPHIA AUGUSTA, married Robert White. DEBORAH BRIGGS, born in Little Compton, R. I. August 1, 1822; married Gershom Bradford Weston CORNELIA PRUDENCE, married Felix G Matthers. RICHARD SYLVESTER, married Mabel Stuart ELIZABETH LOUISA

He made three journeys on horseback from Rhode Island to Cayuga Lake, to visit his brothers and sisters.

THOMAS CHURCH BROWNELL.

(163771).

Thomas Church Brownell, son of Sylvester and Mercy Church Brownell, born October 19, 1779, died January 13, 1865, married August 6, 1811, Charlotte Dickinson, born in St Johns, Nova Scotia, April 12, 1787, and had eight children SARAH F, born September 17, 1813; died September 11, 1869 THOMAS S., born September 9, 1815, died May 5, 1841. CHARLOTTE D., born August 4, 1817; died May 23, 1825 H TUDOR, born August 15, 1819, died August 2, 1887, married Gertrude Kissam FRANCES I, born January 15, 1822, died September 4, 1890, married Thomas Holland. M

LOUISA, born June 15, 1824, died October 5, 1883, married Gordon W Burnham. HARRIET P, born September 25, 1826, married Edward I Thomas, (2) Charles R Chapman ELIZABETH S, born September 25, 1826, died September 26, 1828

His father was a farmer and he was educated at Bristol Academy, Taunton at Rhode Island College (now Brown University), and at Union College, where he graduated in 1804 The next year he became a tutor in Union College, in 1807 professor of Belles-lettres and moral philosophy, and in 1809 was chosen the first professor of chemistry and mineralogy. The following year was spent in traveling through Great Britain and Ireland, and in gathering material and apparatus for the department under his charge. In 1813 he began to turn his attention to preparation for the ministry, and having become an Episcopalian was ordained by Bishop Hobart, in Trinity Church, New York, April 11, 1816 In connection with his professional duties he gave himself to the work of a missionary in Schenectady and its vicinity. In the summer of 1818, he became an assistant minister in Trinity Church, New York. He was consecrated bishop of Connecticut October 27 1819, and removed at once to his new field of labor Washington (now Trinity) College, at Hartford, Conn., took its rise under his auspices in 1824, he was its first president, resigning in 1831 He became presiding bishop in 1852, upon the death of Bishop Chase of Illinois. He was author of "The Family Prayer Book," which contains a commentary, historical, explanatory, doctrinal and practical, on the liturgy of the Episcopal Church In 1839-40 he prepared the "Religion of the Heart and Life" (5 vol 12 mo), a compilation from the best writers on experimental and practical piety, with introductions, etc

RUTH BROWNELL CHURCH

(163772)

Ruth Brownell daughter of Sylvester and Mercy Church Brownell, born in Little Compton, R I August 3, 1781, died January 26 1861, married Joseph Church, and had seven children. SUSAN PERRY THOMAS BROWNELL GAMALIEL THADUS HERBERT ABBY TAYLOR CHARLES HENRY JOHN EDWIN

Her mother, Mercy Church, was great-granddaughter of Colonel Benjamin Church, famous in the Indian wars, and who led the party which killed King Philip at Mount Hope, Bristol R I, in 1676

Mercy Brownell Almy Cory

(163773)

Mercy Brownell, daughter of Sylvester and Mercy Church Brownell, born in Little Compton, R. I., July 28, 1783; died January 22, 1860, married Samuel Almy, and had two children SAMUEL. CAROLINE BARTLETT

She married second Isaac Cory, and had five children. ALEXANDER HAMILTON. ELIZABETH BLIGH ALBERT BROWNELL. ISAAC. MARY CODMAN

Sylvester Brownell

(163774).

Sylvester Brownell, son of Sylvester and Mercy Church Brownell, born in Little Compton, R. I., August 12, 1785; died June 12, 1863; married Abby Taylor, and had four children. SOPHIA TAYLOR. FREDERIC HORATIO. ABBY MARIA. CLARA MARIA

Pardon Brownell

(163775).

Pardon Brownell, son of Sylvester and Mercy Church Brownell, born in Little Compton, R. I., January 13, 1788, died in East Hartford, Conn., March 10, 1846, married December 1, 1815, Lucia Emilia DeWolf, daughter of Charles and Elizabeth Rogerson DeWolf, born in Bristol, R. I., November 23, 1795; died in Bristol, R. I., September 25, 1884 and had six children. FRANCIS DEWOLF, born in Providence, R. I., December 28, 1817, died in East Hartford, Conn., September 16, 1833 HENRY HOWARD, born in Providence, R. I., February 6, 1820, died October 31, 1872. CHARLES DEWOLF, born in Providence, R. I., February 6, 1822, married Henrietta Knowlton Angell EMILIA DEWOLF, born in Providence, R. I. December 10, 1823, died in East Hartford Conn, November 19, 1838. EDWARD ROGERSON, born in East Hartford, Conn., October 2, 1825; died in the West Indies, December 30, 1889. CLARENCE MELVILLE, born in East Hartford, Conn, May 2, 1828, died on the White Nile, Africa, May 2, 1862

He was a physician and practiced his profession in Providence,

R I until 1824, when he moved to East Hartford, Conn, where he remained until his death He was surgeon on the privateer Yankee in the war of 1812 which ship was fitted out by his wife's family, the "DeWolf's"

RICHMOND BROWNELL

(163776).

Richmond Brownell, son of Sylvester and Mercy Church Brownell, born in Little Compton, R I, March 4, 1790; died October 29 1866, married Harriet Bayhes Church and had seven children GEORGE EDWARD , ALBERT AUGUSTUS , WILLIAM RICHMOND , CHARLES FREDERIC , MARY CHURCH ; FRANCIS SEYMOUR , HARRIET CHURCH

He was a physician and practiced his profession with much success

JONATHAN BROWNELL

(163777)

Jonathan Brownell, son of Sylvester and Mercy Church Brownell, born March 31, 1792, died August 29, 1877; married November 2 1815, Elizabeth Hall Simmons, daughter of Davis Simmons, born September 25, 1790, died May 4 1862 and had seven children MARIA LOUISE born January 1, 1817, died March 8, 1888 WALTER SIMMONS born September 30 1820, died November 20, 1904, married Delana Ann Pierce. MARY, born June 16, 1823, died August 10, 1857, married Leslie Combs SYLVESTER, born June 28, 1825, died April 24 1884 CHARLOTTE, born July 11, 183 married A. S Talbot JAMES F S, born October 3, 1833, died July 25, 1873 FREDERICK R born November 28, 1837, died February 5 1903 married Annie Dykes Coggeshall

He served in the war of 1812, attaining the rank of Colonel. He was a farmer and lived upon a farm located near Little Compton, R I, which is still in possession of the family

Lydia Brownell Richmond Wendell

(163778).

Lydia Brownell, daughter of Sylvester and Mercy Church Brownell, born in Little Compton, R. I., April 10, 1794; died September 17, 1882; married William Richmond. She married second Judge John L. Wendell.

Prudence Brownell Brown.

(163779)

Prudence Brownell, daughter of Sylvester and Mercy Church Brownell, born in Little Compton, R. I., March 31, 1796, died June 21, 1878, married William Augustus Brown, and had ten children. William Augustus, Julia Elizabeth, Frederic Horatio. Lucia Emilia Clarke. Theodore. John Shaw, Harkift Church, Helen Wallace Rebecca

Isaac Brownell.

(163922)

Isaac Brownell. son of William and Elizabeth Pearce Brownell, born in Little Compton, R. I. July 1, 1774; married in Little Compton, R. I., September 28, 1800, by Lemuel Taber, J. P., to Betsey Wood, daughter of Abner and Mary (surname unknown) Wood, born 1779, and had four children. Elisha, born in Little Compton, R. I., October 14, 1801 Abner, born September 18, 1803. Nancy born December 8, 1805 Elizabeth, born August 15, 1808

Sylvester Brownell

(163924)

Sylvester Brownell, son of William and Eunice Palmer Brownell, born in Little Compton, R. I, July 31, 1782, married in Newport, R. I., October 14, 1804, by the Rev Michael Eddy, to Sarah Weeden Wilson daughter of Jonathan Wilson, Jr, born in Newport, R. I. 1778, died in Newport, R. I., September

10 1819, and had seven children HARRIET, born August 1, 1805 WILLIAM, born January 1, 1807, died in Newport, R I, January 9, 1892 HENRY MUMFORD, born June 19, 1808 JONATHAN WILSON, born May 2, 1810; died in Newport, R I, October 24, 1814 HENRY MUMFORD, born April 28, 1812 HANNAH WILSON, born March 2, 1815 SARAH WILSON, born October 2, 1818

CLARKE BROWNELL

(163929)

Clarke Brownell, son of William and Betsey Grinnell Brownell, born October 16, 1793, married Sarah Tompkins, daughter of Benjamin and Deborah Simmons Tompkins, and had eight children. WARREN, born 1815 OLIVER C., born October 27, 1819, married Ann B Brownell BENJAMIN P born February 17, 1823, married Amy Pierce. ISAAC T., born December 25, 1826, married Roby Peirce. DEBORAH ANN, born October 20, 1829, married Ichabod Wilbur EBEN, born September 28, 1834 WILLIAM, born March 14, 1837. RICHMOND, born June 30, 1840

DANIEL BROWNELL

(163962).

Daniel Brownell son of George and Elizabeth Peckham Brownell, born March 14, 1782, married November 11, 1810, Hannah Allen, daughter of David and Elizabeth Butler Allen, born March 11, 1780, and had five children. FREDERICK R., born September 15, 1811, married Jane Simmons LEONARD, born May 20, 1813; married Mary A Howland ANDREW P, born January 26, 1815, married Eliza Dyer ELIZABETH, born 1818; died 1836 GEORGE L, born July 15, 1823, died January 13, 1903.

PELEG BROWNELL

(163968)

Peleg Brownell, son of George and Elizabeth Peckham Brownell, born in Little Compton, R. I., March 13, 1798, died in Little Compton, R. I, November 24, 1876, married in Little Compton, R.

I., January 25, 1819, by Mase Shepard, to Lydia Randall Church, daughter of Caleb and Hannah Wilbur Church, born in Little Compton, R. I ; died in Fall River, Mass., and had six children. LAURA A. C., born in Little Compton, R. I., April 7, 1821 ; died in Fall River, Mass., June 1, 1889, married Captain Thomas J Smith. RACHEL A , born in Little Compton, R. I , January 9, 1823, died in Fall River, Mass, 1894, married Richmond P Woodman. MARIA, born in Little Compton, R I , May 26, 1825, died in Fall River, Mass, February 26, 1897, married Jonathan I Hillard HORATIO H., born in Little Compton, R. I., June 6, 1830, married Cynthia B Tompkins ESTHER W., born in Little Compton, R. I., 1832, died in Little Compton, R I , September 28, 1859. ALVIN C , born in Little Compton, R. I , September 28, 1834, married Amelia Leonard.

He was a farmer and always resided in Little Compton, R. I. In politics, he was a Whig, and later a Republican. He was a member of the Congregational Church at Little Compton, R I , many years

WRIGHT BROWNELL.

(163972)

Wright Brownell, son of Stephen and Mary Coggeshall Brownell, born in Little Compton, R. I., December 17, 1806, died March 1, 1880 married Naomi Beecher, daughter of Erastus and Naomi Crowell Beecher, born in Martha's Vineyard, Mass, March 10, 1811, died in New Bedford, Mass., July 3, 1880, and had five children MARY J, born in New Bedford, Mass, September 9, 1829, died December 23, 1904 ELIZABETH M , born in New Bedford, Mass., September 28, 1833, died February 13, 1891 CHARLES WRIGHT, born in New Bedford, Mass, November 26, 1839, died in New Bedford, Mass, March 19, 1895, married Martha Bourne Tripp FREDERICK B., born in New Bedford, Mass, March 8, 1841, died in New Bedford Mass, September 8, 1843 EMMA I. C , born in New Bedford, Mass, October, 1844: died October 30, 1869

He was a contractor and stone mason, and always resided in New Bedford, Mass He was a member of the Congregational Church, and took and active interest in church work He was a lifelong Republican, and was much interested in the formation of that party   He is buried beside his wife in New Bedford, Mass

Perry Brownell

(163973)

Perry Brownell, son of Stephen and Mary Coggeshall Brownell, born November 9, 1808, died July 20, 1885, married 1828, Susan Russell Howland, daughter of Abner and Susan Sherman Howland, and had six children. Hannah, born October 7, 1830, died September 2 1831 Sarah M born September 5, 1831, married William T. Lavare. Charles, born April 29, 1833; died July 30, 1833 Abner Howland, born September 6, 1834, died November 17, 1900, married Elizabeth Russell Susan, born July 23, 1836 died in infancy. Susan, born April 30, 1838, died in infancy

He married second May 30 1839 Sarah A Vinal, and had seven children Gideon V., born June 17, 1840, died 1841 Gideon V., born October 3 1842, died April 10, 1892 William H. P, born January 30, 1845, married Julia Almy John F., born March 3, 1847, died March 27, 1893, married Sarah M Dunham. Susan Amelia, born December 24, 1848, died March 24, 1894, married John L Osborn. Mary Ann, born May 22, 1851; died in infancy Mary Ann, born October 7, 1856, married Albert Steffen

Edith W. Brownell Wilbur

(163974)

Edith W Brownell, daughter of Stephen and Mary Coggeshall Brownell, born July 24, 1811; died November, 1895, married James Wilbur, and had four children Stephen B. James L. Albert C Charles F.

Artemas Brownell.

(164223).

Artemas Brownell, son of Gideon and Phœbe Brown Brownell, born 1781, died at sea, married 1802-3, Sarah Grinnell, daughter of Zebedee and Abigail Brenton Grinnell, born June 29, 1779, died August 28, 1849 and had nine children Clarissa Richmond, born November 23, 1803, died September 29, 1890; married Isaac Wilcox BENJAMIN BRENTON, born September 26, 1806, died November 4, 1874, married Elizabeth Holden EZRA, born December 22, 1809, died in infancy. EZRA STILES, born October 12, 1810, died November 4, 1875, married a Suydam ZEBEDEE G, born November 26, 1812, died April 16, 1870, married Mary Ann Stowe. ABIGAIL G., born February 21 1815, died November, 1898; married Daniel Martin LUCRETIA, born May 20, 1817, died 1904, married Charles C. Lee ASA COOKE, born in Little Compton, R I, April 10, 1819; died in Brooklyn, N Y., September 25, 1903, married Caroline Snow Field CLARK SAWYER, born January 4, 1821, died November 21, 1839

His wife was a great-great-granddaughter of Governor William Brenton and of Governor John Cranston of Rhode Island, and also a great-great-great-granddaughter of Roger Williams, whose granddaughter, Mary Hart, was the wife of Sarah's great-grandfather, Governor Samuel Cranston. He was a seagoing man and captain of a ship when lost at sea

BERIAH SOUTHARD BROWNELL.

(164712).

Beriah Southard Brownell, son of Edward and Susannah Wells Brownell, born in Canaan, Conn 1776, died in Williston, Vt, 1869; married in Williston, Vt, 1804, Lucinda Sanford, and had seven children. ALICE, born in Williston, Vt; died in infancy. ALMON S., born in Williston, Vt, September, 1807, died in Williston, Vt, November, 1854, married Ruby Downer. EDWARD, born in Williston, Vt, October, 1809, died in Colchester, Vt., November 5, 1894, married Mary Maria Byington, (2) Josephine Irish. NORMAN, born in Williston, Vt, September, 1811, died in Elmhurst, Ill, February, 1878; married Mary Ann Myers MARTHA, born in Williston, Vt, 1813; died in New Haven, Vt, 1902, married Charles Blair. ELIAS S., born in Williston, Vt, 1816, died in Burlington, Vt, 1890 LYMAN, born in Williston, Vt.; died at the age of three years

255

SAMUEL AARON BROWNELL

(164713).

Samuel Aaron Brownell, son of Edward and Susannah Wells Brownell, born in Canaan, Conn., June 7, 1778, died in Williston, Vt., May 6, 1869, married October 5, 1801, Zeruah Forbes, born June 18, 1782, died January 6, 1849, and had eight children WILLIAM PIERCE, born in Williston, Vt., July 26, 1802; died April 23, 1824. POLLY FORBES, born in Williston, Vt., August 12 1804, died July 18, 1822 LUCY A, born in Williston, Vt., June 2, 1806, died September 22, 1880 MARY ANN, born in Williston, Vt., June 3, 1808, died 1858, married S. S. Douglass. CHAUNCEY WELLS, born in Williston, Vt., September 13, 1811, died in Williston, Vt., June 4, 1892, married Laura C. Higbee, (2) Martha M. Van Sicklen GEORGE WASHINGTON born in Williston, Vt., February 22, 1814, died September 24, 1905; married Almira Barry Benham. ADELIA HANNAH, born in Williston, Vt., April 13, 1817, married Charles C Holton PHILO FORBES, born in Williston, Vt., March 28, 1823, died November 29, 1872, married Emily Stevens.

HANNAH BROWNELL SANFORD

(164714).

Hannah Brownell, daughter of Edward and Susannah Wells Brownell born in Canaan, Conn., 1780, married Joseph Sanford, and had three children SUSANNAH, died in youth MINERVA, married a Pierce. EDWARD, died in youth.

CHAUNCEY WELLS BROWNELL

(164715).

Chauncey Wells Brownell son of Edward and Susannah Wells Brownell born in Canaan, Conn., 1782, died in Williston, Vt., July 1850 married Belinda Beech, and had ten children LYSANDER NELSON born in Williston, Vt., January 20 1817, died in Colerain, Mass December 3 1888 married Mary Smith Russell ELIZABETH B born in Williston, Vt., married Myrtle McGee EDWARD WELLS born in Williston, Vt., married Louisa A Allen CHARLES P, born in Williston, Vt., married Mary (surname unknown). MARY, born in Williston, Vt., died at the age of sixteen years. WILLIAM, born in Williston, Vt., married Sarah Rogers. FANNIE E., born in Williston, Vt., September 18, 1828, married Henry P. Barton. JAMES T., born in Williston, Vt., October 4, 1830, died in Burlington, Vt., September 6 1894, married Julia Maud Macfarlane. MINERVA T., born in Williston, Vt., married Alfred Pierce GURLEY.

IRA BROWNELL.

(164716)

Ira Brownell, son of Edward and Susannah Wells Brownell, born in Sharon, Conn., 1784; died in Winterset, Iowa, 1869, married June, 1813, Betsey Clark, and had eight children. PATIENCE, died in infancy. IRA CLARK, died in infancy. BELINDA BEECH, born in Colchester, Vt., 1817; died in Muscatine, Iowa, June, 1904; married Ephriam Kirby. DENNIS died in youth. SUSAN, died in youth. BETSEY CLARK, born in Colchester, Vt., 1826, died in Winterset, Iowa, 1889, married Dr. David Hutchinson. HARRIET LUCY, born in Colchester, Vt., March 21, 1828, married Joseph S. Mulford. IRA WELLS, born in Colchester, Vt., June, 1831, died in Macksburg Iowa 1902, married Elizabeth Hawley.

HARVEY BROWNELL.

(164717)

Harvey Brownell, son of Edward and Susannah Wells Brownell, born in Sharon, Conn., 1787, died in Essex, Vt., 1862, married Alma Rogers, and had two children. CAROLINE, born July 16, 1814, died March 23, 1900, married Henry Loran Stowe. BENJAMIN R., born July 22, 1820, died May 15, 1899; married Maria Webb Case

He married second 1823, Maria Delano, and had five children. ALMA A. born October 19, 1824, died September 30, 1860, married Hiram Hill. HENRY M., born April 21, 1829; died October 5, 1855, married Ann M. Willey. WILLIAM H. born July 5 1832, died August 31, 1839. MINERVA M., born March 23, 1836, married William Jennings. SUSAN L., born January 8, 1839, died August 31, 1839

REV. GROVE LAWRENCE BROWNELL.

(164718).

Rev. Grove Lawrence Brownell, son of Edward and Susannah Wells Brownell, born in Canaan, Conn., March 1, 1790; died in Sharon, Conn., April 10, 1855; married in Cornwall, Conn., April 8, 1818, Harriet Burnham, died in Woodbury, Conn., May 3, 1831, and had three children SARAH ANN, born June 11, 1819, died February 28, 1826. EDWARD FRANKLIN, born December 24, 1820; died December 28, 1824 HARRIET EMILY, born October 30, 1827, died in Polo, Ills., December 25, 1900, married Rev. J. R. Herrick

He married second in Danbury Conn., April 24, 1832, Mary Ann Whittlesey, daughter of Matthew Beale and Hannah White Whittlesey, born February 9, 1805, died in Sharon, Conn., May 14, 1877, and had seven children MARY WHITTLESEY, born in Woodbury, Conn., February 1, 1833, married Rev. D. D. T. McLaughlin. GROVE LAWRENCE, born June 14, 1834. WILLIAM AUGUSTUS, born March 7 1836; died in Rochelle, Ill., March 25, 1874; married Sylvia Post. EDWARD FRANKLIN, born in Woodbury, Conn., March 3 1838 RUSSELL BOTSFORD born December 5, 1839, died on the Nile Egypt January 21, 1867. ALBERT JUDSON, born August 28, 1841, died in Sharon, Conn., September 13 1855 CHARLES HOLLY, born August 8, 1844, died in Sharon, Conn., January 2, 1857

He moved with his parents to Williston, Vt, about 1800 He was graduated from the University of Vermont, in 1813 The degree of M A was conferred upon him by Yale College in 1816 In 1817, he was ordained to the work of the ministry and was installed as the first pastor of the North Church at Woodbury, Conn In May, 1840, he removed to Sharon Conn, and became pastor of the Congregational Church, and continued about eight years. After retiring from this charge, he, with his two daughters, opened a select school which was successfully carried on until his death

WILLIAM BROWNELL

(164735)

William Brownell, son of Jeremiah and (given name unknown) Copp Brownell, died in Northport, N S aged 92 years He married Anna Davis, and had two children and possibly others. JERE-

258

MIAH, born in Northport, N. S., April 4, 1817, married Margaret Amelia Davis. WILLIAM GEORGE, born in Northport, N. S., married Cordelia Elizabeth Peacock

He always lived in Northport, N. S., and was a farmer.

AMY BROWNELL MUNSON.

(164741).

Amy Brownell, daughter of Ichabod and Elizabeth Stanley Brownell, born probably in Connecticut in 1778; died in Colchester, Vt., March 22, 1844, married in Colchester, Vt., 1795, William Munson, born in New Hampshire, 1766; died in Colchester, Vt., 1830, son of Richard Munson, and had three children and possibly others CLARA, born in Colchester, Vt., married Lemuel Platt. FANNY, born in Colchester, Vt.; married James Platt. ARTEMESIA, born in Colchester, Vt., 1797; died July 19, 1866; married John Warren Weaver.

Her husband was a lumberman and a man of prominence in his community It is stated that his father, Richard Munson, was a sea captain and moved from Portsmouth, N. H., to Colchester, Vt., in 1810, where he died 1813 The Muson homestead was in the vicinity of the "Stone Tavern" built by her father.

MARTHA BROWNELL BENNETT.

(1649a33).

Martha Brownell, daughter of Aaron and Mary Gardner Brownell, born May 30, 1791, married a Bennett, and had two children. MARY ELIZA.

JOSHUA BROWNELL

(1649a34)

Joshua Brownell, son of Aaron and Mary Gardner Brownell, born June 9, 1793, died 1865, married Esther Denton, daughter of Amos and Elizabeth (surname unknown) Denton, born in Beekman, Dutchess County, N. Y., November 18, 1803; died in Union Vale, Dutchess County, N. Y., February 4, 1871, and had two children. SAMUEL DENTON born in Dutchess County, N. Y., June 1, 1828;

died in La Grangeville, Dutchess County, N Y, July 19, 1906, married Mary Crouse   GEORGE H., born in Dutchess County, N. Y, April 18, 1831, married Isadore E Barlow, (2) Frances T Sherman, (3) Ruth Noxon.

NATHANIEL BROWNELL

(1649a35).

Nathaniel Brownell, son of Aaron and Mary Gardner, born December 7, 1795, married Eunice Emigh, and had one child   JOHN L, born June 10, 1824.

DEBORAH BROWNELL TRUESDELL

(1649a51)

Deborah Brownell, daughter of Joshua and Elizabeth Reasoner Brownell, born in Dutchess County, N Y, May 3, 1788, died in Pawling, Dutchess County, N Y, March 2, 1872, married Jeremiah Truesdell, and had five children.   ELIZA JANE, born in Dutchess County N. Y, March 26, 1812, died in Stanford, Dutchess County, N Y, July 28, 1839, married William Butts   CORDELIA born in Troy, N. Y, May 11, 1815; died in Seneca County, N Y, April 24, 1905, married Edward B Brownell   HELEN, born in Dutchess County, N Y, September 7, 1816, died in Junius, Seneca County, N Y, April 30, 1893, married William Barrett. OLIVER P, born in Dutchess County, N Y., October 18, 1819, died in Beekman, Dutchess County, N Y, February 10, 1844   MARIA, born in Dutchess County, N. Y., September 16, 1822, died in Pawling, Dutchess County, N. Y, March 30, 1895, married Nehemiah D Worden

MORDECAI BROWNELL

(1649a53)

Mordecia Brownell, son of Joshua and Elizabeth Reasoner Brownell, born in Beekman, Dutchess County, N. Y, 1792, died in Wyoming County, N. Y, married Betsey Esmond, and had three children   LORENZO, born February 24 1826, married Maria Cornell   MARY L A, born January 11, 1829, married A D Hawthorne.   HELEN E., born October 4, 1836, married John Marion

Maria Brownell Emigh.

(1649a55).

Maria Brownell, daughter of Joshua and Elizabeth Reasorer Brownell, born in Beekman, Dutchess County, N. Y., January 25 1796, died in Matteawan, Dutchess County, N. Y., March 16, 1880, married in Beekman, N. Y., December 31, 1821, by Rev. Foss, to Nicholas U. Emigh, son of John N and Elizabeth Champlin Emigh, born in North Clove, Dutchess County, N. Y., August 21, 1793, died in North Clove, N Y, January 18, 1856, and had seven children HILEN MARIA born in North Clove, N Y., October 8, 1822, died March 7, 1907 JANE ELIZA, born in North Clove, N. Y., August 11, 1824; died August, 1902, married Sidney Mitchell GILBERT, born in North Clove, N Y., January 1, 1827, died in Poughkeepsie, N Y., June 2, 1872, married a Moran FREDERIC AUGUSTUS, born in North Clove, N Y, December 13, 1829, died in Poughkeepsie, N Y April, 1863; married Adaline Roberts MARGARIT ELIZABITH, born in North Clove, N. Y., March 22, 1834, died in Glenham, Dutchess County, N Y., March 19, 1898, married William H Haight. JOHN N born in North Clove, N Y, April 15, 1836, married Amanda Duncan ANN, born in North Clove, N. Y, March 16, 1839, died at North Clove, N. Y, August 16, 1855

ANN BROWNELL THOMPSON.

(1649a56).

Ann Brownell, daughter of Joshua and Elizabeth Reasoner Brownell, born in Beekman, Dutchess County, N. Y., February 14, 1798; died in Webster Station, Madison County, N. Y., April 2, 1881; married January 1, 1828, Henry Thompson, son of Gideon and Hannah Wooley Thompson, born June 19, 1802; died in Cazenovia, Madison County, N. Y., February 16, 1872, and had seven children. AMANDA, born in Beekman, N. Y., March 6, 1829; died in Ann Arbor, Mich., March 10, 1895; married Noah Gifford

ANN BROWNELL THOMPSON.

Butts. HORACE, born in Beekman, N. Y., September 12, 1830; died in Buffalo, N. Y., November 13, 1859. HANNAH M., born in Beekman, N. Y., February 13, 1832; died in Cazenovia, N. Y., July 19, 1891. ALEXANDER, born in Beekman, N. Y., February 27, 1834; died April 10, 1860. MARY F., born in Beekman, N. Y., March 18, 1836; died in Cazenovia, N. Y., March 30, 1904. WILLIAM H., born in Beekman, N. Y., April 4, 1838; died in Cazenovia, N. Y., June 28, 1845. JANE E., born in Cazenovia, N. Y., December 11, 1840.

JOSHUA BROWNELL.

(1649a57).

Joshua Brownell, son of Joshua and Elizabeth Reasoner Brownell, born in Beekman, Dutchess County, N. Y., April 8, 1800; died in Spencertown, Columbia County, N. Y., December 2, 1881; married in Orange County, N. Y., Susan Moon, daughter of Archibald and Abiah Cunningham Moon, born in Orange County, N. Y., February 16, 1805; died in Spencertown, N. Y., September 4, 1884, and had ten children. ERASTUS, born in Beekman, N. Y., January 16, 1824; died July 6, 1896. LORENZO, born in Beekman, N. Y., September 20, 1826; married Louisa Maria Welles. MARY, born in Beekman, N. Y., March 16, 1829; died October 10, 1890, married Horatio Lewis Smith. MELISSA C., born in Beekman, N. Y., June 18, 1832; married John D. Trimper. WILLIAM, born in Beekman, N. Y., July 10, 1834, died April 6, 1896. EVELINE E., born in Austerlitz, Columbia County, N. Y., September 18, 1836; died December 10, 1848. LEWIS CHARLES, born in Austerlitz, N. Y., March 12, 1838; married Janette Strong. CYNTHIA, born in Austerlitz, N. Y., April 5, 1840; died October 21, 1887. STEPHEN, born in Austerlitz, N. Y., August 12, 1845. LORENA S., born in Austerlitz, N. Y., September 25, 1848; died June 18, 1865.

He was a farmer and moved from Beekman, N. Y., to Austerlitz, N. Y., about 1835, and settled upon a farm, residing there the balance of his life. He is buried beside his wife in the village cemetery in Spencertown, N. Y.

JACOB REASONER BROWNELL.

(1649a58).

JACOB REASONER BROWNELL.

Jacob Reasoner Brownell, son of Joshua and Elizabeth Reasoner Brownell, born in Beekman, Dutchess County, N. Y., January 10, 1802; died in Ellery, Chautauqua County, N. Y., April 20, 1871; married in Pittstown, Rensselaer County, N. Y., August 30, 1827, Mary Brownell, daughter of Reuben and Alice Sherman Brownell, born in Pittstown, N. Y., January 5, 1807; died in Pittstown, N. Y., June 13, 1830, and had one child, MARY MARGARET, born in Pittstown, N. Y., May 27, 1830, died in Ellery, N. Y., October 22, 1872; married John Hale.

He married second in Hoosick, Rensselaer County, N. Y., March 13, 1832, Hannah Harrington, daughter of Philip Harrington, born in Hoosick, N. Y., June 15, 1805, died in Ellery, N. Y., July 25, 1862, and had two children WILLIAM OSCAR, born in Ellery, N. Y., May 18, 1834; married Armena M. Wallis. (2) Lucinda R. Jones (3) Addie Stowell. GILBERT KNOX, born in Ellery, N. Y., January 12, 1840; died in Ellery, N. Y., August 6, 1840. He married third in Harmony, Chautauqua County, N. Y., November 14, 1867 Eliza Bemus Parner (a widow), daughter of Thomas and Jane Atkin Bemus.

He received his education in the public school at Pittstown, N. Y. He came with his brother Peter R. Brownell from Pittstown, N. Y., to Ellery N. Y., in 1832 and settled on lot 43 in the town of Ellery, N. Y., residing there until 1868 when he moved to North Harmony, N. Y., where he lived the remainder of his life. He united with the Ellery Center Baptist Church in the spring of 1844, and soon became one of the leading members, giving liberally of his means for the support of the Gospel as well as to charitable works. He was elected to the office of deacon, made vacant by the removal of Reuben Parker, a position he held until his removal to the town of Harmony, about three years before his death. A short time after changing his residence, he was elected deacon of the North Harmony Church, a position he held at the time of his death. He was known and respected by the denomination of which he was a member throughout the entire county.

In politics he was a Republican, having been elected to the office of Highway Commissioner for the town of Ellery, N. Y. for a term of three years. He is buried beside his second wife in the Bemus Point Cemetery at Bemus Point N. Y.

(1049a59).

PETER REASONER BROWNELL.

Peter Reasoner Brownell, son of Joshua and Elizabeth Reasoner Brownell, born in Beekman, Dutchess County, N. Y., April 20, 1806; died in Ellery, Chautauqua County, N. Y., March 31, 1895; married in Ellery, N. Y., August 31, 1834, Rhoda Putnam, daughter of Ephriam Putnam, died in Ellery, N. Y., July 3, 1880, and had three children. SMITH HARRINGTON, born in Ellery, N. Y., June 4, 1835; married Mary Annar Strong, (2) Minerva Dunn. MARY ANN, born in Ellery, N. Y., September 5, 1837; married John B. Rush. ELIZABETH M., born in Ellery, N. Y., September 11, 1840; died in Jamestown, N. Y., September 25, 1884; married John Pereguin.

He married a second time in Jamestown, N. Y., in January, 1886, Mary Van Dusen (a widow), who died in Jamestown, N. Y. He received his education in the public school at Pittstown, N. Y., and when he left his paternal home, he began life as a laborer, working by the month until he was twenty-eight years of age. He then bought a farm in the town of Ellery, N. Y., upon which he lived until 1880, a total of thirty-six years. He bought property in Jamestown, N. Y., where he resided until a short time before his death, when he went to live with his daughter, Mrs. Mary A. Rush, at her home in Ellery, N. Y.

In politics, he was a Republican. At the age of thirty-five years, he united himself with the Methodist Episcopal Church at West Ellery, N. Y., and continued in that faith until his death. He is buried beside his wife in the Bemus Point Cemetery at Bemus Point, N. Y.

ALICE BROWNELL VAN NAMEE

(1649a71)

Alice Brownell, daughter of Simeon and Sarah Hoag Brownell, born April 4, 1781, died October 16, 1859, married February 7, 1802. Moses Van Namee, son of Abner and Mary (surname unknown) Van Namee, born February, 1778, died February 20, 1862 and had ten children DERRICK, born November 22, 1802, died February 17, 1884, married Sarah Mosher SARAH, born November 20, 1805, died June 26, 1860, married William Stilwell. MARY, born November 5, 1807, died October 4, 1875, married Russell D Mead ABNER, born September 20, 1809; died August 1, 1896; married Aurilla Lamb, (2) Julia Dayton SIMEON, born October 4, 1811, died May 26, 1887, married Anna Cronkhite ALBERT, born December 30, 1813; died December 30, 1815 PHOEBE, born February 21, 1816, died October 9 1887 married David Allen ANN, born October 7, 1818, married Charles D Worden CHARITY, born 1820 died 1905; married Seeley Scofield ALICE, born 1823, died young.

JOSEPH BROWNELL

(1649a72)

Joseph Brownell, son of Simeon and Sarah Hoag Brownell born January 14, 1783, died in Ellery, N. Y., June 10, 1849, married December 19, 1803, Prudence Sherman, and had six children CYNTHIA, born August 20, 1804, married Oliver Carpenter THANKFUL, born in Pittstown N Y, October 18, 1805, died in Ellery, N Y, April 9, 1846, married David Brownell ISRAEL, born in Pittstown, N Y., July 16, 1807, married a Lamb LUVILLA, born in Pittstown, N. Y. September 5, 1809, died in Jamestown, N Y, September 18 1883, married Stephen Pratt ELSIE, born in Pittstown, N Y, March 9, 1811, married Daniel Felton JOSEPH, born in Pittstown, N Y, May 8, 1813, married Eunice Weaver (2) Henrietta M Weaver.

He married second Elizabeth VanWert and had four children BARNEBUS CLAPP, born in Pittstown, N Y, December 29, 1815; died in Ellery, N Y February 9, 1893, married Martha Scofield. NANCY MARIA, born in Pittstown, N Y, January 12, 1818, died

1895; married Reuben Downing. JANE JEMIMA, born in Pittstown, N. Y., January 16, 1820, died in Panama, N. Y., December 17, 1891, married Telemichs Burch, (2) David Brownell, (3) Reuben F Randolph SARAH, born September 30, 1821; married Barnard Flinn

He married third Mrs. Phoebe Smith (a widow), and had two children. PHOEBE, married Perry Dayton ELIZABETH, born December 20, 1826.

STEPHEN BROWNELL.

(1649a73)

Stephen Brownell, son of Simeon and Sarah Hoag Brownell, born September 4, 1784; died October 18, 1840, married January 17, 1802, Esther Norton, and had eight children DAVID NORTON, died 1886, married Jane R Hunt STEPHEN JACOB GILBERT WILLIAM H. SARAH ELSIE

DANIEL BROWNELL.

(1649a74).

Daniel Brownell, son of Simeon and Sarah Hoag Brownell, born July 3, 1786, died April 5, 1857; married February 7, 1820, Esther Miller, and had one child. JANE, born in Cambridge, N Y; married William J. Harrell.

It has been stated that his wife was a granddaughter of Colonel Elisha Miller of the Revolutionary Army, and that her mother, Martha Miller "won distinction for her brave act of carrying dispatches, when fourteen years of age, from White Plains through the British lines when the British occupied Manhattan Island General Washington had headquarters at the Miller homestead at Cambridge and himself wrote the dispatches and delivered them to the girl, the safe delivery of three of which resulted in the joint action of the American troops and the evacuation of the island by the British."

SIMEON BROWNELL.
(1649a75).

Simeon Brownell, son of Simeon and Sarah Hoag Brownell, born

April 14, 1788, died 1862, married April 21, 1813, Betsey Ann Churchill, born December 1, 1793, and had nine children. LORENZO M., born March 1, 1814. MARY ANN, born July 24, 1815. CHARLES H., born November 24, 1818. EDWARD J., born April 19, 1821, died October 4, 1851. SIDNEY M., born April 6, 1823. JANE H., born July 15, 1825. CAROLINE E., born December 26, 1827, died September 29, 1830. GEORGE W., born April 21, 1831. SIMEON, born May 26, 1833.

MOSES BROWNELL

(1649a76)

D   Moses Brownell, son of Simeon and Sarah Hoag Brownell, born January 1, 1790, died March 11, 1879, married January 1, 1816, Mary Brown, daughter of Andrew and Sarah Cobb Brown, born February 2, 1794, died January 7, 1874, and had six children ELEANOR M., born August 12, 1817, died July 11, 1883, married Joseph Newland. (2) Ebenezer Baker Cobb OLIVIA M., born March 24, 1819, married Rev. Alfred Pinney. ANTIONETTE SARAH, born February 2, 1823, died December 12, 1842 AMELIA A., born October 23 1825; died May 23, 1841. CHARLES A., born June 30, 1828, died June 6, 1877, married Mary Denton. SILAS B born October 11, 1830, married Sarah Stoddard

SARAH BROWNELL WING

(1649a77).

Sarah Brownell, daughter of Simeon and Sarah Hoag Brownell, born January 15 1792, died March, 1836; married July 29, 1810, Thomas Wing, son of Abraham and Lydia Brownell Wing, born in Dutchess County, N. Y., March 27, died October 14, 1854, and had thirteen children. BROWNELL, born May 15, 1811, died May 6, 1874, married Desire Gifford MORDECAI, born August 1, 1813, died in Ellery, N. Y., October 17, 1890, married Polly Jane Furlow RUSSELL, born December 29, 1814, died in Lisbon, Ill., January 23, 1876; married Mary Ann Hoag MARTHA, born October 27 1816, died 1838, married Edson Gifford NATHAN born November 27, 1818 died July, 1837 ABRAHAM, born April 19, 1821, died in Wilson, Kan., February 8, 1897, married Mehitabel Jones SENECA, born April 6, 1823, died 1838. LYDIA, born October 8,

1825; died March, 1855; married Oliver Dix PHOEBE JANE,
born February 26, 1827, died about 1843. SARAH ANN, born
March 29, 1830, died July 31, 1884, married Hiram Derby.
MARY, born December 27, 1833, died 1847 THOMAS, born February 17, 1837, married Caroline Close. SIMEON, died young

Her husband was a farmer and miller, and in 1806, moved to
Pittstown, Rensselaer County, N. Y., remaining there until about
1820, when he went to Ellery, Chautauqua County, N Y, locating
on a farm. He later built what was known as the Liscom Weeks
grist mill, and also the grist mills at Dewittville and Mayville,
Chautauqua County, N. Y. He was a Quaker in early life, but
later united with the Methodist Episcopal Church He married in
1838, as his second wife Mrs Electa Halleck Strang, (a widow).
In the spring of 1844, accompanied by several of his children, he
journeyed to Kendall County, Ill., and settled on a farm near Lisbon He was twenty-three days on the road.

MARY BROWNELL BROWN
(1649a79).

Mary Brownell, daughter of Simeon and Sarah Hoag Brownell,
born November 23, 1795, died 1877, married October 12, 1816,
David Brown, and had six children. ISAAC NEWTON, born August
15, 1817. SIMEON, born September 9, 1820, married Caroline Haskins SARAH, born July 29, 1823. MARY ANN, born April 8, 1830.
EDWIN, born February 12, 1835, married Catherine Vreeland.
PHOEBE, born February, 1837

NATHAN BROWNELL
(1649a79a).

Nathan Brownell son of Simeon and Sarah Hoag Brownell, born
May 7, 1797, died in Cambridge, N Y, December 4, 1859, married June 8, 1822, to Aleha Case born May 10, 1792, died in Pittstown, N Y., March 8, 1842, and had nine children CAROLINE,
born June 13, 1823; died in Lockport, N. Y., August 9, 1854, married Henry H Hoag MINERVA A., born September 29, 1824, died
in Pittstown, N Y, June 19, 1860 MOSES HOAG, born January
26, 1826· died in Pittstown, N Y November 29, 1894, married
Elizabeth Hoag, (2) Anna Brownell Stilwell CHARLES E., born

August 28, 1827, died in Pittstown, N Y, October 3, 1828. SIMEON C, born July 2, 1829, died in Pittstown, N Y January 26, 1852 AARON WADDLE, born in Pittstown, N Y., March 4, 1831, died in Salem, Oregon, February 12, 1896, married Martha B Fernandez. (2) Angene Ruth Chilson SMITH HARRINGTON, born February 28, 1833; died in Shushan, N Y., January 21, 1877, married Isabelle Smart. FRANKLIN, born August 29, 1835, died in Chillicothe, Ohio, February 25, 1854 PHILETT J., born October 9, 1837, died in Pittstown, N Y., November 13, 1838.

He married second October 25, 1843, Orpha Case, born February 7, 1808; died in Cambridge N Y, February 20, 1883, and had two children ALCHA A, born November 2, 1844 ADELADE A, born February 8, 1847, died in Cambridge, N. Y. September 19, 1897, married Andrew B McNish

He was a farmer and breeder of Merino sheep, which business was continued by his son Moses Hoag Brownell and is now carried on by his grandson, Irving M Brownell. He was a man of much energy and enterprise, of great firmness of character, deservedly popular and respected

ISAAC BROWNELL.

(1649a79b).

Isaac Brownell, son of Simeon and Sarah Hoag Brownell, born January 29, 1799; died June 26 1886, married January 17, 1821, Anna Eddy Barker, born March, 1803, and had six children AMY, born October 17 1821 died January 4, 1853 SARAH ANN, born January 13, 1824, died July 11, 1848 SIMEON, born January 30, 1826; married Mary Rose. LEWIS, born March 13, 1828, married Jane Dorr GERMAN, born June 9, 1833; married Delia Lockwood JANE, born June 13 1837; married Walter Howell

LUTHAN BROWNELL.

(1649a79d).

Luthan Brownell, son of Simeon and Sarah Hoag Brownell, born March 28, 1803, died August 26, 1866, married Mary Ann Husted, and had four children ANNA, married William Stilwell (2) Moses Hoag Brownell SARAH JANE, married Lewis Curtis REUBEN SIMEON

PHOEBE BROWNELL WEAVER.

Phoebe Brownell, daughter of Simeon and Sarah Hoag Brownell, born in Pittstown, Rensselaer County, N. Y., July 9, 1805; died in Ellery, Chautauqua County, N. Y., July 24, 1883; married in Pittstown, N. Y., September 9 1829, to Morrison Weaver, son of Samuel and Hannah (surname unknown) Weaver, born April 25, 1806; died in Ellery, N. Y., September 17, 1880, and had six children. SIMEON, born in Pittstown, N. Y., 1831; died in Pittstown, N. Y., 1834. SAMUEL, born in Pittstown, N. Y., January 16, 1833; died in Ellery, N. Y., May 7, 1893; married Eveline Medorah Lazell. LUVILLA, born in Ellery, N. Y., July 10, 1835; died in Ellery, N. Y., November 3, 1903; married Charles Austin Bowen. ARVILLA, born in Ellery, N. Y., July 10, 1835; died in Ellery, N. Y., July 10, 1835. SIMEON BROWNELL, born in Ellery, N. Y., August 8, 1840; died in North East, Pa., November 26, 1904; married Anna Delora Bickford. DELOSS MORRISON, born in Ellery, N. Y., October 24, 1845; died in Ellery, N. Y., November 26, 1870; married Maryette Bickford.

She came from Pittstown to Ellery, N. Y., in the spring of 1835, living upon the farm of Thomas Wing one year. Then she moved upon the farm in Ellery, N. Y., where she resided until her death. She was an attendant of the Methodist Episcopal Church at West Ellery, N. Y., to which she contributed liberally. She is buried beside her husband in the Bemus Point Cemetery at Bemus Point, N. Y.

ALLEN BROWNELL DURFEE

(1649b96)

Allen Brownell Durfee, son of Samuel and Anna Brownell Durfee, born in Little Compton, R. I., July 27, 1807, married October 15, 1831, Phebe Ann Robinson, daughter of Seth and Anna Swift Robinson, born in Falmouth, Mass., December 18, 1809, died in Bourne, Mass., August 4, 1884, and had ten children. MELISSA A, born in New Bedford, Mass., August 28, 1833, married James J. Besse MATILDA E, born January 1, 1835 died January 16, 1905. SAMUEL B, born December 26, 1838, died at sea December 26 1847 SETH R, born March 19, 1840 ANNA R, born December 23, 1841, died August 2, 1901 HENRY M, born August, 1842. EDWARD M, born February 2, 1844. JOSEPH C, born April 7, 1847. DAVID S., born October 23, 1849 LEWIS C, born April 9, 1851 died November 2, 1856

He was a farmer and lived in New Bedford, Mass., until 1851, when he moved to Fairhaven, Mass. where he resided until his death. In politics, he was a Democrat It is said of him that he was of a quiet disposition and was characterized by his strong love for the country and nature in all of its moods

ALLEN BROWNELL

(1649b9d1)

Allen Brownell, son of Robert and Roby Fuller Brownell, born February 16, 1801, died June 16, 1884; married October 19, 1837, Rebecca Delano, born August 2, 1814, died March 24, 1897, and had five children. HELEN MAR, born in Fairhaven, Mass., August 27, 1838 ROBY FULLER, born March 11, 1840, died September 7, 1841 FREDERICK STEVENS, born February 13, 1842, died on board of ship Philippe Delanove, April 12, 1861, and was buried at sea PETER FULLER, born June 26, 1846; died February 20, 1891 ALLEN FULLER, born May 14, 1849, died January 25, 1890, married Addie L Stevens

He was engaged in both the merchant and whaling service until 1849 when he and others purchased the schooner John Allyne and sailed to the gold regions of California He later returned and located upon a small farm in Fairhaven Mass., residing there until his death

273

Henry H. Brownell

(1649b9d5)

Henry H. Brownell, son of Robert and Roby Fuller Brownell, born February 22, 1808; married Harriet Terry, daughter of Phineas and Betsey (surname unknown) Terry, born May 23, 1819, and had four children MARY LOUISE, born August 27, 1839. SILAS, born March 2, 1851 PHINEAS TERRY, born in Fairhaven, Mass, March 5, 1855, married Louise Gertrude Hill HARRIET T, born April 21, 1859

Mabel Brownell Smith

(166612).

Mabel Brownell, daughter of Thomas and Milly Grey Brownell, born in Hoosick, Rennselaer County, N Y, December 4, 1805, died in Batavia, Genessee County, N. Y., September, 1881, married in Sandgate, Bennington County, Vt, March 13, 1828, Guy Smith, son of Mathew and Anna Hurd Smith, born in Sandgate, Vt, August 2, 1800; died in Elba, Genesee County, N Y., September 30, 1852, and had four children. JOHN, born April 2, 1832, died April 14, 1833 ANN AMELIA, born in Ellisburg, Jefferson County, N Y., May 7, 1834 MARY, born in Ellisburg, N Y., March 3, 1836: married Miles H. Bierce EVELINE BROWNELL, born in Ellisburg, N. Y., February 9, 1841, died February, 1861

After living in Ellisburg Avon and Elba, she moved to Batavia, N Y, where she resided until her death. She was a member of the Episcopal Church She and her husband are buried in Batavia, N. Y.

(166614).

DANIEL LYON BROWNELL.

Daniel Lyon Brownell, son of Thomas and Milly Grey Brownell, born in Hoosick, Rennselaer County, N. Y., September 20, 1809; died in Avon, Livingston County, N. Y., May 11, 1890; married in Seaghticoke, Rennselaer County, N. Y., November 14, 1832, by Rev. R. Kelly, to Caroline Blasdel, daughter of Jerry and Sally Van Ness Blasdel, born in Hoosick, N. Y., August 20, 1813; died in Sandy Hill, N. Y., February 4, 1843, and had two children. JOHN WESLLY, born in Sandgate, Bennington County, Vt., October 8, 1833; died June 22, 1892. FRANCES ANN, born in Sandgate, Vt., April 19, 1841; married Adrian R. Parish.

He married second Amelia Barnard, born June 10, 1820; died November, 1875.

He received his education in the public schools in Rennselaer County, N. Y. When a young man he engaged in farming and continued to follow that occupation through life. After residing at Glen Falls, N. Y., Rochester, N. Y., and West Liberty, O., he moved to Avon, N. Y., where he remained for sixty years. In politics, he was a Republican. He was a member of the Methodist Episcopal church for seventy years, and was one of its ardent supporters.

WILLIAM SHAW BROWNELL.

(166034).

WILLIAM SHAW BROWNELL.

William Shaw Brownell, son of Jedediah and Eunice Watkins Brownell, born in Trenton, Oneida County, N. Y., October 27, 1818; died in Smethport, McKean County, Pa., July 21, 1900, married in Clermont, McKean County, N. Y., August 22, 1852, Octavia C. Howard, daughter of Eliphlet Morgan and Patty (surname unknown) Howard, born in Adams, Jefferson County, N. Y., October 13, 1822; died in Smethport, Pa., November 21, 1882, and had five children. FITZ WILLIAM, born in Alden, Henry County, Ill., May 1, 1853; died in Smethport, Pa., January 7, 1863. MARY ALBINA, born in Alden, Ill., November 13, 1854; died in Chemung, Ill., September 25, 1859. GEORGE RALEIGH, born in Smethport, Pa., October 8, 1857; died in Smethport, Pa., December 16, 1904. FRED WILLIAM, born in Smethport, Pa., November 20, 1859; married Hattie Adelaide Foote. ADDIE OCTAVIA, born in Smethport, Pa., October 10, 1864; married William Frederick Specht.

In 1837, at the age of nineteen years, he in company with his brother-in-law, Rasselas Wilcox Brown, started on foot from Oneida County, N. Y., for the purpose of locating a home in the wilderness of the state of Michigan. After a long and tedious journey they reached their destination. Not liking the "wild west" they only remained there a short time, when they retraced their steps to New York state. One year later the young adventurers again started on foot in search of another location. This time their fortunes took them to Jones Township, Elk County, Pa., where they immediately commenced to clear up a farm. From Elk County, he drifted to Sergeant Township, McKean County, Pa., where he taught school for some time at Bunker Hill, now known as Clermont. It was here that he met his future wife.

Shortly after his marriage, he moved to Alden, Henry County, Ill., where he located upon a farm. After remaining there about four years, he sold his farm and returned to Elk County, Pa., locating at Ridgway. In 1857, he went to Smethport, Pa., and purchased a mercantile business, beginning in the old Brownell homestead on State Street. Later he moved into the store now occupied by his son, Fred William Brownell. In 1882, he turned his business over to his two sons, George R., and Fred W. Brownell. It was a proud boast of his that he never sued a creditor or ever intentionally distressed the poor. He was an honorable and just man in all his business dealings. He was twice elected Associate Judge of McKean County, Pa., serving in that capacity for ten years. He was also one of the oldest Masons in the county at the time of his death. Judge Brownell was a man of sterling traits of character, and was of the type that look upon the shams of life with contempt.

GARRETT BROWNELL

(166651).

Garrett Brownell, son of Aaron Brownell married and had three children. WILLIAM, was in the Union Army. AARON, married and had several children. SARAH.

JOHN BROWNELL

(166652).

John Brownell, son of Aaron Brownell, married and had daughter MARY. He was a boat captain on the Erie Canal and run between Rochester and New York City.

EPHRIAM BROWNELL.

(166653)

Ephriam Brownell, son of Aaron Brownell, married and had several children of whom two are: JOHN. FRANCES

Elizabeth Brownell Lewis.

(166656).

Elizabeth Brownell, daughter of Aaron Brownell, married Benjamin Lewis, and had a son CHARLES Her husband was a contractor on the canal

Robert Pattee Brownell.

(171421)

Robert Pattee Brownell, son of Robert and Abigail or Priscilla Pattee Brownell, born February 14, 1784. died in Fort Wayne, Ind, December 28, 1845; married Hannah Colby, daughter of Rowell Colby, and had a son ALSTEAD, born December 24, 1809; died November 9, 1887, married Lucy Eaton Jackson, (2) Harriet Whittsmon

He married second in Fort Wayne, Ind., Catherine Webb, and had five children MARY C., born April 29, 1821 NATHANIEL WEBSTER, born February 15, 1824 ARMINDA, born January 10, 1826. ARMIRA, born March 26, 1828, died November 27, 1830 HARRIET, born May 15, 1830 died in Richland, Wis, 1902.

After his first marriage a few years, he became financially embarrased and was confined in jail for his debts, as was common and lawful at that time. During his confinement his wife and children went to live with her father When he was released from jail, he went to his father-in-law's after his wife and children, but his father-in-law would not have him around and drove him away, allowing him only a place to sleep over night He then went to Indiana Soon after his disappearance, his wife received a letter from near Buffalo, N. Y, stating that a man supposed to be Robert Pattee Brownell had been drowned in Lake Erie After receiving this letter his wife married again. Later it was found that this letter had been written by her father and another party, with the idea of deceiving her and make her contented to stay at home, as they needed her there After twenty years or more, Robert Pattee Brownell, met a man in Indiana, who was going to the next town from the one in which he left his wife and children and asked him to inquire about them He did so, and his son, Alstead Brownell, was thus put in communication with his father, whom he supposed dead. He never returned east although he corresponded with his son until his death.

ABNER BROWNELL

(172132).

Abner Brownell son of Benjamin and Phoebe Potter Brownell, born in Westport, Mass., June 21, 1756, died January 13, 1851, married September 5, 1784 to Hannah Crary, daughter of Nathan and Dorothy Wheeler Crary born November 1, 1761, died March 4 1837, and had ten children DOROTHY, born June 11, 1785, died July 4, 1871 NATHAN CRARY, born January 28, 1787; died January 8, 1862, married Hannah B Wilbur FREDERICK, born February 14, 1789, died April 9, 1872, married Charlotte Almy Sisson, (2) Hannah A Gifford ELIPHAL born October 14, 1790, died January 10, 1881 JAMES HARVEY, born January 8, 1792, died November 8, 1876, married Louisa W Canfield HANNAH, born May 24, 1794, died April 2, 1796 ISAAC WATTS, born March 19, 1796, died July 5, 1867, married Abigail White EDWARD PARKER, born August 27, 1798, died December 3, 1875, married Anstis Cole EPHRIAM WOODBRIDGE born June 16 1802· died July 30, 1876, married Sarah H Hicks. GILES HATHAWAY, born August 9, 1807; died July 12, 1808.

PHEBE BROWNELL MILKS

(172133)

Phebe Brownell, daughter of Benjamin and Phoebe Potter Brownell, born in Westport, Mass., November 6, 1758; died November 29, 1811, married November 8, 1781, Job Milks, born February 22, 1763 and had three children ALICE, born July 9, 1783 JOHN, born August 30, 1786 ELIZABETH, born January 12, 1797

BENJAMIN BROWNELL

(172134).

Benjamin Brownell son of Benjamin and Phoebe Potter Brownell, born February 2, 1760, died April 14, 1830; married March 18, 1784, to Abigail Milks, daughter of Lemuel and Mary (surname unknown) Milks, born September 28, 1765, died August 29, 1837, and had eleven children PHOEBE born January 7, 1785, married Peleg Gifford JIRAH, born June 17, 1787, died January 13, 1864, mar-

278

ried Sarah Kirby PRUDENCE, born February 24, 1788; died 1854, married Levi Gifford LEMUEL, born February 13, 1790, died May 24, 1885, married Elizabeth Brightman DAVID, born May 9, 1793, married Patience Briggs LYDIA, born December 3, 1794, married Amos Baker CYNTHIA M., born September 17, 1795, died June 8, 1817 RUBY, born May 6, 1799, married Thaddius Manchester HOLDER WHITE, born October 16, 1800, died 1861, married Love G Baker. WILLIAM T, born May 2, 1802, married Mary Devol ALMEDIA, born January 20, 1806, married Asa Potter

MARY BROWNELL HANDY.

(172136).

Mary Brownell, daughter of Benjamin and Phoebe Potter Brownell, born July 18, 1772, died February 20, 1876, married Dr Eli Handy, born 1764, died February 15, 1812, and had four children MIRA E, born October 1, 1790, died July 24, 1803. JAMES HARVEY, born November 13, 1792 died May 15, 1868, married Hope White HANNAH, born July 31, 1797. POLLY, died January, 1874

JUDITH BROWNELL MAYHEW.

(172142).

Judith Brownell, daughter of George and Mary Tripp Brownell, born May 1, 1777, died February 17, 1869, married Jonathan Mayhew, and had four children. EDWIN L, born February 25, 1809 died December 3, 1861, married Nancy Hicks JEREMIAH BROWNELL, born March 27 1811, died September 26, 1849, married Dorothy Manchester MATTHEW, married Clarissa Davol CHARLES M, born October 16, 1818; died January 30, 1841

NATHANIEL POTTER.

(172164).

Nathaniel Potter, son of Ephriam and Judith Brownell Potter, died December, 1766, married Sarah (surname unknown), died February, 1785, and had six children FREELOVE, born February 6, 1729, married Caleb Hathaway. EPHRIAM, born April 17, 1731

PHEBE, born August 21, 1733, died November 29, 1811, married Benjamin Brownell ABNER, born November 23, 1736, married Patience Macomber ZILPHA, born August 4, 1739. PATIENCE, born November 18, 1740, married Stephen Tripp.

JOSEPH BROWNELL

(173111).

Joseph Brownell son of Stephen and Margaret Church Brownell born May 14, 1773, died in Hanover, Chautauqua County, N Y, April 29, 1844, married Rachel Putney, born July 12, 1771, died September 12, 1854, and had five children. STEPHEN, born June 6, 1796, died 1881, married Terza Day ESTHER, born December 12, 1798, died September 20, 1870, married Simeon Bunce HICK, born April 24 1800, died May 5 1873, married Rachel McKee. (2) Nancy Reed. SABIN C, born May 14, 1802; married Julia Black. MARGARET, born August 8, 1805, married Earl Eaton

He settled in the town of Hanover, Chautauqua County, N Y, in 1809 and was chosen the first Supervisor of the town in 1812 He also served in 1814-16-17-19 He was the first deacon of the First Baptist Church of Hanover, and served for many years He was a man of strong character and prominent in the community.

BENJAMIN BROWNELL

(173114)

Benjamin Brownell, son of Stephen and Margaret Church Brownell, born August 19, 1778; married November 4, 1798, Mary Record, born April 1 1780, died December, 1859, and had eight children MARY ANN. ALMIRA CORNELLIUS. JAMES RACHEL DENNIS. RUTH. BENJAMIN FRANKLIN, born September 21, 1815, married Catherine Knight Briggs

Oliver Hazard Perry

(1126331).

Oliver Hazard Perry, son of Christopher Raymond and Sarah Wallace Alexander Perry, born in South Kings Town, R I, August 23, 1785; died in Port Spain, Isle of Trinidad, August 23, 1819; married May 5, 1811, Elizabeth Champlin Mason, and had six children CHRISTOPHER GRANT, born April 2, 1812, married Fanny Sargent. OLIVER HAZARD, born February 23, 1813 died March 4, 1814. OLIVER HAZARD, born February 23, 1815, died August 30, 1878, married Elizabeth Ann Randolph, (2) Mary Ann Morley CHRISTOPHER RAYMOND, born June 29, 1816, died October 8, 1848 ELIZABETH MASON, born September 15, 1819, died 1842, married Rev Francis Vinton

He entered the United States Navy as midshipman, April 7, 1799, cruised with his father, a naval officer, in the West Indies, 1799-1800 He was engaged in the war against Tripoli, 1804-5, and became a lieutenant, January 15, 1807, and at the outbreak of the War of 1812 was in command of a flotilla of gunboats on the Atlantic coast. In February 1813, he was transferred at his own request to serve under Commodore Isaac Chauncey on Lake Ontario

He took an active part in the attack upon Fort George, and was appointed to fit out a squadron upon Lake Erie, which he successfully accomplished at Presque Isle, (now Erie) Pa Having equipped nine small vessels, he attacked and captured the British fleet near Put-in-Bay, Ohio, September 10, 1813. This action, known as the "battle of Lake Erie," or more commonly as "Perry's Victory," obtained him an immense popularity, partly attributable to the manner in which it was announced by the famous dispatch "We have met the enemy and they are ours." Congress rewarded him with a vote of thanks, a medal, and the rank of Captain He co-operated with General Harrison in his operations at Detroit and at the battle of the Thames, October 5, 1813, and in the following year was employed upon the Potomac and in the defense of Baltimore.

He commanded the Java in Decatur's squadron in the Mediterranean, in 1815 He was sent to the Spanish Main in command of a squadron, June, 1819 He ascended the Orinoco to Angostura in July, was seized with yellow fever, and died at Port Spain on the Island of Trinidad, the day of his arrival there, August 23, 1819 His remains were removed to Newport R I in a ship of war, by order of Congress, and buried in the cemetery of that city, December 4, 1820, where an imposing obelisk was erected by the State of Rhode Island. In September, 1860, a marble statue of Commodore Perry was erected in Cleveland, Ohio, and on September 10, 1885, a fine bronze statue was unveiled at Newport, Rhode Island.

RAYMOND HENRY JONES PERRY.

(1126332)

Raymond Henry Jones Perry, son of Christopher Raymond and Sarah Wallace Alexander Perry, born in South Kings Town, R. I., February 11, 1789, died March 12, 1826, married May 16, 1814, Mary Ann DeWolf, daughter of James DeWolf of Bristol, R. I., and had four children. JAMES DEWOLF, born September 2, 1815, died September 9, 1876, married Julia Sophia Jones. RAYMOND HENRY, born June 25, 1817, died July 2, 1817. NANCY BRADFORD, born January 13, 1819, died July 12, 1883; married Robert Lay. ALEXANDER, born May 4, 1822, died November 9, 1888; married Lavinia Cady Howe.

MATHEW CALBRAITH PERRY.

(1126334)

Matthew Calbraith Perry, son of Christopher Raymond and Sarah Wallace Alexander Perry, born in Newport, R. I., April 10, 1794, died March 4, 1858; married October 24, 1819, Jane Slidell, daughter of John Slidell of New York, N. Y., born in New York, N. Y., February 29, 1797, died in Newport, R. I., January 14, 1879, and had nine children. JOHN SLIDELL. SARAH, married Colonel Robert S. Rogers. JANE HAZARD, died December 24, 1882, married John Hone. MATTHEW CALBRAITH, died November 16, 1873, married Harriet Taylor. SUSAN MURGATROYD, died August 15, 1825. OLIVER HAZARD, died in London, England, 1870. WILLIAM FREDERICK, died March 18, 1884. CAROLINE SLIDELL, married August Belmont. ISABELLA BOLTON, married George Tiffany.

He entered the United States Navy in 1809, and was appointed lieutenant in 1813. In 1819, while cruising, he settled the question of the location of the first occupation of Liberia. In 1821-24, in command of the schooner Shark he captured several pirates near the West India Islands. In 1833 after a three years' cruise in the

282

Mediterranean, he became the superintendent of a school for gun practice in the Brooklyn Navy Yard, and superintended the application of steam to war vessels. In 1837, he was made captain and in 1838 went abroad to visit the dock-yards, and inspect the danger signals on the coast. In 1839-41, he was commandant at the Brooklyn Navy Yard, afterwards of the African Squadron and the Gulf Squadron, and gallantly co-operated with the land forces at the battle of Vera Cruz. In 1852-54, he went on an expedition to Japan. He was one of the first public men in this country who looked for the peaceful opening of Japan, and long before he was appointed to command the fleet, March, 1852 he had carefully studied the land, the people, and the problem from every side. He arrived off Uraga in the bay of Yeddo, July 7, 1853, and after leaving letters for the Tycoon, sailed away July 17, and returned in February, 1854. On March 8, the formal articles of convention between the United States and Japan were exchanged at Yokohoma, on the spot now occupied by the Union Christian Church. His one mistake was in not treating with the true sovereign, the Mikado, from Osaka, instead of with his lieutenant the Tycoon.

Commodore Perry was a cultivated scholar and the "Narrative of the Expedition of an American Squadron to the China Seas and Japan," though nominally edited by Dr. Francis L Hawks, is, in the main, an exact reprint of Perry's diary and autograph narrative. He died in New York City, and a superb bronze statue of him, with four bas-reliefs in bronze illustrating scenes in his public life by J Q A. Ward, stands in Truro Park, Newport, R I, erected by his son-in-law, August Belmont, of New York

MERCY CHAMPLIN ROGERS

(1126341)

Mercy Champlin, daughter of Stephen and Elizabeth Perry Champlin, born September 19, 1783, died August 14, 1857, married 1806, Rev. James Rogers, and had six children. RUTH HAYWARD, born May 13, 1809, married Elisha Harmon. JOSHUA PERRY, married Electa Baldwin. CAROLINE HAYWARD, married Rev. Tucker. ELIZABETH, married Robert Pomeroy. FRENAH R., married John Keeney. RYLAND J., married Eliza Pomeroy, (2) Eunice Goddard

AMANDA MASON CHASE.

(114151 9b).

Amanda Mason Chase, daughter of John and Mary Davis Chase, born January 5, 1816; died April 3, 1893; married April 26, 1835, James Luther Peirce, son of Obadiah and Susan Luther Peirce, born in Somerset, Mass., May 3, 1808; died in New Bedford, Mass., March 25, 1853, and had eight children. AMANDA M., born Feb. 7, 1836; married Captain William Jenkins Macy. SUSAN LUTHER, born March 8, 1838; married William Shepard Mosher. JAMES MASON, born June 4, 1840; married Mattie Beardsley. MARY JOSEPHINE, born December 2, 1842; married Thomas Edwards. CLARA VERNON, born December 22, 1845; married Edward H. Mason. EMMA EUDORA, born November 30, 1848. JEANETTE, born May, 1850; died young. HERBERT SUMNER, born April 18, 1852; married Annette Blanchard. (2) Jennie C. Howland.

She united with the Fourth Street Methodist Episcopal Church at the age of nineteen years. She was a woman of most sterling character, always a firm expounder of the right, and a conformer in the strictest sense to her views. Her charitable nature and many

POLLY WILCOX BROWN.

(1153611).

Polly Wilcox, daughter of Isaiah and Polly Pendleton Wilcox, born in Preston, Conn., January 4, 1789, died May 17, 1813, married November 22, 1806, Isaac Brown, son of Isaac and Esther Barrington Brown, died October 27, 1834, and had three children. RASSELAS WILCOX, born September 30, 1809, died June 27, 1887; married Mary Potter Brownell. MARY ANN, born June 22, 1811; married Noah Merriam. ISAAC, born August 3, 1812; died December 9, 1832.

They moved early in life to German Flats, and later to Cicero, Onondaga County, N. Y.

WILLIAM PENDLETON WILCOX.

(1153613)

William Pendleton Wilcox, son of Isaiah and Polly Pendleton Wilcox, born in Danube, N. Y., May 30, 1794, died in Port Allegany, Pa., April 13, 1868, married Betsey Payne, and had three children. ELVIRA ZEVIAH, born in Danube, N. Y., December 29, 1815; died October 5, 1900; married Chester Irons Medbery. ALONZO ISAIAH, born in Danube, N. Y., March 22, 1819, died in Hackensack N. J., July 28, 1899, married Lovisa Horton. CLARISSA PRUDELIA, born in Danube, N. Y., 1821; died January 9, 1845.

He married second 1834 Esther Swift, born in Tolland, Conn., 1802, died in Port Allegany, Pa., January 5, 1881.

He was a soldier in the War of 1812, and was at one time sheriff of Allegany County, N. Y. He moved in 1822 to Nunda, N. Y., and in 1831 to McKean County, Pa., where he became sales agent for Benjamin and Andrew M. Jones, later the McKean and Elk Land and Improvement Company. His work was the inducing of immigration and development of the agricultural and mineral resources of the properties of the company, and he naturally became identified with many of the enterprises of that section of the state. In 1835, he was elected to the Pennsylvania House of Representatives and was re-elected for three successive terms, serving through Governor Ritner's administration and the "Buckshot War." He was then elected to the Senate and in 1845, to the speakership of that body. In 1858 and 1859, he was again a member of the House

285

ot Representatives He also served one terms as Associate Judge
The latter part of his life was spent on a farm near Williamsville,
McKean County Pa The newspaper notices of his death speak of
his public services, the purity of his public and private life, his
abilities, generosity, commanding appearance and the evenness of his
cheerful, genial disposition

Asa Wilcox

(1153614)

Asa Wilcox, son of Isaiah and Polly Pendelton Wilcox, born in
Danube N Y, March 9, 1797, married and had two children and
probably others George Pendelton, of Little Falls, N Y, and
Hon Isaiah Alonzo, of Santa Clara, California He was a member of the New York State Legislature

Nathan Pendelton Wilcox

(1153617)

Nathan Pendleton Wilcox, son of Isaiah and Polly Pendleton
Wilcox, born in Danube, N Y, May 3, 1804, died April 24, 1833,
married October 9, 1828, Lurancie Richardson, daughter of Lieutenant William and Sarah Norton Richardson, died in Sewickley,
Pa, December 10, 1893, and had two children Thomas Jefferson, born in Nunda, N Y., April 29, 1830, died in Nunda, N Y
July 30, 1830 Nathan Pendelton, born in Nunda N Y, May
16 1832, died April 25, 1904, married Celestine Birge

He moved to Nunda, N Y, where he became the architect and
builder of the Baptist Church known as the "Brick Church."

Thomas P Estes

(1231163).

Thomas P Estes, son of Philip and (given name unknown)
Gage Estes, born February 28, 1778, died September 17, 1845, mar-
ried in Schoharie Schoharie County, N Y June 25, 1801, Mary
Burlingham, daughter of Philip and Elizabeth, (surname unknown)
Burlingham, and had ten children Elizabeth born March 16,
1803, died August 20, 1881, married William Ball Charlotte,

286

born April 3, 1806; died April 18, 1880   EDMUND, born July 9, 1808, died July 27, 1842; married Esther H. Toppings.   PHILIP, born June 27, 1810, died June 20, 1863, married Rebecca Ball   REBECCA ANN, born September 24, 1815; married Moses De Line   PHLBL H., born December 7, 1817, died August 7, 1874, married James H. Earle   FRANCIS H., born August 5, 1819, married Phoebe Ann Howe.   SUSAN, born March 17, 1822, died May 18, 1882, married John Horton   MARY B., born July 5 1824; died February 16, 1883, married G. V. Pulver   GEORGE D., born September 28, 1827, married Mary E. Moyer.

He was a farmer and a member of the Friends Society.

REBECCA ESTES GAGE

(1231172).

Rebecca Estes, daughter of Thomas and Sarah Tripp Estes, born July 5, 1776, married in Duanesburg, N. Y., Daniel Gage, and had six children   EZEKIEL   ELKANAH.   JARVIS   MORTIMORE   DANIEL   PHEBE.

She moved to Pennsylvania soon after her marriage and resided there the balance of her life

ANNE ESTES OLIN

(1231173).

Anne Estes, daughter of Thomas and Sarah Tripp Estes, born December 30, 1779, married Henry Olin of Florida N. Y., and had seven children   WILLIAM.   VANRENSALEAR   GILES.   SARAH.   RUTH   CATHERINE   ANNI.

THOMAS ESTES

(1231175)

Thomas Estes son of Thomas and Sarah Tripp Estes, born January 7, 1784, died September 9, 1812, married and had three children.   JOSEPH   RACHEL.   SARAH.

JERUSHA ESTES McDONALD

(1231176)

Jerusha Estes, daughter of Thomas and Sarah Tripp Estes, born March 20, 1786; married James McDonald of Duanesburg, N Y, and had seven children THOMAS NATHANIEL MARGARET ANNA REBECCA. EDMOND. ESTES

NATHANIEL ESTES

(1231177)

Nathaniel Estes, son of Thomas and Sarah Tripp Estes, born May 31, 1788, died September 3, 1819, married July 2, 1807, Ruth Gage, daughter of Isaac and Lydia Sowle Gage, born February 16, 1789, died August 17, 1871, and had seven children Lois, born in Duanesburg, N. Y., May 6, 1808, died April 2, 1882; married Forus Kellogg. JOSEPH N., born in Duanesburg, N. Y., September 17, 1809; died in Missouri. September, 1858, married Mary Sowle. LYDIA G., born in Duanesburg, N Y., April 14, 1812, married Killson Lout Isaac, born in Duanesburg, N. Y., December 9, 1813 MARY, born in Duanesburg N Y, January 13, 1816, died September 28, 1853; married Thomas Williams. PATIENCE G. born in Duanesburg, N Y June 27, 1817, married Nathaniel Douglas. NATHANIEL, born in Duanesburg, N. Y., August 26, 1819

MARY ESTES THOMPSON

(1231192)

Mary Estes daughter of Benjamin and Phebe Borland Estes, born in Rinebeck, N. Y., May 20, 1782, died in Canada, 1860, married March 27, 1800, Joel Thompson, son of John Thompson, born March 19, 1775, died in Canada, 1850, and had nine children PHEBE, born in Palatine, N Y July 17, 1801, died in Canada, 1870, married Alexander Rutter REBECCA, born in Palatine N Y., March 31, 1803, married William F. Diamond SILAS, born in Palatine, N Y, April 29, 1805; died 1854, married Jane Ann Canniff. CHARLES B, born in Palatine, N Y, September 29, 1807, married Abigail F Gilbert ANN, born in Palatine, N Y, February 13, 1810, died 1850; married Edward H. Curlette ANDREW, born in Palatine, N. Y., July 9, 1812, died young HORATIO N , boin in Palatine, N. Y, April 10, 1814, married Julia Bussing. ANGELINE, born in Palatine, N. Y, November 26, 1816, married William Denyke. JAMES ESTES, born in Palatine, N. Y., February 2, 1819; died 1879, married Mary Hall.

BETSEY ESTES BARBER

(123119a9)

Betsey Estes, daughter of Benjamin and Phebe Borland Estes, born in Rinebeck, N Y., April 6, 1801, married in Schoharie County, N Y, 1816, Alsbro Barber, son of Alsbro and Patience (surname unknown) Barber born in Rhode Island, 1793, and had nine children. SARAH, born 1817. ELI, born in Cape Vincent, N. Y, August 19, 1819. LUCINDA, born August 12, 1821. AMANDA, born 1823 LORENZO A , born 1826. HARRIET, born 1828. PATIENCE, born 1830, died 1855. CALVIN, born 1832, died 1878. ELIZABETH, born in Hamilton, N Y, 1834

LUCINDA ESTES WRIGHT

(123119a9b).

Lucinda Estes, daughter of Benjamin and Phebe Borland Estes, born in Rinebeck, N Y, October 27, 1805, married Calvin Wright, died March 9, 1872, and had four children. MINERVA, born in Lyme, N. Y., February 2, 1829. CHARLOTTE A , born in Cape Vincent. N Y., August 14, 1836; died December 27, 1879 FRANCES T., born in Cape Vincent, N. Y., September 15, 1839 VOLNEY, born in Cape Vincent, N Y, August 31, 1841, died November 1, 1848

MARY ESTES HERRICK.

(123119c1)

Mary Estes, daughter of James and Catherine Pearce Estes, born March 4, 1788; married Roswell Herrick, and had one child HIRAM.

HANNAH ESTES EMPEY.

(12311903)

Hannah Estes, daughter of James and Catherine Pearce Estes, born August 17, 1791, married Jacob Empey, and had one child. CHARLES.

BETSEY ESTES CLINE

(12311908).

Betsey Estes, daughter of James and Catherine Pearce Estes, born May 14, 1800, married Epenetus Cline, and had one child. JOHN HENRY

ROSINA ESTES LEONARD

(1231190gb)

Rosina Estes, daughter of James and Catherine Pearce Estes, born September 20 1805, died January 6, 1844, married in Lyme, N. Y., July 5, 1824, Charles Leonard, born September 29, 1800, died April 26, 1865, and had eight children RACHEL, born in Lyme, N. Y., March 24, 1825 married Rev Ashel J Cooley AMASA, born in Lyme, N. Y., April 30, 1827 died May 30 1880 SALLY M, born in Lyme N. Y., March 30, 1830, married Isaac Norton. EDGAR, born in Lyme, N Y, August 15, 1832 married A Huntington MARY J, born in Lyme, N. Y., March 12, 1835 married Daniel B Rood LaFAYETTE born in Lyme N. Y., March 18, 1837 married Ella J Conant CAROLINE, born in Lyme, N. Y., August 31, 1839, married John C Broadbent. CHARLOTTE, born in Lyme, N. Y., March 20, 1842, married George Cantley.

Her husband was a mechanic, merchant wool carder, etc.

JANE ESTES ROGERS

(1231190c)

Jane Estes, daughter of James and Rachel Odell Estes born July 3 married January 1 1843, Jeremy W Rogers, son of Jeremy W. and Caroline Porter Rogers, born April 21, 1814, and had six

children   GEORGE N., born October 5, 1843; married Philena A.
Fuller   ALBERT V., born October 9, 1845, married Alice Sawyer
ORLANDO N., born October 12, 1847, married Cepha June   HEN-
RIETTA A., born November 12, 1849, married James H. Birtland
CHARLES O., born November 15, 1852, married Mina M. Hodges
JOHN F., born February 15, 1856, married Martha Snyder

HANNAH THOMAS DENNIS

(1231221)

Hannah Thomas, daughter of Joseph and Ruth Tabor Thomas,
born in Portsmouth, R. I., March 20, 1770, died in Portsmouth,
R. I., March 5, 1849; married in Portsmouth, R. I., November 6,
1793, George Dennis, son of Robert and Hannah Coggeshall Dennis,
born January 26, 1769, died in Portsmouth, R. I. March 10, 1837,
and had six children   JOSEPH, born September 29, 1794   AMEY,
born October 29, 1795, died July 21, 1840   NATHAN, born March
26, 1798, died in Portsmouth, R. I., December 7, 1869, married
Patience Seabrook Cook   JOHN.   DORCAS, born July 23, 1802
JONATHAN, born October 10, 1808.

DAVID ESTES

(1231315).

David Estes, son of Robert and Prudence Bennett Estes born in
Tiverton, R. I., June 3, 1783, died in Savoy, Mass., April 19, 1842
married in Tiverton, R. I., Eliphal Durfee, daughter of Benjamin
and Rhoda Brightman Durfee, born in Tiverton, R. I. September
15, 1781, died December 25, 1852, and had five children.   FRED-
ERICK, born in Tiverton, R. I., June 15, 1806, died June 16, 1849
PETER, born in Tiverton, R. I., August 6, 1807   MARY A., born
in Tiverton, R. I., December 16, 1809, died July 11, 1872, married
Joseph Joslin.   HANNAH, born in Tiverton, R. I., October 13, 1812
EMELINE, born in Tiverton, R. I., June 27, 1822, died March,
1854

Elizabeth Estes Sisson.

(1231331)

Elizabeth Estes, daughter of Joseph and Edith Wood Estes, born in Dartmouth, Mass., March 12, 1789, died June 19, 1872, married in Dartmouth, Mass., July 28, 1812, Allen Sisson, son of William and Sylvia Allen Sisson born February 15 1790, died October 11, 1860, and had six children SARAH H, born in Dartmouth, Mass., July 15 1813, married Joseph Crapo. HANNAH H, born in Dartmouth, Mass., April 6, 1815, died young WILLIAM, born in Dartmouth, Mass., April 6, 1817, married Susan Russell SYLVIA A, born in Dartmouth, Mass. November 2, 1819, married Elisha Chase EDITH C, born in Dartmouth, Mass., November 16, 1823. ELIZABETH ESTES, born in Dartmouth, Mass., April 6, 1825, married John H Nickerson

Sarah Estes Smith

(1231332).

Sarah Estes, daughter of Joseph and Edith Wood Estes, born in Dartmouthh, Mass., April 22, 1791, died July 5, 1867, married in Dartmouth, Mass., February 13, 1812 George Smith, son of George and Mary (surname unknown) Smith, born in Dartmouth, Mass., April 26, 1790; died May 8, 1870, and had twelve children ALMIRA, born in Dartmouth, Mass., June 18, 1811; married David Sisson GEORGE, born in Dartmouth, Mass., November 13, 1813, married Mary R Wood. HENRY born in Dartmouth, Mass., November 15, 1815, married Ruth L Wilcox JOSEPH ESTES, born in Dartmouth, Mass., October 8, 1817, married Sarah Howland, (2) Annie E Swift SARAH E, born in Dartmouth, Mass., September 16, 1819, married George P Potter DAVID, born in Dartmouth, Mass., August 25, 1821, married Phebe A Tripp A son, born in Dartmouth, Mass., January 30 1824, died young. LEANDER, born in Dartmouth, Mass., April 4, 1825, married Rubie H Sherman HANNAH W, born in Dartmouth, Mass., November 30, 1827, married William H Cummings FRANKLIN S., born in Dartmouth, Mass., March 9, 1832, died young EMILY, born in Dartmouth, Mass., September 5, 1834, died young CHARLES F, born in Dartmouth, Mass., June 14, 1837, married Ella C Borden.

Hannah Estes Hull

(1231333).

Hannah Estes, daughter of Joseph and Edith Wood Estes, born in Dartmouth, Mass., May 10, 1794, died April 21, 1869; married in Dartmouth, Mass., October 1, 1810, Captain John Hull, son of Captain John and Abigail Carr Hull, born April 14, 1786, died in Baltimore, Md., May 1830, and had five children   John, born in Dartmouth, Mass., January 8, 1812; died April 25, 1875, married Lydia Sherman.   Mary A., born in Dartmouth, Mass., January 8, 1814; married Edward Chase   Eliza born in Dartmouth, Mass., October 14, 1819, died October 5, 1868   Hannah, born in Dartmouth, Mass., June 24, 1822, married Elihu Howland   Charles F., born in Dartmouth, Mass., December 27, 1824, married Caroline B. Bumpas, (2) Maria L. Palmer

Joseph Estis

(1231335)

Joseph Estes, son of Joseph and Edith Wood Estes, born in Dartmouth, Mass., October 26, 1801; died March 26, 1889, married in Dartmouth, Mass., December 9, 1830, Eunice Chase, daughter of Anthony and Isabel Buffington Chase, born October 2 1808, and had seven children   Joseph Anthony, born in Fall River, Mass., August 29, 1831.   James, born in Fall River, Mass., January 16, 1833.   Darius B., born in Fall River, Mass., March 28, 1834, died May 13, 1845.   Thomas G, born in Fall River, Mass, April 2, 1839   Nathan C., born in Fall River, Mass January 1, 1841   Sarah, born in Fall River Mass., October 15, 1843, died October 11, 1845.   Charles, born in Fall River, Mass., June 14, 1849

Sarah Estes Lake.

(1231345).

Sarah Estes, daughter of Elisha and Sarah Bennett Estes, born in Tiverton, R. I. October 27, 1791, died August 28, 1878, married March 18, 1825, Christopher Lake, son of David and Susan (surname unknown) Lake, born March 13 1782 died March 6, 1864, and had two children   David H., born July 12, 1826, died

Young LYDIA B, born January 18, 1829, married John W Dennis.

JOSEPH TRIPP.

(1231303).

Joseph Tripp, son of Edmund and Sarah Estes Tripp, born in Westport, Mass, November 23, 1785; married May 30, 1811. Elizabeth Davis, born in Westport, Mass, April 8, 1787, and had seven children DEBORAH, born in Westport, Mass, May 28, 1812, married Abial Gardiner NICHOLAS D, born in Westport, Mass, November 5, 1813. SARAH D, born in Westport, Mass, April 30, 1815 JAMES, born in Westport, Mass June 23, 1817; died August 7, 1818 HANNAH W, born in Westport, Mass, July 31 1819 CATHERINE, born in Westport, Mass, April 21, 1823 CHARLES G, born in Westport, Mass, June 24, 1830.

JOB ESTES

(1231372)

Job Estes, son of Edmund and Elizabeth Lawton Estes, born in Tiverton, R I, March 24, 1797: died December 23, 1872, married in Tiverton, R I December 23 1823, Delilah Orswell, daughter of Benjamin and Amy Durfee Orswell, born February 14, 1800, and had ten children ELIZABETH L., born in Tiverton, R. I., February 12, 1825, married Lsek M. Brownell. CHARLES O, born in Tiverton R I October 1, 1826; married Elizabeth Cornell ALZADA, born in Tiverton, R I December 12, 1828, died May 30, 1844. LAVINETT T., born in Tiverton, R I April 13, 1830, died October 23, 1850, married Thomas W Lawton THOMAS W, born in Tiverton, R I, November 4, 1831, died August 18, 1864 JOSEPH D born in Tiverton R I, October 9 1833, married Abbie B Manchester JOHN H, born in Tiverton, R I, June 19, 1835, married Caroline A Ling BENJAMIN F, born in Tiverton, R I, January 1, 1837, married Henrietta Thomas LOUISA J, born in Tiverton, R I, October 27 1837, married Thomas W Lawton ANNA D, born in Tiverton, R I, April 1, 1843, died in Fall River, Mass, July 12, 1899, married Francis H Wixon

He was a wheelwright by trade About 1837 he built the first cotton mill for making sheeting and print goods in Tiverton (now

Brookville), Fall River, Mass, where from 1840 to 1860 he manufactured cotton yarn This mill was destroyed by fire, and about 1862, he built the present stone mill, which since his death has been conducted by his sons under the firm name of John H. Estes & Bros.

ELIZABETH ESTES CHASE.

(1231381)

Elizabeth Estes, daughter of Peter and Mercy Durfee Estes, born in Tiverton, R I., September 16. 1799; married in Tiverton, R I September 7, 1817, Holder Chase, son of Nathan and Annie Sherman Chase, born in Portsmouth, R. I, March 17 1797, died September, 1832, and had seven children. JANE L, born July 23, 1818; married Francis Bourn Read. IRENE A., born October 30. 1819, married James D Albro. HOLDER, born March 11, 1821, married Harriet Petty. ELIZA ESTES born January 26, 1823; married Charles S Kirby THOMAS E, born December 10, 1824, married Clara G Douglass ABBY A., born June 4, 1826; married Josiah T. Ellis OBEDIAH D born March 30, 1851; died young

MARY ESTES COOK.

(1231385)

Mary Estes, daughter of Peter and Mercy Durfee Estes, born in Tiverton, R I, September 29, 1805; died October 8, 1883, married in Tiverton, R. I., August 17, 1825, Captain Samuel T Cook, son of Daniel and Sarah Bennett Cook, born in Tiverton, R. I. March 7, 1799, died in Tiverton, R I, December 1, 1879 and had eight children. ASA, born in Tiverton, R. I, July 2, 1828, married Maria Coggeshall ALBERT J, born in Tiverton, R. I, April 17, 1832; died September 7. 1833 STEPHEN J, born in Tiverton. R I, April 17, 1833 HARRIET M, born in Tiverton, R I. April 1, 1835; married Stephen F. Grinnell. PETER ESTES, born in Tiverton, R. I.. February 22, 1838; married Caroline A Brownell HENRY V, born in Tiverton, R I., August 21, 1840, married Lucretia Mason, (2) Nellie T. Rickerson. MERCY ESTES, born in Tiverton, R. I., January 4, 1843, died September 23, 1843 MERCY ESTES, born in Tiverton, R. I., July 21, 1844, married George H. Fish.

CATHERINE C. ESTES SWIFT

(1231388)

Catherine C. Estes, daughter of Peter and Anna Hicks Estes, born in Tiverton, R. I., February 21, 1812; died in Toledo, O., August 26, 1861, married in Tiverton R. I., September 16, 1832, Albert Swift, son of Charles and Sarah Parker Swift, died in Toledo, O., October 30, 1865, and had two children. EMMA R. born June 19, 1834; died December 31, 1866, married Daniel H. Nye. ANNIE ESTES born November 14, 1835, married Norman Waite

LYDIA ESTES SISSON.

(1231389)

Lydia Estes, daughter of Peter and Anna Hicks Estes, born in Tiverton, R.I., November 7, 1813, married in Tiverton, R. I. June 9, 1831, Thomas R. Sisson, son of Peleg and Hannah Brownell Sisson, born January 30, 1800, died June 20 1848, and had eight children. HENRY W., born March 24, 1832, died young. JAMES F. A., born November 9, 1833, died March 18, 1888. ALBERT H., born August 4, 1836, married Louisa J. Ashley. FRANCIS B., born October 25, 1838, married Retta Snow. ANNA J. born January 14, 1841, married Joseph Estes. SARAH A., born March 28, 1843; married George P. Clark. LYDIA J., born September 7, 1846, died young. THOMAS R., born May 4, 1848

HANNAH H. ESTES CHURCH

(1231389b)

Hannah H. Estes, daughter of Peter and Anna Hicks Estes, born in Tiverton, R. I., March 21, 1818 died April 27, 1888, married in Tiverton, R. I., October 25, 1840, Joseph T. Church, died July 14, 1841, and had one child JOSEPH H., born September 11, 1841; died January 26, 1848

She married second April 11, 1848, Ephriam Willey, son of Ephriam and Mary Noble Willey, and had three children JOSEPH H born December 31, 1848, married Julia Burgess. JOHN F., born September 29, 1852; married Jane E Burbank. HATTIE A., born December 1, 1861, died May 9, 1862

Anna B Estes Swift

(1231389f)

Anna B Estes, daughter of Peter and Anna Hicks Estes, born in Tiverton, R. I., April 28, 1822, died August 21, 1877, married Thomas R Swift, son of Moses Swift, and had one child   Annie Estes, born November 16, 1840, married Joseph Estes Smith

Hiram M Estes

(1231389g)

Hiram M Estes, son of Peter and Anna Hicks Estes, born in Tiverton, R I, February 9, 1826, died July 10, 1854, married Mary A. Jones, daughter of John W. and Ruth B. Welden Jones, and had three children. Mary E, born November 9, 1848, married James G. Case   Francis H, born September 5, 1849, died October 20, 1849   Annie B, born June 12, 1851

John Dennis

(1232311).

John Dennis, son of Gideon and Mary Durfee Dennis, born in Portsmouth, R I, March 31, 1787, died in Portsmouth, R I; married in Portsmouth, R I.; (his wife's name is unknown), and had three children. Eliza, born in Portsmouth, R I; married Lorenzo Kenney.   Hy Franklin   William R, born in Portsmouth, R I 1822, married Abby F Field.

Phebe Dennis Cornell

(1232313).

Phebe Dennis, daughter of Gideon and Mary Durfee Dennis, born in Portsmouth, R. I, November, 1790; died in Portsmouth, R I, married a Cornell, and had one child.   Almira

GIDEON DENNIS

(1232314).

Gideon Dennis, son of Gideon and Mary Durfee Dennis, born in Portsmouth, R. I., February 27, 1793, married Meribah Manchester, daughter of John and Mary (surname unknown) Manchester, and had two children EDWARD. HARRIET, born March, 1816; married Hiram Sherman

JOB DURFEE DENNIS

(1232315)

Job Durfee Dennis, son of Gideon and Mary Durfee Dennis, born in Portsmouth R. I. April 3, 1795, died in Tiverton, R. I., December 13, 1875, married in Newport, R. I., May 2, 1820, Mary Borden Mosher, daughter of Amos and Mary Davol Mosher, born in Tiverton, R. I., March 10, 1802; died in Fall River, Mass., October 16, 1882, and had six children PATIENCE SEABURY, born in Tiverton, R. I. August 18 1821 ELIZA ANN born in Tiverton, R. I., October 20, 1823 AMANDA FITZALLEN, born in Tiverton, R. I., November 10, 1825, married Samuel Allen. JANE ELIZA, born in Tiverton R. I., November 20, 1827, died in Milford, Mass., June 13, 1897 married Rowland Coffin Hussey EDWIN, born in Tiverton R. I., February 19 1830, married Elizabeth Ann Mitchell HENRIETTA B, born in Tiverton, R. I., June 4, 1845, married Jonathan Earl.

He was a farmer and a soldier in the War of 1812.

RICHMOND DENNIS

(1232319)

Richmond Dennis, son of Gideon and Mary Durfee Dennis, born in Portsmouth, R. I., February 27 1803, married Susan E Pearce, and had seven children SARAH ANN, born August 14, 1832, married Samuel Lindsey WILLIAM R, born April 10, 1837 SUSAN E, born July 29, 1839, married Richard Fish Boyd CHARLES E, born November 20, 1841, married Emma Fisher Proctor MARY ELLEN, born April 20, 1845; married a Martin. HARRIET A, born July 19, 1847 CATHERINE A born July 17, 1850

208

JOSEPH CORNELL DENNIS.

(1232319b).

Joseph Cornell Dennis, son of Gideon and Mary Durfee Dennis, born in Portsmouth, R. I., November 10 1807; died in Providence, R. I., June 3, 1866; married in Portsmouth. R. I., May 29, 1832, Mary Brayton Gifford, daughter of Jeremiah and Hannah Hall Gifford, born in Portsmouth, R. I., March 4, 1814; died in Providence, R. I., July 20, 1865, and had eight children WILLIAM ANTHONY, born March 4, 1833, died July 4, 1833. GEORGE HALL, born May 29, 1834; died August, 1834 MARY JANE, born 1836, died 1877, married Nathan B Capon CLARISSA GIFFORD, born October, 1840, died 1876, married a Cole MATILDA ANNA, born September 4, 1842, married Philip D Gibson, (2) Job Dawley. HARRIET GIFFORD, born June 26, 1844, married Silas Davol CHARLES EDWARD, born November 13, 1847. JOSEPH HALL, born December 26, 1848.

He enlisted in the Eleventh Rhode Island Volunteer Infantry, and served nine months His patriotism is well attested by his willingness to serve his country at an age when a draft or involuntary service could not be required His people were among the "well-to-do" farmers of Portsmouth, R. I., where he probably spent the period of his life before the War of the Rebellion

SARAH ANN DENNIS TALLMAN.

(1232319c)

Sarah Ann Dennis, daughter of Gideon and Mary Durfee Dennis, born in Portsmouth, R. I., October 1, 1814, died in Portsmouth, R. I., December 24, 1891, married in Portsmouth, R. I., September 22, 1832, Benjamin Tallman, son of Thales and Priscilla Devol Tallman, born in Portsmouth, R. I., April 21, 1807; died in Portsmouth, R. I., October 9, 1883, and had ten children REUBEN RANSOM, born in Portsmouth, R. I., September 11, 1833, married Eliza Smith JOHN WESLEY, born in Portsmouth, R. I., December 31, 1835; married Almina E Tallman. ELIJAH LOVEJOY, born in Portsmouth, R. I., February 13, 1838, married Mary J Devol. MARY ANN, born in Portsmouth, R. I., February 3, 1840. LETITIA TYLER, born in Portsmouth, R. I., August 20, 1842, married William F Freeborn SARAH CARPENTER, born in Portsmouth, R.

I, November 16, 1844, married William B Fish. (2) James E
Babcock BENJAMIN, born in Portsmouth R. I., November 7,
1846, married Eleanor A. Fish WILLIAM THALIS, born in Portsmouth, R. I., August 19, 1851; married Laura G Carr FRED-
ERICK UPHAM, born in Portsmouth, R. I., September 11, 1853, married Mary Orterson. GEORGE BANCROFT, born in Portsmouth, R.
I., September 11, 1853

WILLIAM HALL

(1232321).

William Hall, son of George and Hannah Dennis Hall, born
in Portsmouth, R I, February 2, 1774; married in Portsmouth, R
I., August 6, 1797, Mary Thomas, daughter of Alexander and Ur-
silla Oldridge Thomas, born in Portsmouth, R I, May 18, 1777,
and had one child. WILLIAM, born in Portsmouth, R I, May 6,
1798.

HANNAH HALL GIFFORD.

(1232322).

Hannah Hall, daughter of George and Hannah Dennis Hall,
born in Portsmouth, R I, August 29 1775, married in Portsmouth,
R. I., March 30, 1797, Jeremiah Gifford, son of Captain David and
Abigail Durfee Gifford, born in Portsmouth, R I., January 15,
1771, died in Portsmouth, R. I., November 21, 1841, and had
eleven children. DAVID, born October 28, 1799. ELIZA, born July
4, 1801 GEORGE HALL, born June 26, 1803 CLARISSA, born June
24, 1805 RUTH, born May 4 1807 HARRIET, born June 24,
1810 WILLIAM HALL, born June 28, 1812 MARY BRAYTON,
born March 4, 1814 JANE born October, 1816 JOSEPH, born
January 18 1818, died September 7, 1822. ELIZABETH, born January 29, 1820
Her husband was a large land owner and kept a tavern at Bristol Ferry, in Portsmouth, R I., and run the ferry boat to and from
the Bristol side.

PARKER HALL.

(1232327).

Parker Hall, son of George and Hannah Dennis Hall, born in Portsmouth, R. I., July 29, 1784; died in Portsmouth, R. I., August 17, 1809, married Hannah Thomas, daughter of Richard and Elizabeth Brownell Thomas, born in Portsmouth, R I, October 6, 1787; died in Portsmouth, R I, October 5, 1871, and had six children. ALMIRA T born May 27, 1810, married a Sowle HANNAH W, born February 16, 1812. ANN JANETTA, born January 1, 1816; married a Carr. CATHERINE SOWLE, born September 30, 1822 WILLIAM THOMAS, born January 9, 1825. BENJAMIN, born March 20 1827, died in Portsmouth, R I, August 5, 1901, married Eliza V Chase.

He was a farmer and was a member of the legislature of the State of Rhode Island during the Dorr War, and it is said he was a friend of Governor Dorr General LaFayette made frequent stops at his father's house during the Revolutionary War He was a leading man in public matters in the town of Portsmouth, R I, and was Associate Judge in the Court of Common Pleas

HANNAH DENNIS HALL.

(1232341)

Hannah Dennis, daughter of Robert and Ruth Anthony Dennis, born July 13, 1784, married in Portsmouth, R. I. January 1, 1807, David Hall, son of George and Charity Fish Hall, born in Portsmouth, R. I, July 16, 1781, and had nine children ISAAC DENNIS, born November 11, 1807 DARIUS born January 21, 1809. HARRIET A., born July 16, 1810 JANE, born April 4, 1812 EDWARD, born January 27, 1814 GARDINER, born October 10, 1815, married Catherine Sowle Hall. RUTH DENNIS, born November 21, 1817 ROBERT DENNIS, born June 18, 1820, married Mary A Cook DAVID FRANKLIN, born February 18, 1828, married Abbie T Chase.

Isaac A Dennis

(1232343)

Isaac A Dennis, son of Robert and Ruth Anthony Dennis, born April 30, 1788, married in Middletown, R. I., December 25, 1814, Sarah Coggeshall, daughter of Joseph and Elizabeth Horsewell Coggeshall, born in Middletown, R I, September 18, 1791, died 1860, and had two children RUTH ANN, married Joseph W Chase. JOSEPH C., married Mary G Chase.

RUTH DENNIS CHASE

(1232346).

Ruth Dennis, daughter of Robert and Ruth Anthony Dennis, born October 16, 1791, married in Portsmouth R I, January 1, 1817, Isaac Chase, son of Isaac and Phebe Hall Chase, born in Portsmouth, R I, August 4, 1791, and had three children MARY, married John H Butler CHARLES, married Elizabeth Clark ALBERT BURR, born October 15, 1824, died March 12 1872, married Emily Henderson

DAVID DENNIS

(1232347)

David Dennis, son of Robert and Ruth Anthony Dennis, born August 4, 1793, married Eliza Gifford, daughter of Jeremiah and Hannah Hall Gifford born in Portsmouth, R. I., July 4, 1801, and had four children BENJAMIN JEREMIAH. HANNIBAL DARIUS

ABIGAIL DENNIS ARNOLD.

(1232362)

Abigail Dennis, daughter of Jonathan and Hannah Sherman Dennis, born May 18, 1794, married in Newport R. I., July 28, 1815, Asa Arnold, son of Benjamin and Isabel Greene Arnold, born in Providence, R I October 1 1788, died in Smithfield, R I December 19, 1833, and had eight children MARY, born December 8, 1816. HARRIET, born December 29, 1818 WILLIAM W, born

September 16, 1820   BENJAMIN, born October 4, 1822   JAMES GREENE, born September 22, 1824   SAMUEL ASA, born January 4, 1827.   ELIZABETH, born May 17, 1829   SARAH GREENE, born May 24, 1832

SAMUEL DENNIS

(1232363)

Samuel Dennis, son of Jonathan and Hannah Sherman Dennis, born February 19, 1796, died in Dover, N. H., married in Portsmouth, R. I., February 1, 1822, Diana Gifford, daughter of Gideon and Bridget Almy Cook Gifford, born in Portsmouth, R. I., July 23, 1794, died in Portsmouth, R. I., February 5, 1835, and had two children.   GIDEON GIFFORD, born June 14, 1823.   SAMUEL JAMES born March 22, 1829, married Addie Bangs

MARY DENNIS CONGDON

(1232365)

Mary Dennis, daughter of Jonathan and Hannah Sherman Dennis born April 27, 1799, died in Providence, R. I., September 29, 1871, married in Portsmouth, R. I., December 11, 1823, Welcome Congdon, son of Jonathan and Elizabeth Arnold Congdon, born in Providence, R. I., April 3, 1794, died in Providence, R. I. August 13, 1874, and had seven children   CALEB, born September 10 1826 married Sarah P Richardson   ABBY, born January 1, 1828, died September 14, 1829.   ABBY, born October 7, 1829, married William H Phillips   ELIZABETH RUDD, born June 8, 1831   RUTH EDDY, born November 12, 1833, married John Sanford   GEORGE, born February 19, 1836   EDWARD ARNOLD, born August 18, 1838, died in Providence, R. I., November 12, 1859.

JAMES DENNIS

(1232366)

James Dennis son of Jonathan and Hannah Sherman Dennis, born February 1, 1801; died in East Providence, R. I., April 9 1889, married in Providence R. I., September 11 1828, Hannah Jackson daughter of Richard and Nabby Wheaton Jackson, born in Providence, R. I., February 6, 1800; died in Providence, R. I., June 26, 1833, and had one child CATHERINE JACKSON, born in Cranston, R. I., December 7, 1829, married Benjamin Barker

RICHARD DENNIS

(1232367).

Richard Dennis, son of Jonathan and Hannah Sherman Dennis, born September 5, 1802 died in Lowell, Mass, February 19, 1860; married September 1826 Lucy Ann Hooper, daughter of John and Jane Lord Hooper, born in Berwick, Me., December 30, 1806; died in Lowell, Mass., December 30, 1890, and had five children. ANNA MARIA born January 13, 1828, married James M McCoy. MARY ABBY, born September 11, 1830, married Henry P Carter. WILLIAM HOOPER, born April 29, 1833 married Angie M Eaton. JENNIE H., born in Lowell, Mass., March 17, 1837, married Alfred Metcalf. SARAH FRANCES born February 8, 1840; married Otis M. Humphrey M. D. EDWARD PAYSON, born April 8, 1843, married Emma L. Robinson.

JONATHAN DENNIS

(1232376)

Jonathan Dennis, son of George and Hannah Thomas Dennis, born October 10, 1808, married and had one child. JOSEPH G, married second Clara E Barker

JOSHUA COGGESHALL

(1232525).

Joshua Coggeshall, son of Joseph and Elizabeth Horsewell Coggeshall born December 25, 1788; died in Middletown R. I., April 7, 1879, married in Middletown, R. I., November 26, 1815, Deborah Allen daughter of John and Hannah (surname unknown) Allen, and had five children. GEORGE C, born October 7 1816. DAVID, born October 28 1818. HANNAH MARY, born January 6, 1820 ANNE ELIZABETH, born November 2, 1822. SARAH DENNIS born September 21, 1824

He spent his life in Middletown, R. I., and was a farmer. He was in early life an old line Whig, but subsequently became a Democrat, and for many years served in the General Assembly of Rhode Island. He was president of the Coucil of Middletown, R. I., and for nearly forty years was the efficient clerk of the township "While liberal toward all sects, he worshipped with the Friends meetings."

ABRAHAM COGGESHALL

(1232528)

Abraham Coggeshall, son of Joseph and Elizabeth Horsewell Coggeshall, born March 15, 1797 married Annie Sisson and had seven children ABRAHAM born 1820, married Sarah G Oman NOEL JANE M, married William Chase. JOSEPH, born 1825; married Mary A Lawton MARY C married William Chase Martha, married William E. Coggeshall JOHN P, born in Portmouth, R I 1836, married Elizabeth Roddy.

PHILIP ANTHONY.

(1232531)

Philip Anthony son of Gideon and Elizabeth Coggeshall Anthony born 1789, died 1873; married in Middletown, R I December 4, 1817, Mary Manchester, daughter of John Manchester and had one child SUSAN ANTHONY.

PARDON BROWN

(1232559b)

Pardon Brown, son of Peleg and Mary Coggeshall Brown born December 24 1801; married in Narragansett, R I., Lucy Armstrong, daughter of Captain Nathaniel Armstrong and had five children GEORGE ARMSTRONG, born October 4 1822, married Elizabeth C. Anthony. PARDON, born January 5, 1825 JOSHUA C, born February 27, 1828, married Jane Smith MARY A NATHANIEL A married Sarah F Carr

He married second 1831 Sarah Sanford daughter of Captain

Peleg Sanford, and had three children   Lucy M , married James
A Brown   Peleg   Lydia

Isaac Manchester

(1232563)

Isaac Manchester, son of Thomas and Mercy Coggeshall Manchester, born February 9, 1792 married in Portsmouth, R I December 31, 1820, Sally Fish, daughter of John Fish, and had three
children Cook, born in Middletown, R I, August 21, 1823.
Freeborn, born in Middletown R I July 5, 1825 Thomas,
born in Middletown, R I, 1839, married Mary Albro

Freeborn Manchester

(1232564)

Freeborn Manchester, son of Thomas and Mercy Coggeshall
Manchester, born November 14, 1793, married in Portsmouth, R
I , July 2, 1816 Ann Slocum, daughter of Stephen Slocum and had
five children Sarah Ann, born November 12 1818 Stephen,
born March 16, 1820 George Tew, born May 23, 1823 Truman, born November 13, 1825   Peter A , born May 19, 1835

Peleg Coggeshall

(1232581).

Peleg Coggeshall, son of George and Cynthia Sherman Cog-
geshall, married in Portsmouth R I January 14 1817 Bridget
Almy, daughter of Peleg Almy, born in Portsmouth, R I, 1796,
died in Portsmouth, R I, 1886, and had four children Cynthia,
born August 20, 1818; died in Providence, R I , married William
B. Chase George B , born January 8, 1820, died June 30, 1828
Peter A , born August 10 1822; married Lucinda Aylesworth
George B , born February 27 1827
    He was a soldier in the War of 1812

BENJAMIN FISH

(1232782)

Benjamin Fish, son of Joseph and Amey Chase Fish, born September 5, 1801; married 1827, Abbie Estes, daughter of Peter Estes, and had two children. A son, born December 24, 1827 A son, born February 24 1831

ELIZABETH MOTT WADSWORTH

(1232823)

Elizabeth Mott, daughter of Benjamin and Sarah Chase Mott, born November 3, 1799, married in Portsmouth, R I October 2, 1822, John A Wadsworth, M D, and had two children EMMA ANN, born November 14, 1824, died March 20, 1825. JOHN LEON born June, 1828, died in Bristol, R I, October 13, 1828

JACOB MOTT

(1232824)

Jacob Mott, son of Benjamin and Sarah Chase Mott, born January 21, 1804 married in Portsmouth, R I, April 14, 1825, Eliza Anthony, and had four children. WILLIAM P, born January 27, 1826 BENJAMIN, born September 7, 1827 JACOB, born December 21, 1831 JOHN C, born December 21 1831

ALEXANDER HAMILTON CHASE

(1232884)

Alexander Hamilton Chase, son of Abner and Deborah Chase Chase, born September 8 1808, he married and had a son, WILLIAM ALFRED CHASE, born 1834, married Sarah C. Thomas

BENJAMIN FRANKLIN CHASE

(1232886).

Benjamin Franklin Chase, son of Abner and Deborah Chase Chase, born November 30, 1811, married in Portsmouth, R. I.,

Priscilla Anthony, daughter of Abraham Anthony, born in Portsmouth, R. I., 1813, and had three children ANN ELIZA, born December 28, 1836. ABNER, born December 27, 1842 RUTH SMITH, born May 8, 1846

GILES MARTINBOROUGH CHASE

(1232887)

Giles Martinborough Chase, son of Abner and Deborah Chase Chase, born August 24, 1813, married Elizabeth Hambly, daughter of John Hambly, and had five children AMANDA H, DEBORAH, PEACE ELIZABETH, FANNIE S, married William H Manchester. SQUIRE.

BORDEN CHASE

(1232893)

Borden Chase, son of Clark and Anna Borden Chase born April 5, 1816, died in Fall River, Mass, 1897, married in Portsmouth, R I December 24, 1838 Elizabeth A Thomas, daughter of Joseph and Hannah Anthony Thomas, born in Portsmouth, R I, and had four children ANNE BORDEN, born January 10, 1840 FREDERICK, born September 13, 1842 CLARK, born January 1, 1846 SIMEON BORDEN born January 10 1849.

He started a coal business in Fall River, Mass in 1871, and established the Fall River Coal Company in 1875, later became interested in the Globe Coal Company.

PHILIP BORDEN CHASE.

(1232894)

Philip Borden Chase son of Clark and Anna Borden Chase, born February 3 1818 married in Portsmouth, R I, Sarah Cook, daughter of William Earl and Eunice Sherman Cook, and had nine children. WILLIAM C, born in Portsmouth, R I EUNICE A, married Doctor Benjamin Green. PHILIP S REBECCA NANCY. CONSTANT C. CHARLES E. ISAAC S. HANNAH.

He filled the office of Town Clerk of his native town for many years.

ALFRED CLARK CHASE

(1232899).

Alfred Clark Chase son of Clark and Anna Borden Chase, born March 21, 1833, married in Portsmouth, R. I, Ruth Anthony, daughter of William Anthony, and had two children EDMUND MAUD A.

BETSEY READ WINSLOW

(1236491)

Betsey Read, daughter of Jonathan and Eleanor Law Read, married in Freetown, Mass, July 30, 1812, Ebenezer Spooner Winslow, son of John and Bethiah Spooner Winslow, born in Freetown, Mass, October 5, 1785, died May 9, 1822, and had two children EBENEZER, born December 7, 1814, married Christiana L Hartwell, (2) Mary Ann Miller DAVID B, born May 24, 1821, married Abigail Church

PHILADELPHIA BORDEN CHURCH

(1237482).

Philadelphia Borden, daughter of Aaron and Mercy Durfee Borden, born in Fall River, Mass, October 16, 1790, died in Fall River Mass, February 20, 1887, married in Fall River, Mass, September 11, 1819, John Church, son of John and Mary (surname unknown) Church, born in Fall River, Mass, July 31, 1794, died in Fall River, Mass, March 15, 1853, and had seven children JOHN, born August 11, 1821 SUSANNAH, born May 30, 1822 MARY M, born October 10, 1824 CHARLES born November 26, 1826 THOMAS E, born March 30, 1829 GEORGE J born January 6, 1832 CAROLINE E, born September 15, 1835

JOHN SHERMAN

(1237931)

John Shearman, son of Samuel and Susannah Pearse Shearman, born in Portsmouth, R. I, September 14, 1791, died in Portsmouth,

R. I., June 9, 1864, married in Portsmouth, R. I., January 31, 1812, Mary Albro, daughter of Robert and Innocent Tabor Albro, born in Portsmouth, R. I., January 11, 1789, died in Portsmouth, R. I., August 11, 1864, and had seven children   CATHERINE TEW born February 5, 1813   STEPHEN D., born November 24, 1814   LYDIA MARIA, born December 14, 1819   ROBERT ALBRO, born October 10, 1822   ELIZABETH ALBRO, born September 22, 1825   MARY HALL, born August 1, 1828.   SUSAN PEARSE, born November 1, 1831.

WAITE DURFEE SHEARMAN SHEARMAN

(1237933).

Waite Durfee Shearman, daughter of Samuel and Susannah Pearse Shearman, born April 4, 1794, married in Portsmouth, R. I., November 20, 1820, David Shearman, son of Samson and Ruth Fish Shearman, born in Portsmouth, R. I., June 2, 1772, and had eight children   ALMIRA born September 5, 1821   OBEDIAH D., born November 28, 1822.   CHARLES F., born February 23, 1824, died March 12, 1825   SUSAN P., born June 2, 1825   MARY A., born August 30, 1826   ABBIE W., born October 13, 1827   CHARLES G., born November 28, 1829, died May 11 1832   DAVID S., born April 18, 1833

IRA SHEARMAN

(1237939d).

Ira Shearman, son of Samuel and Susannah Pearse Shearman, born July 6, 1811; married in Portsmouth, R. I., November 20, 1835, Maria Mason Pearse, daughter of Timothy and Elizabeth (surname unknown) Pearse, born September 6 1812, and had three children   FRANCIS MARION born in Portsmouth, R. I., September 16, 1835.   ANN ELIZABETH, born in Portsmouth, R. I., September 13, 1838   HENRY CLAY, born in Portsmouth, R. I., October 10 1844

Susannah Lawton Lawton.

(12379c11)

Susannah Lawton, daughter of Peter and Waite Borden Lawton, born October 5, 1795, married in Portsmouth, R. I., May 11, 1814, Darius Perry Lawton, son of Giles and Ann (surname unknown) Lawton, born in Portsmouth, R. I., April 7, 1788, and had one child Ann, born in Swansea, Mass., March 6, 1815.

Walter Cornell

(1245113).

Walter Cornell, son of Thurston and Mary Perry Cornell, born in Tiverton, R. I., February 10, 1784, married Theresa Manchester, and had eleven children Alfred. Daniel Edward, born in Tiverton, R. I., married (2) March 14, 1852, Mary Jane Dyer Peleg Andrew Gideon Stephen. Gilbert. Nancy, married an Allen Mary, married a Mosher Elizabeth, married William O. Babbett.

William Cornell

(1245116)

William Cornell, son of Thurston and Mary Perry Cornell, married Betsey Jennings, and had five children. Abraham Anthony Thomas Jennings. Benjamin Warren Eliza Lydia Jennings

Anthony Cornell.

(1245118)

Anthony Cornell, son of Thurston and Mary Perry Cornell, married Sarah Grinnell daughter of Stephen Grinnell, and had three children. Elizabeth Anthony, married Charles O. Fustis. Amy Grinnell. Sarah Anthony, married Jeremiah Hathaway.

CHARLES RUSSELL CORNELL.

(1245561)

Charles Russell Cornell, son of Gideon and Hannah Russell Cornell, born January or June 20, 1806; died September 12, 1866; married Maria Cornell, and had one child. CHARLES WILLIAM, born September 30, 1833

He married second Hannah S. Avery, and had one child ELLA MARIA, born April 22, 1858.

JOHN W CORNELL

(1245721).

John W Cornell, son of Walter and Eunice Hunt Cornell, born in White Creek, N Y., November 16, 1816, died in Chautauqua, N Y., January 6, 1896, married in Cambridge, N. Y., January 24, 1839, Anna Durfee, daughter of Earl and Phoebe Hunt Durfee, born in Cambridge, N. Y September 13, 1819, died in Chautauqua, N Y March 17, 1902, and had six children. WALTER EARL, born in Cambridge, N Y, October 17 1839; died in Chautauqua, N. Y., May 21, 1906 WESLEY M, born in Cambridge, N Y, October 4, 1843, married JANE ANN IRWIN EMILY, born in Cambridge, N Y, May 10 1847, married Robert Hewes MARIA, ANTIONETTE, born in Cambridge, N Y., November 16, 1851 GEORGE J, born in Chautauqua. N. Y., February 8, 1854; married Ida Wilcox WILLIAM JAY, born in Chautauqua, N Y, February 1, 1858, married Laura A Little

He was a farmer and came to Chautauqua County, N. Y., in the spring of 1852, and located upon a farm on the west side of Chautauqua Lake He was a member of the Methodist Episcopal Church. In politics, he was a Republican. He is buried beside his wife in the Chautauqua Cemetery

MERRITT I CORNELL

(1245731).

Merritt I Cornell son of Matthew and Lydia Ford Cornell, born March 5, 1809, died August, 1883 married February 13, 1836,

Mercy Whitman Howard, daughter of Otis and Polly Wellington Howard, born July 23, 1814, died November 17, 1881, and had five children   DUDLEY EMERSON, born in Wilton, Saratoga County, N. Y., January 15, 1837   HOWARD, born in Wilton, N Y., September 10, 1840, married Jessie Kirby.   JOHN AUGUSTUS, born in Wilton, N Y, August 10, 1843, died April 6, 1844   MARY AUGUSTA, born in Wilton N Y, August 10, 1843, married James Sylvester   LYDIA ANTOINETTE, born in Wilton, N. Y., January 24, 1844, died June 17, 1897, married Henry Denison

He was a school teacher and school commissioner in his early life, and later a farmer   He lived most of his life in Hoosick, Hoosick Falls and Lima, N Y   He moved to Wyandotte Kan, in 1881, residing there until his death in 1883   He was a member of the Baptist Church.

HARRIET BROWNELL GARDNER

(1462163)

Harriet Brownell daughter of Isaac and Susan Anthony Brownell, born in Providence, R I, September 13, 1807, died July 13, 1902; married March 31, 1831, Malachi Rhodes Gardiner, and had one child   EDWIN RHODES, born November 26 1834, died June 28, 1903, married Abby Sanford

SUSAN FISH BROWNELL

(1462164)

Susan Fish Brownell, daughter of Isaac and Susan Anthony Brownell, born in Providence, R I, May 30, 1810, died March 29 1835, married April 29, 1834, Abel Lincoln, and had one child   SUSAN FISH, born March, 1835, died December 1890 married Edwin R Gardiner

STEPHEN BROWNELL.

(1462194).

Stephen Brownell, son of Stephen Fish and Mary White Brownell, born in Smithfield, R I, March 14, 1822, married November 12, 1846, Henrietta Hunt, daughter of Seth and Henrietta Hunt, Jr, and had one child, ISABEL SITH

He attended the Academy at Union Village and while a young man went to Providence, R I, and became a commission merchant. In 1859 he was instrumental in forming the firm of Goff, Cranston & Brownell, whose business extended all over this country and into Europe. The Union Wadding Company, an outgrowth of this firm, was the largest manufactory of cotton wadding in the world Since 1879, he has devoted himself to the real estate business. He was trustee of Butler Hospital for the insane nearly twenty years, and has been prominent in financial, educational and philantropic enterprises

JOSEPH BROWNELL

(1463311)

Joseph Brownell, son of Burden and Sarah Earle Brownell, born 1800 died 1874, married Sabrina C Stowell daughter of Nathaniel and Aurelia Bancroft Stowell, born in Pomfret, Conn, 1806, died in Benton, Lackawanna County, Pa, March, 1894, and had two children EDWIN DEFOREST, born in Sauquoit, N Y, April 6, 1829, died in Scranton Pa, April 16, 1874 SARAH AURELIA, born in Sauquoit, N Y, February 17, 1832, married Charles Newcomb

GEORGE MACOMBER BROWNELL

(1463362).

George Macomber Brownell, son of Abner and Susan Macomber Brownell born September 15, 1812, died July 30 1859, married May 1, 1837, Louisa Sweeting, and had four children CHARLES G, born April 8 1838, married Martha Jane Grant. ALBERT ELIPHELET, born October 18 1839, died November 18, 1886 ELIZABETH LOUISA born August 12. 1841, married Henry D Riley Tucker. JOHN JAY, born February 12, 1849; married Mary Elizabeth Starks

JULIETTE V. BROWNELL SAVAGE

(1463363).

Juliette V. Brownell, daughter of Abner and Susan Macomber Brownell, born July 26, 1814, died August 22, 1872, married October 25, 1837, Morris Stephen Savage, died December, 1875 and had seven children. GEORGE FREDERICK, born in Nolin, Ky., April 5, 1839; married Ellen M. Gilbert. MARIA J, born in Nolin, Ky, June 21, 1840, died October 4, 1846. EMMA FRANCES, born in Nolin, Ky, April 4, 1843; married Morris N Johnson SUSAN ELIZABETH, born in Sauquoit, N. Y., June 24, 1845, married George W Burpee KATHERINE JULIA, born in Sauquoit N Y, June 9, 1849. MORRIS DWIGHT, born in Sauquoit, N Y, September 6, 1851; married Fanny Carey. CLARA CORNELIA, born in Sauquoit, N. Y, June 5, 1856, George Herbert Rising.

EBENEZER DEAN BROWNELL

(1463364).

Ebenezer Dean Brownell, son of Abner and Susan Macomber Brownell, born November 13, 1816, died June 2, 1889, married Hannah West, and had two children FRANK ROSELL FANNIE MARIA.

HENRY DWIGHT BROWNELL.

(1463365)

Henry Dwight Brownell, son of Abner and Susan Macomber Brownell, born August 4, 1820, died March 21, 1829, married November 17, 1841 Katherine R Fox.

INDEX

Baker—(Continued)
    Johannah, 184
    Love, G 279
    Mary 184
    Sarah (Butterfield) 184
    William 193
Balch Benjamin 150
Baldwin
    Clarissa, 121 232 234
    Electa, 283
    Elizabeth Parmlee, 131
    Elvira 238
    Nathaniel, 131
    Sarah 131
Ball
    Rebecca, 287
    Thankful 86
    William 286
Bangs, Addie, 303
Barkley Mary, 113
Barlow Isadore, 260
Barnaby Joanna 114
Barnard, Amelia 274
Barnett
    Ann, 150
    Ruth, 229
Barney,
    Elizabeth (Bemus) 133 264
    Isaiah 243
    Sarah, 93 165
Barnum Henrietta 217
Barrett William 260
Barrington, Esther 285
Barber
    Alsbro 180 289
    Amanda 289
    Calvin 289
    Eli, 289
    Elizabeth 289
    Harriet 289
    John 93
    Lorenzo A, 289
    Lucinda 289
    Patience 289
    Patience (   ) 289
    Ruth 222
    Sally 180
    Sarah 289
    Susannah 80
Barker
    Abigail 123 238
    Abbey I , 242
    Anna E 133 270

Barker—(Continued)
    Benjamin, 304
    Clara I 304
    Jacob 144
    James, 160
    Sarah 170
Bartlett,
    Mary 237
    Esther, 184
Barry, Samuel 171
Barton, Henry P 257
Bateman Luther 151
Bates Daniel 175
Beardsley Mattie 284
Beck Elizabeth, 61
Beebe,
    Daniel 198
    Elizabeth, 198
Beech Belinda 129 256
Beecher
    Erastus, 253
    Naomi 253
    Naomi (Crowell) 253
Belmont August 282 283
Bemus, Elizabeth, 133, 264
Besse, James I , 272
Bessy Alice 202
Benham Almira Barry, 256
Bennett
    Curtis, 132
    Daniel 183
    Eliza 259
    Emeline, 218
    John 65
    Jonathan 65
    Maria 217
    Mary 259
    Prudence 98 182 291
    Robert 182
    Sarah 98 108, 183, 293, 295
    Susanna 40
    Thankful 183
Bickford
    Anna Delora 271
    Maryette 271
Biddle,
    Col Clement, 66 112
    Jacob, 112
    James 112
    John 112
    Mary, 113
    Nancy 113
    Rebecca 113

Biddle—(Continued)
Sally 113
Thomas 112
Bierce Miles H, 273
Bigelow, Erastus, D D
Birge Celestine, 273
Bissell. Charlotte, 95, 177
Birtrand, James H 291
Black, Julia 280
Blackman, Mary 71
Blair
Adolphus 236
Charles, 255
Polly 235
Blake Davis A 243
Blanchard Annette, 284
Blanchet Joshua 116
Blasdel
Caroline 274
Jerry, 274
Bliss Nancy, 220
Blinn, ——————— 240
Bly, Ann (Brownell) 47
Boomer,
David 220
Joseph 118, 220
Borden,
Aaron, 104 195
Abigail 195
Abraham, 59
Amey, 64
Anna, 102, 193
Catherine (Turner) 105
Cynthia 191
Daniel 209
David 195
Eleanor, 181
Elizabeth 19 40 55, 106
109, 209
Elizabeth (Wanton) 36
Ella C, 292
George, 21, 41, 219
Hope, 71 124, 240 241
Jeremiah, 202
Job 41
John 41 105, 124 191, 198
Joseph, 21 41, 104, 105 190
191, 195
Lydia. 183
Mary, 144
Mary (Earle) 41
Patience, 81 150
Peace. 195

Borden—(Continued)
Penelope, 74, 117 138, 219
Philadelphia, 195
Rebecca (Church) 219
Richard, 51, 219
Ruth, 106
Sarah 51 59, 79, 80
Sarah (Brownell) 41
Simeon, 193
Stephen 41, 74
Susan M , 195
Susanna 47, 74 108, 138
191, 204
Susanna ( ) 124
Thomas, 191
Waite, 106 198
William, 41, 101 190
Borland Phebe, 180 288 289
Boss,
Abbey, 95, 175
John 160
Bosworth, James 171
Bours,
Ann 84, 158
Rev Peter, 53
Bowdoin,
Mary Preston 52 82
Peter, 82
Bowen,
Anna 64 108, 203 204, 205,
206, 207
Charles Austin 271
Boyd, Richard Fish, 298
Buckover, John, 175
Bradford Gov William 73
Brant
Nathan 91
Mehitable, 99
Brayton
Sarah 64
Patience, 62, 102
Bready, Marcia (Brownell) 24
Brever Delia Roxanna 236
Brenton,
Abigail 254
Harriet 150
William 255
Briant, Rebecca, 78
Brightman
Anna 209
Betsey, 246
Daniel 126 246

Brownell—(Continued)
Alvin C, 253
Amanda 240
Amey or Amy 66 114, 131
    241 259, 270
Amey Ann 247
Amelia A, 268
Amelia S 221
Amos 121 231
Amos Knapp 120, 225
Amy Jane, 217
Amy S, 220
Andrew P, 252
Ann, 17, 20, 22, 23, 26 43
    48 67 76, 77 123 125,
    133, 142 246 247 262
Ann B 252
Ann Eliza 221, 231
Ann Elizabeth Decotee 98
    181 301
Anna 25 26 67 71 74 115
    121 125 126 130 138
    218 242 243 269, 270
    272
Anne 131
Anthony, 114
Antoinette, 120, 224
Antoinette Sarah 268
Ariadne 120 224
Arminda 277
Armira, 277
Artemas 128 254
Asa Cook, 255
Barnabas Clapp 266
Belinda Beech 257
Benjamin 22, 23 25 26, 44
    48 67 68 69 77 115
    117 121 133 141, 143, 216,
    219 228, 229 2331 232
    234 278, 279 280
Benjamin Brenton 255
Benjamin Franklin 225 280
Benjamin Harmon 232
Benjamin Jonathan 120
    225
Benjamin P, 252
Benjamin R, 257
Beriah Southard, 129 255
Betsey 115 120 127 197
    218
Borden 76 115
Burden, 140, 214 215
Bridget 47
Calista 245

Brownell—(Continued)
Caroline 222 257, 269
Caroline A 295
Caroline E, 268
Caroline G 138
Catherine, 224
Charles, 23, 24 47 70 76,
    121, 122 138 140, 232
    233, 234 235, 254
Charles Aranzo, 224
Charles A 268
Charles Carroll 233
Charles DeWolf, 249
Charles F 269
Charles Frederick, 250
Charles F 219
Charles Henry 229
Charles Hoily 258
Charles Homer, 227
Charles H, 222 268
Charles P 256
Charles Wright 253
Charlotte, 124, 215, 218
Charlotte D, 247
Chauncey Wells 129 256
Christopher 219
Clara 234 245
Clara Maria 249
Clarence Melville, 249
Clarissa Richmond 254
Clarissa (Baldwin) 232 234
Clarke 125, 127 252
Clarke, Sawyer 255
Clinton David 221
Comfort 122 234
Comfort (Dennis) (Taylor)
    45
Content 42 68 118 119
    140
Content (Shaw) 47 138,
    140
Cornelia Budlong 246
Cornelia Prudence 247
Cornelius, 280
Cornelius B 245
Cushing 124
Cynthia 73 122 249 262
    268
Cynthia M 279
David 47 69 74, 113, 115
    118, 120 121, 125, 221
    228 229 230 266, 267,
    279
David F 222

322

Brownell—(Continued)
Elizabeth B., 256
Elizabeth (Crandall) 48, 143
Elizabeth (Davol), 44
Elizabeth Harriet, 219
Elizabeth Louisa, 247
Elizabeth M 253, 265
Elizabeth (Richmond) 45
Elizabeth S 248
Elizabeth (Shaw) 45
Elizabeth (Stanley) 131
Elizabeth (Van Wert) 229
Elsie, 266, 267
Emeline Alworth, 217
Emeline E 262
Emilia DeWolf, 249
Emily A., 214
Emily S., 221
Emily W., 138
Emma Genevieve 227
Emma J E, 253
Enos, 234
Ephraim, 76 140 141, 276
Ephraim Woodbridge, 278
Erastus, 262
Esek, 73
Esek M 294
Eslie Maria 229
Esther, 42, 47 74 141 280
Esther Albro, 143
Esther (Tabor) 42
Esther W., 253
Eugene Ellsworth, 233
Eunice 123, 127 132 140 237
Eva, 72
Eva Gardner 227
Eveline 139
Ezekiel, 117 219
Ezra, 71, 124, 128 240 241, 255
Ezra Stiles, 255
Fallec 123, 278
Fally, 123
Fannie E, 257
Fanny Maria 215
Fitz William, 275
Frances Ann 274
Frances I, 247
Francis, 276
Francis De Wolf, 249
Francis Edwin, 232
Francis Seymour 250

Brownell—(Continued)
David I., 120, 121, 222
David M., 221 222
David Norton, 267
David Sherman, 229
Daniel, 74, 118, 128 133 216 252, 269
Daniel Kelsey, 217
Daniel Lyon, 138, 274
Deborah 44, 45, 117 122, 132, 219, 222, 260
Deborah Ann, 252
Deborah Briggs, 247
Deborah (Burgess) 45 74
Delilah 141
Dennis, 257, 280
Dexter, 213
Diadama 219
Dorman Lake 120, 227
Dorman Smith, 120
Dorothy 68, 70, 117, 118, 122, 235 239 278
Dwelley, 128
Eben, 252
Ebenezer, 216
Ebenezer Dean, 215
Edgar Dorman, 227
Edith, 72, 127, 201
Edith W., 128, 254
Edith (Wilbur) 45
Edmund 126 221, 244 246
Edward, 43 73, 74, 128 129, 130 255 256 257 258
Edward B, 260
Edward Franklin 258
Edward J., 268
Edward Parker 278
Edward Rogerson 249
Edward Wells 256
Edwin 121, 231 234
Eleanor M., 268
Electa 223
Elias S., 255
Elijah 44 120 222
Elisha, H 222 251
Eliphal, 74, 278
Eliza, 115
Eliza Ann, 222
Elizabeth 42, 44 45 47 68, 69, 70, 71 72 73 74, 76 114, 118 122 126 127 128 132, 139 140 214, 215, 216 238 244 246 251 252, 267, 277

324

Brownell—(Continued)
Isaac T , 252
Isaac Watts. 278
Isabel, 76
Israel, 120, 222 266
Israel Putnam 124 239
Jabez Barker, 219
Jacob, 267
Jacob Reasoner, 133, 121, 263
James, 47, 69, 70, 115, 122 216 218, 280
James A , 220
James Alvero, 228
James Amatus, 233
James, F S , 250
James Grey. 138
James Harvey, 278
James, T 270
Jane, 267, 270
Jane Ann. 233
Jane Jemima, 121 229, 267
Jason, 218
Jedediah, 76 140, 275
Jeremiah. 23, 24 45 72, 73, 74 130 138 258
Jesse Matilda 233
Jirah, 278
Joan, 141
Job 47, 76 140
John, 23 24 42 44 45 47 74, 124 130, 133 138, 140 141, 221, 276
John Avoy, 219
John B 222
John Davis, 220
John E . 222
John F , 254
John Fletcher, 139
John L , 260
John, Leonard, 224
John Wesley 139, 274
Jonathan, 44, 45, 66 69, 71, 120, 121 125 126 222 223 224 225 226 227 244, 245, 250
Johnathan Wilson, 251
Joseph, 21 41 42, 48, 66, 67 70, 77, 113, 114, 115, 122, 133, 143, 214, 215 216, 229, 230, 234, 266, 267, 280

Brownell—(Continued)
Joseph Arnold, 217
Josiah 117, 219
Joshua, 47, 74, 120, 130 131 132, 133 259 260 261 262, 263, 265
Julia, 221, 223. 231
Juliette V., 215
J Augustus, 214
J S Bradley 222
Katherine, 234
Keziah, 68, 116
Laura, 74
Laura A C , 253
Lavinia, 130
Lawrence, 245
Leah, 121 232
Lemuel, 279
Leonard 252
Leverett, 239
Levi, 221
Lewis, 270
Lewis Charles, 262
Lois 72
Lorena 262
Loring 239
Loring Richmond. 124 239
Lorenzo, 260, 262
Lorenzo M , 268
Louisa W , 222
Louise, 216
Lucinda, 229
Lucretia, 254
Lucy, 73, 123, 124, 125, 235, 239, 245
Lucy A , 256
Lucy R , 240
Luvilla, 266
Luthan, 74 133, 270
Lydia, 71. 74, 120 121 122, 126, 222 228, 245 251 268 278
Lydia Ann, 225
Lydia Sanford 143
Lyman, 255
Lysander Nelson 256
Mabel 139, 273
Major 219
Marcus, 225
Margaret 25, 26 77 216, 234 280

Brownell—(Continued)
Maria, 132, 139, 216, 221, 253, 261.
Maria Louise, 250
Martha, 20, 21, 22, 23, 25, 41, 42, 43, 44, 45, 67, 116, 117 120, 125, 132, 141, 216, 219, 255, 259
Martha (Peckham), 47, 74, 132, 133
Martin VanBuren, 223
Marquis Lafayette, 217
Mary, 21, 22, 23, 25, 26, 41, 42, 44, 45, 47, 66, 69, 70, 72, 77 120 122, 123, 124, 126 127, 128, 132, 133, 141, 142, 213, 222, 224, 225, 235 240, 244, 245, 250, 257 263, 269, 276, 279
Mary Ann 115, 218, 219, 254, 265, 268, 280
Mary Albina, 275
Mary B., 246
Mary (Brownell), 133
Mary (Cary), 45
Mary (Crandall), 44
Mary Church, 250
Mary Davis, 221
Mary (Eldridge), 45
Mary France, 234
Mary Freeborn, 234
Mary Jane, 231
Mary J 253
Mary Louise, 273
Mary L V 260
Mary Margaret 263
Mary M 133
Mary Potter 140 285
Mary (Thurston) 45
Mary (Wilbur) 44, 47
Mary (Wood), 47
Mary Whittlesey, 258
Melissa C 253
Mercy, 68, 115 126, 249
Mercy Church, 246
Mercy (Shaw) 214
Milly, 139
Minerva A 269
Minerva M, 257
Minerva T, 257
Mordecai 132 260
Moses, 113, 133, 213 268

M Louisa, 248
Nancy, 128, 140, 216, 221, 251
Nancy Maria, 266
Nathan, 66, 113, 124, 133, 240, 269
Nathan Crary, 278
Nathan C, 126.
Nathaniel, 71, 125, 132, 242 260
Nathaniel Webster, 277
Nicanor, 240
Norman, 255
Oliver, 66, 114, 215
Oliver C, 252
Olivia M, 268
Oscar Lavaldin, 225
Osmin, 242
Osmin B, 125
Pardon 71 122 126, 141, 244, 245, 246, 247, 249
Paris R, 240
Parker, 122, 124
Paul, 45, 72, 123
Patience 25 26, 68, 74, 115, 117, 118, 217, 257
Peace 141
Pearce 45, 72, 128
Peckham 126
Peleg, 128, 143, 252
Penelope (Borden), 138
Percy, 124
Peris Richmond, 124, 239
Peris R 240
Perez, 71, 126, 244
Perry, 128 254
Peter 113 214
Peter Fuller, 272
Peter Reasoner, 133, 264, 265
Philadelphia, 42, 66, 67, 113, 115
Philip, 220, 242
Philip II, 221 279
Philo Forbes, 256
Phineas Terry 273
Phillet J, 270
Phoebe, 42 44 45 47, 67, 70 72 76, 116, 124, 134, 141, 222, 267, 271, 278,
Phoebe Macomber, 241
Phoebe Shaw 246
Polly 118, 141 220

Brownell—(Continued)
Polly Forbes, 256
Prince, 77, 141
Priscilla 69, 71, 76, 128, 141
Priscilla (Pattee) 47, 140
Prudence, 77, 126, 143, 221, 279
Prudence Jane, 229
Putnam Cushing, 240
Rachel, 120, 223, 240, 280
Rachel A , 252
Ralph Platt 223
Rebecca, 42, 66, 113, 114, 118, 120, 121, 214, 215, 220, 231
Rebecca (Davol), 43, 48, 141, 142, 143
Rejoice, 44
Reuben, 120, 221, 263, 270
Rhoda, 69, 74, 115, 120, 121, 122, 128, 217, 221, 222, 228
Rhoda Jane 222
Rhoda (Milk) 220, 221
Rhoda M , 219, 221
Richard, 44, 69, 124
Richard Grinnell, 246
Richard Sylvester, 247
Richmond, 74, 126, 246, 250, 252
Robert, 21, 22, 23, 25, 47, 74, 76, 138, 140, 272, 273, 277
Robert Pattee, 140, 277
Robert Smith, 245
Roby, 122
Roby Fuller, 272
Rosilla, 228
Roxylania, 214
Ruby, 141, 279
Russell 238
Russell Botsford, 258
Ruth, 47, 67, 71, 72, 115, 121, 126, 238, 248, 280
Ruth (Cornell), 66, 67
Ruth (Irish) 45
Ruth Jane, 223
Ruth Louise 221
Ruth (Manchester) 47, 76,
Sabin C , 280
Sally, 118, 125, 128
Samuel, 24, 47, 70, 123, 125, 129, 235, 236, 237, 238

Brownell—(Continued)
Samuel Aaron, 129, 130, 256
Samuel Clarke 242
Samuel Denton, 259
Sara Elizabeth 229
Sarah 17, 21, 22, 41, 42, 44, 71, 72, 77, 123, 130, 133, 141, 142, 216, 220, 236, 242, 267, 268, 276
Sarah Ann, 217, 258, 270
Sarah (Bailey), 45, 122
Sarah E , 247
Sarah Jane 270
Sarah Maria, 231
Sarah M 254
Sarah Wilson, 252
Sidney M , 268
Sherman 221
Silas 138, 234, 273
Silas B , 268
Simeon, 74, 133, 229, 266, 267, 268, 269, 270, 271
Simeon C , 270
Sophia Taylor, 249
Stephen, 21, 42, 45, 55, 66, 67, 72, 77, 113, 127, 128, 133, 143, 213, 214, 254, 262, 267, 280
Stephen Duane 227
Stephen Elton 213
Stephen Fish 113, 213
Stephen Foster, 120, 227
Susan 124, 213, 242, 245, 254, 257
Susan E 215
Susan Emeline 215
Susan L 257
Susanna, 21, 22, 40, 42, 45, 47, 65, 66, 72, 74, 76, 111, 113, 114, 123, 209, 210, 211, 237
Susanna (Borden)
Susannah (Fish) 213
Sylvester 72, 126, 127, 246, 247, 248, 249, 250, 251
Thankful 47, 68, 116, 121, 229, 266
Theodore 214
Thomas, 17, 20, 21, 22, 23, 24, 25, 41, 42, 44, 45, 47, 66, 67, 68, 69, 71, 24, 25, 41, 42, 44, 45, 47, 66, 67, 68, 69, 71

Chase—(Continued)
Deborah 102 192
Durfee, 200
Edmund, 200
Edward, 293
Elisha, 292
Eliza, 102 192 193
Eliza Estes 295
Eliza V 301
Elizabeth, 64 183, 247
Eunice, 183, 293
Fannie Smith 193
Freeborn, 102
Gideon, 107
Giles Martinborough 192
George, 118, 220
George B, 220
George Washington, 192
Hannah 107, 191
Henry, 126, 200, 247
Henry B 185
Holder, 102, 185, 191, 192, 193 295
Ira, 214
Irene V 295
Isaac 187 302
James Scott 193
Jane Eliza 192
Jane L, 295
Job 68 117
John 93 171, 284
Jonathon 95
Joseph, 107
Joseph W 302
Lucinda, 200
Mary 117 192, 302
Mary Ann 192
Mary Davis, 171
Mary G 302
Mason, 200
Mason Champlin, 193
Nathan, 102, 171 191, 295
Nathaniel Perdon, 193
Obadiah 192
Obadiah D 295
Phebe, 102
Philip Perden 193
Purley, 200
Rowland 192
Ruth Ann, 192
Samuel West 193
Sarah, 102 107 191, 201, 247,
Sarah Ann, 193
Sarah Barney 171

Chase—(Continued)
Stephen 107 198
Simeon B, 193
Thomas B 295
Wesley, 171
Willard 200
William, 220
William, 220
Chauncey Com Isaac, 281
Cheesboro Eunice, 112
Cheesborough, Abigail, 165
Child, Rebecca 114 214
Childs,
Ann G, 161
Emeline, 239
Chilson
Eugene Ruth, 270
Eliza 238
Christopher Elizabeth, 54
Church,
Abby Taylor, 248
Abigail, 85
Benjamin 24 248
Caleb, 253
Charles Henry, 248
Gamaliel 248
Grace, 47 48
Hannah (Wilbur) 253
Harriet Bayhes, 250
Harriet B 126
John, 195
John Edwin 248
Joseph 126, 143, 248, 296
Joseph T, 185, 296
Lydia (Randall) 128 253
Margaret 77 143, 280
Mercy 72 126 247 248 249
250, 251
Rebecca 219
Sarah 247
Seth, 72
Susan Perry, 248
Thaddeus Herbert 248
Col Thomas 126
Thomas Brownell, 248
Churchill, Elizabeth Ann, 133
268
Clark
Adam 139
Ann, 154
Betsey, 129, 257
Byron S 217
Elizabeth, 302

Coil—(Continued)
    Mary Ann, 217
    Patience 217
Colby,
    Hannah 140 277
    Rowell, 277
Cole.
    ————— 299
    Abby, 153
    Ann, 153
    Austis, 278
    John 95, 153
    Mary 95 153 177
    Sarah, 153 177
    Susan D 183
    William 82 153
Collier
    Elizabeth 73
    William 73
Collins
    Anna, 150
    John 87
Coleman, Nelson 217
Colt Joseph S 160
Colton Delia 151
Combs Leslie 250
Comstock Dr Joseph, 160
Compton, William 154
Conant, Ella J 290
Condon,
    George 86
    Mary 146 164 166
Congdon
    Abby 303
    Caleb, 303
    Carder Hazard, 164
    Deborah 175
    Edmund Arnold, 303
    Elizabeth Rudd, 303
    George 96 150, 164, 303
    Hannah, 96 150
    Hannah S 177
    Jonathan, 303
    Joseph 96
    Lucy 94, 173
    Margaret, 170
    Martha 175
    Ruth Eddy 303
    Samuel 59, 96
    Sarah 96
    Sarah (Chase) 95 177,
      178
    Sarah (Hazard) 150
    Stephen, 170

Congdon—(Continued)
    Susan, 163
    Welcome, 187, 303
Conklin, Emma, 231
Cook,
    Albert J 295
    Asa, 295
    Bridget Almy 303
    Daniel 295
    Ebenezer, 87
    Harriet M, 295
    Henry V, 295
    Col John 181 203
    Mary A, 301
    Mercy Estes, 295
    Patience Seabrook, 188,
    Peter Estes 295
    Capt Samuel T 185 295
    Sarah, 149, 193
    Stephen J, 295
Cooke Col ————— 129
Cornell
    Abigail, 65
    Adalaide, 212
    Albert 116
    Alfred, 119
    Alice, 210
    Almira, 297
    Amy, 112 212
    Ann 209
    Anna, 210
    Anthony, 209
    Betsey 159
    Charles, 210
    Charles Russell, 211
    Charlotte, 210
    Charlotte M 212
    Clara, 209
    Clark, 67
    Content 119
    Cyrus 212
    Daniel 210
    Daniel V, 119
    Daniel Niles 119
    David 77, 142
    David Earle, 116
    Deliverance 186
    Dollwyn, 210
    Dorr 211
    Edward, 65 111 116 209
      210
    Elijah 211
    Elizabeth, 42 65 67 109 112
      209 210 212 294

Cornell—(Continued)
Emeline, 212
Emma, 211, 212
Esther, 119
Ezekiel, 68, 118
Ezra, 118
Frances 210
George, 19 39 41, 65 111,
112 119 210
Gerves, 210
Gideon, 19 39 65, 66 68,
111 112, 119, 209 210
211
Hannah 65 111 112, 210
Hannah Brownell, 68
Hannah (Mosher), 68
Harriet 210
Isaac, 210
James, 119
Jethro 142
Job 116
John, 112, 116 119, 210
John W, 212
Jonathan, 42, 68 118
Latham, 65, 111, 211
Louisa, 211
Lydia, 189
Maria, 119, 211, 260
Maria Janette, 212
Martha, 19, 20, 40
Martha (Freeborn), 39, 40
64 65, 66
Mary 68, 111 116 119,
209, 210
Mary D 212
Mary Jane, 212
Matthew 65 112 212
Mehitable F, 212
Merritt I 212
Millicent 111, 112 210,
211
Nathaniel, 119
Oliver 68, 119
Patience 68 119
Philadelphia (Estes), 41
Philip, 68 119
Priscilla (Lawton), 67
Rebecca, 66 112
Rhoda 118
Richard 68 118, 119
Ruth, 21, 41 66
Sarah 19, 39, 65 109, 111,
209
Sarah Elizabeth 211

Cornell—(Continued)
Seabury, 119
Silvey 210
Stephen 68, 119
Stephen Brownell 68
Susan Almy, 212
Susanna, 19, 39 64, 65 111,
210, 211
Thomas 17, 19, 39, 64, 65,
66, 109, 119
Thomas F, 212
Thomas J, 212
Thurston, 111
Walker, 210
Walter 65 68 111, 112,
116, 209 211 212
Wanton 111, 211
William, 19, 39 65, 109,
111 142 209 210
William W, 211
Zina 212
Cooley Rev Asahel, 290
Corey
Isaac, 126, 249
Lawton 219
Corliss,
George
Corp Caleb, 122
Cory,
Albert Brownell, 249
Alexander Hamilton 249
Alonzo 171
Ann, 101
Cynthia, 101
Dennis, 101
Elizabeth 101, 190
Elizabeth Bligh 249
John, 190
Joseph 101
Joseph Dennis 101
Mary Codman, 249
Nancy, 101 108 201
Susanna, 101
Thomas, 201
William 101
Cottrell,
Benjamin 177
Samuel C 177
Crandall,
Content (Manchester), 77
Eber, 77
Elizabeth, 48 77, 143
Jane 26 48
Margaret 174
Mary 23, 44, 69

333

335

Dorn.
Alexander. 240
Nancy 124, 240
Dorr, Gov ———,300
Jane. 270
Douglas,
Diama, 168
James 83 154
Margaret. 155
Mary 155
Samuel James 155
Sarah, 155
Susanna Wilson 155
Waitstill Eunice 155
Douglass, Betsey, 114
Clara G 295
Nathaniel 288
S S, 256
Dow, Susanna, 40
Downer Ruby 255
Downing Reuben 267
Drake, Eliza L, 241
Doering Freelove 65
Dring Nathaniel 72
Dulcina Mary, 78
Duncan Amanda, 261
Dunham, Sarah M 254
Dunlap Eunice 422
Dunlop, Thomas, 113
Dunn, Minerva 265
Dunning Mary, 246
Dunwell Jacob 179
Durfee,
Aaron 204
Abel, 206
Abigail 201 300
Abner 108 201
Abraham 203
Addison 208
Albert G 198
Allen, 138, 207
Allen Brownell, 272
Amanda 206
Amey 209
Amy, 294
Ann, 19 20 37 61 63 97,
98 106
Ann (Freeborn) 37 61 62
63, 64
Anna, 109, 204
Anna (Brownell) 138 272
Anna B 206
Anna R 272

Durfee—(Continued)
Anne, 203 207, 212
Austin, 205
Bailey, 203
Barton, 207
Barton Brownell, 138
Barzilla, 205
Benjamin, 64, 106, 198, 203,
204, 208, 291
Betsey. 198, 201, 204, 208
Catherine, 201
Catherine Stanton, 198
Charles 200, 206
Chloe, 207
Christina, 138
Christopher, 63
Cynthia, 206
Daniel 109, 208
David 109, 208
David S, 272
Delana, 208
Deliverance, 101
Dwelly 208
Earle, 64, 108, 203 204
Edward, 108, 204, 205, 206
Edward M 272
Eleanor, 63, 105, 198, 202,
208
Ehas, 206
Eliphal 182, 291
Elisha 207
Elizabeth, 19, 37, 39, 40, 63,
64, 104 105 106, 107,
108 195 196, 198, 200,
201, 202, 205, 207
Elizabeth (Cannon) 194
Elizabeth C, 208
Eliza Seabury, 199
Emily 207
Emory, 207
Freeborn 37 63
George, 109, 205, 208
Gideon 19 37 63 64, 67
69 103, 104, 105, 108,
112, 193, 203, 204, 205,
206 207
Gideon C 208
Goodwin Halverson, 200
Hannah 103, 106, 108, 194,
204 205
Hannah Beebe 198
Hannah C 138
Hannah ( ), 138
Harriet, 201, 206

336

337

Gatchell, William, 205
George Dinah, 210
Gerry Lydia 153
Gibbs Robert, 103
Gibson, Phillip D, 299
Gifford,
    Clariss 300
    Capt David, 300
    Deborah 26, 49
    Desire, 268
    Diana, 187, 303
    Edson 268
    Eliza, 187, 300, 302
    Elizabeth, 300
    Ephraim, 100
    George Hall, 300
    Gideon, 111, 112 303
    Hannah A, 278
    Harriet 300
    Jane, 300
    Jeremiah 186 299 300, 302
    Joseph, 300
    Levi 279
    Mary Brayton 299 300
    Peleg 278
    Ruth 300
    William, 102
    William Hall 300
    Henry 221
Gilbert,
    Abigail F 288
    John, 231
Giles
    Elizabeth, 241
    Phebe, 241
Gilmore, Arunah. 236
Goddard
    Abigail, 219
    Eunice 283
Goodrich
    Armitta, 231
    Caroline 231
    Charles, 231
    Darwin 231
    Francis 231
    Henrietta, 231
Goodyear Joseph 244
Gough Joanna, 240
Gould, Daniel 171
Graves Dorothy 70
Gray
    Archimedes 243
    Desire, 204
    Emeline 214

Gray—(Continued)
    Phebe 64, 108, 200, 201, 202
    Phebe A 71
    Richard 223
    Sarah (Bennett) 108
    Thomas 108
Greene,
    Elizabeth 84 157
    Dr Daniel Howland, 163
    Gideon, 67, 115
    Hannah 58 94 174
    Isabel, 302
    John 115
    Gen Nathaniel, 73, 115
    Patience, 54
    Richard 157
    Sally 114
    Sarah (   ) 157
    Sarah M, 158
Greenman,
    Hannah (   ) 225
    Lester, 225
    Marietta 225
Gregg
    John 207
    Lucinda C 200
Grey,
    James, 138
    Mabel (Hall) 138
    Milley 76 138 273, 274
    Phebe 185
Griffin
    Charlotte R 167
    Evan Malbone, 167
    Hannah Hazzard, 167
    Joseph Hazard 167
    Mary C, 167
    Dr Stephen, 90 167
    Dr Stephen Augustus 167
Griggs, Elijah 160
Grinnell
    Anna (Tillinghast) 126 244
    Betsey 72 127 252
    Daniel 127
    Grace (   ) 127
    Isaac, 202
    Mary 244
    May 126
    Matilda (Sherman) 98 185
    Sarah. 128 209 254
    Stephen 185
    Stephen T 295
    Zebedu 254

Groves, Prudence 237
Guinsey
    Frances Spencer, 234
H ———
Haight William H 261
Hale, John 263
Hall
    Anne, 186
    Ann Janetta, 301
    Benjamin 41, 186, 301
    Benjamin Dennis, 186
    Catherine Sowle, 301
    Darius 301
    David 187 301
    David Franklin 301
    Edward 301
    Frances (Parker) 41
    Gardiner 301
    George 99 146 186, 300 301
    Hannah, 186 209 300, 302
    Hannah W 301
    Harriet A 301
    Isaac Dennis 301
    Jane 301
    Joseph 186
    Lorenzo 171
    Mabel 138
    Mary, 289
    Parker 181 186 301
    Phebe 53 302
    Robert Dennis 186 301
    Ruth 186
    Ruth Dennis 301
    Susanna 186
    William 21 41 181 186, 300
    William Thomas 301
Halleck Electa, 269
Hamblin Maria 168
Hambly Elizabeth 192
Hammond,
    Benjamin 175 178
    Benjamin Franklin 178
    Chloe ( ) 178
    Eliza Ann 178
    Elizabeth 175
    George Newton, 178
    Joseph, 96, 178
    Joseph Willett 178
    Ruth 178
    Waity Frances 178
    William 175
Hampton William 158
Handy
    Eli 141, 279

Handy—(Continued)
    George, 221
    Hannah, 279
    James Harvey, 279
    Mira E, 279
Haner, Ezra, 221
Harmon Elisha, 283
Harley Solomon, 168
Harrall, William J, 267
Harrington
    Cornelia, 232
    Hannah 133, 264
    Horace 211
    Philip 264
Hart,
    Barsheba 109 208
    Eunice 112
    Jonathan 43
    Joseph 208
    Mary 255
    Phebe Ann, 223
    Richard 43
    Rosella 240
    Samuel, 22 43
    Smiton 43
Haskin,
    Caroline 269
    Delilah, 77 141
Hathaway, Prudence 108 203
Hathway
    Isaac 125
    Col 123
Havens Susannah 156
Hawes, John A, 74
Hawks Dr Francis L, 283
Hawley Elizabeth 257
Hawthorne A D 260
Hazzard
    Abby 92 149 152 158 169,
      173 175
    Abby M 156
    Abigail 28 29 52, 53, 56 80
      82, 83 84 85 92, 94 95,
      145 153 156 157
    Abraham 152
    Alice 53 54 80, 81 86 145,
      147, 150 162, 163 164,
      166 174
    Alice Robinson 150 166
    Alice Joanna Fitzgerald, 163
    Almira Jane 161
    Amey, 34 58, 174
    Amey, ( ) 34 57
    Amy Susan 156
    Angeline Margaret 161

343

344

Hazard—(Continued)
 Rouse, 92
 Rowland, 79, 95, 145 146,
  175
 Rowland Gibson, 144
 Rowland Robinson 150
 Ruth, 81, 90, 94, 151, 152 166,
  175 177
 Samuel, 31, 56 91 92, 144,
  152 162 168 169 177
 Samuel Green, 87
 Sally, 92 161
 Sarah 27 29, 31 35 50 51,
  52 53, 54, 56, 58 78 79,
  80, 81 83 85, 86 89, 92
  143, 144 145, 146, 147,
  149, 150 152 161 162,
  163 166 175, 178
 Sarah Eliza 162
 Sarah Louisa 154
 Sarah Lucretia, 54
 Sarah M , 156
 Sarah (Odell) 143
 Sarah Robinson 150
 Sarah (Smith) 34, 58 59
 Simeon, 51, 80, 145, 147, 149
 Sophia Freelove 85
 Stanton, 56 90 91, 167 170
 Stephen 27 31 32 50 51, 54,
  55 56 57 78, 89 90 92
  95 143, 165, 166 168 170,
  171 178
 Susan, 61, 175, 177
 Susanna 31, 34, 35, 51, 52, 55,
  58 79 82 83, 91, 94 145,
  153 173
 Susanna (Nichols) 27 51 52
 Sylvester, 149
 Sylvester Gardner, 84 157
 Sylvester Robinson 166
 Thomas, 17, 27 28 29 31, 33,
  34 50, 51 52 54, 56, 58
  79, 81, 82 86 87, 91 92
  94 143 144 150, 152, 154
  162 170 173
 Thomas A 145
 Thomas Arnold
 Thomas Cranston 161
 Thomas Edward, 152
 Thomas George 151
 Thomas Jefferson, 83, 155,
  174
 Thomas Rhodes 82 153

Hazard—(Continued)
 Thomas Robinson 144
 Thomas R , 144
 Varnum, 177
 Waitstill Curtis, 83, 154
 Waitstill Douglass, 154
 Wilbur 95
 Wilbour, 177
 Wilbur, 177
 Willard, 174
 William, 29, 53, 83, 84, 86,
  143, 144 150 154, 156 162,
  169, 170 177
 William Coggeshall, 161
 William Henry 163
 William Jones 154
 William Robinson, 144
 William Sylvester 158
 William Tweedy, 85
 William Wilbur, 149

Head
 Harvey, 237
 Lysander, 237
 Miranda, 237

Helme
 Elizabeth, 31 54, 55 56, 57
 Mary ( ) 31
 Rouse, 31

Henderson Emily 302

Herendeen,
 Anne, 205
 Durfee, 205
 Gideon 205
 Huldah, 205
 Mercy 207
 Nathan, 205, 206
 Welcome 108, 205
 Wilkinson 205

Herrick
 Hiram, 289
 Rev J R , 258
 Leonard 181
 Roswell 180 289

Hicks
 Anne, 98, 185 296 297
 John, 76
 Nancy 279
 Sarah H 278
 Stephen 185
 Capt William 123, 124

Higbee Laura C 256
Hight, James, 175

Hill
 Hiram 257

345

Hill—(Continued)
    Louise Gertrude 273
Hiller, Hannah, 69, 120 121
Hilliard
    Deborah Pierce 128
    Jonathan, 26
    Jonathan I 253
Hines Sylvester 219
Himrod Lewis 245
Hitchcock
    Eunice 238
    Fally 237
    Hannah, 237
    Hannah (Livermore) 237
    Isaac 238
    Joseph 123 237
    Merea, 237
    Mary 238
    Ruth 237
    Samuel 237
    Seth 237 238
    William, 2338
Hiscox Thomas 171
Hix, Robert N 111
Hoag,
    Elizabeth 269
    Henry H 269
    Mary A 268
    Philen r 222
    Sarah 74 133, 266 267 268,
        269 270 271
Hobson Mary 57
Hodges
    Mina M, 291
    William 154
Holcomb Chester 235
Holder Elizabeth 255
Holland Thomas 247
Holloway Liam 152
Holmes
    Almira 200
    Nicholas 143
Holton Chas C 256
Holway, Elizabeth, 57
Hone
    John 282
    Phillip T, 144
Hooper
    Lucy Ann 187 304
    Mary 154
    Thomas 154
Hopkins
    Isaac, 170

Hopkins—(Continued)
    Mary 119
    Dep Gov Stephen, 55
Horsewell
    Deborah 111
    Elizabeth 100 189 302 304
Horton,
    John 287
    Louisa 285
Hotchkiss Heman, 238
Howard
    Deborah 219
    Eliphlet Morgan 275
    Mercy Witman 212
    Octavia C, 275
    Patty ( ) 275
    Stephen, 224
Howe
    Lavinia Cady 282
    Phebe Ann 275
Howell
    Lt Col Gilbert 206
    Hannah 109 206
    Walter 270
Howland
    Abigail (Goddard) 219
    Abner 254
    Amy W 243
    Benjamin 36 61
    Daniel 67 115
    Deborah 117, 219
    Elihu 293
    Henry 219
    Jennie C 284
    John H, 144
    Mary A 252
    Mercy 67 115
    Patience 52 78
    Prince 142
    Rhoda (Allen) 220
    Samuel 47
    Sarah, 62 292
    Susan Russell 254
    Wanton 36
    William 42
    William P 219
Hoxie
    Anne 58
    Elizabeth, 111 209
    Gideon 94
    Hazard 173
    Mary 86, 162, 173
    Sarah 241

Moyer, Mary E., 287
Mudge Nathaniel 124
Mulford, Joseph S 257
    Abigail 51, 80 145 147, 149
    Abigail (   ), 55
    David 170
    Hannah 31
    John, 92
    Joseph, 55
    Mary, 56, 92, 169, 170
    Paul, 85
    Stephen, 55
    Thomas, 55
Munro
    Bateman, 195
    Elizabeth Pease 195
    Mary, 195
    Sarah Easton, 195
    Thomas, 195
Munroe,
    Elizabeth, 104
    Mary 105
    Sarah, 104
Munson
    Artimesia 259
    Clara 259
    Fanny, 259
    Richard, 259
    William 259
Myres, Mary Ann, 255
Negus,
    Nancy Butts, 219
    Sarah 117, 219
Nelmes, Susanna Jane, 153
Nelson, John, 243
Newbold, Caroline, 144
Newland, Joseph 268
Newman, John, 92 170
Niblo, Ann, 246
Nichols
    Elizabeth, 91
    Andrew, 101
    Hannah 59 90, 167
    John, 163
    Jonathan, 89, 90 91
    Mary, 68
    Sarah, 55 89, 165 166
    Susanna 50
Neckerson, John H, 292
Niles
    Charles 157
    Ebenezer 29 53

Niles—(Continued)
    Elizabeth 90 157, 167
    Hannah 168
    Mary 157
    Nathaniel, 58
    Penelope, 29 53
    Robert Hazard 157
    Sarah 29 53
    Sarah (Sands) 53
    Silas, 84 157 167
    William, 157
Noble, Mary, 296
Northrup
    Mary 178
    Mary (Thomas) 59
    Patience 59, 94 95
    Stephen, 59
Norton
    Esther, 133, 267
    Isaac, 290
    Sarah 286
Noxon, Ruth, 260
Noyce, Lorette 220
Noye, Col Joseph, 172
Nye
    Daniel H 296
    William H, 152
Oatley
    Abigail 159
    Benedict 170
    Betsey 170
    Betsey (Ladd) 170
    Hannah 170
    Jonathan 170
    Joseph 92 170
    Mary 170
    Nancy 170
    Rouse 170
    Stephen 170
    Susan 170
Odell,
    Rachel, 181 290
    Sarah 143
Ogden
    Charles 231
    Harlon M 231
Oldbridge Ussilla, 98 181,, 300
Olin,
    Anne 287
    Catherine 287
    Giles, 287
    Henry, 180, 287
    Ruth 287

Perry—(Continued)
    Raymond Henry Jones 164, 282
    Ruth, 55
    Samuel, 55, 57
    Sarah 55 57 160 282
    Sarah Wallace 164
    Simeon 55
    Stephen 55
    Susan, 165
    Susan Murgatroyd 282
    Susanna 31 55 57, 91
    William Frederick 282
Pettey Ephraim 185
Petty,
    Abby 219
    Harriet 295
Philips William H 303
Pierce,
    Alfred, 251
    Amanda 284
    Amy 252
    Anstice 238
    Catherine, 219
    Clother 171
    Delana Ann 250
    Elizabeth 72 127
    Emma Ludora 284
    Ezekiel 178 238
    Frances 97
    George, 238
    Giles 127
    Hannah 185
    Herbert Sumner 284
    James Luther, 171 284
    James Mason, 284
    Jeanette 284
    Jeremiah 55
    Laura Vernon, 284
    Lydia 177
    Lydia G 171
    Martha, 23 35
    Mary 97 179 180
    Mary Josephine 284
    Nathaniel, 237
    Obadiah, 284
    Philip 97
    Roby 252
    Samuel 177
    Susan Luther 284
Pierson Louisa M 193
Pinney Rev Alfred 268
Pippey, Joseph 154
Pitts
    Henry 171

Pitts—(Continued)
    Louisa 171
    Lydia 171
Place
    Enoch, 33, 51
    Hannah, 32 33
    Mary, 51, 80, 81
    Mary (Sweet) 51
    Sarah 52
Platt,
    James 259
    Lemuel 259
    Tracy 69
Pomeroy,
    Eliza 283
    Miriam 165
    Robert 283
Pope,—— Col 123 124
Porter Catherine, 290
Pratt Stephen, 266
Prentice Alice, 237
Preston Mary 152 153
Proctor Emma Fisher 298
Post
    Manson, 171
    Sylvia 258
Potter
    Abigail 89 167
    Abner, 280
    Alice, 53 86 87 150
    Ann, 166
    Asa, 279
        90 166
    Benedict Arnold 86
    Christopher 90
    David, 107 142
    Edmund, 142
    Edward 87 142
    Elisha 175
    Elizabeth 78 90 166
    Elizabeth S, 150
    Ephraim 77 142 279
    Fenner 166
    Freelove 279
    George 90
    George, P 292
    Henry 57 90
    Ichabod 28, 50 77 89
    Jeremiah Niles 81 150
    John 55 77 81 86 87 89
        90, 166
    Joseph 166
    Lydia 169
    Martha 79, 90 94, 142
    Mary 52 81 145 150 166
        175 184
    Mary Niles 150

Sherman—(Continued)
   Cynthia 100, 190
   Catherine 68
   Daniel, 185
   David, 204
   Durfee, 204
   Eber 58
   Elisha W 156
   Elizabeth (   ), 190
   Enoch, 83, 156
   Francis T, 260
   Gideon 204
   Hannah, 99, 187, 302, 303, 304
   Hiram, 298
   Humphrey, 108, 204, 205
   James Harvey, 221
   Job, 204
   Lemuel 204
   Lydia 293
   Patience 156
   Peleg 190 192
   Prudence 133 229 266
   Rubie H 292
   Sampson, 182, 191
   Stephen 204
   Susan 95 254
   Susannah 42
Sheffield Phebe 150
Sheldon Mary 82
Shepard Mase 253
Shore, Phila, 184
Shove Joshua, 187
Shrieve,
   Abigail (   )112
   Daniel, 112
   Elizabeth, 65 112 205, 212
Shrives, Benjamin 47.
Simmons
   Adam 123 237
   Alanson 237
   Benjamin, 237
   Calista, 237
   Carlos, 237
   Clarissa, 237
   Davis, 250
   Deborah, 252
   Eliza, 126
   Elizabeth Hall 250
   Fally 238
   Gamaliel, 237
   George, 129
   Isaac 242

Simmons—(Continued)
   Jane, 252
   Lucy L, 239
   Mary 238
   Mary A 235
   Mary Brownell, 125, 242
   Mary A 238
   Mehitabel, 237
   Melissa, 238
   Otis 237
   Pelig 44, 109
   Philip, 237
   Phoebe, 238
   Ruth 237, 238
   Samuel, 237
   Susannah 237
   William 123 238
Simpson, Andrew, 218
Sisson
   Albert H 296
   Allen, 183, 292
   Anna J 296
   Annie 188
   Asa 100, 188
   Charlotte Almy, 278
   David 292
   Edith C, 292
   Francis B 296
   Grizzel 113
   Hannah 117 219
   Hannah H 292
   Henry W, 296
   Isaac 188
   James, 113
   James F A, 296
   Joseph 188
   Lydia J 296
   Mary 188
   Nancy 219
   Pelig, 113, 118, 296
   Rebecca 113
   Richard 66, 113
   Robert 118
   Ruth, 113 188
   Sarah A 296
   Sarah H 292
   Sylvia A 292
   Thomas R 185 296
   William 292
Slade
   Deborah 103
   Edward 102, 103
   Gideon 103
   Joseph 103
   Louisa 107

Starr,
    Amisa Ives, 229
    Charles, 157
    Elizabeth 157
    Francis Henry, 157
    George 157
    Henry 157
    Jared, 84 157
    Mary, 157
    Nancy 157
    Robert, 157
Stedman
    Mary Ann 149
    Sarah Ann 149
    Stephen M 149
Steffens Albert 254
Stephens
    Calista 228
    Charles, 144
    Elisha 228
    George 218
    Jacob 218
    John 115 218
    Louise, 218
    Martha 218
    Mary 218
    Sarah Kennedy, 228
Sternberg,
    Margaret 240
    Martha, 241
Stevens,
    Addie L, 272
    Elizabeth Frances 235
    Gen Isaac Ingalls, 151
Stewart,
    Abby 165
    Jane 207
Stillwell
    Anna Brownell 269
    William 270
Stocum Anna 231
Stoddard
    Christine 125, 242
    Israel 71 72
    Julia 207
    Sarah, 268 s
Stone J P 174
Stork, Elliott G 244
Stowe,
    Henry Loran, 257
    Mary Ann, 255
Stowell Addie, 264
Strang Esther Halleck 269

Strong
    Henry Wright 211
    Janette, 262
    Mary Anna 265
Strunk Salma, 229
Stuart, Mabel, 247
Sutherland Pamela 156
Sweet,
    James 17
    Jane, 17
    Mary 51
    Miriam, S 231
    Thomas, 22
Sweeting Louise 215
Swift,
    Abbey E, 243
    Albert, 185 296
    Anna 272
    Anna E, 292
    Anne Estes 296, 297
    Charles 296
    Esther, 285
    Moses 297
    Thomas R, 185 297
    Lt Col, 205
Taber,
    Esther 22 42 68
    Lemuel 2, '
    Mary Cook 42
    Philip 42 70
Tabor,
    Christopher 128
    David, 196
    Elizabeth 208
    George, 208
    Gideon, 179
    Capt Jonathan 142
    Rebecca, 105 196
    Ruth, 98 188, 291
    Samuel 159
Talbot, A S, 250
Tallman
    Almina E, 299
    Benjamin, 299, 300
    Elijah Lovejoy 299
    Frederick Upham 300
    George Bancroft 300
    John Wesley 299
    Jeremia, 101 113
    Lettitia Tyler 299
    Mary Ann, 299
    Reuben Ranson, 290
    Sarah Carpenter, 299

360

Tillinghast—(Continued)
    Phebe 58, 95, 174
    Thomas 174
Tilton Francis W 221
Todd William, 245
Tompkins
    Benjamin, 252
    Brownell 235
    Cynthia B 253
    Gilbert 123, 235
    James B. 235
    John B 238
    Joseph 235
    Lucy 235
    Mariah 235
    Martha Pierce 235
    Mathilda 235
    Mary 235
    Philip, 235
    Phoebe 123, 235
    Ruth 235
    Samuel, 235, 236
    Sarah, 71 125 242 252
    William B, 235
Toppings, Esther H, 287
Townsend
    Thomas 68
    William, 83
Trafalgar Jane 246
Trax Rev I 228
Trimper John D, 262
Tripp
    Abbie 202
    Abiel 63 66
    Abigail 43 142
    Abraham 184
    Benjamin, 184
    Catherine 294
    Charles G 294
    Daniel 184
    Deborah, 294
    Delilah, 76
    Edith 184
    Edmund, 98, 184, 294
    Eleanor 63, 67, 69 105
    Eleanor Waite, 63 66
    Elias, 202
    Elizabeth, 142 184
    Emma, 202
    Esther 219
    Fallie Davol 221
    George 108, 201
    Hannah 184

Tripp—(Continued)
    Hannah W 294
    Isaac 68 117
    James, 117, 294
    Job 202
    John 141, 202
    Jonathan, 22, 43
    Joseph 43 184 294
    Maria, 142
    Martha Bourne 253
    Martha Brownell 43
    Mary 63 77, 106, 117, 141,
        184 202 279
    Nancy, 202
    Nicholas D 294
    Philip 184
    Phebe, 202
    Phebe A 292
    Priscilla, 202
    Rebecca 41 66 113, 114.
    Reuben 184
    Robert 168
    Ruth 184
    Ruth Mosher, 43
    Sarah 180 287 288
    Sarah D, 294
    Silvia, 184
    Susanna, 43
    Thomas 43, 68
    Waite, 63 103 104
    William 43, 202
Truesdell
    Codcha, 260
    Eliza Jane 260
    Helen 260
    Jeremiah, 260
    Maria, 260
    Oliver P, 260
Truman, Rebecca, 84, 158
Tucker
    Hannah, 183
    Rev 283
Turner, Catherine, 105, 190
Tuttle John 125
Tweedy Jane 53 85, 161, 162
Underwood,
    Damaris 199
    Harriet E, 199
    John 77
    John Holcome 231
    Joseph, 50, 77
    Ruth 28

363

www.ingramcontent.com/pod-product-compliance
Lightning Source LLC
Chambersburg PA
CBHW080226270326

41926CB00020B/4161